The Founding of
THOMAS JEFFERSON'S
UNIVERSITY

JEFFERSONIAN AMERICA

Peter S. Onuf
and Andrew O'Shaughnessy,
Editors

The Founding of
THOMAS JEFFERSON'S
UNIVERSITY

———————————— *Edited by* ————————————

JOHN A. RAGOSTA, PETER S. ONUF, AND
ANDREW J. O'SHAUGHNESSY

UNIVERSITY OF VIRGINIA PRESS

Charlottesville and London

University of Virginia Press
Printed in the United States of America on acid-free paper

First published 2019

1 3 5 7 9 8 6 4 2

LIBRARY OF CONGRESS CATALOGING-IN-PUBLICATION DATA

Names: Ragosta, John A., editor. | Onuf, Peter S., editor. | O'Shaughnessy,
Andrew Jackson, editor.

Title: The founding of Thomas Jefferson's university / edited by John A. Ragosta,
Peter S. Onuf, and Andrew J. O'Shaughnessy.

Description: Charlottesville : University of Virginia Press, 2019. | Series: Jeffersonian
America

Includes bibliographical references and index. | Identifiers: LCCN 2019001721 (print) |
LCCN 2019011096 (ebook) | ISBN 9780813943237 (ebook) | ISBN 9780813943220
(cloth : alk. paper)

Subjects: LCSH: University of Virginia—History. | Jefferson, Thomas, 1743–1826—
Political and social views. | Education, Higher—United States—History—19th century.

Classification: LCC LD5678.3 (ebook) | LCC LD5678.3 .F68 2019 (print) |
DDC 378.755/481—dc23

LC record available at https://lccn.loc.gov/2019001721

For the students of the University of Virginia, past, present, and future

Contents

Illustrations

Acknowledgments

The Thomas Jefferson Foundation wishes to acknowledge additional financial support for the conference on which this volume was based from the J. F. and Peggy Bryan Fund. The conference and its sequel in Philadelphia were greatly facilitated by the assistance of Patrick Spero, Librarian at the American Philosophical Society. This volume was made possible in part by the generous contribution of the Jefferson Legacy Foundation. We are also very grateful for logistical support from Whitney Pippin, the executive assistant for the Robert H. Smith International Center for Jefferson Studies; Mary Scott-Fleming, Director of Enrichment Programs; Megan Justice Howerton, Director of Events; Danielle de Almiñana in the Department of Events, and Lacey Hunter, intern. Of course, this volume would not have been produced without the excellent support of Dick Holway and the entire team at the University of Virginia Press.

Abbreviations

Adams Family	L. H. Butterfield et al., eds., *Adams Family Correspondence* (Cambridge, MA: Belknap Press of Harvard University Press, 13 vols. to date, 1963–).
APDE	*The Adams Papers Digital Edition*, ed. Sara Martin (Charlottesville: University of Virginia Press, Rotunda, 2008–2018). http://rotunda.upress.virginia.edu/founders/default.xqy?keys=ADMS.
Founders Online	*Founders Online*, National Archives, https://www.founders.archives.gov/.
Notes	Thomas Jefferson, *Notes on the State of Virginia*, ed. William Peden (Chapel Hill: University of North Carolina Press for the Omohundro Institute of Early American History and Culture at Williamsburg, 1982).
PJM-SSS	Robert J. Brugger et al., eds., *The Papers of James Madison—Secretary of State Series* (Charlottesville: University of Virginia Press, 11 vols. to date, 1986–).
PTJ	Julian P. Boyd et al., eds., *The Papers of Thomas Jefferson* (Princeton, NJ: Princeton University Press, 43 vols. to date, 1950–).
PTJRS	J. Jefferson Looney et al., eds., *The Papers of Thomas Jefferson, Retirement Series* (Princeton, NJ: Princeton University Press, 15 vols. to date, 2004–)
VMHB	*Virginia Magazine of History and Biography*
WMQ	*William and Mary Quarterly*

The Founding of
THOMAS JEFFERSON'S
UNIVERSITY

A Look Back at Jefferson's Forward-Looking Mission for the University

FOR THOMAS JEFFERSON, the University of Virginia was not an end in itself. It marked instead the culminating achievement of a career dedicated to promoting the ongoing progress of enlightenment and republican self-government in America and the world. With his authorship of the Declaration of Independence and the Virginia Statute for Religious Freedom, the founding of the University was one of the three accomplishments he asked to have inscribed on his tombstone. Each was essential for a functioning republic; each was essential to end the "tyranny over the mind of man" that had plagued mankind for millennia and bedeviled Jefferson throughout his life. Together those achievements—political liberty, religious freedom, and public education—would empower the people to make their own history, a better history. He and his fellow Founders would not rule from the grave; Jefferson believed that they had no right to do so and could not possibly comprehend the challenges that their progeny would face. If they succeeded, every subsequent generation of Americans would govern itself, looking toward an ever better and more enlightened future. But their success depended on a broadly and properly educated populace.

Today, the centrality of educating new generations for a functioning democracy may seem self-evident, but Jefferson believed that there was a fundamental battle in the early republic between those who looked to the past (tradition, hierarchy, the old world) and those who looked to an improving, enlightened future, one in which the nation that he helped to create would be a beacon. This battle threatened both the republic and education. Jefferson the revolutionary was dedicated to liberating the "living generation" from the "dead hand of the past" and the old structures of knowledge and power

controlled by "kings, nobles, and priests." While Jefferson loved history and
believed that the study of history was essential to identify and tackle the problems of the present, he was equally adamant that the past should not control the
present and that excessive reliance on the past for wisdom about the present
was both impractical and ill advised in a dynamic world. He referred dismis-
sively to the "sanctimonious reverence" of those who saw in the past unchange-
able mandates that cannot adapt to new times and new challenges. Monarchs
and aristocrats looked backward; republicans must look to the future.[1]

True self-government depended on demolishing hierarchy and hereditary
authority in order to free the people and permit them to reach their potential.
There was no place for monarchs or aristocrats or state-sponsored priestcraft
in the land of the free, where "all men are created equal." Jefferson celebrated
the American Revolution as the epochal triumph of the Sons of Liberty over
the tyrannical rule of King George III, an unnatural father who betrayed his
own children by restricting their commerce, saddling them with taxes and
regulations, and undermining their control of their own destiny.

By contrast, Jefferson would be a different kind of father, and nowhere
was this more evident than in his dedication to education and to the University. In our republic, educated citizens would participate broadly in government and control their own destiny and write their own future. By founding
a university rather than a dynasty, he would not perpetuate his power and
privilege across the generations, exalting his family over all other families.
The "dead have no rights," no claims on the future. Rather, conforming to nature's dictates and recognizing their own mortality, Jefferson and his fellow
Revolutionary fathers instead prepared the way for succeeding generations of
Americans to take their place, to govern their nation, and to continue improving the human condition.

This was not to say that there was no responsibility across generations.
"[T]he earth belongs in usufruct to the living," Jefferson famously wrote his
dear friend James Madison in 1789. But by using the word "usufruct"—a civil
law term meaning the use or stewardship of property belonging to another—
Jefferson underscored the responsibility of each generation for the welfare of
its successors. The earth only "belonged" to the living temporarily, in trust.
The living were not bound by the past, but they had an obligation to the
future. This obligation was nowhere more immediate than in the area of
education.[2]

Defining the mission of the University of Virginia in the Rockfish Gap Report of 1818, Jefferson urged Virginia's legislature to provide for "the gratifica-

Jefferson, a republican father, by Rembrandt Peale, 1805. (Oil on linen, 28 × 23 1/2 in. 71.1 × 59.7 cm. frame: 37 3/4 × 33 1/2 × 4 in. 95.9 × 85.1 × 10.2 cm., New York Historical Society, gift of Thomas Jefferson Bryan, 1867.306)

tion and happiness of their fellow citizens, of the parent especially, and his progeny, on which all his affections are concentrated." When Virginia's lawgivers and taxpayers founded the University, they exemplified the enlightened paternalism that should secure the future progress and ultimate success of the Commonwealth's experiment in republican government.[3]

Enlightenment was synonymous with progress, and so much of Jefferson's lifework was creating a continuing opportunity for progress. Speaking of the Declaration of Independence, in June 1826, Jefferson wrote in his life's penultimate letter about the possibilities embodied in the Declaration. "All eyes are opened, or opening, to the rights of man." The same goal of perpetual progress was at the heart of the University. With the "general spread of the light of science," future generations—particularly students at the University— would see more clearly and thus be better able to discharge their responsibilities to their future generations. Educated republican patriots could look hopefully to the future. This is why, for Jefferson, education, along with political and religious freedom, was a foundational pillar for the republic.[4]

"Freedom of the Human Mind"

Jefferson planned for, and hoped for, this vision to be realized at the University of Virginia.

Jefferson wanted to be remembered for the disinterested role he played as the "Father of the University of Virginia." The University was, in the language of the Enlightenment, a "project" whose promise would be fulfilled in the progress of time, in ways the father could not possibly fully anticipate. Those other two tombstone-worthy achievements—"Author of the Declaration of American Independence" and "of the Statute of Virginia for religious freedom"—also looked to the future. They would only be worth remembering, however, if successive generations, educated generations, redeemed their promise. Jefferson's legacy, as he imagined it, was not an "inheritance," a property to be distributed among privileged heirs. It would instead be a living faith in the future, the "spirit of 1776" and "sacred fire of liberty" that animated him through his long life of public service, and the opportunity for new generations to capitalize on that faith in a society with political freedom, religious freedom, and public education.

For nearly a half century, from 1779 when he offered his unsuccessful "Bill for the More General Diffusion of Knowledge" until his death, he understood that education and enlightenment were vitally important for all Virginians, not just the aristocratic few or the wealthy. His 1779 bill was a revolutionary, comprehensive, bottom-up scheme for public schools, envisioning broad popular participation in local "hundreds" or "wards"—a jurisdiction that did not then exist. Jefferson envisioned that grammar schools would provide three years of public education for all free children—girls and boys, presumably white and black (although there were very few free blacks in Virginia in 1779, and Jefferson did not discuss the issue expressly in his writings). Young men might then attend the district schools and the university, the brightest at public expense. Nowhere else in the world was such a system of public education available; while Russia, Austria, and Prussia had proposed broad systems of public education in the eighteenth century, the reality fell far short of their plans, with only Prussia making any real effort and that not bearing significant fruits until the nineteenth century. New England had a public primary school system that Jefferson admired, but he hoped to do better. Had his 1779 bill been adopted, Virginia would have had one of the finest educational systems in the world.

In his idealistic vision, he imagined that war-torn Virginians would be willing to take on a substantial tax burden to achieve this goal. In fact, Jefferson was emphatic that if he had to choose between a broad, publicly available education for the masses or a university, he would choose the former. "It is safer to have a whole people respectably enlightened, than a few in a high state of science and the many in ignorance," he explained. In subsequent decades, when he argued for reforming the College of William and Mary or establishing a new university for the Commonwealth as the capstone of the educational pyramid, the larger civic context remained paramount. Alas, with politicians in the nineteenth century (no less than today) having a shortsighted view concerning the costs of public education, Jefferson was left with the University as an achievable goal, meaning that the University took on an outsized role.[5]

Advocating for a "natural aristocracy" of talents, Jefferson initially hoped that the University would provide a free education and that students would be chosen based on merit. (Today, while hardly free, the University is consistently rated one of the best values in public higher education, a fact with which its Founder would be inordinately pleased.) In any form, though, the University would produce graduates for, not simply of, Virginia. It would produce "the statesmen, legislators & judges, on whom public prosperity, & individual happiness are so much to depend." The University would inspire "habits of reflection, and correct action" among students, making them "examples of virtue to others & of happiness within themselves." Its influence would pervade the state and nation.[6]

With such an important function, it was essential that the curriculum and faculty of the new University promote those ideals. While Jefferson spent an enormous effort on having the University approved and funded by the state and supervising its construction, he also was very careful and particular to ensure that the curriculum of his new academy would encourage the forward-looking search for truth that would help to propel the nation, and its people, forward. To facilitate that search for truth, Jefferson's University introduced the elective system of education, allowing students to concentrate in areas of study that they found of most interest and in so doing to expand knowledge. For similar reasons, most of the professors would define the course of study in their own discipline, and faculty was chosen based on their ability to serve the broader goals.

That search for truth not only required the best faculty—with the majority of the first professors coming from Europe in spite of nativist criticism—but also required that the University not be controlled by religious dogma as were other American colleges at the time, including those that were ostensibly public. In the midst of an ultimately losing battle to retain Thomas Cooper, a presumed deist, as the University's first professor, Jefferson explained that "this institution will be based on the illimitable freedom of the human mind. [F]or here we are not afraid to follow truth wherever it may lead, nor to tolerate any error so long as reason is left free to combat it." While public pressure threatening the University's funding meant that Cooper had to go, Jefferson would continue to fight for the principle.[7]

The only areas in which Jefferson insisted on particular control of the curriculum and faculty were in law and political science, for there he viewed a sound republican education—recognizing the causes of American independence, the limits on the powers of its governments, and the nature of political power in general—as requiring the utmost attention.

His Doubts, His Prayer

As he struggled to establish the University, Jefferson could not avoid knowing that Virginia was far from being—or even becoming—a perfect commonwealth. Dreams of the future exposed his own limitations and failures as well as those of his countrymen. Jefferson recognized that the monstrous injustice of slavery would not soon be redressed, that the institution was instead becoming ever more deeply entrenched in Virginia and in the expanding American "empire of liberty." He was also profoundly disturbed by economic uncertainty and an acquisitive culture that made invocations of old-fashioned virtue and patriotism seem increasingly archaic. He may sometimes have wondered if the sacrifices of the Revolutionary fathers were for naught. Indeed, his insistence on a southern university for southern leaders was, in part, to try to ensure that southerners would ultimately control resolution of the issue of slavery, an insistence that would be resolved only in a bloody Civil War and more than a century of struggle for civil rights.

In his last years, Jefferson nonetheless reaffirmed his faith in the fundamental principles of republican self-government that he had so memorably articulated in the Declaration of Independence. Jefferson's crusade to establish the University was a testimonial to his republican faith—a prayer for the future, not only for succeeding generations of Virginians but for all mankind. Perhaps, too, it was a hope for redemption for all his own dreams, and those of his Revolutionary colleagues, which had never quite achieved their promises.

In that June 1826 letter declining an invitation to attend a celebration of the fiftieth anniversary of American independence—on July 4, 1826, the day he would die at his mountain-top home—Jefferson eloquently expressed his most fervent hopes. "May" the Declaration of Independence—the creed of his faith—

"be to the world what I believe it will be, (to some parts sooner, to others later, but finally to all.) the Signal of arousing men to burst the chains, under which Monkish ignorance and superstition had persuaded them to bind themselves, and to assume the blessings & security of self government." Jefferson knew, as well as anyone, that the creed had not then succeeded, but as he told his old friend John Adams, "I like the dreams of the future better than the history of the past."[8]

The University was, and is, and always will be, a dream of the future.

The Burden on Us

Jefferson laid a heavy burden on future generations. Finding that he fell so conspicuously short of the values he so ostentatiously celebrated, critics might well question his good faith and dismiss him as a hypocrite; disenchanted with the Enlightenment that he claimed to promote, they might wonder if there is such a thing as "progress" in the affairs of men and women. But the point of thinking about Jefferson's long-past hopes for the future should not be to settle intergenerational scores with the "Father of the University." Jefferson instead calls us to take the measure of where we are now, by whatever lights now guide us. How well are we, the "living generation," preparing the way for those who follow?

Now, two hundred years after its founding, studying the University must have that same vision in mind: a realistic understanding of the University's past, not to build a monument to our achievements, nor simply to criticize its past, but because the academy is essential for our dreams of the future.

The Conference

The essays in this volume, offered to encourage that realistic understanding, are the product of a conference held by the Thomas Jefferson Foundation as part of its commemoration of the bicentenary of the University of Virginia, which took place at its Robert H. Smith Education Center at Montalto on May 24–25, 2018. The conference was cohosted by the American Philosophical Society, of which Jefferson was a long-term president, which held a sequel conference in Philadelphia on June 7–8, 2018.

The location, with its commanding view of the Blue Ridge Mountains, is well-known to generations of University law students and those who attended "Kite Day" when what Jefferson referred to as Montalto was called Brown's Mountain. Although he never built any housing on the heights looming above his Monticello, Jefferson began the process of purchasing those parts of the mountain in his viewshed on the eve of the Revolutionary War. From its summit, he could look west toward the expanding nation that he had helped to form.

It was during his retirement from the presidency while at Monticello that Jefferson planned the University of Virginia. His little mountain was where he drew up the architectural drawings, drafted the Rockfish Gap Report, and held many of meetings of the Board of Visitors, as well as invited faculty and the first cadre of students to dine with him.

The conference was initially conceived to deal more broadly with education in the early republic as both background and context for the founding of the University of Virginia. Yet it became clear that there were a sufficient number of scholars working on various aspects of the University's founding to devote the sessions almost entirely to that subject. Nevertheless, the original idea was retained in the first panel, which looked more broadly at educational ideas and initiatives in the early republic and, particularly, examined their influence on the University's beginnings. The final program represented the most comprehensive and ambitious academic event marking the bicentenary of the University. It attempted to cover all aspects, including the architecture, the selection of faculty, the curriculum, the library, the role of enslaved labor, and some of the early academic departments. All the presentations were filmed and are available online. To conclude the conference, Alan Taylor, the Thomas Jefferson Foundation Professor of History at the University of Virginia, gave the keynote address in which he discussed student life, southern interest in education in the period, and the reasons that Jefferson rejected his alma mater, the College of William and Mary, as a foundation for his educational scheme.

Despite such wide coverage, the conference also highlighted some of the research needs and opportunities for scholarship on the early history of the University of Virginia. In his essay suggesting a pioneering role for the early medical school, Robert S. Gibson offered an example of the kind of research that needs to be undertaken by every department. It is particularly to be lamented, for both academic and personal reasons, that J. Gordon Hylton passed away before the conference while working on an important monograph about the early law school. While Cameron Addis's essay provides important insights, it would be good to see more work on the religious arrangements at the University that made it so distinctive and that were the cause of sustained opposition in the state assembly. There is need for more systematic study of the correspondents, writers, and institutions that influenced Jefferson's vision for the University. Finally, the comparative domestic and international context requires greater elaboration to help us understand what was unique about the University in relation to other universities. The essays do, though, provide an important platform for understanding and further study.

The Book

This volume begins with a section that considers the students who would embark on Jefferson's imagined vision. The human material on which Jefferson placed his dreams for paragons was often deeply flawed. As he elsewhere anticipated, the sons of wealthy southern plantation owners were more schooled in tyranny than in his own Enlightenment philosophy. He hoped to build an Academical Village where they might join in his vision, separated from many southern realities, but this proved to be too much to ask.

A series of essays concerning the location and construction of the University follows. Jefferson convinced himself, and the state legislature, that Charlottesville was the best location for the new University of Virginia, while he also convinced the legislature to adopt an innovative (and expensive) building plan that would integrate students and faculty into a learning community. At the same time, his architectural plan and regulations for the University would tend to hide the necessary and inevitable presence of the enslaved population that played such a prominent role in building the school and making it work.

Today, in visiting the University, one tends easily to associate Jefferson with its extraordinarily beautiful architecture and design. This, though, can lead us to miss a broader point, as the next series of essays makes clear. Admittedly, Jefferson's architectural design for the University was more than just a practical consideration—roofs, walls, classrooms, and dormitories; still, to see only that material design is to miss his larger vision, which fixated on the critical nature of the curriculum, library, and faculty that would populate his temple of learning.

Jefferson's University was based on a principle of learning that was grounded in the Enlightenment: students came not just to study the classical knowledge of man, important as that was, but to create new knowledge, as discussed in the final set of essays. Here, too, though, the students could not leave the reality of the nineteenth century in which the ability to present one's learning, and oneself, as a southern gentleman would continue to take precedence.

Much more could be written, other topics explored. All of these are presented with the same hope that Jefferson had for his new University: that they will encourage further search for understanding.

Notes

This introduction is based on an earlier essay, written by Peter S. Onuf, printed in *Virginia: The UVA Magazine* (Spring 2017), http://uvamagazine.org/articles/thomas_jeffersons_prayer_for_the_future.

1. Jefferson to "Henry Tompkinson" (Samuel Kercheval), July 12, 1816, *PTJRS*, 10:226–27.

2. Jefferson to James Madison, September 6, 1789, *PTJ*, 15:392.

3. Jefferson, Draft of the Rockfish Gap Report of the University of Virginia Commissioners, ca. June 28, 1818, *PTJRS*, 13:193.

4. Jefferson to Roger C. Weightman, June 24, 1826, *Founders Online*, https://founders.archives.gov/documents/Jefferson/98-01-02-6179.

5. Jefferson to Joseph C. Cabell, January 13, 1823, *Founders Online*, https://founders.archives.gov/documents/Jefferson/98-01-02-3266.

6. Rockfish Gap Report of the University of Virginia Commissioners, August 4, 1818, *PTJRS*, 13:212 (ftnt. omitted).

7. Jefferson to William Roscoe, December 27, 1820, *Founders Online*, https://founders.archives.gov/documents/Jefferson/98-01-02-1712.

8. Jefferson to Roger C. Weightman, June 24, 1826, *Founders Online*, https://founders.archives.gov/documents/Jefferson/98-01-02-6179. Jefferson to John Adams, August 1, 1816, *PTJRS*, 10:285.

From Academy to College to University

The Prehistory of the University of Virginia

J. JEFFERSON LOONEY

IN OCTOBER 2017 the University of Virginia (UVA) began a fifteen-month celebration of its bicentennial, running through January 2019. The decision to celebrate *two* founding dates may seem unusual. The United States has gotten by quite comfortably celebrating a single birthday of July 4, annoying as this would have been to John Adams who famously wrote a letter to his wife, Abigail, imagining the future celebrations, including fireworks, that would surely take place each year on July 2, the day that the Continental Congress voted for independence.[1] No one at the time would have expected that July 4 would win out, since the Declaration of Independence was not to achieve iconic status for decades.[2]

Indeed, the dates chosen as the birthdays of great institutions often have interesting histories. Businesses founded much more recently snap up some small but venerable firm and adopt its much earlier year of origin for their "Selling Great Widgets since Year X" signs. This process of acquired seniority can simply be intended to give the company an air of solidity and permanence. Other times there is a more tangible reason for the choice of a founding date. The 1746 date used by Princeton University is reasonably straightforward. It received a charter as the College of New Jersey in 1746, began admitting students the following year, awarded its first degrees in 1748, and has been in operation ever since, having changed its name to Princeton University on its own sesquicentennial.[3]

The University of Pennsylvania has a much more complex origin story. Benjamin Franklin led a group that began planning what it originally called an "Academy" in 1749, secondary education commenced two years later, and the school was not chartered as a college until 1755. Penn duly celebrated its centennial in 1849. Fifty years later, however, on what would have been its own sesquicentennial and three years *after* Princeton's, Penn's trustees voted to change the official year of its founding to 1740. The ostensible reason was that the land acquired in 1749 contained a structure that had been built in 1740 to be a charity school, although it was never operational. The stakes were high. By changing its founding date to 1740, Penn jumped ahead of Princeton as the nation's fourth-oldest college, and thus gained priority in academic processions involving both institutions.[4]

UVA's early years are at least as complex as Penn's. The year 1819 is on the seal, and the official celebration has now added 1817 as a second date of origin. The waters can be muddied even further by examining UVA's prehistory and focusing on a number of important dates and happenings. This reveals that many more events can arguably be regarded as the moment that UVA history begins, and in so doing one can learn a lot about the earliest years of the institution and Thomas Jefferson's role in its creation.

I

The first key date is January 12, 1803, the day on which the Virginia General Assembly issued a charter to the Albemarle Academy.[5] Since Thomas Jefferson was busy being president in Washington, there is no evidence that he was involved in this, and he was not initially named as a trustee. Nonetheless, a clear line of succession runs from the creation of the Albemarle Academy in 1803 to today's University of Virginia. As has been shown, Penn began as a secondary school and still dates its origin from this earlier incarnation, and this is by no means unusual. In Virginia, Washington and Lee University was founded as the Augusta Academy in 1749 and did not become Washington College until 1813. Mary Baldwin University was founded as the Augusta Female Seminary in 1842 and did not become a junior college until 1916 and a four-year institution until 1923. Each school claims the earlier founding date.[6]

II

Whatever the initial plan of the trustees, the Albemarle Academy seems to have been a dead letter almost from the start, with no building, no funds, no faculty, and no students. Still, if UVA *did* adopt 1803 as its founding date, it would jump ahead of quite a few institutions, including Ohio (1804), Maryland (1807), Miami of Ohio (1809), Hamilton (1812), Colby (1813), Allegheny (1815), Michigan (1817), and Saint Louis (1818).[7] However, whatever it would gain in seniority it would lose in the splendor of its founder, which leads to the next important date, March 25, 1814, when Thomas Jefferson enters the picture.[8] On that day, the five surviving original trustees of Albemarle Academy met and acted by electing thirteen new members for their board. One of the new trustees was Thomas Jefferson. According to legend, he attended this meeting quite by chance. As Jefferson happened to pass through town on his daily horseback ride, one of the trustees saw him go by, knew of his interest in education, and suggested that he be asked to dismount and join them. Jefferson cheerfully complied, joined the meeting, became a trustee, and the rest is history. The story is charming, but dubious. Jefferson's nephew Peter Carr chaired the meeting. Knowing Jefferson's penchant for quiet lobbying behind the scenes, which was to be exerted again and again in the years ahead, it seems at least as likely that Carr called the meeting to breathe new life into the institution at Jefferson's suggestion. It is not even known with certainty that Jefferson was at the meeting where he was selected. But he was certainly at the next one, on April 5, 1814, and he immediately became the leading spirit on the Board of Trustees. He was quickly placed on a committee to draft rules and regulations and seek out funds for what he shortly began calling the "Academy or College."[9] Jefferson soon persuaded his fellow trustees that they should set their sights higher than a mere secondary school, and at their suggestion,

III

Jefferson submitted a plan on September 7, 1814, of such fundamental importance that this becomes another key date in UVA's founding. Writing to Peter Carr, who had been chosen as board chairman, Jefferson began by stating that Virginia should provide three years of free education to every citizen, an extraordinarily ambitious proposal at this time and one that the Commonwealth did not even begin to realize for another half century. As for the new Albemarle institution, Jefferson proposed that it start out by teaching both secondary-school and collegiate topics, gradually expanding its scope as resources increased and eventually including a law school, a medical school, even a school for the hearing and vision impaired, and a technical school at which artisans could catch up on the latest scientific and industrial advances. Jefferson identified a dichotomy between a broad liberal-arts education, open to all students but especially intended to nurture the state's future political leaders, and specialized professional education for law and medicine. He intended his school to serve *both* needs. Jefferson seems to have felt that any well-rounded citizen should have a reasonable grasp of mathematics, physics, chemistry, anatomy, medicine, zoology, botany, mineralogy, ethics, law, political science, history, and, of course, Latin and Greek. In its ambition and commitment to citizen education, Jefferson's letter to Carr is surely the intellectual founding document of the University of Virginia.[10]

IV

Jefferson next began taking practical steps to make his vision a reality. Later in 1814 he submitted funding estimates and an architectural design (probably the first draft of Pavilion VII, the current home of the Colonnade Club), and he drafted a bill to turn the Albemarle Academy into Central College.[11] Unfortunately, the draft legislation was delayed in the mail and reached the legislator who was supposed to submit it too late for action in the 1814/1815 legislative session.[12] This frustrating delay was just one of many parts of this story in which Jefferson was called upon to exercise his talent for patience and perseverance. However, the bill was duly submitted in the following legislative session, and on February 14, 1816, the legislature passed an act chartering Central College.[13] A good case can be made for this date as UVA's birthday, since it turned a secondary school into a college presumably able to award degrees. The act authorized the governor to select six visitors, and Jefferson was chosen on October 18, 1816, along with two other United States presidents, former president James Madison and then-president James Monroe.[14]

V

More than a year later, May 5, 1817, the Board of Visitors held its first business meeting, with much publicity and with all three American presidents in attendance. Jefferson had made a special plea to Monroe to find time in his official schedule to come to this meeting, regarding the presence of the three presidents as a key way to instill public confidence in the new college. The Board immediately began a major fundraising campaign, centering on a three-year subscription drive but also including a possible lottery and obtaining the assets of local Anglican church property that had been claimed by the state. The Board also approved the purchase of what would become the nucleus of UVA's grounds. When it toured this property, Jefferson suggested that an observatory could be built on Carter's Mountain with a line of sight from the college. This

prompted Madison to indulge himself in a rare witticism: he "playfully remarked that this point shou'd be denominated the Apex of Science."[15]

VI

As the college visitor closest to the scene, Jefferson oversaw day-to-day operations, and on July 18, 1817, actual construction began. His overseer, Edmund
Bacon, recalled that on that day he followed Jefferson's instructions and
brought "ten able-bodied hands" (while the document does not specify, they
were presumably enslaved persons) "to commence the work." Bacon got a ball
of twine, the builder James Dinsmore made pegs from some old shingles, and

> we all went on to the old field together. Mr. Jefferson looked over the ground
> some time, and then stuck down a peg. He stuck the very first peg in that
> building, and then directed me where to carry the line, and I stuck the second.
> He carried one end of the line, and I the other, in laying off the foundation of
> the University. He had a little rule in his pocket that he always carried with
> him, and with this he measured off the ground, and laid off the entire founda-
> tion, and then set the men at work.[16]

So, there it is: July 18, 1817, is the real rather than the ceremonial day that
construction of UVA began. All through the summer and early autumn, the
ground was leveled and foundations dug, and Jefferson began preparing for
the formal cornerstone laying.

VII

The ceremony took place on another key date, October 6, 1817, and UVA
began observing its bicentennial exactly two hundred years later with appropriate fanfare and revelry. The event in 1817 was conducted with elaborate
Masonic ritual. All the Central College visitors, including Jefferson, Madison,
and Monroe, were present, as well as hundreds of spectators. Surviving descriptions indicate how the invited participants were to approach the site, with
due attention paid to precedence for the various dignitaries. The right wor-
shipful grand master approved the cornerstone after testing it with square,
plumb, and level. He then asked if one of the college visitors present wished to
do the same. James Monroe stepped forward and did so, either because he had

precedence as the sitting American president, or because, unlike Jefferson and Madison, Monroe was a Mason himself and would have known what to do. He was thus able to agree with the presiding Masonic officer that the stone was "True and Trusty," after which corn, wine, and oil were scattered, further speeches were made, and the ceremony concluded.[17]

Jefferson had been anxious that the Masons officiate. The two local lodges initially asked if they could participate, but they then advised Jefferson that they might not be able to get ready. He persuaded them that there was time enough and expressed his desire "to see the inauguration of our institution commence under the regular auspices of this antient fraternity."[18] Whatever he thought of these rituals, Jefferson recognized the symbolic importance of having Masons bless the commencement of work on a major public building, just as they did in 1793 at the cornerstone laying for the United States Capitol.

VIII

Building operations were now well under way, but, it is important to remember that the ceremony in October 1817 was *not* the laying of the cornerstone for Pavilion VII. Central College certainly did not have the funds for more than three or four pavilions, and no one was thinking as yet of a large central Rotunda. By now, however, Jefferson had begun scheming to get his college's hands on state funding and to turn Central College into *the* state university. After many false starts and initial failures, including legislative defeat of an ambitious Jefferson-drafted bill to establish a statewide system of public education that would have included primary schools, nine colleges, and a university, on February 21, 1818, legislation was passed creating a commission to meet and consider the feasibility of establishing a state university and recommend a venue for it.[19] The following month Jefferson was chosen to sit on this twenty-four-member commission, which met at Rockfish Gap, rejected Staunton and Lexington as locations, and issued a report on August 4, 1818 (another key date) that called for creation of a state university in Charlottesville. Jefferson would have been surprised by none of its specific proposals about the new school's buildings, curriculum, or organization, because he had drafted the report weeks in advance of the commission's meeting. He had also lobbied a number of the influential members of the commission in advance and arranged to travel with some of them to Rockfish Gap.[20]

IX

The action then moved to the Virginia General Assembly, where two battles occurred simultaneously. Some members saw no need for a state university, certainly not one with state funding, and some sentiment still existed for providing at least some state support to William and Mary. The town of Staunton also had supporters, but the key struggle was between proponents of Charlottesville and those advocating for Lexington. On paper Lexington's claim was far stronger. Its Washington College (now Washington and Lee University) had similar ambitions to Central College and the advantage of an actual operating school, with land, a building, faculty, and students, plus a new subscription by its citizens and the promise of a very sizable bequest of land and enslaved people. While Charlottesville had a somewhat larger promised subscription, much of which proved impossible to collect, its buildings were unfinished and it had no faculty and no students. But it did have Thomas Jefferson. His trump card was his argument that Charlottesville was closest to the geographical center of white population in Virginia, a point he sought to prove with some tables he constructed using census data in ways he found convincing but that, to say the least, others had great difficulty replicating.[21]

X

After much tense legislative back and forth, on January 25, 1819, the Virginia General Assembly passed a law (also drafted by Jefferson) that granted a charter turning Central College at Charlottesville into the University of Virginia and providing it an annual allocation of $15,000 in state funds.[22] This is the date generally given for the University's founding, and it was the terminal date of its bicentennial celebration. However, Jefferson immediately recognized that the proposed $15,000 annuity would not be sufficient, and within days of passage of this act he was already lobbying for more.[23] On more than one occasion he and his devoted legislative allies, of whom Joseph Carrington Cabell was the most important, did not scruple to argue for the diversion to UVA of money allotted to primary education for the poor.[24] Their problems were greatly enhanced by the fact that this year is known to historians less for the chartering of UVA than for the Panic of 1819, the first great economic depression following American independence, which made bankruptcies commonplace (including one that led to Jefferson's own financial downfall[25]) and private subscriptions hard to collect. The state of Virginia encountered funding troubles of its own, including the discovery that the treasurer of Virginia had made large, uncollectible loans of state funds to his friends.[26] Instead of an increased subsidy, UVA had to settle for loans and plead for extended repayment schedules. Additional funding crises, legislative hurdles, logistical difficulties, labor struggles, and disappointments in faculty recruitment needed to be overcome before

XI

March 7, 1825, when the University of Virginia quietly and somewhat unceremoniously opened its doors to students, a full six years after it obtained its charter, but with a largely European faculty with reasonably impressive-sounding credentials and a set of buildings (designed by Jefferson) of such architectural beauty that they were worth waiting for and are still celebrated today.[27]

XII

Thus, eleven legitimate possibilities can be proposed as the founding date of the University of Virginia. Even this array leaves out some dark horses, such as January 18, 1800, when Jefferson sought advice from the eminent scientist Joseph Priestley on his plans to "establish in the upper & healthier country, & more centrally for the state an University on a plan so broad & liberal & *modern*, as to be worth patronising with the public support, and be a temptation to the youth of other states to come, and drink of the cup of knolege & fraternize with us." Or May 6, 1810, when Jefferson advised a group considering establishing a college in Tennessee that they should not plan a single building but "an academical village" (a phrase that has become beloved in Charlottesville), "instead of a large & common den of noise, of filth, & of fetid air."[28]

But in closing, an even more intriguing possibility is worthy of consideration. On December 15, 1778, Jefferson's Bill for the More General Diffusion of Knowledge was presented to the Virginia House of Delegates. In this proposal, justly celebrated now but not approved at the time, Thomas Jefferson was already calling for universal public schooling and for access to college education for an aristocracy of talents rather than one of wealth. Fully forty years before the University obtained its charter, he argued that it was "expedient for promoting the publick happiness that those persons, whom nature hath endowed with genius and virtue, should be rendered by liberal education worthy to receive, and able to guard the sacred deposit of the rights and liberties of their fellow citizens, and that they should be called to that charge without regard to wealth, birth or other accidental condition or circumstance" and that those "whom nature hath fitly formed and disposed to become useful instruments for the public, . . . should be sought for and educated at the common expence of all, [rather] than that the happiness of all should be confided to the weak or wicked."[29] Even though a university in Charlottesville was not yet even a gleam in his eye, in many ways this language sets the tone for all of Jefferson's efforts to come. He was so confident that he had succeeded that he named the founding of the University of Virginia as one of the three acts for which he wished to be remembered. Insofar as it continues to live up to these goals, Jefferson's confidence will not be misplaced.

Notes

1. John Adams to Abigail Adams, July 3, 1776, *Adams Family*, 2:29–33.

2. Pauline Maier, *American Scripture: Making the Declaration of Independence* (New York: Alfred A. Knopf, 1997), 160–75.

3. Thomas Jefferson Wertenbaker, *Princeton, 1746–1896* (Princeton, NJ: Princeton University Press, 1946; repr. 1996), 22–28, 368–73.

4. Edward Potts Cheney, *History of the University of Pennsylvania, 1740–1940* (Philadelphia: University of Pennsylvania Press, 1940), 45–52.

5. "An Act to establish an academy in the county of Albemarle, and for other purposes," January 12, 1803, *Acts passed at a General Assembly of the Commonwealth of Virginia: begun and held at the Capitol, in the City of Richmond, on Monday, the sixth day of December, one thousand eight hundred and two* (Richmond: Meriwether Jones, [1803]), 23–24.

6. Emily J. Salmon and Edward D. C. Campbell Jr., *The Hornbook of Virginia History*, 4th ed. (Richmond: Library of Virginia, 1994): 262, 267; Mame Warren, ed., *Come Cheer for Washington and Lee: The University at 250 Years* (Lexington, VA: Washington and Lee University, 1998); Mary Watters, *The History of Mary Baldwin College, 1842–1942* (Staunton, VA: Mary Baldwin College, 1943).

7. Betty Hollow, *Ohio University: The Spirit of a Singular Place, 1804–2004* (Athens: Ohio University Press, 2003); George H. Callcott, *A History of the University of Maryland* (Baltimore: Maryland Historical Society, 1966); Curtis W. Ellison, ed., *Miami University, 1809–2009: Bicentennial Perspectives* (Athens: Ohio University Press, 2009); Maurice Isserman, *On The Hill, 1812–2012: A Bicentennial History of Hamilton College* (Clinton, NY: Hamilton College, 2012); Earl H. Smith, *Mayflower Hill: A History of Colby College* (Waterville, ME: Colby College, 2006); Jonathan E. Helmreich, *Eternal Hope: The Life*

of Timothy Alden, Jr. (New York: Cornwall Books, 2001); Howard Henry Peckham, *The Making of The University of Michigan, 1817–1967* (Ann Arbor: University of Michigan Press, 1967); William Barnaby Faherty, *A Concise History of Saint Louis University* (Saint Louis: Reedy Press, 2009).

8. A similar instance of the importance of an eminent person in choosing a founding date occurred at the College of New Jersey in 1820. In that year the Cliosophic Society, one of the school's two literary societies, used a connection to an earlier club to move its founding date from 1770 to 1765. Its bitter rival, the American Whig Society, could have made a similar claim and also moved its own birth year to 1765, but doing so would have meant that James Madison would no longer have been its founder. Rather than give up that claim to fame, the Whigs grudgingly relinquished their chronological priority and stuck with a 1769 founding date (Jacob N. Beam, *The American Whig Society* (Princeton, NJ: American Whig Society, 1933), 13–17; J. Jefferson Looney, *Nurseries of Letters and Republicanism: A Brief History of the American Whig–Cliosophic Society and its Predecessors, 1765–1941* (Princeton, NJ: American Whig–Cliosophic Society, 1996), 4–5).

9. Meeting minutes and editorial note in *PTJRS*, 7:264–68, 282–83; horseback-ride anecdote repeated in Philip Alexander Bruce, *History of the University of Virginia 1819–1919: The Lengthened Shadow of One Man* (New York: Macmillan, 1920–1922), 1:121, and disputed in Dumas Malone, *Jefferson and His Time* (Boston: Little, Brown, 1948–1981), 6:241–42; "Academy or College," *PTJRS*, 7:636.

10. *PTJRS*, 7:636–42.

11. *PTJRS*, 8:86–94.

12. *PTJRS*, 7:266.

13. "An Act for establishing a College in the county of Albemarle," February 14, 1816, *Acts passed at a General Assembly of the Commonwealth of Virginia, Begun and held at the Capitol, in the City of Richmond, on Monday, the Fourth day of December, in the year of our Lord, one thousand eight hundred and fifteen, and of the Commonwealth, the fortieth* (Richmond: Thomas Ritchie, 1816), 191–93.

14. *PTJRS*, 10:473–74.

15. *PTJRS*, 11:314–35.

16. *PTJRS*, 11:544–45.

17. *PTJRS*, 12:59–72.

18. *PTJRS*, 11:669–70, 12:36–37, 40–41, 45.

19. *PTJRS*, 12:114–33; "An Act appropriating part of the revenue of the Literary Fund, and for other purposes," February 21, 1818, *Acts passed at a General Assembly of the Commonwealth of Virginia, Begun and Held at the Capitol, in the City of Richmond, on Monday, the first day of December, in the year of our Lord one thousand eight hundred and seventeen, and of the Commonwealth the forty-second* (Richmond: Thomas Ritchie, 1818), 11–15.

20. *PTJRS*, 12:610–11, 13:108–09, 110, 111–12, 179–225.

21. *PTJRS*, 13:185–88, 514–17, 535–36.

22. *PTJRS*, 13:401–5; "An Act for establishing an University," January 25, 1819, *Acts passed at a General Assembly of the Commonwealth of Virginia, Begun and Held at the Capitol, in the City of Richmond, on Monday, the seventh day of December, in the year of our Lord*

one thousand eight hundred and eighteen, and of the Commonwealth the forty-third (Richmond: Thomas Ritchie, 1819), 15–18.

23. *PTJRS*, 13:613, 614–15.

24. See, for example, Jefferson to Cabell, November 28, 1820, *Founders Online*, https:// founders.archives.gov/documents/Jefferson/98-01-02-1660, which proposed reducing the annual state contribution to primary schools by one-third in order to double its donation to the University, with Jefferson's suggestions for ways to organize elementary education so much more efficiently that he argued the reduction would not even be felt.

25. *PTJRS*, 12:649, 13:14, 14:586–88, 631–34.

26. *PTJRS*, 15:350–52.

27. University of Virginia Matriculation Books, 1825–1855 (University of Virginia Library: Special Collections); Bruce, *History of the University of Virginia*, 2:59–60; Malone, *Jefferson and His Time*, 6:422.

28. *PTJ*, 31:319–23; *PTJRS*, 2:365–66.

29. *PTJ*, 2:526–35.

YOUNG LEADERS OF THE REPUBLIC

The "earth belongs in usufruct to the living," Thomas Jefferson wrote James Madison from Paris in 1789. In this great exposition of his theory of generational sovereignty, the American minister to France expressed his vaulting hopes for the future of republican Virginia and its sister states. The present, "living" generation exercised rule over a vast, bountiful continent, but the legitimacy of its title depended on fulfilling its obligation to the next, "rising" generation. The Roman law term "usufruct," or stewardship, defined that obligation: to preserve the great estate of the people from waste, to spare future generations from the burden of debt ("the dead hand of the past"), and, looking forward, to prepare them for the responsibilities that would come with their inheritance. Education was the pivot between generations: grateful for the sacrifices of the fathers and their gifted inheritance, enlightened heirs would recognize the need to educate and enlighten their own children, from generation to generation, time out of mind.

Jefferson's hopes were shadowed by misgivings. By fighting a great war to secure American independence, the Revolutionary generation modeled the farsighted disinterestedness of fathers who risked everything to guarantee the happiness and well-being of future generations. Would their sons rise to this exalted standard? The revolutionaries' obsession with education betrayed the same profound anxieties. For many, those anxieties focused less on the common people, who had displayed such extraordinary patriotism in the war, than on the children of the patriot elite, the sons of the "sons of liberty." When the new republic faced the next—and inevitable—existential threat, would a new generation of patriot leaders rise to the occasion?

For anxious revolutionaries looking to an uncertain future, the patriotism and enlightenment of the sons of the wealthy and privileged took on a portentous, world-historical significance. There was nothing new, however, as Neven Leddy shows, about paternal and parental anxieties regarding the education and socialization of elite children in the Anglophone Atlantic world. Jefferson was an engaged participant in an ongoing transatlantic conversation about the proper education of those sons (who had the luxury of worrying about such things) that antedated the American Revolution. Without sons of his own, Jefferson's concern was not narrowly familial or dynastic, but embraced a more inclusive "generation" of future leaders, a generation that would of course include his own daughters. Throughout his life, Jefferson was a font of wise counsel on what young men—relatives, sons of friends, strangers—should read and where they should study. Stay away from Europe, he wrote one correspondent from Paris in 1785: "an American coming to Europe for education loses in his knowledge, in his morals, in his health, in his habits, and in his happiness."[1] The urgency of Jefferson's injunction suggests that much beyond the life choices of one privileged young man was at stake. Collectively, the choices fathers made about their sons' educations would shape the new nation's future.

Location mattered. Although Jefferson would keep young Americans from Europe, he also acknowledged that some places there were better than others—and that, until Virginia and the other American states created adequate institutions of their own, ambitious boys would have to go *somewhere*. London, the old imperial metropolis and destination of choice for provincial Anglo-Americans with resources, was now unacceptable, as were Oxford and Cambridge. Edinburgh continued to attract American students, including Jefferson's future son-in-law, Thomas Mann Randolph. By the end of his embassy to Paris in 1789, Jefferson overcame misgivings about Geneva's aristocratic revolution of 1782 and endorsed educational opportunities in that Swiss canton. Geneva appealed to Jefferson, Leddy suggests, because education there "focused on immersive language training, in a gender-segregated environment under clerical oversight." The small city's remote location resonated with Jefferson's agrarian, antiurban values. There was no place like Geneva in America, and American boys might find a safe and salubrious home there until one could be provided.

The revolutionary paradox that Jefferson addressed was one that became increasingly familiar to growing numbers of parents in postrevolutionary America. How could poorly disciplined, rambunctious, often ungovernable adolescent males who were sent away to school and no longer subject to parental

Jefferson saw William and Mary as a relic of the old regime; Sir Christopher Wren Building. (Image courtesy of Stephen Salpukas, William and Mary)

discipline be taught to govern themselves—and then assume leadership roles in a self-governing republic? Ambitious American parents "across the Colonial, Revolutionary, and Early National periods" faced difficult choices as they negotiated contradictory pulls between home and world, "cosmopolitan 'finishing' and national or parochial ambitions." Sent away they must be, particularly in the plantation South. Before the Revolution, the College of William and Mary was the only institution of higher education in the region—and even it was located far away from the homes of most of its rowdy students. Jefferson, who had studied there, was well aware of the College's inadequacies. William and Mary epitomized the hopelessly corrupt provincial old regime; it was beyond reformation, as he discovered over the course of his subsequent career. Far from being the site of enlightenment and a vital link to the larger world, Alan Taylor shows, the College was a benighted backwater in a sleepy old capital where students customarily confused liberty with license, freedom from parental control with self-indulgent irresponsibility. A new university was needed.

Jefferson's plans for "a new and improved university" in his own neighborhood reflected growing disenchantment with his own class. The "peer culture" that flourished in the hothouse of student life at William and Mary constituted a cruel caricature of planter privilege. By incorporating impressionable boys into professors' families and isolating them from evil influences, Jefferson's "Academical Village" would offer an idealized, enlightened model of intergenerational relations. Taylor aptly summarizes the old patriot's fervent prayer, that his university would "rescue Virginia from the generation created by the unanticipated consequences of revolution." Jefferson's hopes for the continuing progress of revolutionary republican enlightenment hinged on a generation of privileged, ungovernable boys, hell-bent on degradation and debauchery. This was Jefferson's nightmare, the betrayal of his inspiring conception of generational sovereignty and stewardship.

Creating a place where the character of future republican leaders could be shaped was the great project of Jefferson's retirement years. That he should choose Charlottesville as the best location for this republican seminary seems extraordinarily self-serving. Yet it also reflected his careful consideration and ultimate rejection of other possible sites. It was, he thought, imperative to remove the rising generation from the baneful influence of home plantations while protecting them from the temptations of the great European metropolises (and their politically corrupt counterparts in states to the north). Perhaps, he imagined, his own presence would make a difference in the culture of an institution in which he would invest so much of himself.

While young men were the hope of the future, they also represented the greatest potential threat to the republic's survival. The cheery optimism of Jefferson's faith in the rising generation was shadowed—and often subverted— by riot and mayhem at colleges across the continent, especially in the South. Adolescent males were notoriously impressionable. Scions of the planter class "nursed, educated, and daily exercised in tyranny" over enslaved people, as Jefferson famously put it in his *Notes on Virginia*, were predictably incorrigible.[2] Slaveowners like Jefferson who were keenly aware of their own patriarchal prerogatives recognized, resisted, and revolted against the tyrannical King George III. But young masters would only recognize the tyranny of their own mastery when—and if—they were sufficiently enlightened to the Commonwealth's ultimate, long-term self-interest.

In his retirement years, Jefferson's anxieties about the character and values of Virginia's future leaders were heightened by what he saw as threats to the Commonwealth's rights and interests from the "consolidation" of authority in the federal government. Virginia's dominant position in the federal union could no longer be taken for granted. Nor could Republicans be complacent about their great victory over the Federalists, with their subversive aristocratic and monarchical tendencies, in the "Revolution of 1800" when Jefferson ascended to the presidency. After his return to Monticello in 1809, Jefferson focused on a reform agenda for Virginia: the Commonwealth needed a new, more democratic constitution that would expand the ambit of the people's participation in their own government; it was also imperative to prepare a new generation of republican leaders to guide the Commonwealth through increasingly dangerous times at home, within the Union, and in the world beyond as, yet again, it descended into war. For Jefferson, commitment to principle meant defending Virginia's autonomy as a self-governing republic and thus securing the state's vital interests—including the institution of slavery—from outside interference. The flood of southerners educated in northern universities risked returning home with sympathy for Federalist politics or, equally troubling, northern abolitionism. Jefferson did not abandon his principled opposition to the "peculiar institution" and his understanding that the system would have to end. But he insisted, in retrospect benightedly, that Virginians would have to implement voluntarily the scheme for emancipation and expatriation that he outlined in his *Notes on Virginia*, and that, in turn, required the enlightened leadership that his university ultimately would supply.

How could anyone possibly imagine that the University would produce a new generation of leaders who would defend slavery against the rising tide of antislavery sentiment in the northern states while at the same time preparing the way for its eventual abolition? How could such leaders ever emerge in a flourishing slave society, particularly when students were recruited exclusively from the wealthiest and most privileged classes? (There were no scholarships when the University opened, although Jefferson had earlier hoped that the education would be free.) Given the well-publicized antics of such students at William and Mary, Jefferson's hopes seem wildly misplaced, even delusional. More generously, we might conclude that Jefferson's great, deeply personal investment in the University testified eloquently to his enduring faith in republican government, the world historical significance of the American Revolution itself, and his hope for continuing progress.

There was no getting away from slavery at the University of Virginia when it finally opened its doors in 1825. As Ervin L. Jordan Jr. powerfully shows in his essay, enslaved people were everywhere on Grounds and played an essential role in the institution's ongoing operation. If anything, the ban against students bringing their own slaves to Charlottesville and the absence of accommodations for the slaves owned or hired by the University or by hotelkeepers charged with catering to the needs (and whims) of student-clients, made the pathologies of mastery and white racial domination more conspicuous than on home plantations. Enslaved workers served members of the master class who did not own them, and who did not therefore feel constrained by any self-interest, custom, or sentiment from abusive displays of mastery. "All whites," Jordan notes, "had the right to discipline slaves and so-called 'uppity' free blacks, as surrogate masters" and that right was repeatedly on conspicuous display at the University. Slaves and free blacks might benefit from serving an illicit market in alcohol and other mainstays of student life. But they had little reliable protection against the casual violence and abuse of young white men asserting their honor, race privilege, and mastery.

The free air of Charlottesville enabled adolescent masters-in-training to do their worst. The quasi-familial bonds that Jefferson hoped would attach students to professorial proxy-fathers to encourage educational intercourse and curb youthful indiscretions proved radically ineffectual. The kind of patriarchy Jefferson modeled at Monticello could not be effectively exercised by a largely foreign-born faculty that failed to engage the fleeting attention, much less command the respect, of lazy and self-indulgent students. Vain efforts to impose discipline provoked scions of the plantocracy to mobilize against despised, would-be authority figures. Nighttime revels and riots, blatant defiance of University rules, and routine harassment and displays of contempt kept beleaguered professors and their families on the defensive. The kind of peer culture that tormented college authorities at William and Mary characterized the early years at the University as well, perhaps in an even more extreme form. Virginia students achieved generational solidarity, forming strong bonds with one another and demonstrating their honor by upholding a code of silence on transgressions of University rules or the laws of the Commonwealth. Needless to say, this was not the sort of solidarity Jefferson envisioned in advocating a student honor code and governance system. At the University, the generations did not collaborate in the transmission of knowledge and transfer of cultural capital as hoped. Quite the contrary, the University Grounds were—sometimes quite literally—an intergenerational battlefield, with enslaved and free black workers often caught in the crossfire.

Living with students could be a demoralizing, disillusioning experience. Riotous students helped turn refugee radical Thomas Cooper—who, upon being dismissed as the University's first faculty member for his unorthodox religious views, became a member of the faculty and then second president at South Carolina College—into a reactionary. Disgusted by his defiant young charges, he dubbed them "the *offspring* of Democracy run mad." Jefferson hoped things would be different at his university.[3] An "Academical Village" in a wholesome rural environment, organized in family units headed by learned and inspiring professors, would enable sons of the Revolution to chart an enlightened course into the future: from generation to generation, the republic would be reborn and renewed. Jefferson lived long enough to see his hopes sorely tested. The privileged young men who passed through Charlottesville—many staying for only a brief period—proved impervious to the benign influence of would-be father figures and heedless of the world beyond Grounds; they were impetuous, masterful, prone to rise in righteous defense of their honor. With characters already formed, they defied reformation. With the success of the University so central to him, and to Virginia, he was willing to impose stern discipline after riotous behavior, even to the point of expelling a young grandnephew. Yet Jefferson kept the faith, overlooking—and looking beyond—the facts on Grounds, identifying with both the Revolutionary fathers and their wayward sons. Young leaders had come to the fore in 1776, and surely they would—they must—come forward again, in future crises that would shape his beloved Commonwealth's history and fulfill its destiny. In fact, while the intergenerational, familial bonds between students and faculty that Jefferson had sought largely eluded the University community, the intragenerational solidarity among the students would evidence itself again and again as students from "the University" became political, business, legal, military, and religious rulers.

Jefferson recognized that his own legacy was inextricably linked to the fate of Virginia and its University, and therefore to the ultimate success of the American Revolution itself. In darker moments, he despaired. With the Union on the verge of collapse in 1820 during the Missouri crisis, he regretted that "the useless sacrifice of themselves by the generation of 1776, to acquire self-government and happiness for their country, is to be thrown away by the unwise and unworthy passions of their sons." The Union's demise would be nothing short of "treason against the hopes of the world," negating and obliterating everything he had hoped to achieve.[4] When the crisis passed and the University welcomed its first students, a chastened Jefferson regained his equilibrium and renewed his faith in the rising generation, however much the privileged boys in Charlottesville might also be led astray by their "unwise and unworthy passions."

Notes

1. Jefferson to John Banister Jr., October 15, 1785, *PTJ*, 8:637.

2. *Notes*, Query XVIII (Manners), 162.

3. Thomas Cooper to Jefferson, February 14, 1822, *Founders Online*, https://founders
.archives.gov/documents/Jefferson/98-01-02-2662.

4. Jefferson to John Holmes, April 22, 1820, *Founders Online*, https://founders
.archives.gov/documents/Jefferson/98-01-02-1234.

American Education and Atlantic Circulations

NEVEN LEDDY

In England, it becomes every day more and more the custom to send young people to travel in foreign countries immediately upon their leaving school, and without sending them to any university. Our young people, it is said, generally return home much improved by their travels. [. . .] By travelling so very young, by spending in the most frivolous dissipation the most precious years of his life, at a distance from the inspection and controul of his parents and relations, every useful habit, which the earlier parts of his education might have had some tendency to form in him, instead of being rivetted and confirmed, is almost necessarily either weakened or effaced.
—Adam Smith, *Wealth of Nations*

A N AMERICAN EDUCATION during Jefferson's lifetime was an Atlantic affair. Particularly in the southern states, higher education frequently involved travel, sometimes transatlantic. With the exception of William and Mary, the South lacked functional institutions of higher education until the nineteenth century, with the result that Americans from the states south of Virginia were generally obligated to travel abroad to pursue professional credentials. This situation presented American parents with difficult choices, which varied across the Colonial, Revolutionary, and Early National periods, but always rested on a tension between cosmopolitan "finishing" and national or parochial ambitions. The process of educating an American reads like a Goldilocks story in which just the right amount of cosmopolitan finishing would cement elite status in America, but too much exposure to European culture could dissolve a fragile nascent American identity.

Jefferson was broadly in step with other Founders who had responsibility for the education of elite American youths. Along with John Adams and Henry Laurens especially, Jefferson was deeply engaged in the search for a cosmopolitan education that would serve American ambitions. Jefferson, unlike most of his peers, continued this investigation throughout his life to the extent that it seems plausible to suggest that the University of Virginia was Jefferson's answer to questions that he had been asking about American education and Atlantic circulations since the 1780s. In the Colonial period the South Carolina planter Henry Laurens settled on Geneva as the best available site for the education of his sons, and in the Revolutionary period the diplomat Benjamin Franklin and the Philadelphia merchant Robert Morris followed that example. Jefferson took longer to come to the same conclusion, but it is significant that he continued to look to Geneva as a model for American education later in life. In correspondence with Littleton Tazewell when the Virginia legislature was considering an endowment for a state college in 1805, Jefferson drew on five sources to model his vision: synopses of useful education provided by Joseph Priestley and Pierre Samuel Dupont de Nemours, the University of Edinburgh, the French "national institute," and a plan for the College of Geneva.[1]

Jefferson was consistent in his assessment of Edinburgh as the world's finest medical school, and he further endorsed study outside the medical faculty for American boys. During his years in Europe, Jefferson had reservations about the Genevan political context and did not offer a wholehearted endorsement of that city as an educational center until the 1790s. In his first year as American minister, Jefferson recommended Rome as the best option for private study, on the condition that boys board with a French-speaking family while in Rome.[2] By 1791, confident that the political context had improved, Jefferson wrote to Archibald McCalester that "[o]n the continent of Europe no place is comparable to Geneva. The sciences are there more modernised than anywhere else. There too the spirit of republicanism is strong with the body of the inhabitants." Significantly, Jefferson added the caveat that the Genevan aristocracy should be eschewed by the young, lest their questionable politics prove detrimental to American republican identity.[3] Jefferson's continued esteem for the College of Geneva is evident in his involvement with a scheme to transplant the college to the United States following the disruptive and radical revolution that engulfed Geneva in 1794.[4]

Like all the Founders in question, Jefferson worried that a European education would dilute American identity; he had a deeply antiurban worldview, and a special loathing of London. While he sharply defended a classical education—unlike Henry Laurens—Jefferson clearly hoped that the classics would be a buttress for an agricultural republicanism. He worried that exposure to the courts of Europe would confuse the rustic simplicity of American youths. And finally, he worried that unchaste European women, especially London prostitutes and the French in general, would debase American men. Regarding the travel required to reach European centers of education, Jefferson believed that it infected the young with a kind of melancholy that would leave them unsatisfied with a life in an agricultural republic. In his correspondence with William Short, Jefferson explained these dangers. In response, Short acknowledged that his own predicament was the result of too great an exposure to the dangers of Europe:

> I feel that those pleasures which are within the grasp of every body in Europe are transient and not at all adapted to captivate me. I know as little of them as most people, but enough to teach me that they are what no rational person can count on when he is taking measures for permanent happiness. On the contrary the enjoyments which all those who are properly settled in America may with certainty count on are such as I should look forward to with ecstasy, and with impatience, if I could persuade myself they would be within my reach. Nothing less than my doubts on this subject could have rendered my stay in Europe of so long duration. Long before this I should have bidden a final adieu to Paris and those charms for which it is so much celebrated. I can say more I should have left it without a sigh.[5]

With the exception of the dangers of travel itself, Geneva seemed to mitigate all of Jefferson's concerns, and override Short's binary distinction between Paris and America. The appeal of Geneva was often as a kind of anti-Paris, where elite American boys might imbibe European culture while avoiding the problematic European metropoles of Paris and London.

The Genevan hosts of these elite American were aware that a cosmopolitan education might present some unique problems for elite American boys. The case of Jefferson's grandnephew Dabney Terrill is telling on this point. Dispatched to Geneva after killing a fellow student in a duel at college in Pennsylvania in 1815, in a move choreographed by Jefferson, Terrill was immersed in the Genevan culture of education. At Jefferson's request his education was overseen by Professor Marc Auguste Pictet in Geneva, who wondered about the utility of such an education upon Terrill's return to America: "I don't know what degree of civilization exists in the part of Kentucky where he resides, but I must confess that I fear a little for him the contrast he might feel between the resources of the mind that were provided to him for four years by old Europe, and the kind of Society he will encounter in the back country, which perhaps has been only barely touched by education, and where it will be hard for him to find, as we say in Europe, 'somebody with whom to talk.'"[6] Jefferson's involvement in sending his sister's grandson to Geneva over any other foreign alternative suggests that he continued to hold Genevan education in especially high regard, even as he was working toward the establishment of the University of Virginia.

Jefferson's initial recommendation of Rome over Geneva marks out his views from those of the other Founders, in that Jefferson certainly seemed less phobic of Catholicism than many of his peers. Given that the sample group includes the descendants of French Huguenots (Laurens and John Jay), as well as the Adams family, it is not difficult to characterize Jefferson as the least anti-Catholic of the bunch, which is evidenced in his suggestions for boys and in his decisions regarding his own daughters. This points to the greatest imagined danger of a cosmopolitan education for American boys: Catholicism.[7] On this reading, education of whatever stripe was understood as an inoculation against the aesthetic and cultural lures of Catholicism, and on this question the respectable—if largely nominal—Calvinism of the Genevan republic once again answered American concerns.

In their disinclination to send their boys to London or any other metropolitan urban center, the Founders were in agreement—in this Jefferson may have been the most deeply antiurban in outlook. His reference to cities both European and American as "the sinks of voluntary misery" is only one of many quotable denigrations of urban life to flow from Jefferson's pen.[8] Jefferson's nonurban educational preferences were based on a more specific anxiety, which touches on the site of the University of Virginia. Writing to James Breckenridge in 1822, Jefferson explained that *capital* cities and education are a poor mix: "[T]hey [legislators] seem not to have considered that the seat of the government and that of the University are incompatible with one another that if the former were to come here [Charlottesville], the latter must be removed. [E]ven Oxford and Cambridge placed in the middle of London they would be deserted as seats of learning, and as proper places for training youth."[9] On this score, Geneva and Edinburgh offered an alternative to the great imperial capitals of Europe.

American Cohorts: Planters, Diplomats, and Merchants

The students who are the focus of this investigation were drawn from three specific groups: In the Colonial period a cosmopolitan education was largely reserved for the planter class, which included most of the South Carolina boys in this study. In the Revolutionary period the planter cohort was joined by the children and kin of the diplomatic corps and American merchants trading with Europe. Henry Laurens is the seminal figure in the formation of the earlier cohort, since he seems to be the originator of the American practice of Genevan education in the early 1770s. Eventually the Boston grandsons of Samuel Cooper and Benjamin Franklin, the sons of Robert Morris of Philadelphia, and many others found their way to Geneva in the Revolutionary and Early National periods.

When American diplomats and merchants arrived in Europe as agents of the Revolution, they began to cast around for suitable educational arrangements for their kin, in which the Genevan alternative to the schools of suburban Paris was a live and occasionally disputed option among American planters, diplomats, and merchants. The distinction between the polish and education offered in Paris and the more rigorous practice in Geneva was one component of the patriarch's selection process. The question of where to place their sons and wards was in many ways an expression of the anxieties of the Founders' generation: confessional, political, moral, financial, and dynastic.

American Identity and Cosmopolitan Anxieties

Writing in 1776, Adam Smith offered a scathing critique of university education in England: "In the university of Oxford, the greater part of the publick professors have, for these many years, given up altogether even the pretence of teaching."[10] To Smith's everlasting dismay, the failures of English education encouraged the substitution of the Grand Tour for a formal higher education in the Atlantic World. At the same time that the Founders worried about the nefarious outcomes of foreign travel and education in which boys might fall into dissipation, bad habits, poor health, the clutches of Catholic or undowried women, lapses in accounting, or tyrannical attitudes and foppish dress, Smith endorsed their anxieties:

> He commonly returns home more conceited, more unprincipled, more dissipated, and more incapable of any serious application either to study or to business, then he could well have become in so short a time, had he lived at home. By travelling so very young, by spending in the most frivolous dissipation the most precious years of his life, at a distance from the inspection and controul of his parents and relations, every useful habit, which the earlier parts

of his education might have had some tendency to form in him, instead of being rivetted and confirmed, is almost necessarily either weakened or effaced.[11]

Smith's objection to displacement in pursuit of education seems to have resonated with American elites both in the North, where respectable institutions of education were available, and in the South, where travel was essential in pursuit of professional credentials.

The northern case is perhaps more curious and speaks to the quest for gentility through education. The correspondence between a New York diplomat and a Philadelphia merchant on the question would seem to settle the matter in favor of national or parochial education. Writing to Robert Morris in 1782, John Jay explained:

> I think the youth of every *free* civilized Country should, if possible, be educated in it; and not permitted to travel out of it, 'till age had made them so cool and firm, as to retain their National and moral Impressions. . . . American Youth may possibly form proper and perhaps useful Friendships in European Semenaries, but I think not so *probably* as among their Fellow Citizens with whom they are to grow up, whom it will be useful for them to know, and be early known to, and with whom they are to be engaged in the business of active Life; and under the Eye and Direction of Parents, whose Advice, Authority and Example are frequently of more worth than the Lessons of hireling Professors, particularly on the subjects of Religion, Morality, Virtue and Prudence.[12]

The recipient of these insights, Robert Morris, had nevertheless sent both of his sons to Europe for further education, where they mixed with dozens of other American boys. John Jay's nephew Peter Jay Munro (1767–1833) spent at least one of his teen years in Paris, while Jay himself participated in American diplomacy—sometimes from his base in New York, but sometimes also in Europe. In neither case was there any obvious necessity for the Jay or the Morris boys to study in Europe, especially as they were not accompanied by their immediate families.

Jefferson was equally adamant that a cosmopolitan education or the accompanying European travel was unnecessary and dangerous, especially to the young. Jefferson's letters to Peter Carr make his position abundantly clear: "Travelling. This makes men wiser, but less happy."[13] To John Banister, Jefferson enumerated the many dangers of a European education: the peculiarities of the English, aristocratic privilege, youthful friendships with only foreigners, unchaste behavior, profligacy, and poor grammar.[14] Jefferson was nevertheless willing to encourage European travel in some very specific cases—notably that of his future son-in-law, Thomas Mann Randolph Jr.—and he allowed that in exceptional cases even young men might benefit from a cosmopolitan education.[15]

Atlantic Circulations: Education as Migration

If American education is conceived of as something necessarily ambulatory, it can be framed as a kind of migration, an educational sojourn. American motives and strategies in the education of succeeding generations can then be productively interrogated through the lens of migration and diaspora studies. In these terms, four questions present themselves. What were the push factors that drove Americans away from home for higher education? What were the pull factors that drew Americans inexorably toward London? Why were parents and guardians of the founding generation so leery of London and Paris? What motivated these parents and guardians to favor Geneva and Edinburgh specifically over the metropoles? Jefferson's correspondence is illuminating on each of these points.

The push factor that drove Americans to Europe from the Colonial period until the early nineteenth century was not addressed until the establishment of state colleges in the early republic. In the absence of credential-granting institutions in America, a flow of young men was directed toward London where those credentials were available. This hardly exhausts the question of the Atlantic gentility that could most easily be acquired through residence in London specifically and to a lesser extent in other European capitals. The third component examines the antiurban bias of American parents and guardians, and their fears of exposing their children to the dangers and temptations of European capitals. Finally, this essay touches on the emergence of a European alternative in Geneva to the major metropolises that was endorsed by Henry Laurens and Benjamin Franklin for their own progeny, which provided high-quality education for boys, immersive language training, gender segregation, and clerical oversight.

This last component will receive a cursory treatment in this essay, which only touches on the unique arrangement of Genevan education whereby few foreigners enrolled at the much-vaunted academy but hundreds boarded with private tutors. Hundreds of British youths and a surprising number of Americans passed through or paused at Geneva in pursuit of an Enlightenment education. As the object of historical inquiry, Geneva has been both marginalized and poorly represented. As a provincial Francophone city outside of French

sovereignty, Geneva is an orphan among national histories. When Geneva is
included in accounts of Early Modern Europe, it is overwhelmingly in its status as the "Protestant Rome" with a strong emphasis on Calvinism or the
French Protestant diaspora. This project instead hinges on the status of Geneva as a hub of teaching and research in the Enlightenment.

In an American context, higher education usually implied a sojourn
abroad, near or far. In the particular case of South Carolina, leaving the state
was a requirement for pursuing training in the liberal professions: Anglican
ministers could only be ordained in London; attendance at the Inns of Courts
was obligatory in order to practice law in the state; medical training was un-
available locally, as was any respectable course of study resulting in a creden-
tial or respectable qualification. Virginian education was a mitigated version
of this southern example, with a law degree available from William and Mary
beginning in 1779. In the North, conditions for higher education were very different; yet many young men from those states nevertheless traveled abroad for
further education, as we have seen with the sons of Robert Morris.

In the recent historical scholarship on the British Empire,[16] Carolinians
have been identified more closely with the West Indies than with the northern
colonies, which is borne out in the patterns of expatriation and education. For
the purposes of this case study, it is worth observing that most of the boys in
question came from the pinnacle of South Carolina's elite merchant planters,
and in their cultural and economic ambitions they closely resembled their Caribbean counterparts. Carolinians had been overrepresented among American students in London, ever since attendance at the Inns of Court had been
made a prerequisite for practicing law in South Carolina.

Beyond the credentials available exclusively in London, the Anglo-Atlantic
metropolis was the barometer by which American gentility would be measured. Julie Flavell does an excellent job of explaining the position of London
in an Atlantic network, and ably teases out the often conflictual motives of
Americans in the metropolis.[17] Daniel Kilbride outlines an attempt to buy
gentility off the shelf, which included sitting for portraits by British painters as
well as acquiring British-sanctioned luxury goods to take home.[18] Given the
age and immaturity of the boys in question, however, pedagogy rather than
gentility was the explanation for their time in London.

The correspondence between boys and parents is informative: the parents
have an educational agenda, which the boys attempt to assimilate and exe-
cute. As explained by (grand)father to son, it is an exacting and intimidating
agenda, fraught with moral and spiritual hazards. In the correspondence among

(grand)fathers, while no less anxious, this agenda is tempered by a measure of realism and a greater indulgence for dancing. Among the boys themselves, the pedagogical agenda is the source of pride, deference, and some bafflement—with the Inns of Court a particular source of puzzlement. While a number of published correspondences have been consulted in this investigation, the Laurens's papers have been especially fruitful in assessing parental motives. On the one hand, there is nothing exceptional in the Laurens family's pursuit of gentry status through the acquisition of a gentleman's education. On the other hand, Laurens was exceptionally hands-on in his approach to the education of his sons following the death of their mother in 1769.

Laurens is the key figure in this exploration, since he seems to be the originator of the American practice of Genevan education that eventually included the scions of many wealthy Carolina families. There is little doubt that the Laurens boys forged the first link in this chain of Genevan sojourners. Such was his persuasive capacity that he—along with John Laurens as a kind of factor on the ground in Geneva—organized the journey to Geneva for the sons of many of his business partners in the 1770s. John Laurens served as an able and enthusiastic agent in this process, with oversight of several younger boys during his years in Geneva and continuing after his departure for London—by organizing connections, tutors, and accommodation for the Manigault boys (sons of the wealthy Peter Manigault of South Carolina) in the 1780s.

Beginning in Charleston, Laurens continued his conversations about education in epistolary form from London, elaborating on the costs, dangers, and distortions of an English education. In the process Henry Laurens became a widely consulted oracle on boys' education. Laurens reasoned from the premise that Charleston lacked the public or private institutions to properly educate a boy of John Laurens's caliber; Henry Laurens suggested that for many others—including his own middle son, Henry Jr.—that the expense was a poor return on investment. For boys like Henry, classical education was overkill: "Hundreds of Men have their Mouths fill'd with jabbering Latin, while their Bellies are empty, whereas, if they had been taught to write good hands, and made perfect in Figures, they might every day meet with Employment which would give them bread, and put them in a way to Affluence. I don't object to learning Latin, but to a Latin and Greek Education in a commercial Country, without having a foundation of English, Reading, Writing, and Cyphering first well laid."[19] One of the great pleasures of a close reading of Laurens's account of his sons' performance is watching the "blockhead," Henry Jr., outperform expectations. The boys, for their part,

rarely questioned the formal classical curriculum but were more skeptical of
the value of attendance at the Inns of Court.

Laurens made himself at home in London, but kept his sons out of reach of
the British metropolis—in Birmingham, Shropshire, and Geneva—until the
eldest was twenty years old. This strong suspicion of London was not con-
fined to American parents and is also seen in Europeans, certainly Scots, and
many of the English themselves. Part of this antipathy stems from London's
reputation throughout the Atlantic World for vice and dissipation, but actual
experience of London living was common among the (grand)fathers in
question—Henry Laurens specifically, but also Benjamin Franklin and Peter
Manigault. Laurens had apprenticed in London as a young man and returned
with his sons in 1771 following the death of their mother in 1769. While Laurens set himself up in London, he initially placed his sons at the school of Richard Clarke, formerly of Charleston, who was a known quantity who hosted
several other Carolina boys. Upon the realization that the boys were often free
to roam the streets of the city without supervision, Laurens began to liquidate
Clarke's school, by removing first his own sons, but eventually all the Carolin-
ian students, who mostly found their way to Geneva.[20]

Push factors from Paris tended more toward the political and confessional,
but also included the antiurban biases of the Founders. While Franklin originally kept his grandson Benjamin Franklin Bache near to him in Passy, he
eventually determined that a French education presented two specific dangers
that resulted in Bache's evacuation to Geneva.[21] He elaborated on this in a
note to John Quincy Adams, explaining, "[A]s he [Bache] is destined to live in
a Protestant Country, & a Republic, I thought it best, to finish his Education,
where the proper Principles prevail."[22] When Franklin informed his daughter,
Sally, of his decision later that year, he returned to these two criteria: "[A]s I
intend him for a Presbyterian as well as a Republican, I have sent him to finish
his education at Geneva."[23] Franklin, given his stature and long residence near
Paris, was frequently consulted by fathers and guardians on matters of education and, like Henry Laurens before him, emerged as a strong advocate of
Genevan education.

As to the selection of Geneva specifically, we must begin with the (grand)
fathers and their expectations of their (grand)sons. From this perspective
Geneva was as notable for what it was not—London—as for what it offered. For
Henry Laurens in particular, Geneva was a kind of anti-London. The fathers and
guardians of these boys seem to have sought a compromise between the benefits of cosmopolitan finishing without unnecessary exposure to metropolitan

corruption, so that Edinburgh, Geneva, and other provincial towns were preferred destinations over the major centers of London and Paris.

Geneva boasted an exceptional class of pastor-tutors, who provided lodging and lessons as a means to supplement their clerical income. David Chauvet was the foremost of the pastor-tutors. Many of these Genevan hosts were ordained ministers of the Genevan Reformed Church and thereby members of the Company of Pastors along with all instructors at the Geneva Academy. The economics of this public-private organization are explained in Jennifer McNutt's recent book *Calvin Meets Voltaire*. Briefly, since Geneva produced more scholars and ministers than it could absorb, there emerged a class of pastor-tutors who drew many students to Geneva.[24] This arrangement was appealing to parents, one imagines, because they were confident of the moral and social standing of any member of the Company of Pastors. For the Carolinians, more so than their northern counterparts, this arrangement represented a continuity with their private education in Charleston, which was provided mostly by Anglican clergy.

The Genevan scholar-ministers would provide the core curriculum, especially for the younger students, while specific instructors in advanced topics would be hired for subjects like math. On some occasions, a respected scholar affiliated with the college might be convinced to give private lessons in his field of expertise, as was the case with the historian Paul-Henri Mallet. The boys might also attend public lectures at the College, as Joseph Manigault did. The mountaineering expeditions led by David Chauvet and other tutors always provoked substantial epistolary accounts.[25] These expeditions no doubt featured in Chauvet's geography course—which was substantially stripped of this "applied" element when Chauvet moved to London after 1782.

There was also significant social overlap between the mostly Genevan boys enrolled at the College and the American boys studying privately. In most cases the American boys shared lodgings with Genevan boys their own age, British students, and of course their fellow Carolinians. This occasionally mitigated the immersive language experience so valued by the Founders, as some of the boys surrounded themselves with fellow English speakers whenever possible. For many boys, Geneva served as a kind of hub for a more modular form of the Grand Tour, often with travel to and from London via France and Germany substituting for an extended circuit to France and Italy. As a consequence—and equally likely, the intention—these more circumscribed tourists spent most of their time in Protestant Europe. For the Huguenot boys of London and Carolina, as well as Genevans, this pattern reflected concentrations in the Huguenot diaspora.[26]

Laurens seems to have first considered a Genevan education for his sons in 1769–1770, but this remained only one among other options until John gave his consent to these arrangements after inspecting the situation on the ground in Geneva. Once arrived in England, Laurens's scheme was applauded and encouraged by his English connections—which was only reinforced by the departure of the Duke of Hamilton for Geneva in 1772, anticipating the Laurens party by a few months. In the 1770s British families heeded the ungenerous comments of Adam Smith and other Enlightenment luminaries that English universities were rotten. Aristocratic families with serious academic credentials increasingly turned to Geneva as an alternative, most notably the Stanhope family. In this sense the Laurens were on-trend. But all of this came to a sudden stop with the Genevan Revolution of 1782, and the exile of the ablest tutors of best reputation, David Chauvet among them. Having witnessed the revolution firsthand, Joseph Manigault confirmed the consequences of the subsequent repression: "Mme. Chauvet's Home was quite fallen, there was nobody at it. He is banished for ten years from the Republick. . . . There are not so many good Masters at Geneva as there were formerly, and it is deservedly fallen in its Reputation."[27]

Chauvet consequently moved his operation to London, which made a Genevan-style education more readily available to Americans and Britons alike. These developments go some way to explaining Jefferson's initial ranking of Rome ahead of Geneva as a site of private education for Americans. Jefferson explained that his initial reservations were political in nature, referring to its government as "a tyrannical aristocracy" that would be dangerous to American youths.[28] Letters from Geneva in 1788, however, presented a different picture to Jefferson. John Rutledge Jr. wrote that "[t]he wealthy and contented appearance of these happy people declares this to be the land of liberty. Everything here is gay chearful and happy and everything proclaims the superiority of the republican over every other sort of government."[29] William Short addressed the impact of the 1782 Geneva revolution on education explicitly: "I was convinced there that the late revolution had had less influence than I imagined on Geneva as a place of education, and when I saw the different light in which Professors are viewed at Geneva from Paris and other parts of Europe and considered the importance of youth respecting and seeing respected those by whom they are to be taught, I had no hesitation in determining that Geneva was to be preferred above any place I have yet seen."[30] Following these communications, Jefferson seemed satisfied that Geneva was less politically corrupt than he had earlier believed. The events of 1782 in Geneva, which preceded and foreshadowed the moderate constitutional revolution in France, would have been even more encouraging for Jefferson.

Gender and Class

American parents and guardians therefore carefully deliberated the scope of their charges' exposure to European culture. The generation of the Founders expressed strong preferences for Protestant educational contexts, but a sustained aversion to London. The Founders' preferences were differentiated by gender, which is most evident among the American diplomatic corps based in Paris and London. While boys were generally sent away from European metropoles to peripheral villages or to provincial cities, girls were kept closer to home, even at the risk of exposure to Catholicism in France or to a variety of degradations in London. A closer examination of these gendered choices, however, reveals that the educational arrangements for boys in Geneva and Edinburgh were analogous to the cloistered environment in which Jefferson's daughters passed their Paris years: American youths were both housed with, and educated by, clergy. Obviously the experience of a Parisian cloister and a Geneva host family were sharply different lived experiences for the youths in question, but the intentions of their parents in placing them in those situations were remarkably similar for boys and girls. The Parisian cloister and private education with a Genevan host family provided "respectability" in accommodation, gender segregation, and immersion in a Francophone environment coupled with language training, along with the kinds of chaperoned social training favored by anxious and absent parents.

Jefferson's choice of the Panthemont convent for his daughters' education seems obviously gendered, as American boys were certainly not habitually entrusted to French monks for their education. On closer examination, however, education preferences for boys do not seem all that different: in Geneva especially, the education of American boys focused on immersive language training, in a gender-segregated environment under clerical oversight. There are, however, some significant differences: girls did not travel unaccompanied, and even though Jefferson was not always a regular visitor, his girls were kept nearby.

On this point, Paris and Geneva were at opposite ends of a spectrum of gender integration: visitors to France often remarked on the astonishing extent of gender mixing in both public and salon contexts, while social life in Geneva was largely segregated by gender.[31] The Genevan institution of the *cercle* formalized the kind of gender segregation that was equally characteristic of Enlightenment Scotland. In Scotland an exclusively masculine sociability was organized around clubs, which met usually in a public tavern; in Geneva the same practice was organized around privately rented space in which groups of men and women socialized separately. While it is not clear that the Founders were aware of this particular characteristic of Geneva social life, they were certainly aware of—and troubled by—the presence of French women in the social life of Enlightenment Paris. So promiscuous were the French *salonnières* that even the least couth of Scottish philosophers, Adam Smith, won the lasting admiration of a French novelist when in Paris as a traveling tutor in 1766. From the perspective of an American dynast, Geneva consequently offered fewer opportunities for a bad marriage than did Paris.[32]

The transatlantic travels of American sons in pursuit of a higher education were a source of numerous anxieties for their parents and grandparents, as reflected in the choices those parents made for—or in collaboration with—their children. Along with his fellow Founders, Jefferson favored Protestant, Francophone, provincial, and gender-segregated environments for the education of American boys. While Jefferson committed his daughters to a Catholic convent in Paris, these preferences were modulated, but not entirely abandoned: Panthemont was a cloistered environment, with the result that Paris was not a part of the daily experience for Martha or Maria Jefferson. It provided immersive language training in a gender-segregated environment at least as effectively as a Genevan host family would, while maintaining strict gender segregation and excluding any possibility of a bad marriage. With these preoccupations in mind, Henry Laurens's choices for his sons do not seem much different from Jefferson's choices for his daughters.

Notes

1. Jefferson to Littleton W. Tazewell, January 5, 1805, *Founders Online*, https://founders.archives.gov/documents/Jefferson/99-01-02-0958.

2. Jefferson to John Banister Jr., October 15, 1785, *PTJ*, 8:635–36; Jefferson to Thomas Elder, November 25, 1785, *PTJ*, 9:58.

3. Jefferson to Archibald McCalester, December 22, 1791, *PTJ*, 22:430.

4. See Nicholas Hans, "The Project of Transferring the University of Geneva to America," *History of Education Quarterly*, 8 (1968): 246–51, and Jennifer Powell McNutt

and Richard Whatmore, "The Attempts to Transfer the Genevan Academy to Ireland and to America, 1782–1795," *Historical Journal*, 56 (2013): 345–68.

5. William Short to Jefferson, April 3, 1789, *PTJ*, 15:27.

6. Marc Auguste Pictet to Jefferson, November 1, 1819, *Founders Online*, https://founders.archives.gov/documents/Jefferson/98-01-02-0851.

7. For the context on American anxieties about Catholicism, see Maura Jane Farrelly, *Anti-Catholicism in America, 1620–1860* (New York: Cambridge University Press, 2018) (esp. chs. 3 and 4).

8. Jefferson to David Williams, November 14, 1803, *PTJ*, 41:728; "New York, for example, like London, seems to be a Cloacina of all the depravities of human nature," is perhaps the most evocative. Jefferson to William Short, September 8, 1823, *Founders Online*, https://founders.archives.gov/documents/Jefferson/98-01-02-3750.

9. Jefferson to James Breckenridge, April 9, 1822, *Founders Online*, https://founders.archives.gov/documents/Jefferson/98-01-02-2756.

10. Adam Smith, *An Inquiry Into the Nature and Causes of the Wealth of Nations*, R. H. Campbell and A. S. Skinner, eds., Glasgow Edition of the Works and Correspondence of Adam Smith, vol. 2 (Indianapolis: Liberty Fund, 1981 / Oxford University Press, 1976 [1776]): V.i.f.ii.8 / 760.

11. Ibid., V.i.f.ii.36 / 773–74.

12. John Jay to Robert Morris, October 13, 1782, *The Papers of Robert Morris, 1781–1784. Volume 6*: July 22–October 31, 1782, John Catanzariti and James E. Ferguson, eds. (Pittsburgh: Pittsburgh University Press, 1984), 577 (ftnts. omitted).

13. Jefferson to Peter Carr, August 10, 1787, *PTJ*, 12:17.

14. Jefferson to John Banister Jr., October 15, 1785, *PTJ*, 8:636–37. At that time Jefferson included the dangers to American republicanism that would be encountered in Geneva specifically.

15. For Thomas Mann Randolph's education in Edinburgh, see William H. Gaines Jr., *Thomas Mann Randolph: Jefferson's Son-in-Law* (N.p.: Louisiana State University Press, 1966), 13–24.

16. See, e.g., Andrew Jackson O'Shaughnessy, *An Empire Divided: The American Revolution and the British Caribbean* (Philadelphia: University of Pennsylvania Press, 2000).

17. Julie Flavell, *When London Was Capital of America* (New Haven, CT: Yale University Press, 2010).

18. Daniel Kilbride, *Being American in Europe, 1750–1860* (Baltimore: Johns Hopkins University Press, 2013).

19. Henry Laurens to John Rose, December 28, 1771, in *The Papers of Henry Laurens, Volume Eight: Oct. 10, 1771–April 19, 1773*, George C. Rogers Jr. and David R. Chesnutt, eds. (Columbia: University of South Carolina Press, 1980), 141.

20. See George C. Rogers Jr., *Evolution of a Federalist: William Loughton Smith of Charleston (1758–1812)* (Columbia: University of South Carolina Press, 1962), 56–96.

21. For Franklin's operation in Passy, see Jeffrey A. Smith, *Franklin & Bache: Envisioning the Enlightened Republic* (New York: Oxford University Press, 1990).

22. Benjamin Franklin to John Quincy Adams, April 21, 1779, *Founders Online*, https://founders.archives.gov/documents/Franklin/01-29-02-0292.

23. Benjamin Franklin to Sarah (Sally) Franklin Bache, June 3, 1779, *Founders Online*, https://founders.archives.gov/documents/Franklin/01-29-02-0496.

24. Jennifer Powell McNutt, *Calvin Meets Voltaire: The Clergy of Geneva in the Age of Enlightenment, 1685–1798* (Farnham, VT: Ashgate, 2013). See also Lenore O'Boyle, "The Problem of an Excess of Educated Men in Western Europe, 1800–1850," *Journal of Modern History* 42 (1970): 471–95.

25. Peter H. Hansen, *The Summits of Modern Man: Mountaineering after the Enlightenment* (Cambridge, MA: Harvard University Press, 2013).

26. Discussed in Kilbride, *Being American*, 21, 61. See also Hugh Trevor-Roper, "The Scottish Enlightenment," *Studies on Voltaire and the Eighteenth Century* 58 (1967): 1635–58.

27. Joseph Manigault to Gabriel Manigault II, June 21, 1783, University of South Carolina, South Caroliniana Library, Manigault Family Papers, box 1: November 7, 1747–February 13, 1797, folder 12.

28. Jefferson to John Banister Jr., October 15, 1785, *PTJ*, 8:636.

29. John Rutledge Jr. to Jefferson, August 30, 1788, *PTJ*, 13:552.

30. William Short to Jefferson, October 18, 1788, *PTJ*, 14:26–27.

31. On gender integration in French salons, see Dena Goodman, *The Republic of Letters: A Cultural History of the French Enlightenment* (Ithaca, NY: Cornell University Press, 1994); on public life in travel accounts, see Joan Dejean, *How Paris Became Paris: The Invention of the Modern City* (New York: Bloomsbury, 2014).

32. The novelist Marie-Jeanne Riccoboni is discussed in Neven Leddy, "Grave, Philosophical and Cool Reasoner: Mary Wollstonecraft on the Use of Gender in Adam Smith," *The Adam Smith Review* 7 (2013): 8–17.

Premature Men

Honor, Jefferson, and the College of William and Mary

ALAN TAYLOR

A MERICANS RARELY elect philosophers as their presidents. In the run-up to the pivotal election of 1800, Federalists denounced Thomas Jefferson's learning as showy but idiotic and dangerous. In a July 4, 1799, oration, a Connecticut Federalist mocked Jefferson's science as folly by titling the speech, "Sun-beams May Be Extracted from Cucumbers, But the Process Is Tedious." More than just silly, Jefferson's ideas were menacing, allegedly spreading the anarchic beliefs of French Jacobins who undermined law, order, and religion in the name of bloody revolution. Federalists urged voters to defend inherited traditions, particularly in religion, by rejecting Jefferson as a dangerous radical. Noah Webster exhorted, "Never let us exchange our civil and religious institutions for the wild theories of crazy projectors; or the sober, industrious moral habits of our country, for experiments in atheism, and lawless democracy. *Experience* is a safe pilot; but experiment is a dangerous ocean, full of rocks and shoals."[1]

While Federalists defended the past, Jefferson claimed the future. He assured a William and Mary student that the human "mind is perfectible to a degree of which we cannot as yet form any conception." Jefferson derided "as cowardly the idea that the human mind is incapable of further advances." Dismissing Federalists as retrograde bigots fond of medieval barbarism, Jefferson insisted that his election vindicated free and wide-ranging inquiry seeking new knowledge, which would enable humans to achieve a better and brighter future. This is what he meant by "science," which included all forms of inquiry.[2]

The culture war between Jefferson's philosophy and Federalist tradition persisted after the presidential election of 1800–1801. Federalists denounced Jefferson for supporting two young Virginians, William A. Burwell and Lewis

Harvie, ousted from Princeton for leading disturbances and promoting "atheism and infidelity." Both came from distinguished families well known to Jefferson, particularly the Harvies who had lived in Albemarle. At Princeton, Republican students from Virginia offended the college president and faculty, who were strict Presbyterians, staunch authoritarians, and firm Federalists. The Virginians insisted that their defiance served the larger cause of intellectual freedom. Indeed, they disdained the Princeton faculty as wedded to antiquated modes of teaching, which relied on memorizing and repeating the dogmas of professors. The college expelled Burwell and Harvie as ringleaders of protest and vandalism, but they landed on their feet by finding employment as secretaries for the new president. Disgusted Federalists thought the country was going to hell when young men reaped rewards after disrupting a traditional college.[3]

While defending Princeton, Federalist cultural critics blasted William and Mary, which so conspicuously supported Jefferson's cause. They alleged that the writings of the English radical William Godwin, particularly *Political Justice*, served as core readings at the College. They blamed Godwin and Jefferson for the concept that people could perfect themselves by a process of liberation from tradition. The primary response to the critics came from the College's president and a bishop of the Episcopal Church, James Madison, who was also a cousin of the more famous James Madison. In an essay published in November 1801, Bishop Madison insisted that William and Mary neither taught nor proscribed Godwin, but allowed every student to engage in "free and candid investigation." In that Jeffersonian spirit, Madison asserted that William and Mary offered a "system of rational education, calculated to disseminate truth in morals and politics, and to form wise and virtuous citizens."[4]

A few months later, the students discredited Madison's case for their wisdom and virtue. In February, two students fought a duel, with one suffering a minor wound. The faculty ousted both young men—the first expulsions of the Madison regime that had begun in 1777. The ousters outraged the other students, who were used to getting away with much worse. Charging arbitrary injustice by the faculty, the protestors demanded restoration of the evicted young men. When the faculty refused, the students boycotted classes and vandalized College and town. They targeted the homes of professors, particularly the law professor, St. George Tucker, smashing windows. The protestors also broke up a village shop and attacked both the College chapel and parish church to tear apart Bibles and prayer books. St. George Tucker's son, Henry St. George Tucker, concluded, "The College has been a complete scene of confusion. It has received a blow from which I fear it will never recover." Tucker blamed the foolish student "idea that dissipation and disorderly conduct" best demonstrated a young man's "reputation for talents!"[5]

The northern, Federalist press gleefully seized on the episode as evidence for the malign influence of Godwin and Jefferson at the College. The student riot vindicated the conservative view of human nature as innately depraved—and not remotely perfectible. If unleashed from the restraints of Christianity, Federalists argued, young men produced violent anarchy. The *New York Evening Post* warned, "Thus dies one of the oldest and wealthiest seminaries of learning in the United States of America. These may be considered as some of the blessed effects of the modern, or Jeffersonian, system of religion."[6]

Once again, Bishop Madison engaged in damage control by posing as an impartial observer in an anonymous newspaper essay. He correctly reported that the College had not closed, but he misled readers by insisting that the riot involved only five or six students. In conclusion, Madison vindicated Jefferson's influence at the College as promoting "virtue, & science, and pure republicanism, & the best interests of America."[7]

While the bishop publicly insisted that the trouble was overblown, the Board of Visitors privately assembled in a crisis session. In March, they authorized the faculty to expel any student who failed to adopt studious habits within a month. The Visitors specified that a good student "devotes to his studies at least six hours out of every twenty-four, independently of the time spent in the Lecture Rooms."[8]

A second new statute directed the faculty to "compel a Student to give Evidence on his honor against any Student accused of an offense." If he refused to testify, the faculty could suspend him. The Visitors sought to redirect honor, so cherished by students, away from protecting one another, instead, to recognizing a duty to tell the full truth. Students, however, rebuffed that redirection as insulting. One explained, "There is an idea of dishonor connected with the name of an informer, which no student will ever be willing to attach to himself." In April, nearly half of the College's seventy-one students resigned and returned home, damaging the school's finances, which depended on tuition. In November 1802, Bishop Madison again posed as a student in a newspaper essay to insist that all was well thanks to the new statutes: "Our college is now the emblem of a well-regulated family. Everyone sees his duty, and knows that a parental authority will enforce that duty."[9]

Student defiance contradicted the bishop's insistence on a new reign of harmony and order. On March 31, 1803, the faculty expelled four students for participating in a duel: two as principals and two as seconds. The expulsions outraged their peers. On April 1, they attacked the Williamsburg parish church of Reverend John Bracken, who also served as the most despised professor at the College. According to a Norfolk newspaper, students "broke into the church, played on the organ for nearly two hours, and then went to the church yard, dug up the body of a female that had been buried for many months, took it from the coffin, and placed it on the floor of an empty house in a situation too shocking to describe!!!"[10]

In an odd and anonymous response published in a newspaper, the bishop insisted that the purloined corpse was male and came from the burial ground for the insane asylum rather than from the parish churchyard. He refused to confirm or deny that the culprits were students but insisted that they had dug up the corpse for medical study—which seems unlikely unless the diggers were students. "Similar cases have frequently occurred in every part of the world, without exciting any extraordinary abhorrence," Madison huffed. The bishop told less than the full truth, for a student later confirmed, "[t]he Students in their last *insurrection* broke into the Church, beat the windows down, and nearly completed the destruction of the organ. Such frequent behavior has discouraged the inhabitants, and they have abandoned both the Organ and Church."[11]

Another spate of tough new statutes followed upon the newspaper denial of any real problem at the College. Passed in July, the latest regulations increased the frequency of course examinations and imposed a review of each student's moral behavior at the end of the first year. Only the worthy could return for a sophomore year. In December, the bishop assured the other James Madison that the College was "in a state of perfect order" because of the strict new regime: "[W]e will never again permit a student to continue here, a single Day, after he has shewn the least Disposition to Idleness & Irregularity." It must have been hard, however, for students to take seriously the bishop's new pose as a tough disciplinarian.[12]

The new statutes alienated the leading professor, St. George Tucker. He bristled at the mandate that every professor conduct bed checks twice a week to enforce a curfew on students. He also took offense at a second statute meant to increase faculty presence: "That no professor shall absent himself from college during the terms prescribed for lecturing, nor on the times of public examinations or exercises." Serving as a state judge as well as a college professor, Tucker went to Richmond for court sessions during the winter term. He made up for his College absences with a hurried spate of lectures upon his return home. Often he held those sessions in the convenience of his home rather than at the College.[13]

Always proud and increasingly irritable, Tucker resigned in December 1803 (effective March 1804). He blasted the new statutes as fit only for "the superintendents of the little truants of a country village" and beneath his honor as "a professor of liberal science, honoured with the important trust of assisting the studies" of young men "destined to fill the most conspicuous stations, and the highest offices of the state." To accept the regulations "must degrade the professor in the eyes of his pupils, and of the public, & the man in his own eyes." Tucker had his own robust sense of wounded honor.[14]

Tucker's resignation further damaged William and Mary's decaying reputation. The visitors appointed a local judge, William Nelson, of gray hair and scant accomplishment, to replace the College's most distinguished faculty member. The best that another professor could say of Nelson was that he "danced very merrily, though he had silvered locks." The change of law professor and the authoritarian new rules irritated the students. Henry St. George Tucker reported, "The laws are at present very strict and the bishop very arbitrary. The young men are not yet rebels, yet this is the way to make them so."[15]

William and Mary reached a new low in March 1808, when the faculty sought to suppress drunken parties and balls. Angry students vandalized the College and threatened the bishop and his home. Ellen Randolph informed her grandfather, Thomas Jefferson: "[T]here has been a terrible riot at Williamsburg 15 boys were expelled and 5. thrown in Jail and fined 20. dollars a piece." The city militia had to patrol the streets for several nights. A resident reported that a few students "refused to join in the conspiracy" and, instead, helped guard Bishop Madison's house. One of them, Samuel Myers, denounced his riotous peers as having "arrived at a state of depravity and insensibility."[16]

The son of a leading merchant in Norfolk, Myers resolved to study hard and avoid dissipated company, save, he conceded, for two or three times a week. He welcomed the latest round of strict new regulations and hoped for better enforcement than in the past. Myers cherished the friendship of his housemate, William C. Somerville of Richmond: "[A] better one I believe I could not have possibly chosen. . . . He is a clever young man and well spoken, but is rendered far more respectable by his fortune, reported to be a hundred thousand pounds." They shared "the same desire and intention of applying closely to our studies and avoiding company as much as possible."[17]

Three months later, however, Myers wrote to his father: "Several insults which I had received from Somerville compelled me on Saturday morning to call on him for an explanation." They met at a meadow on the margins of town, where Somerville called Myers a liar, which "drew from me a blow." Somerville refused to back down, so Myers offered to fetch two pistols from a friend "that we might decide it on the spot." When Somerville refused, Myers put up a public notice "to post him in the College as a poltroon"—which meant a coward. Although he violated College rules, Myers insisted that "the dictates of honor impelled" his action. A magistrate arrested Myers and Somerville, compelling both to post bond to keep the peace. The faculty held a hearing but settled for admonishing the two young men.[18]

Honor culture could divide the best of friends and cast even dedicated students on a deadly path. Genteel people loved to gossip about duels, closely judging the conduct of the participants to assess their performance. Youths felt compelled to adhere to public expectations and shape the circulating talk by their subsequent descriptions of encounters. Rather than hide their participation in duels, as either principal or second, students gloried in proving their genteel manhood and devotion to their best friends.[19]

After leaving college, Myers returned to Norfolk to study law. One day in May his father, Moses Myers, a merchant, visited the city market, where he ran into Mr. Bowden, a former business partner. Resuming an old quarrel, Myers called Bowden "a Rogue, upon which Mr. Bowden gave him several blows with a Cane." With a bloody head, Moses staggered home, fainting from the loss of blood just as he met his son. Thinking his father dead, Samuel angrily rushed down to Bowden's countinghouse and accosted him: "How have you dared, Sir, to insult my Father[?]" Firing a pistol, Myers shot Bowden dead. Just twenty-eight years old, the dead man left behind a wife and four children. Thanks to the best lawyers and indulgent judges, Myers escaped trial and later became a leading lawyer in Norfolk.[20]

In Williamsburg, Lelia Tucker, St. George Tucker's wife, reported in 1811 that student-on-student violence had increased: "Dirks & pistols are carried in the Pockets and Challenges are sent to & from." She wished that the students would heed the "excellent Sermon" recently given by Reverend Bracken on the merits "of meek resignation in opposition to human feeling." But Bracken was the last man that any student would follow. Trained to assert their honor as the essence of masculinity, young gentlemen balked at submitting their souls to Christian conversion, which seemed feminine to them.[21]

Dead and Buried

The College suffered from the violent episodes. Enrollment stagnated at about fifty, two-thirds of its peak in early 1802 when parents and students had felt a surge of optimism about William and Mary in the wake of Jefferson's electoral triumph. The College compared poorly to Princeton, Harvard, and Yale, all of which attracted at least 150 students. Few William and Mary students persisted for more than a year or two, and almost none met the daunting requirements for a degree. From 1800 through 1805, the College graduated only three students, although more than 150 attended courses during some of that time. William and Mary also struggled to attract and retain good professors. In March 1807, Joseph Cabell reported that the College had only five of its six professors, and they were "more miserably compensated for the services they render, than any five men in America."[22]

Many genteel Virginians disdained the strict new regulations as degrading to the honor of students, while other parents distrusted enforcement as ineffectual, leaving the young men as wild and impious as ever. In 1804, one student explained, "That there are so few [students] is attributable in a great measure to the dissipation of the place. Parents are afraid to send their children here, lest their morals should be perverted." William Wirt, a prominent attorney, insisted that the students "run riot in all the wildness of dissipation; while the venerable professors are forced to look on, in the deep mortification of impotence." They could only watch and mourn "the ruin of their pupils and the destruction of their seminary."[23]

Almost alone among Virginians, Joseph C. Cabell believed that the College could rally with a little help from its many distinguished alumni, especially Jefferson. Born into a wealthy and prestigious family of Amherst County in the Piedmont, Cabell was a sickly but brilliant student, who attended the College in 1796 to 1798 and returned in 1800 to study law with St. George Tucker. A fellow student praised Cabell's winning combination of a "most ardent love for Science" and "easy and respectful manners which never fail to seize upon the affections." Jefferson was an old family friend who helped Cabell by providing a reading list on law, politics, religion, math, astronomy, geography, poetry, oratory, philosophy, literary criticism, and chemistry. When his health took a turn for the worse, Cabell toured Europe from 1803 to 1806 to investigate educational systems, geology, politics, and ancient sites. Returning to the United States and Williamsburg in 1806, he courted Polly Carter

Tucker, an heiress and one of St. George Tucker's stepchildren. They married in January 1807 and spent most of the next two years lodging in the rambling Tucker house, while Cabell prepared to launch his political career in Nelson County, recently created in a division of Amherst.[24]

In Williamsburg, Cabell befriended the new professor of modern languages, Louis Hue Girardin, "an ingenious Frenchman" with an interest in natural history. They proposed a "museum of nature" located at the College and supported by a new Natural History Society. "It is time the Virginians should dispel the shades that hover over our country," Cabell wrote to his old friend and classmate, Isaac A. Coles, who had become President Jefferson's secretary. Cabell hoped that the museum and Natural History Society could help revive the College. He conceded that William and Mary suffered from insufficient funding and "the want of an overawing population in the town . . . to suppress the riotous disposition of the students." Still, he concluded, "we ought to make the best of it, as it is all we have."[25]

Coles and Jefferson disagreed, deriding the College as a lost cause and the Natural History Society as a nonstarter in a state indifferent to intellectual life. They preferred to push for a "great new University" in the Piedmont. Five years later, Cabell considered accepting an appointment as a professor at William and Mary, but his brother dissuaded him. William Cabell insisted that Joseph instead should "keep up the idea that you are still in the world. You would indeed be dead and buried" at the College.[26]

The College's decline accelerated after the death of its longtime president, Bishop James Madison, in March 1812. The new president, John Bracken, was an elderly and often drunken Episcopalian minister whom a visitor thought "looks more like a tavern keeper than a divine." Noting Bracken's limited support for the Revolution and subsequent Federalism, Jefferson disdained the new president as a "tory" and "simpleton." In December, Cabell led a push among the Visitors to force Bracken's resignation and replace him with Peter Carr, Jefferson's nephew. But Jefferson persuaded Carr to decline, deeming the College a lost cause. Bracken persisted as president.[27]

The College also suffered from the War of 1812, which exposed the Tidewater to British raids. The students melted away to avoid militia drafts to serve in the malaria-ridden camps of men defending Norfolk. In 1814, a mere twenty-one students attended the College, which had only one professor left. Fed up with the decline, the Visitors pressured the decrepit president to resign in October 1814. They replaced him with Dr. John Augustine Smith, born in Virginia and briefly educated at the College in 1800, but recently a medical professor in

New York. Energetic, he doubled as the professor of moral philosophy and taught law and political economy as well. He repaired buildings and upgraded the scientific apparatus. From a mere twenty-one enrolled in 1814, the student body grew to ninety-two in 1817. In a newspaper puff piece, Smith boasted, "Contemplate now the great, the rapid, the delightful change, and the heart of every Virginian and of every Republican must exult at the recollection that WILLIAM & MARY IS AGAIN RESTORED."[28]

Although the College attracted more students, they remained as dissipated and disorderly as ever. A frequent visitor to Williamsburg, Cabell, sighed, "Whilst here, I am probably a closer student than any at the college." In a diary entry for May 3, 1816, Powhatan Robertson reported partying from dusk until three the next morning: "As we danced all night, we were not very well prepared for a lecture room, of course did not reap much benefit from the lecture." Once that lecture ended, he had his friends returned to the tavern to resume dancing and drinking for another evening. Robertson concluded, "However strong may be the resolutions of the mind, they will and must give way to the feelings of the heart."[29]

Smith vowed to control the students, rejecting the popular belief "that young Virginians were absolutely uncontroulable; that they sucked in with their mother's milk, such high spirited notions, as to be ever after ungovernable." Smith "would much prefer" that the faculty "should be ourselves the sole occupants of this venerable pile, than see it crowded with a lawless host of ungovernable students." He nearly succeeded. During his first ten years as president, the College expelled or suspended seventy-seven students, about a fifth of the total attending, and more than twice as many as those ousted during the previous thirty years. The expulsions showed Smith's determination, for the College refunded the fees paid by the ousted—a great sacrifice for an institution so dependent on tuition.[30]

Smith's bustling energy impressed Cabell, who praised his friend in 1815: "Smith has a happy turn for the Government of young men. He is very ardent and entirely devoted to the welfare of the College." Cabell's nephew Nicholas put that confidence to the test by entering the College that fall. His father William, a former governor of the state, had both hopes and fears for Nicholas as a student: "I believe he went down with good determinations, but I know he will yield to the first temptation" to become idle and drunken.[31]

In May 1816 Nicholas tangled with a larger and more popular classmate, Robert Douthat. Feeling insulted by Nicholas, Douthat threatened him with a humiliating caning, so Nicholas obtained a pistol and put up notices at the

College accusing his rival of cowardice. The faculty intervened and suspended both for the rest of the term.[32]

News of Nicholas Cabell's conduct spread statewide in the gossip of Virginia's gentry, which embarrassed the former governor. William H. Cabell sought to spin the story to his son's credit by drafting a statement that vindicated Nicholas for resorting to a pistol to avoid "the degradation of being caned . . . and so would any other man, whatever professors as such may say to the contrary." Disgusted by his son's suspension, Cabell vowed, "I shall never place another son under the guardianship of men who are capable of such injustice." While urging colleges to discipline their students in general, genteel parents fiercely defended their own sons who reaped punishment. Governor Cabell criticized Nicholas in family letters but could never abide public shame inflicted by professors on his boy.[33]

Smith tried to suppress the nocturnal pranks of breaking into the College belfry or parish church steeple to clang the bells to disquiet town and faculty. In 1817 he complained "[t]hat night after night the repose of the town had been disturbed by whooping and shouting, by the ringing of the church-bell, and the firing of cannon." When summoned to testify, no student would confess or implicate others. Smith sputtered that "these deliberate violations of truth, so far from exciting the indignation of the virtuous part of the *students*, were becoming matters of mirth." Nothing so enraged the vain Smith as to become the butt of student mockery, so he suspended ten suspects in February. Yet the nocturnal disorders persisted. One night in May 1822, Smith ventured out to trap the culprits. Instead, he charged into an ambush of hurled plaster and blows from sticks. Able to identify four assailants, he secured their expulsion, but bell ringing resumed in early 1824, when Smith suspended another eight students.[34]

In February 1818, students protested that a new professor of chemistry had overcharged them. When the faculty rejected their petition, students resorted to their nocturnal tricks: firing a cannon in the main street to disturb the inhabitants after pulling down the gate and breaking the windows of a local judge who served on the Board of Visitors. A scuffle followed between a student, waving a knife, and an angry townsman. The faculty demanded a written apology from every signer of the petition. Twenty-six, a third of the students, refused, which led to their suspension. Resorting to the *Richmond Enquirer*, the expelled students denounced Smith; "Deluded man! Know that Virginians" possess "a spirit of prompt resistance to any encroachment on their just rights."[35]

To break that resistance, Smith required any suspected student to swear under oath to his innocence or guilt. If none confessed to a violation, then in stage two, Smith could demand of any student whether he knew anyone to have lied under oath. The faculty suspended any student who refused to respond. "There is no alternative, order must be maintained, or the Institution must sink," he explained. When many fathers sided with their sons, Smith replied that no student had to testify "to the disadvantage of a Fellow-Student, until that Fellow-Student has *told a public, deliberate, solemn falsehood*. Let him object to the law who wishes his son to acquire or to retain a friend capable of such an act." Smith tried to turn the concept of honor against the students, for there was no greater dishonor than exposure in a lie. He claimed to correct their "abuse of that sacred, but most hackneyed and perverted term HONOR." But students despised the informer statute as a threat to their honor, by compelling them to betray a peer or to lie.[36]

The expulsions and informer statute soured many genteel Virginians on the College, reversing the revival of William and Mary. One ousted student assured his uncle, "The College is in great confusion. They are suspending students every day there." From the peak in 1817 of ninety-two, enrollment plummeted to fifty in the fall of 1818 and to half of that by 1824. Most elite Virginians refused to send their sons to a college that coerced them to become informers, imperiling their sacred honor. Soured on the College rules by his son's punishment, William H. Cabell preferred to tolerate student disorder rather than compromise honor:

> The Professors *must* give over the idea of compelling the students to give evidence against each other & themselves. I have always believed that the disorderly spirit prevailing in our Colleges has proceeded from the effort to enforce this regulation. The students revolt at it & rush into excesses in order to show their determination not to submit. They lose all respect for men who endeavor to enforce upon them what they believe to be dishonorable and this want of respect & spirit of resistance produce most of the disorders which disgrace our Colleges. If the authors of offences cannot be discovered, the offences must remain unpunished. The remedy, & the only proper one, is to punish very severely the few that are detected.

Virginian opinion further turned against Smith's informer policy, when he foolishly cited the similar statutes enforced at Harvard, Princeton, and Yale: the bastions of Yankeedom.[37]

Black Rides

During the early nineteenth century, disorder affected every American college, North and South. That problem, however, seemed especially associated with southerners, often considered the ringleaders of turmoil at northern schools. The most troubled northern university was Princeton, which Jefferson "held in great contempt as ... the most licentious and unruly seminary on the continent." It had the largest proportion of southern students, usually a third, which struck observers as no mere coincidence with the school's troubles.[38]

The student tumult proved especially deep and pervasive at southern universities. At the University of North Carolina, students shaved the tail of the president's horse, toppled his outhouse, and stole and hid away deep in the woods his cart and garden gate. A student there thought his peers the most drunken, profane, and defiant in the land. His father partially disagreed: "The dissipation you speak of pervades all the States where Slavery abounds. Were you conversant with the habits of So[uth] Carolina or Georgia University, you would find darker traces there than at Chapel Hill." To rile their professors, South Carolina students staged "blackrides," when they blackened their faces, stole the horses of faculty, and galloped about campus while holding flaming torches. After exhausting a horse and drawing a cheering crowd, a "blackrider" dismounted and slipped into the midst of his fellows to hide from investigation. The Carolina students delighted in demonstrating the impotence of frustrated professors.[39]

Most observers regarded southern students as more undisciplined, dissipated, and defiant than their northern peers. Thomas Cooper was well positioned to compare northern and southern students, for he had taught in Pennsylvania before becoming president of South Carolina College. In February 1822, Cooper reported that students stole his horse for a "blackride," broke his house windows, and even fired guns to startle him.[40]

A former radical democrat, Cooper became more reactionary in disgust at student defiance, which he deemed "the *offspring* of Democracy run mad. No professors of any reputation will stay at an institution where their authority is so disputed inch by inch and their lives put in jeopardy if they resist the encroachment of a hot headed set of boys." Writing to his friend Jefferson, Cooper declared, "In my own opinion, the parental indulgence to the south renders young men less fit for college government than the habits of the northern people; and the rigid discipline of the northern seminary must be put in force inexorably in the south." Jefferson must have been astonished to read this from his radical old friend, for the philosopher of Monticello wanted his university to defend Virginia against social change on northern terms.[41]

Southern students built a powerful peer culture that pressured all to seek approval from one another instead of professors. A South Carolina College graduate recalled that the student "sees his professors for an hour or two only every day. There is no social relation between them. The student herds with the boys alone." Seniors set a tone that new students emulated. The graduate recalled, "The raw freshman . . . is ambitious to emulate the high spirited example of his senior. He makes rapid advances in smoking, chewing, playing billiards, concocting sherry cobblers, gin slings and mint juleps . . . ." A Virginian at Princeton attributed the frequency of disturbances there to the southern-inflected student culture: "There is something wonderfully inflammable in the nature of young men, which is fostered and promoted by the manner of living together . . . . A feeling of resentment or indignation communicates itself like electricity, and what I most wonder at, is that we have not more riots." Peers shunned and insulted the rogue student who failed to join them in defying the morality preached by professors. A few painful examples prodded the rest of the new students into line with the peer culture.[42]

Above all, students covered for one another by refusing to testify against a peer accused of any infraction. Nor would any student admit to his own misdeed when pressed by a faculty investigation. He deemed any questions about others as impugning his sacred honor never to betray them. At Yale, a Virginian denounced northern students who did testify against peers. "If a young man so far violated the laws of propriety as to go and inform against a fellow student, the very fact would blast his every prospect of living, much less of distinction, in the South; it should be so; the name character and votaries of Judas Iscariot will ever be condemned and despised, for shame! For shame!"[43]

Colleges, particularly in the South, became trapped in a spiral where defiant students provoked faculties and Visitors into imposing stricter codes meant to forbid every behavior seen as triggering that defiance. Those rules banned drinking, gaming, dueling, wearing dandy clothes, keeping guns, dogs, and slaves on campus, frequenting prostitutes, staying out late, sleeping in to skip classes, and making a racket to rouse sleeping townspeople. By mandating expulsions for violation, the new codes increased the stakes of that conflict. Enforcement fell on the beleaguered faculty. In addition to their full days in the classroom, they had to become the nocturnal monitors of a large number of younger and spryer malcontents. By defying the new rules, the students defended their own turf, where they could more readily humiliate professors as ineffectual. Students insisted that the faculty lacked "rightful authority to restrain them in their pleasures and amusements, or interfere at all with their moral conduct."[44]

During the 1810s, college leaders tried to enlist parental support by sending home reports after every term on every student. More often, however, parents sided with sons, favoring their stories of innocence persecuted by bullying and dishonorable professors. When push came to shove, genteel parents blamed the faculty for failing to set genteel examples that could inspire students without resorting to coercion. Few southern fathers wanted their sons to forfeit the esteem of genteel peers by submitting to strict rules that compromised personal honor. The honorable and genteel student reflected better on his parents than did the mean fellow who studied in his room and told a professor what he wanted to hear. And family ties were too sentimental and precious to southern parents to consider siding with any outsiders at the expense of a son's reputation.[45]

Premature Men

St. George Tucker blamed William and Mary's decline on impetuous young men bred by Virginia's honor culture. In 1809, Tucker commiserated with another son-in-law, John Coalter, on the birth of a son, for "unless the manners of our Youth, or the management of their Tutors, shall undergo a most surprising & happy change in this Country, I had rather he should never hear of an *Academy* or a *College* than enter the walls of one." After raising six sons and step-sons, Tucker exulted: "I have no young son to educate." A few years later, the childless Cabell reached the same conclusion after the College expelled his nephew: "When I see so many instances of kind Parents rendered miserable by thoughtless or ungrateful sons, I am not very sorry to have my skirts clear of such troublesome appendages."[46]

A relative of St. George Tucker, George Tucker, had attended the College during the 1790s. Later he published a satire featuring a young man named Harry Whiffler, the son of a Tidewater planter who sent his boy "to the college of William and Mary, where he soon went thro' the whole circle of *vices* taught in that polite seminary. It is true, he didn't make quite so great a progress in the sciences. He passed, however, for a lad of great genius, principally upon the ground of his laziness." Harry "played cards all night and lay abed all day" save for on the Fourth of July, when he gave a bombastic and patriotic address at the courthouse in Williamsburg. An elderly listener noted, "It was a mighty learned piece indeed, as she was sure nobody (except the Bishop) could understand a single word, from beginning to end." Harry abruptly left the College after picking "a quarrel with one of his companions, about something or other, challenged him to a duel, and got a slight flesh wound by way of diploma." He returned home to practice law and felt qualified for "the House of Delegates and Congress" by delivering pompous speeches to loungers at the post office and tavern.[47]

Virginia's leaders worried that young men lacked the self-discipline to learn enough to lead the state after the Revolutionary generation passed away. In 1818, the state's leading Presbyterian minister, John Holt Rice, lamented the arrogance of collegians, who "pronounce their opinions with an air of infallibility; and although their reading extends to little more than a newspaper paragraph, or . . . the titles of a few books, they speak as though they knew all that is knowable, and could do all that is possible." Worse still, they "swear like privateersmen; and are very apt to make a display of this admirable gift, if they happen to travel with a minister of the gospel, or other pious person. It is really mortifying to find such creatures thriving on our republican soil."[48]

Thomas Jefferson and John Randolph agreed on almost nothing except that genteel young Virginians were too wild and full of themselves. In 1807, Randolph warned a young kinsman: "A petulant arrogance, or supine, listless indifference, marks the character of too many of our young men. They early assume airs of manhood; and these premature men remain children for the rest of their lives. Upon the credit of a smattering of Latin, drinking grog, and chewing tobacco, these striplings set up for legislators and statesmen." Given Randolph's misspent youth, which featured a duel at the College, his advice boiled down to: do as I write and not as I did. The more scholarly Jefferson had more credibility. In 1814 he wrote a sarcastic letter to John Adams, with whom he had reconciled in old age: "[O]ur post-revolutionary youth are born under happier stars than you and I were. they acquire all learning in their mothers' womb, and bring it into the world ready-made. the information of books is no longer necessary; and all kno[w]le[d]ge which is not innate, is [held] in contempt." All men may have been born equal, but they were not born educated. Jefferson did hope that a new and improved university could rescue Virginia from the generation created by the unanticipated consequences of revolution.[49]

Notes

This essay is taken, in slightly different form, from *Thomas Jefferson's Education* by Alan Taylor. © 2019 by Alan Taylor. Used by permission of W. W. Norton & Company, Inc.

1. Linda K. Kerber, *Federalists in Dissent: Imagery and Ideology in Jeffersonian America* (Ithaca, NY: Cornell University Press, 1970), 19–22, quoting Noah Webster on 21.

2. Jefferson to Elbridge Gerry, January 26, 1799, *PTJ*, 30:645–53; Jefferson to William G. Munford, June 18, 1799, *PTJ*, 31:126–30 ("mind" and "cowardly"); Jefferson to Joseph Priestley, January 27, 1800, and March 21, 1801, *PTJ*, 31:339–41, 33:393–95, and Jefferson to Moses Robinson, March 23, 1801, *PTJ*, 33:423–24.

3. Garrett Minor to Joseph C. Cabell, July 8, 1800, Cabell Papers, Swem Special Collections Library, College of William and Mary (SSCL-CWM hereafter); Manasseh Cutler, *Life, Journals, and Correspondence or Reverend Manasseh Cutler* (Cincinnati: Robert Clark & Co., 1888), 2:172 ("atheism"); Gerard W. Gawalt, "'Strict Truth': The Narrative of William Armistead Burwell," *Virginia Magazine of History and Biography* 101 (January 1993): 103–4; Mark A. Noll, *Princeton and the Republic, 1768–1822: The Search for a Christian Enlightenment in the Era of Samuel Stanhope Smith* (Princeton, NJ: Princeton University Press, 1989), 126–51; Thomas Jefferson Wertenbaker, *Princeton, 1746–1896* (Princeton, NJ: Princeton University Press, 1946), 134–38.

4. Theodore Dwight, *An Oration Delivered at New-Haven on the 7th of July, A.D. 1801, Before the Society of the Cincinnati, for the State of Connecticut* (Suffield: Edward Gray, 1801), 45; Bishop James Madison to James Madison, October 24, 1801, *PJM-SSS*, 2:196–97; [Bishop James Madison], "Late a Student of William & Mary," *National Intelligencer*, November 20, 1801; Steven J. Novak, *The Rights of Youth: American Colleges and Student Revolt, 1798–1815* (Cambridge, MA: Harvard University Press, 1977), 98.

5. Thomas L. Preston to Andrew Reid Jr., February 22, 1802, *WMQ*, 1st ser., 8 (April 1900): 216; Charlotte Balfour to Eliza Whiting, February 23, 1802, Blair, Braxton, Horner, Whiting Papers, ser. 1, box 1, SSCL-CWM; Joseph S. Watson to John Hartwell Cocke, March 26, 1802, John Hartwell Cocke Papers, box 3, Albert and Shirley Small Special Collections Library, University of Virginia (ASSCL-UVA hereafter); Henry St. George Tucker to Joseph C. Cabell, March 28, 1802, Cabell Papers, box 2, ASSCL-UVA; *New York Evening Post*, April 3, 1802; "A Student," *National Intelligencer*, May 31, 1802; Ruby Orders Osborne, *The Crisis Years: The College of William and Mary in Virginia, 1800–1827* (Richmond: Dietz Press, 1989): 57–58.

6. *New York Evening Post*, April 3, 1802 ("Thus dies"), and April 16, 1802.

7. Bishop James Madison to Thomas Jefferson, April 15, 1802, *PTJ*, 37:241–42; [Bishop Madison], "An Inhabitant of Williamsburg," *Virginia Argus*, May 5, 1802, reprinted in *WMQ*, 2nd ser., 5 (January 1925): 61–62 ("virtue"); [Bishop Madison], "A Late Student," *Richmond Examiner*, May 8, 1802, reprinted in Osborne, *Crisis Years*, 64; "A Student," *National Intelligencer*, May 31, 1802.

8. Statute quoted in Osborne, *Crisis Years*, 59–60.

9. Statute quoted in ibid.; Paul Carrington quoted in Lorri Glover, *Southern Sons: Becoming Men in the New Nation* (Baltimore: Johns Hopkins University Press, 2007), 76;

Thomas L. Preston to Andrew Reid Jr., April 15, 1802, *WMQ*, 1st ser., 8 (April 1900): 217; [Bishop Madison], "Extract of a Letter from a Student at William and Mary," *Virginia Argus*, November 17, 1802, College Chronology File, 1802–1819, SSCL-CWM.

10. "A College Prank," *Norfolk Herald*, April 18, 1803, College Chronology File, 1800–1820, SSCL-CWM; John Hartwell Cocke to Joseph C. Cabell, April 18, 1803, Cabell Papers, box 2, ASSCL-UVA.

11. [Bishop James Madison], "Gentleman at Williamsburg," *Virginia Argus*, April 30, 1803; Benjamin Crowninshield to B. L. Oliver, May 30, 1804 ("The Students"), Benjamin Crowninshield Papers, one folder, SSCL-CWM; Charles William Janson, *The Stranger in America, 1793–1806* (New York: Press of the Pioneers, 1935, reprinted from London, 1807), 304; Osborne, *Crisis Years*, 78; Joseph C. Robert, "William Wirt, Virginian," *Virginia Magazine of History and Biography* 80 (October 1972): 404.

12. [Bishop James Madison], "Gentleman at Williamsburg," *Virginia Argus*, April 30, 1803; J. P. Galt to Polly Galt, August 4, 1803, Galt Papers, ser. 2, box 1, SSCL-CWM; William Russell, "Communication," *National Intelligencer*, August 24, 1803; Bishop James Madison to James Madison, December 11, 1803, *PJM-SSS*, 6:158–59; Ludwell H. Johnson, "Between the Wars, 1782–1862," in *The College of William and Mary: A History*, ed. Susan H. Godson et al., 2 vols. (Williamsburg: King and Queen Press, 1993), 184.

13. For the new statutes, see William Russell, "Communication," *National Intelligencer*, August 24, 1803. For Tucker's erratic teaching schedule, see Joseph C. Cabell to William B. Hare, January 4, 1801, *WMQ*, 1st ser., 8 (April 1900): 215; Tucker to John Ambler, December 16, 1801, Ambler Family Papers, sec. 2, folder 6, Virginia Historical Society.

14. St. George Tucker to Joseph C. Cabell, January 23, 1804, Byran Family Papers (BFP hereafter), box 1, ASSCL-UVA; William Taylor Barry to John Barry, February 15, 1804, *WMQ*, 1st ser., 13 (October 1904): 113; L. Johnson, "Between the Wars," 174; St. George Tucker quoted in Novak, *Rights of Youth*, 104; Osborne, *Crisis Years*, 85–86.

15. Henry St. George Tucker to Joseph C. Cabell, December 27, 1803, Joseph Carrington Cabell Family Papers (38–111), box 3, ASSCL-UVA; Osborne, *Crisis Years*, 85; George Blackburn quoted in L. Johnson, "Between the Wars," 175 ("danced").

16. Jane C. Charlton to Sarah C. Watts, January 10, 1808, Sarah C. Watts Papers, box 1, SSCL-CWM; Eliza Prentis to Joseph Prentis, March 9, 1808 ("those young Men"), Webb-Prentis Papers, box 37, ASSCL-UVA; Ellen Randolph to Jefferson, March 11, 1808, *Founders Online*, https://founders.archives.gov/documents/Jefferson/99-01-02-7597; James Eyle to Charles S. Todd, March 16, 1808, College Subject File, Chronology, 1800–1820, SSCL-CWM; Samuel Myers to John Myers, April 10, 1808, Samuel Myers Papers (SMP hereafter), one file, SSCL-CWM; Albert Allmond to Andrew Reid Jr., *WMQ*, 1st ser., 8 (April 1900): 222–23.

17. Samuel Myers to John Myers, April 10, and October 26, 1808, SMP, one file, SSCL-CWM.

18. Samuel Myers to Moses Myers, January 30, 1809, Littleton Tazewell to John Myers, February 5, 1809, SMP, one file, SSCL-CWM.

19. George Blow to Richard Blow, March 20, 1804, Blow Family Papers, ser. 2, box 33G, SSCL-CWM.

20. St. George Tucker to Frances Coalter, May 31, 1811, Brown, Coalter, Tucker Papers, ser. 1, box 3, SSCL-CWM; *Richmond Enquirer*, June 4, 1811, and November 29, 1811.

21. Lelia Tucker to Francis Coalter, April 12, 1811, Brown, Coalter, Tucker Papers, ser. 1, box 3, SSCL-CWM; Glover, *Southern Sons*, 19–20.

22. Joseph C. Cabell to Isaac A. Coles, 1 March 1807, Cabell Papers, box 4, ASSCL-UVA; Richard Beale Davis, *Intellectual Life in Jefferson's Virginia, 1790–1830* (Knoxville: University of Tennessee Press, 1972), 53; L. H. Johnson, "Between the Wars," 187–88, 300n134; Osborne, *Crisis Years*, 107–8, 117.

23. Sterling Ruffin to Thomas Ruffin, December 29, 1803, in *The Papers of Thomas Ruffin*, 3 vols., ed. J. G. de Roulhac Hamilton (Raleigh: Edwards & Broughton Printing Co.), 1:48; William T. Barry to John Barry, January 30, 1804, *WMQ*, 1st ser., 13 (October 1904): 109 ("That there are"); Thomas Lomax to St. George Tucker, December 20, 1804, Tucker Coleman Papers, reel M-21, SSCL-CWM; William Radford to Andrew Reid Jr., December 26, 1805, *WMQ*, 1st ser., 8 (April 1900): 219; George Tucker, *Letters from Virginia Translated From the French* (Baltimore: Fielding Lucas, Jr., 1816), 129–30; William Wirt, *The British Spy, or Letters to a Member of the British Parliament* (Newburyport, MA: Repertory Office, 1804), 71–72.

24. Lynn A. Nelson, "Joseph Carrington Cabell," in *Dictionary of Virginia Biography*, ed. Sara B. Bearss et al. (Richmond: Library of Virginia, 1998–), 2:488–89; Jefferson to Joseph C. Cabell, ca. September 1800, *PTJ*, 32:176–81; Joseph S. Watson to David Watson, October 26, 1800, *Virginia Magazine of History and Biography* 29 (April 1921): 155 ("most ardent"); St. George Tucker to Joseph C. Cabell, January 23, 1804, Bryan Family Papers, box 1, ASSCL-UVA; Joseph C. Cabell to W. H. Cabell, October 23, 1806, Cabell Papers, box 4, ASSCL-UVA; Phillip Hamilton, *The Making and Unmaking of a Revolutionary Family: The Tuckers of Virginia, 1752–1830* (Charlottesville: University of Virginia Press, 2003), 130, 140.

25. Joseph C. Cabell to William H. Cabell, November 27, 1806 ("which I find"), Joseph C. Cabell to Isaac A. Coles, February 17, 1807 ("ingenious" and "It is time"), February 22, 1807, March 1, 1807 ("first-rate"), and March 16, 1807 ("the want" and "we ought"), Cabell Papers box 4, ASSCL-UVA.

26. Joseph C. Cabell to Isaac A. Coles, March 16, 1807, William H. Coles to Joseph C. Cabell, March 17, 1807, and Coles to Joseph C. Cabell, May 27, 1807, Cabell Papers, box 4, ASSCL-UVA; William H. Cabell to Joseph C. Cabell, June 22, 1812, Cabell Papers, SSCL-CWM; Nathaniel Francis Cabell, ed., *Early History of the University of Virginia as Contained in the Letters of Thomas Jefferson and Joseph C. Cabell* (Richmond: J. W. Randolph, 1856), xxx.

27. Samuel Mordecai to Ellen Mordecai, May 25, 1812 ("looks"), Chronology File, 1802–1819, SSCL-CWM; Jefferson to James Semple, October 2, 1812, *PTJRS*, 5:373–74; Semple to Jefferson, November 28, 1812, *PTJRS*, 5:469–70 ("rude shock"); Jefferson to William Duane, January 22, 1813, *PTJRS*, 5:577–79 ("tory"); Jefferson to William Short, November 9, 1813, *PTJRS*, 6:604–06 ("simpleton"), and Jefferson to Thomas Cooper, January 16, and August 25, 1814, *PTJRS*, 7:124–31, and 606–7; L. H. Johnson, "Between the Wars," 200–03; Osborne, *Crisis Years*, 150–53, 167–72; Joseph C. Cabell to William Wirt, December 8, 1812, and William H. Cabell to Joseph C. Cabell, December 16, 1812,

Cabell Papers, SSCL-CWM. For Bishop Madison's decline, see Richard Beale Davis, *Francis Walker Gilmer: Life and Learning in Jefferson's Virginia* (Richmond: Dietz Press, 1939), 35.

28. John Augustine Smith, "William and Mary," *Richmond Enquirer*, August 12, 1817 ("Contemplate"); Elizabeth B. Kennon to Rachel Mordecai, May 1, 1814, *Virginia Magazine of History and Biography* 36 (April 1928): 173–74; Robert Saunders to Joseph Prentis Jr., July 1, 1814, Webb-Prentiss Papers, box 38, ASSCL-UVA; William C. Rives to John C. Cabell, July 21, 1814, Cabell Papers, box 11, ASSCL-UVA; Osborne, *Crisis Years*, 181–97, 206, 210, 231.

29. Powhatan Robertson, Diary, *WMQ*, 2nd ser., 11 (January 1931): 61 and 68; Joseph C. Cabell to John Hartwell Cocke, March 5, 1823, Cabell Papers, box 15, ASSCL-UVA; Samuel M. Garland to Sarah A. Garland, March 13, 1824, *WMQ*, 2nd ser., 11 (April 1931): 139–40.

30. John Augustine Smith, "Extract from the Address of the President of William and Mary College, at the Commencement," *Richmond Enquirer*, November 24, 1814 (quotations); Smith, "Commencement Address," *Richmond Enquirer*, July 20, 1816. For the number of expulsions, see Smith, "Address to the House of Delegates," *Richmond Enquirer*, February 5, 1825. For negative commentary, see "William and Mary College Again," *Richmond Enquirer*, October 19, 1824. For faculty grumbling over the refunds, see Ferdinand S. Campbell to John Campbell, July 10, 1818, Campbell Family Papers, folder 2, Virginia Historical Society.

31. William H. Cabell to Joseph C. Cabell, November 12, 1815, and Joseph C. Cabell to Isaac A. Coles, December 18, 1815, Cabell Papers, box 11, ASSCL-UVA.

32. William H. Cabell to Joseph C. Cabell, November 12, 1815, and May 7, 1816, and Joseph C. Cabell to Isaac A. Coles, December 18, 1815, Cabell Papers, box 11, ASSCL-UVA; Powhatan Robertson, Diary, *WMQ*, 2nd ser., 11 (January 1931): 62.

33. "Philodemus," in *Evangelical and Literary Magazine*, ed. John Holt Rice, 10 vols. (Richmond: N. Pollard, 1816–1827), 9:350–51; William H. Cabell to Joseph C. Cabell, May 7, 14, and 16, 1816, and John Augustine Smith to Joseph C. Cabell, November 10, 1816, Cabell Papers, box 11, ASSCL-UVA. President Smith stood by the suspension, despite the irritation it gave to his powerful friend Joseph C. Cabell.

34. John Augustine Smith, "William and Mary College," *Richmond Enquirer*, August 12, 1817 (quotations); Elizabeth Trist to Catharine Wistar Bache, September 12, 1817, Bache Papers, box 2, American Philosophical Society; Osborne, *Crisis Years*, 263, 275.

35. "William and Mary," and "Williamsburg," *Richmond Enquirer*, March 13, 1818 ("Deluded man!") and March 24, 1818; Margaret Page to Mrs. Lowther, March 18, 1818, Page-Saunders Papers, box 1, folder 3, SSCL-CWM; "William and Mary College," *The Union* (Philadelphia), March 21, 1818; Osborne, *Crisis Years*, 223, 226. For the student with a knife, see John J. Ambler Jr. to John J. Ambler Sr., March 9, 1818, Ambler Family Papers, sec. 3, Virginia Historical Society.

36. John Augustine Smith, "Commencement Address," *Richmond Enquirer*, July 20, 1816 ("There is no"); Smith, "William and Mary College," *Richmond Enquirer*, August 12, 1817 ("to the disadvantage"); James Kirke Paulding, *Letters from the South By a Northern Man*, 2 vols. (New York: Harper & Brothers, 1835), 58–62.

37. John J. Ambler Jr. to John J. Ambler Sr., March 9, 1818 ("confusion"), Ambler Family Papers, sec. 3, VHS; William H. Cabell to Joseph C. Cabell, May 16, 1816, Cabell Papers, box 11, ASSCL-UVA; John Augustine Smith, "William and Mary College," *Richmond Enquirer*, August 12, 1817; John T. Barraud to John Hartwell Cocke, December 1, 1818, Cocke Papers, box 27, ASSCL-UVA. For the declining enrollment, see Smith, "Communication: William and Mary College," *Richmond Enquirer*, July 18, 1823; Smith, "Address to the House of Delegates," *Richmond Enquirer*, February 5, 1825.

38. Elizabeth Trist to Nicholas P. Trist, May 2, 1819, Jefferson Family Letters, International Center for Jefferson Studies, http://tjrs.monticello.org/letter/1505; Jefferson quoted in E. Trist to Catharine Wistar Bache, September 12, 1817, Bache Papers, box 2, American Philosophical Society; David F. Allmendinger Jr., "Dangers of Ante-Bellum Student Life," *Journal of Social History* 7, No. 1 (October, 1973): 75–85, 75–76; Fitzgerald Flournoy, "Hugh Blair Grigsby at Yale," *Virginia Magazine of History and Biography* 62 (April 1954): 178; Glover, *Southern Sons*, 77; Noll, *Princeton and the Republic*, 126, 151–58; Novak, *Rights of Youth*, 17–23, 176n1; Wertenbaker, *Princeton*, 134–43. During the period 1820–1860, Southerners accounted for 9 percent of Harvard students, 11 percent at Yale, and 36 percent at Princeton. See Michael O'Brien, *Conjectures of Order: Intellectual Life and the American South, 1810–1860*, 2 vols. (Chapel Hill: University of North Carolina Press, 2004), 1:29; Edgar W. Knight, ed., *A Documentary History of Education in the South Before 1860*, 5 vols. (Chapel Hill: University of North Carolina Press, 1945–1953), 5:279–80.

39. William C. Preston to Samuel M. Reid, February 3, 1810, *WMQ*, 1st. ser., 8 (April 1900): 213–27; Lorri Glover, "'Let Us Manufacture Men': Educating Elite Boys in the Early National South," in *Southern Manhood: Perspectives on Masculinity in the Old South*, ed. Craig Thompson Friend and Lorri Glover (Athens: University of Georgia Press, 2004), 39–42, George Swain quoted on 42; Glover, *Southern Sons*, 64–72; Robert Pace, *Halls of Honor: College Men in the Old South* (Baton Rouge: Louisiana State University, 2004), 65–67; Louis P. Towles, "A Matter of Honor at South Carolina College, 1822," *South Carolina Historical Magazine* 94 (January 1993): 6–18.

40. Ferdinand S. Campbell to John Campbell, Campbell Family Papers, folder 2, Virginia Historical Society; Thomas Cooper to Jefferson, February 14, 1822, *Founders Online*, http://founders.archives.gov/documents/Jefferson/98-01-02-2662; Glover, "'Let Us Manufacture Men,'" 36–37; Glover, *Southern Sons*, 77; Dumas Malone, *The Public Life of Thomas Cooper, 1783–1839* (New Haven, CT: Yale University Press, 1926), 251–58; Towles, "Matter of Honor," 6–18.

41. Thomas Cooper to Jefferson, February 14, 1822, *Founders Online*, http://founders.archives.gov/documents/Jefferson/98-01-02-2662; Glover, *Southern Sons*, 45–46, 64; Craig Thompson Friend and Lorri Glover, "Rethinking Southern Masculinity: An Introduction," in Friend and Glover, *Southern Manhood*, x–xi; Glover, "'Let Us Manufacture Men,'" 29; Glover, *Southern Sons*, 22–34.

42. William J. Grayson quoted in Towles, "Matter of Honor," 12 ("sees his professor"); James W. Alexander to unnamed, December 24, 1824, in *Forty Years' Familiar Letters of James W. Alexander, D.D.*, ed. John Hall, vol. 1 (New York: Charles Scribner, 1860), 71 ("There is"); Glover, *Southern Sons*, 2–3, 64–71, 98–110; Joseph F. Kett, *Rites of Passages:*

Adolescence in America, 1790 to the Present (New York: Basic Books, 1977), 58–59; Stowe, "Rhetoric of Authority," 921–22.

43. William D. Lowther to Maria L. Skinner, April 7, 1814, Skinner Family Papers, box 1, Southern Historical Collection-University of North Carolina; Thomas Cooper to Jefferson, February 14, 1822, *Founders Online*, http://founders.archives.gov/documents /Jefferson/98-01-02-2662; Glover, *Southern Sons*, 76; Hugh Blair Grigsby quoted in Flournoy, "Hugh Blair Grigsby," 174: John Augustine Smith, "Commencement Address," *Richmond Enquirer*, July 20, 1816.

44. Roger L. Geiger, "Introduction: New Themes in the History of Nineteenth-Century Colleges," in *The American College in the Nineteenth Century*, ed. Geiger (Nashville: Vanderbilt University Press, 2000), 10–12; Glover, *Southern Sons*, 59–60; Novak, *Rights of Youth*, 21–22; Towles, "Matter of Honor," 13–16; "Convention of the Visitors and Governors of William & Mary College," *Richmond Enquirer*, September 22, 1809; Osborne, *Crisis Years*, 203; "Philodemus," in Rice, *Evangelical and Literary Magazine*, 9:354 ("rightful authority").

45. Sterling Ruffin to Thomas Ruffin, May 5, 1803, in Roulhac Hamilton, *Papers of Thomas Ruffin*, 1:45; Geiger, "Introduction," 12; Glover, "'Let Us Manufacture Men,'" 39; Glover, *Southern Sons*, 12–14, 42, 60–62; Osborne, *Crisis Years*, 203.

46. St. George Tucker to John Coalter, June 14, 1809, Brown, Coalter, Tucker Papers, ser. 1, box 3, SSCL-CWM; Joseph C. Cabell to S. G. Tucker, December 30, 1816, Tucker Coleman Papers, reel M-28, SSCL-CWM.

47. Tucker, *Letters from Virginia*, 54–58. For a similar satire by one of Tucker's close friends, see William Wirt, *The Old Bachelor* (Richmond: Thomas Ritchie & Fielding Lucas, 1814), 100–101 and 166.

48. J. H. Rice, "The University of Virginia," in Rice, *Virginia Evangelical and Literary Magazine*, 3:587.

49. John Randolph, *Letters of John Randolph, to a Young Relative: Embracing a Series of Years, from Early Youth, to Mature Manhood* (Philadelphia: Carey, Lea & Blanchard, 1834), 25–26; Jefferson to John Adams, July 5, 1814, *PTJRS*, 7:454, and Jefferson to Francis W. Gilmer, November 23, 1814, *PTJRS*, 8:101.

"Chastising a Servant for His Insolence"
The Case of the Butter Bully

ERVIN L. JORDAN JR.

Musings of a University Slave, 1828

"Minor's servant" was bone tired. Every day, all day, he and other dining hall slaves were kept busy at the beck and call of the University's student-gentlemen. Fetching and removing plates, tableware, napkins and tablecloths, keeping wine glasses full, hoping the food would arrive hot enough to the students' liking—these were endless worries. At first, after Massa Warner Minor announced they were going to that new Jefferson school in Charlottesville, all the slaves thought it would mean lighter workloads. Massa and Mistress had promised they would be working indoors as "dormitory" and dining room servants.

Well, that was three years ago, and the sweat on their dark skins caused by their labors made it seem more like "Jefferson's Plantation" than school. "Waiters," he grunted to himself. After they'd arrived there was almost no time spent "waiting". Life seemed easy for the white students—they attended classes when they felt like it, bad-mouthed the professors, smoked, drank, and came and went as they pleased. They were quick-tempered, foul-mouthed, nitpicking, and spoke harshly, sometimes even to Massa Warner but he as a white man could talk back—and gave as good as he got. Students cursed and thumped his slaves because he didn't buy first-rate food or enough of it. The dim, smoky cellar kitchen and its damp floor reeked of food scraps and bugs. So, it was the slaves' fault the butter was bad, the biscuits hard, the beef tough, the potatoes undercooked, the coffee muddy, the tea bitter, and the wine watered-down.

But there were side benefits. Pocket money could be had when hungry students almost politely requested late night secret deliveries of fried chicken, buttered dough cakes and spirituous liquors. They paid in cash as slaves didn't offer credit and weren't supposed to know their numbers or read and write anyway. Massa Warner didn't know his larders allowed slaves to make a little side money; the students kept silent to avoid missed-meal cramps. Extra hard cash could be made by running errands across the school, in Charlottesville or in the countryside. And the students paid well and quietly but grudgingly if they lost while gambling at cards or cock-fights with slaves. Still, the slaves viewed them and all whites with veiled contempt. Some of them foreign professors seemed sympathetic but said nothing within earshot of other whites.

"Minor's servant" ached to be free and wondered if freedom would come someday. He frowned as he recalled colored women scandalously mistreated by the so-called young white student-gentlemen who also threatened their menfolk with pistols and knives. Another grim reminder of past wrongs was the whipping post near the Grounds, site of many a flogging with thirty-and-nine lashes on colored folks' backs. He shuddered at those brutal memories; thanks to a bit of luck, he'd avoided such treatment—for the moment.[1]

Dining Room Drama

One evening in June 1828, shortly after his twenty-fourth birthday, University of Virginia student Thomas Boyd was seated in Hotel C's student dining room. When rancid butter was served, and despite Boyd's requests for fresh butter, the slave-waiter ignored him, walking away without offering further service. After Boyd left the room, the male waiter "in an insolent tone of voice" sarcastically muttered to a fellow slave that "he was surprised that Mr. B. having read so many books should not know the difference between water & butter." Another student, James Neal, and thirty-five-year-old hotelkeeper Warner Minor, the slave's owner, both overheard those remarks; Neal reported them to Boyd, whose follow-up written complaint to Minor the next morning was ignored.

Encountering the same dining room waiter later that evening (Wednesday, June 25), Boyd brusquely ordered him to leave; when the slave refused, Boyd and fellow student Andrew Johnston assaulted and tried to forcibly eject him from the room, then attempted to flee before the arrival of University officials. Minor and his wife, Maria, hearing the loud altercation, rushed into the room to see blood "running freely from the servant's head" and Boyd holding a broken stick. Angry and embarrassed yet mindful of society's etiquette expectations, Boyd apologized to Mrs. Minor and withdrew.[2]

Two centuries later, race and public spaces seem incompatible. As a *Washington Post* reporter recently observed, "Black people in this country have long known that disturbing white Americans in white spaces can mean death."[3] The Boyd–Minor incident merits attention as among the earliest documented episodes of contested spaces, proslavery ideology, prickly personalities, and race privilege at the University of Virginia, with underlying social status and intergenerational issues: "Generation Post-Revolutionary"—those born the first decade after the American Revolution (post-1783), and, "Generation Early Republic"—those born the first decade of the nineteenth century (post-1801). Both antagonists were white male slaveholders who doubtless had punished disobedient slaves. Under the antebellum South's social customs and laws, all whites had the right to discipline slaves and so-called "uppity" free blacks, as surrogate masters.

"A Suitable Person"

Twenty-one-year-old Albemarle County resident Thomas Jefferson Boyd (1804–1893) matriculated in February 1826, without identifying a parent or guardian (both parents were deceased by 1827), and took courses in medical jurisprudence, moral philosophy, and law. His signature in the University's matriculation book pledged on his honor as a gentleman "to conform to its laws." (Edgar Allan Poe enrolled that month but dropped out by year's end.) Boyd's father, Colonel Thomas Duckett Boyd (d. 1820), moved to Virginia from Maryland in 1802, and a decade later he and his wife, Mary (d. 1827) purchased a 230-acre popular and profitable Albemarle establishment they renamed Boyd's Tavern, which hosted the Marquis de Lafayette during his 1824 American tour. Thomas Senior served in the Virginia cavalry during the War of 1812. The Boyds' eighth and last child was named for family friend Thomas Jefferson (1743–1826). In April 1812, eight-year-old Thomas and four of his siblings were apprenticed to their Albemarle uncle John Bowie Magruder Sr. and Fluvanna County resident Walker Timberlake (1781–1863), a relative of Warner Minor's wife, Maria.[4]

Warner Washington Minor (1792–1831), formerly of Caroline and Hanover Counties and a distant relative of George Washington, was among the University's six original hotelkeepers. His initial appointment by proctor Arthur Spicer Brockenbrough (1780–1832) was confirmed by the Board of Visitors in December 1826 as "a suitable person." Minor's appointment possibly resulted from social and military networks with fellow War of 1812 veterans Captain Brockenbrough and General John Hartwell Cocke (1780–1866), a Fluvanna County planter and University board member. During this period, students made their own arrangements based on recommendations of fellow students, faculty, or staff. Minor's Hotel was one of two favorably recommended by

University bursar Alexander Garrett (1778–1866) to the general's son Phillip St. George Cocke (1809–1861, class of 1828). William Wertenbaker (1797–1882), University librarian and faculty secretary, was married to Minor's sister-in-law; three of Minor's daughters later married at Wertenbaker's University residence.

Minor proved a conscientious though contentious proprietor who communicated grievances in vitriolic letters. He repeatedly grumbled it was "impossible to realise a profit," cover expenses, and support his wife, Maria Timberlake Minor (b. 1799), and their eventual fifteen children (four sons and eleven daughters).When the board was not in session (it met annually in July and October), board secretary, Nicholas P. Trist (1800–1874), and Cocke communicated its wishes to Brockenbrough and other school officials. Minor shrewdly signed letters to him as "your friend." Cocke later characterized Minor as a quiet man who abhorred students' drinking, gambling, and cavorting with prostitutes. This did not endear him to the unruly sons of Virginia elites, many of whom were anything but sober, quiet, or orderly at Mr. Jefferson's University; they detested Minor, his slaves, his hotel, and his sanctimoniousness.[5]

"Impossibility of Pleasing Every Body"

In 1828 the Academical Village comprised twenty-eight acres. By the time of the school's fourth session (1827–1828), there were 131 students, 109 dormitory rooms, and thirty faculty and administrative officers. Warner Minor's Hotel C, a West Range dining hall built in 1822 behind Pavilion V at a cost of $3,600, was also the home of the Jefferson Literary and Debating Society (founded 1825). Hotels contained a dining room, a garden, and the hotelkeeper's office. There were female—usually married women or widows—as well as male hotelkeepers. Slaves were housed in attics, outbuildings (barns and stables), and cellar kitchens susceptible to "shoe deep" rain-produced flooding, making them "impracticable . . . to cook in." Hotelkeepers leased hotels from the school and were assigned several dormitory rooms to maintain; students were required to take their meals at assigned hotels.[6]

A common problem involved student-boarders who left Minor's hotel without paying what they owed, leaving him "to receive nothing for the expenses I had incurred." He plaintively added in a letter to Cocke, "I am well aware of the impossibility of pleasing every body." He was responsible for ten dormitory rooms whose rental profits increased during 1825–1826, though he often groused of too many competing hotels and "the profit & risk will induce no man who is qualified to keep one." He owned "five robust Negroes" (adult

males); a "boy Moses" was hired out to the University's waterworks at fifty
cents per day. The duties of hotel and dormitory servants (slaves and free
blacks) included boot polishing, running town errands, washing tobacco-
splattered walls, and delivering food to students too tardy or too lazy to take
their meals at the hotels. They were unfairly vilified when unable to perform
their duties because of hotelkeepers' neglecting to provide them with fresh
bedding and cleaning supplies. Daily dirty jobs such as cleaning chamber pots
and privies required slave labor at a cost to the school of nearly $3,000 in ex-
penditures during the 1820s. Free black employees were banned from residing
on Grounds as of an April 1828 faculty resolution.[7]

Minor was not alone in grumbling about the high costs of living. Eighteen
months prior to his violent encounter with Minor's slave, Thomas Boyd complained to board member and family friend John Hartwell Cocke that the
school's unjust enactments increased his expenses, and of hotelkeepers' charging students for extra services though they provided their own furniture, beds,
and bedding for their dormitory rooms: "I can furnish myself with the other
necessaries much less than the present law requires me to pay the Hotelkeeper." As a subtle reminder to Cocke of his family's high social status in Albemarle County, Boyd mailed his letter from the "Boyd's Tavern" manor.[8]

Students Behaving Badly

A maelstrom of verbal and physical clashes marred the University's first two
decades. Relations between students and hotelkeepers were the most antago-
nistic. Before the Boyd–Minor incident, Minor quarreled with other students,
including Andrew Johnston and Boyd, who successfully complained to the
faculty of Minor's refusal to furnish adequate fuel and firewood, escalating
long-standing tensions between them.

Slaves, free blacks, faculty, townspeople, or anyone else who dared interfere with students behaving badly risked physical attacks, insults, or death.
One student, engaged in a dispute with a mathematics professor, heatedly protested during a subsequent faculty investigation that "he was spoken to in an
authoritative manner, as an overseer speaks to a negro slave." As members of
wealthy slaveholding Virginia families, the hot-tempered gentlemen scholars
treated the mostly nonslaveholding English faculty with disdain and disrespect and demanded racial deference from African Americans.[9]

Although Virginia law since 1792 permitted blacks to respond in self-
defense if "wantonly assaulted," it was largely ignored; de facto racial customs

and white supremacy forbade any black from assaulting any white, even in self-defense, without resulting in severe consequences, including death. Minor's battered slave had no choice except to stoically swallow his resentment and seek medical treatment, probably at the twice-weekly medical and surgical dispensary (clinic) offered by the medical school at the Rotunda since February 1828 free of charge for poor whites, fifty cents for free blacks and slaves.

"Minor's servant" was not a unique victim; blacks regardless of gender or status were subjected to white violence and were vulnerable to sexual violence during the Age of Slavery, as typified by two philosophy students. One broke into a faculty residence one night and attacked its female slave during the 1830s. Another beat a ten-year-old slave girl into unconsciousness during the 1850s after she challenged his right to whip her for chasing a pigeon across Grounds. Neither assailant was punished as both asserted their rights as white men to punish black "impertinence."[10]

"You or I Shall Die"

Historian Lorenzo Greene argues that the economics of American slavery were disincentives for the killing of slaves by their owners but a driving force in seeking legal remedies for damages to their human "movable goods" by others. Slaveholding faculty and staff objected to students' extralegal punishing and abuse of their slaves without their permission, warranted or not. After interrogating his injured slave, who denied any disrespect to Boyd, an irate Minor formally accused Boyd of "assaulting & beating one of his servants" in a written protest to the school's fourth faculty chairman—moral philosophy professor George Tucker (1775–1861), who promptly called a faculty meeting at Pavilion VII, the school's first building, first library, and now faculty meeting room. Boyd was not particularly bookish, having visited only five times during 1826–1827.[11]

Convening on Thursday evening, June 26, the nine professors summoned Boyd to explain himself. He duly appeared, expressing "astonishment & Indignation at being called before the Faculty for so trifling an affair as that of Chastising a servant for his insolence." Boyd considered his actions justified, given that Tucker and most whites affiliated with the University owned, hired, or supervised slaves.

Boyd claimed to have complained verbally and in writing of his dormitory room not being cleaned for six weeks, water served only twice daily, and of poor service by Minor's servants. (Contemporary correspondence and accounts euphemistically referred to slaves as "servants.") The reluctant testimony of student eyewitness James Neal confirmed Minor's version of events and that the hotelkeeper maintained adequate control over his dining room servants but not those assigned to dormitories.

Minor countercharged students too often interfered with his servants' supervision in the dining room and dormitories. He employed six dormitory and dining room servants in addition to a cook, assistant cook, and washerwomen, for all of whose clothing and sustenance he had to pay, and he netted little profit due to belated reimbursement by the school. Minor contended he was short-staffed as most of his slaves were sick, and that even when healthy they were overwhelmed as each was expected to attend to twenty students. He had declined to respond to Boyd in writing but denied his slave had been insolent.

Boyd and Minor's testimony failed to impress the faculty, which issued a unanimous wishy-washy decision: "Mr. Minor has the proper remedy in his own hands against Mr. Boyd for his Disorderly conduct. The Faculty decline acting upon it." Boyd went unpunished while Minor, to his mortification, received what amounted to a vote of no confidence: "Resolved that Mr. Minor be requested to have his Dormitories attended to."[12]

The antagonists did not consider the matter closed; after the June 26 faculty evening meeting, Boyd accosted Minor "under the arcade" near Hotel C and "demanded in a very imperious manner . . . how dared he complain of him to the Faculty," adding "[i]f you ever cross my path again you or I shall die." He was egged on by fellow student John Augustus Gretter who loudly exhorted him to horsewhip Minor ("whip him, Boyd, whip him"). Three student bystanders did not interfere. Outnumbered, Minor calmly replied by promising lawsuits for any violence against him. Chairman Tucker remarked in the faculty minutes: "Mr. Boyd was very abusive descending to the usual threats & menaces of a bully but finally went off muttering threats of taking satisfaction" (challenge to a duel).

Unintimidated, Minor sent yet another written grievance against Boyd "for insulting him" and disturbing his family's peace of mind. Two days later (Saturday, June 28) a second faculty meeting at Pavilion VII summoned Boyd, Minor, Gretter, and the three student bystanders. Boyd vehemently denied any intent to insult Minor or to disrespect the faculty but admitted calling the hotelkeeper a coward and "ungentlemanly" after Minor had called him "a puppy." Gretter coolly admitted urging Boyd to horsewhip Minor and insisted the hotelkeeper deserved it: "[I] was anxious Minor should be whipped because he had treated Boyd ungentlemanly in not suffering him [Boyd] to take his servant out to chatise him." ("Puppy" was a fighting word often pre-ceding and accompanying assaults and duel challenges; to ignore such an insult was considered cowardly and disgraceful.)

Student miscreants were inconsistently punished with suspensions or ex-pulsions, perhaps by reason of an irregular unwritten policy of extreme leni-ency for those from prominent families like Boyd's; moderate admonitions were preferred so as to avoid risk of insult or loss of tuition revenue. The fac-ulty, having "maturely deliberated upon, and considered the cases of Messrs. Boyd and Gretter," issued four mild resolutions critical of and unsatisfactory to all parties—mere slaps on the wrists. It decided against "the severe punish-ment" Boyd deserved and limited itself to "expressing . . . [its] high disappro-bation of his conduct." Minor's request that Boyd no longer board at his hotel was granted and Gretter's conduct formally "disapproved in the strongest manner." Yet as late as July 1828 Boyd remained in good academic standing.

The June 28 faculty meeting concluded with a tough-sounding resolution that "any student who insults a Hotel Keeper or other officer for presenting a complaint to the Faculty will be visited with the severest punishment permit-ted by the Enactments." The following day (Sunday, June 29), Boyd appeared at Chairman Tucker's Pavilion IX residence to demand "an explanation of the resolutions of the Faculty in his case." Wanting to save face among his peers by avoiding the appearance of being "turned out of his house" by Minor, Boyd also delivered a written ultimatum for the faculty to reconsider its decision. He withdrew it the next day (June 30) after again meeting privately with Tucker, who advised him to "let the matter rest."[13]

For his part, Minor did not let the matter rest; in early July he sent another letter to Tucker with further evidence of Boyd's misconduct and asked him and Proctor Brockenbrough for the right not to allow any student to board at his hotel "against his will." Moreover, he grumbled about another student's refusal to pay for damages to a dormitory room and hinted "that he might have to take other steps" if the faculty did not act.

Faculty interest in the Boyd–Minor controversy waned partly because of final examinations and a measles outbreak; Tucker referred the case to the seven-member Board of Visitors. However, the board was more interested in a state convention on internal improvements in Charlottesville that month (July). Although the Visitors met for two weeks, they ignored the Boyd–Minor dispute and instead attended the convention for five days, "no business done by them in relation to the University." The board's October meeting also did not take up the matter, passing the buck back to the faculty.[14]

"Disrespectful Conduct of the Gentlemen"

Students increasingly boycotted Minor's unpopular Hotel C for "want of neatness & cleanliness" and its hot-tempered proprietor, so much so that by September, alarmed board secretary Nicholas Trist, writing from Jefferson's Monticello, informed John Hartwell Cocke that "the anticipations of a full session are not realised" as less than a hundred students were enrolled. Warner and Maria Minor sent additional separate, simultaneously written denunciations to the faculty about Boyd and their mistreatment by student boarders; Faculty Chairman Tucker referred the matter to the Board of Visitors. Minor's quarrelsome reputation caused boarders assigned to his hotel to refuse matriculation because of other students' allegations about it and its assigned slaves' lack of cleanliness.

Concerned about how this might affect the school's enrollment, the faculty questioned Minor's few remaining boarders (nine students), who offered mixed reviews about the food, confirmed his servants' uncleanliness, especially a "very dirty" cook, but admitted tableware and tablecloths were always clean. Criticisms of its "wretched fare" continued; Proctor Brockenbrough's inspection found no "great cause for complaint" except rancid butter. During a September faculty meeting, Minor was sent for "but was absent from the precincts." Summoned before the faculty in early December during her husband's absence to answer accusations about Hotel C's food, Maria Minor scornfully condemned "the disrespectful conduct of the Gentlemen." When a sample of the hotel's butter was provided to professor of medicine and new faculty chairman Robley Dunglison (1798–1869) for his personal tasting, he declared, "it was not good—it was rancid."[15]

Even before his wife's cross-examination by the faculty, Warner Minor had had enough. Dissatisfied by his treatment by the board, students, and faculty, he officially resigned in November 1828 prior to the official expiration of his hotel lease on New Year's Day 1829. The remaining hotelkeepers scrambled to take in his boarders, and this strained the availability of accommodations, and required hiring more slaves and securing additional provisions. In his fawning farewell letter, Minor told Cocke, "as I shall not probably see you again before I leave the University . . . I was in hopes you would have called & seen us," and although in arrears for three months' rent sought reimbursement for "moving house." Three days before Christmas Day 1828, his mounting debts occasioned a public auction at the University of "many articles of Household and Kitchen

Furniture—among other things a number of Beds, Mattresses, Blankets, etc."
Minor urged his debtors to settle their owed balances before the auction, otherwise unsettled accounts would be "left with an attorney for collection."[16]

Students took parting shots at Minor. A law student representing remaining student boarders at Minor's Hotel C cheekily sought faculty permission
for a party to celebrate Minor's departure. Permission was denied, though two
weeks later (December 17) students received faculty permission "to give a
Party on Christmas Eve at Mr. Minor's hotel."[17]

The Minors gladly shook the dust of the University from their feet, removing to Spotsylvania County where Warner Minor was entitled to a federal land
bounty as a militia veteran and headed a household of sixty people including
slaves and free blacks. He died in 1831, aged thirty-nine, in Dinwiddie County,
Virginia, while employed as a canal contractor.[18]

Thomas Jefferson Boyd withdrew from the University by September 1828
without earning a degree (a mere formality in those times); having studied
law, he opened an office in Charlottesville and briefly practiced in Albemarle
and Fluvanna Counties, pledging "unremitted attention to all business." He
married in 1833, fathered ten children, and initially prospered through extensive holdings in hotels and mining until bankruptcy caused by the Panic of
1857 reduced his fortunes. Boyd went into politics, representing Pulaski and
Wythe Counties in the Virginia General Assembly during the 1840s–1850s,
and served as a Confederate quartermaster during the Civil War. He became town mayor and was known as "the Father of Wytheville" by the time
of his death in 1893, aged eighty-eight. Two of his sons were Louisiana State
University presidents during the 1870s and 1920s. Boyd Tavern was added to
the National Register of Historic Places and the Virginia Landmarks Register
in 2009 and 2014.[19]

Slaves as Generics

The volatile social dynamics of students versus faculty verbal and physical
clashes in the University's first decades were threats to faculty governance and
domestic tranquility on Grounds. These turbulent dramas were dominated by
malevolent forces of racism, slavery, and white supremacy as students brooked
no insolence from African Americans, slave or free; this was a perilous era of
students behaving badly largely because of the excesses of slavery. Students believed they had the right and personal duty to morally and physically "stand

their ground" against anyone including faculty, staff, or slaves. All this challenged Jefferson's hopes of making the University a leading academic institution that would contribute to prosperity and enlightenment of the American republic—a noble idea that has never been fully realized.

Caught between two strong-willed white males' uncompromising sense of personal honor and self-importance, what of the anonymous male slave whose beating precipitated a racially tinged tempest at the Academical Village two centuries ago? Boyd's assault of Minor's slave was merely deemed property damage. Astoundingly, nowhere in surviving contemporary records is he identified by name. Whatever his name, the University's powers that be were only concerned with damage control by resolving the acrimony between his owner and a privileged student that imperiled institutional tranquility, not the infringement of a defiant slave's personal dignity.

This certainly does not mean to suggest that "Minor's servant" lacked a name; it just was not customary to record slaves' names in every instance in every document. Genteel collective generics including "boys," "hands," "servants," or "laborers" were favored in ledgers linking slaves' labor with sums paid to their owners. "Minor's servant" was a nonperson, damaged property unentitled to compensation for pain and suffering. His formal testimony as the dispute's real victim was never considered; under Virginia laws of 1705 and 1818, blacks could only give evidence against each other, Native Americans, and mulattoes. Lost to history, the name and fate of "Minor's servant" remains unknown and, perhaps, unknowable.[20]

White supremacy's racism and its de jure and de facto violence sustained slavery (and racial segregation). This aggrieved slave knew he had been egregiously assaulted. His indignation can be more imagined than described; the butter-induced beating must have been publicly, physically, and psychologically humiliating even though he initially resisted. Did he and other slaves retaliate by spitting in Boyd's—and other students'—coffee, wine, and food? Undoubtedly, similar covert microresistance and disguised defiance occurred across and despite the Old South's racial order.

African Americans played active roles in the University's first half century by their labors while overcoming peculiar obstacles, not the least of which was slavery's coercive exploitation. Fleshing out African American lives is a profound responsibility; if scholars sift through their stories and ask new questions of them, the results will surely be new and notable answers.

Notes

This essay is a revision of "'Chastising a Servant for His Insolence': The Case of the Butter Bully," Panel 4: "Contested Spaces: Slavery and Peoples," Education in the Early Republic and the Founding of the University of Virginia conference, cosponsored by the Robert H. Smith International Center for Jefferson Studies (Charlottesville, VA) and a Program of the American Philosophical Society (Philadelphia), the Robert H. Smith Center at Montalto overlooking Monticello, Charlottesville, May 24–25, 2018. I am indebted to John A. Ragosta, historian, Robert H. Smith International Center for Jefferson Studies, for thought-provoking questions that subsequently refined my analysis.

1. Ervin L. Jordan Jr., "Blacks and the University of Virginia: An Overview 1819–1987" (unpublished manuscript, 1987–2017, in author's possession): 45–67; Rex Bowman and Carlos Santos, *Rot, Riot and Rebellion: Mr. Jefferson's Struggle to Save the University That Changed America* (London and Charlottesville: University of Virginia Press, 2013), 47 (slave whipping post). The actual name of Minor's slave is absent from contemporary records, and he is only referenced with the generic "servant," hence my referring to him as "Minor's servant."

2. University of Virginia General Faculty Minutes, RG-19/1/1.461, Albert and Shirley Small Special Collections Library, University of Virginia, Charlottesville (hereafter U.Va.), vol. 2, June 26, 1828, 149–55 ("he was surprised," "running freely from"); Jordan, "Blacks and the University," 45–47, 49–51. The actual date of the assault against Minor's servant is only indicated in two daily records of the University-related activities and events including the testimony of a student eyewitness. University of Virginia General Faculty Minutes, RG-19/1/1.461, U.Va., vol. 2, June 26, 1828, 150 (James Neal use of the term "yesterday"); Journals of the Chairman of the Faculty, RG-19/1/2.041, U.Va., vol. 1, 1827–1830, June 25, 1828, 13: "A note was received from W. Minor complaining of T. J. Boyd, a student, striking one of his servants in his dining room."

3. Karen Attiah, "Calling the Police on Black People Isn't a Starbucks Problem. It's an America Problem," *Washington Post*, April 19, 2018, https://www.washingtonpost.com/opinions/calling-the-police-on-black-people-isnt-a-starbucks-problem-its-an-america-problem/2018/04/18/e871d504-4330-11e8-ad8f-27a8c409298b_story.html?noredirect=on&utm_term=.c01e7d610369 ("Black people").

4. University of Virginia Matriculation Books, 1825–1905, RG-14/4/2.041, U.Va., vol. 1, 1825–1856, Thomas J. Boyd signed entry, February 3, 1826, 6 ("conform to its laws"); Sam Towler, *"The Court Doth Order": Guardianships, Apprenticeships/bound outs, African-American Subjects, Citizenship References, Revolutionary War, War of 1812 and Civil War, and Miscellaneous Orders Extracted from Albemarle County & Charlottesville, Virginia Order, Law Order and Minute Books, 1800–1900* (Athens, GA: New Papyrus, 2009), 12; Edgar Woods, *Albemarle County in Virginia: Giving some account of what it was by nature, of what it was made by man, and of some of the men who made it; Includes index compiled by Roger L. Goodman* (Charlottesville: Mitchie Co., 1901; reprint ed., Bowie, MD: Heritage Books, 1991), 260–62 (Boyd family); Jordan, "Blacks and the University," 46–47.

5. University of Virginia, Board of Visitors, Facsimile Minute Book, 1817–1828, RG-1/1/1.101, U.Va., December 16, 1826, 19 ("a suitable person"); Virginia, Auditor of Public Accounts, *Muster Rolls of the Virginia Militia in the War of 1812, Being a Supplement to the Payrolls printed and distributed in 1851, Copied From Rolls in the Auditor's Office at Richmond* (Richmond: W. F. Ritchie, printer, 1852), 27, 171; Therese Fisher, *Marriages of Caroline County, Virginia, 1777–1853* (Bowie, MD: Heritage Books, 1998), 151; John B. Minor (no. 417), *The Minor Family of Virginia* ([Lynchburg: J. P. Bell Company, Inc., 1923), 19, entry no. 104; Justin Glenn, *The Washingtons: A Family History: Volume One: Seven Generations of the Presidential Branch* (El Dorado Hills, CA: Savas Beatie, 2014), 318; *Richmond Whig & Public Advertiser,* September 5, 1843, 2, col. 5; October 31, 1843, 2, col. 6, and May 21, 1844, 2, col. 6 (Boyd daughters' marriage notices); National Archives Roll 19-195, 1830 U.S. Census-Virginia, Lunenburg County-Richmond City: Spotsylvania County, head of family "Warner W. Minor," 91 (last page entry), October 20, 1830; John Hartwell Cocke Papers, 1725–1931, Accession no. 640, U.Va. (hereafter Cocke Papers), box 33, folder "[1820–1830] November 20 [1826 or 1827], W. W. Minor to General John H. Cocke ("your friend," "impossible to realise a profit"); Philip Alexander Bruce, *History of The University of Virginia: 1819–1919,* Centennial Edition, 5 vols. (New York: MacMillan Company, 1920–1922), 2:226–27, 228–29 (Minor disapproval of student drinking and gambling).

6. John B. Richeson Letter, October 2, 1826, Accession 11925, U.Va. ("shoe deep," "impracticable"); Bruce, *History of the University,* II:206–10 (hotelkeepers' duties and their slaves), 220–23 (number of hotels and their leasing).

7. Cocke Papers, box 49, folder "1827 January 31 W.W. Minor to J.H. Cocke" ("Impossible to please" and "to receive nothing for the expenses") and box 48, folder "1826 October, W. W. Minor to J. H. Cocke" ("the profit & risk"); Bruce, *History of the University,* II:206–10, 220–23, 228–29, 236–37 (Minor's slaves and expenses); University of Virginia General Faculty Minutes, April 23 and 25, 1828, vol. 2, 138–39, RG-19/1/1.461, U.Va.; "Privies" account, November 2, 1822–February 8, 1825, Proctor's Ledger, 1819–1825, vol. 2, RG-5/3/2.961, U.Va., 270.

8. Cocke Papers, box 49, folder "1827 January 18 Thomas J. Boyd to John H. Cocke" ("I can furnish myself").

9. University of Virginia General Faculty Minutes, RG-19/1/1.461, U.Va., February 11 and 28, 1828, 100–01 (Botts and Johnston's fuel complaints); February 29, 1828, 108 (firewood quantity); March 1, 1828, 110 (Boyd's firewood supply); University of Virginia General Faculty Minutes, RG-19/1/1.461, U.Va., vol. 5, February 23, 1842, 346, February 24, 1842, 348–49, and March 19, 1842, 353 ("he considered he was imposed upon and spoken to . . . as an overseer speaks to a negro slave") (dispute between student William H. Ballard and mathematics professor J. J. Sylvester).

10. "Dispensary of the University of Virginia," discussed in Todd L. Savitt, *Medicine and Slavery: The Diseases and Health Care of Blacks in Antebellum Virginia* (Urbana: University of Illinois Press, 1978), 214, 215n63; June Purcell Guild, *Black Laws of Virginia: A Summary Of The Legislative Acts of Virginia Concerning Negroes From Earliest Times To The Present* (Whittet & Shepperson, 1936; reprint ed., New York: Negro Universities Press, 1969), 159–60; Jordan, "Blacks and the University," 76 (1830s assault); University

of Virginia General Faculty Minutes, RG-19/1/1.461, U.Va., vol. 7, May 2 and 3, 1856, 475–78.

11. Lorenzo J. Greene, *The Negro in Colonial New England, 1620–1776* (New York: Columbia University Press, 1942), 168–75 ("movable goods"), 231–34, 322–23; University of Virginia General Faculty Minutes, RG-19/1/1.461, U.Va, June 26 and 28, 1828, 149–55; Journals of the Chairman of the Faculty, RG-19/1/2.041, U.Va, vol. I, 1827–1830, June 25, 1828, 13; University of Virginia Library List of Books Borrowed, 1825–1827, RG-12/12/1.113, U.Va., year 1826, 48, 51, and year 1827, 1, 14, 26 (Boyd).

12. University of Virginia General Faculty Minutes, RG-19/1/1.461, U.Va., vol. 2, June 26, 1828, 149–50 ("astonishment & Indignation," "Mr. Minor has the proper," "Resolved that Mr. Minor"), 150 (James Neal testimony of "yesterday" during this meeting identifies the Boyd–Minor incident date as June 25, 1828).

13. University of Virginia General Faculty Minutes, RG-19/1/1.461, U.Va., vol. 2, June 28, 1828, 151–54 ("If you ever cross," "Mr. Boyd . . . threats & menaces of a bully," "whip him, Boyd," "a puppy," "maturely deliberated upon," "the severe punishment," "disapproved in the strongest"), December 1, 1827, 91, and July 23, 1828, 173–74 (Boyd's academic standing); Bruce, *History of the University*, II:291–92 ("I was anxious"); Journals of the Chairman of the Faculty, RG-19/1/2.041, U.Va., vol. I, 1827–1830, June 30, 1828 ("turned out of his house," "let the matter rest").

14. Journals of the Chairman of the Faculty, RG-19/1/2.041, U.Va., vol. I, 1827–1830, June 30, 1828 ("an explanation," "turned out of his house," "let the matter rest"), July 7, 1828, September 17, 1828 ("against his will") [no pagination for some 1828 entries]; University of Virginia General Faculty Minutes, RG-19/1/1.461, U.Va., vol. 2, June 26 and 28, 1828, 142, 149–55, 153; July 5 and 8, 1828 (measles outbreak), 156; folder "1828 July Course of Examination & Questions . . . in the University of Virginia" ["The Course of Examination and Questions Propounded in the Several Schools of the University of Virginia, at the late Public Examinations in July 1828 "], Joseph C. Cabell Papers, 1706–1920, Accession no. 38-111, U.Va., box 20; Transcripts of the Minutes of the Board [University of Virginia Board of Visitors minute books], 1817–1855, RG-1/1/1.383, U.Va., box 1, Board meetings of July 10, 11, 14, 15, 16, 17, 18, 19, 21, 22, 23, 24, 1828, 163–73, and attendance at Charlottesville convention on internal improvements (meetings of July 14, 15, 16, 18, 19), 164–65 ("no business was done by them").

15. Cocke Papers, box 56, folder "1828 Sept. 24 N. P. Trist to [John Hartwell Cocke]" ("the anticipations of a full session"); University of Virginia General Faculty Minutes, RG-19/1/1.461, U.Va., vol. 2, July 8, 1828, 163 (the Minors' complaints against Boyd); September 15, 1828, 189–92 (nine students, "very dirty cook," "want of neatness & cleanliness"); September 16, 1828, 193 ("but was absent"); December 19, 1828, 224 (student complaints about Minor's food); Journals of the Chairman of the Faculty, RG-19/1/2.041, U.Va., vol. I, 1827–1830, June 30, 1828, and December 6, 8, 9 (Mrs. Minor's testimony, "disrespectful conduct") and Dunglison report ("it was not good").

16. Cocke Papers, box 57, folders "1828 October 25 W. W. Minor to Cocke" ("As I shall not probably," "moving house"); "1828 Nov. 24 A. S. Brockenbrough presumably to Rector of U.Va." (Minor's resignation); "1828 Nov. 25 A. S. Brockenbrough to J. H. Cocke" (Minor's resignation), and "1828 Dec. 22 A. S. Brockenbrough to J.H. Cocke

(Resignation of Hotelkeepers)" [1 of 2 of this date] (reduction of suitable student accommodations caused by Minor resignation); "Warner Washington Minor" auction advertisement, *Virginia Advocate* (Charlottesville), December 20, 1828, 4, col. 5 ("many articles of Household").

17. Journals of the Chairman of the Faculty, RG-19/1/2.041, U.Va., vol. 1, 1827–1830, 1828 entries for December 1 (student party request denied), 10, 17 ("to give a Party"), and 19, 13–16, 19, and 40 (no pagination for December 1828 entries), box 1.

18. "Mr. Warner W. Minor" obituary notice," *Virginia Herald* (Fredericksburg), March 30, 1831, 3, col. 3; Jordan, "Blacks and the University," 53, 54n40; National Archives Roll 19-195, 1830 U.S. Census-Virginia, Lunenburg County-Richmond City: Spotsylvania County, head of family "Warner W. Minor," 91 (last page entry), October 20, 1830.

19. "Thomas J. Boyd, Attorney At Law," *Virginia Advocate* (Charlottesville), September 13, 1828, 3., col. 5 ("unremitted attention"); Cynthia Miller Leonard, comp., *The General Assembly of Virginia, July 30, 1619–January 11, 1978: A Bicentennial Register of Members* (Richmond: Virginia State Library, 1978): 433, 438, 446, 451; Mining Papers of John S. Noble and Thomas J. Boyd, 1868–1882, Accession no. 14221, U.Va., folder "1868–1882, Papers of the Wythe County Iron Company; James S. Presgraves, ed., *Wythe County Chapters: A Gathering of Materials from Scarce, Rare or Out-of-Print Sources about Wythe County, Virginia* (Wytheville, VA: Presgraves, 1972), 215–16 (Boyd as town council member and Boyd's Hotel); United States Department of the Interior, National Parks Service, National Register of Historic Places Registration Form, "Boyd's Tavern, Albemarle County, Virginia," September 30, 2009, 1, 5, 7; Marcus M. Wilkerson, *Thomas Duckett Boyd: The Story of a Southern Educator* (Baton Rouge: Louisiana State University Press, 1935), 37, 50, 78, 132, 147, 347.

20. Guild, *Black Laws of Virginia*, 152 (1705 law), 163 (1818 law).

BUILDING AN IDEALIZED
ACADEMICAL VILLAGE

Throughout his life Thomas Jefferson sought to build a high, impregnable wall between his private life and his public career, home and world. He eloquently testified to his failure to do so in the many letters he wrote to daughter Martha Jefferson Randolph and other family members lamenting the "miseries" of public service. He yearned to be with loved ones, gathered around the hearth, free from the worries of the world. But Jefferson's reveries were rarely fulfilled in reality, even at Monticello; instead, a steady stream of political "friends," foreign dignitaries, admirers, and allies breached the boundary, intruding on the family's privacy and demanding hospitality. In truth, Jefferson protested too much. Home and family did *not* stand in radical opposition to his dreary, self-sacrificial life in public service. Quite to the contrary, Jefferson fulfilled himself through a political career devoted to promoting the cause of republican self-government, and family was foundational to his republican vision. Paradoxically, the family letters in which Jefferson conjured up his idealized vision of domestic tranquility served to connect home and world and so subvert the distinction between them.[1]

Architectural drawings constituted another key construction site for Jeffersonian self-fashioning. The surveyor's son saw the world in spatial terms: inscribing lines on plans for Monticello and other private homes to orchestrate domestic harmony and designing public buildings to facilitate orderly and enlightened civic life. If lines defined functions and separated people, they also brought them together, efficiently coordinating domesticity and productive activity and enabling consenting citizens to form ever more perfect unions. Jefferson was a designer and system builder, distinguishing parts and assembling them into new ensembles. His designs, he imagined, were true to nature, inspired by and conforming to the "intelligent design" of Nature's God.

The University of Virginia represented Jefferson's culminating challenge as a designer and builder. His obsessive concern with even the most apparently trivial details underscored the extraordinary importance of this great "hobby" of his retirement years. Monticello has aptly been called Jefferson's autobiography in architecture. The same can be said of the University, and perhaps more emphatically, for even more was at stake. Jefferson offered the world a flattering self-portrait in his mountaintop home, expressing his vaulting aspirations as an avatar of universal enlightenment. In his ambitious design for the University, the anxious sage identified as a Virginia patriot, determined to save his beloved Commonwealth from external threats and internal corruption while enlightening the citizenry more broadly.

But it was far from clear that Virginia wanted to be saved, and obtaining the Virginia General Assembly's approval of the University was a complicated task. Seeking to mute the hostility of political opponents, Ellen Hickman writes, Jefferson was "careful in disguising his labors" and "showing his opponents as little of his methodology as possible." Ironically, as this excellent example of the value of careful documentary editing demonstrates, the great exponent of democracy and majority rule had to resort to disingenuous behind-the-scenes maneuvering to gain his dearly bought victory. Yet this, by his lights, was the measure of his patriotism. It was also, in complicated ways, the measure of the man.

Jefferson saw university education as the crucial and culminating stage in preparing the rising generation to assume its rightful, ruling place in the world. For too many sons of the plantation elite, however, leaving home to spend a short time at the College of William and Mary in Williamsburg meant liberation from parental control and a life of licentious self-indulgence. Jefferson's solution in the University's design was to seek to sustain family discipline within the context of what Joseph Michael Lasala describes as "a village-like group of small, separate houses where students could meet and converse with their teachers in classroom spaces that are essentially the downstairs parlor in the professor's home," what Jefferson referred to as an "academical village." These quasi-domestic classrooms resembled "the parlors and dining rooms of William Small, George Wythe, and Governor Fauquier," the places where the young Jefferson spent his most productive and edifying hours in Williamsburg. Such "domestically inspired collegiate spaces" would ease the transition from home to world, enabling Virginia's future leaders to navigate the perilous

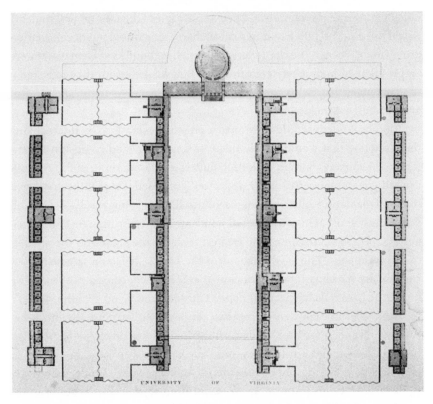

Jefferson intended the "Academical Village" to bring students and faculty together. (Jefferson's design for the Academical Village; John Neilson, draughtsman; Peter Maverick, engraver; University of Virginia [Ground Plan] 1822, revised edition 1825, A Calendar of the Jefferson Papers of the University of Virginia, Jefferson Papers, Albert and Shirley Small Special Collections Library, University of Virginia)

passage to adulthood. Distributed across the "village," students would be kept out of the "large and crouded buildings" in which they were usually "pent up." What would become known as the Wren Building at William and Mary, for example, and its counterparts at other colleges were, Jefferson concluded, "equally unfriendly to health, to study, to manners, morals & order."[2]

Jefferson had no illusions about the unhealthy proclivities of young men at the threshold of the age of reason, particularly when they were thrown into each other's company. Like "[t]he mobs of great cities," an unruly student body added "just so much to the support of pure government, as sores do to the strength of the human body."[3] Jefferson's village design separated students from each other and encouraged them to form attachments with professorial father figures and their families. Their animal spirits thus restrained, students would not descend into licentious debauchery: they would not become a riot-prone "mob," "herd," "beast." Jefferson's anxieties about adolescent males were amply justified and utterly conventional. But, for Jefferson, they reflected a fundamental threat to his conception of generational sovereignty and the progress of enlightenment.

Riotous students could only form a proper "generation" by internalizing the discipline that would enable them to reason for (and so govern) themselves. If Jefferson's faith in education buttressed his commitment to republican self-government, it also betrayed a well-grounded fear that the privileged scions of plantation elite—young men much like his younger self—would fall disastrously short of his own exalted standard. The future masters of Virginia, not the "people," constituted the greatest threat to the success of the republican experiment. "Those who labour in the earth," Jefferson famously concluded, "are the chosen people of God, if ever he had a chosen people, whose breasts he has made his peculiar deposit for substantial and genuine virtue."[4] Jefferson's declaration invites comparison beyond that normally made between rural and urban areas. Sober, industrious, independent, and devoted to the welfare of their own families, ordinary farmers displayed the virtues so conspicuously missing among the elite, including privileged college students.

Jefferson's celebration of the yeomanry seems absurdly hyperbolic, romantically disconnected from the realities of life on the ground. But the author of *Notes on Virginia* did not pretend to be an ethnographer. The idealized farmer was instead the "peculiar depository" of the family values Jefferson considered foundational to the republic. Just as he juxtaposed the felicity of private life to the misery of his public career, Jefferson constructed a stark binary opposition between town (or city) and country that belied his own experience. His point was partly heuristic: that would-be leaders of the Commonwealth must recognize their rural countrymen as equal citizens, deserving of respect as exemplars of homely virtues. These binaries served the reformer's purposes, to bring Virginians together, not to underscore their differences or promote class warfare. Reform began at the top, in Jefferson's own privileged class, and at home, in the renovation of family values. His design for the University constituted an experiment in social engineering at what he saw as a critical moment in the Commonwealth's history and at a critical time in the lives of its future leaders. By creating a homelike environment in his Academical Village, Jefferson hoped to foster a spirited commitment to the ongoing progress of republicanism. As they developed their capacity to see and reason beyond themselves, students would come into their own as a genera-tion ready to take on the responsibilities of leadership.

In his original designs for academical villages, there was no space for a big, dominant building. At architect Benjamin Latrobe's recommendation, Jeffer-son revised his plans to include the Rotunda, a great domed building that would house books, not students or a chapel, and serve as a temple of learning. In designing the Rotunda, the University's founder sought to create an in-spiring space that would facilitate enlightenment. The dome's construction demonstrated what could be done by adapting the best building technology. Jefferson also envisioned using its inside surface as "an enormous astronomi-cal star chart," Douglas J. Harnsberger writes, and locating stars on "a precise grid of longitudinal and latitudinal lines." Yet again, Jefferson would organize space for edifying, uplifting purposes. Raised high on "a thirty-five-foot-long oak boom lifted up by rope and pulley" with a saddle attached on its end, the astronomy professor would guide students through a course in "Celestial Car-tography." The image of enthralled students looking upward to their professor and to the heavens beyond must have been dazzling to Jefferson, but he wisely thought better of his ingenious design. He may have recognized the vulnera-bility of the professor, riding high in the skies. Perhaps, he feared, defiant stu-dents would seize control of the boom and hold the poor pedagogue hostage.

In his new Academical Village, Jefferson hoped to mold the unruly sons of his fellow planters into a generation of republican leaders by subjecting them to the discipline of beloved mentors, like his mentors William Small and George Wythe, while inspiring them to seek self-mastery, independence, and enlightenment. To appreciate and experience "the illimitable freedom of the human mind" was the ultimate goal of a successful university education.[5] It was the destination, not the point of departure for young men—like Jefferson himself—who had to overcome the temptations of privilege, power, and the instant gratification of irresistible appetites. By his own account, Jefferson's victory over adolescent impulses was hard-won, demanding extraordinary self-discipline and denial. But he may have thought that the way forward was more clearly marked and brightly lit for the rising, postrevolutionary genera-tion, and that gratitude for their fathers' wartime sacrifices would inspire for-tunate sons to still greater, more glorious heights. Of course, he was bound to be disappointed. Young men, then and now, live in the moment, only dimly conscious—if conscious at all—of their role in history.

Yet Jefferson had blind spots of his own, things he overlooked, kept out of sight, and did not want to see. His strong tendency to look at the world in

black-and-white terms—to juxtapose private virtue and public vice, rural integrity and urban rot, righteous republicanism and corrupt monarchy, progressive enlightenment and reactionary ignorance—obscured as much as it
illuminated. Similarly, he would not see many of the ways in which slavery fundamentally shaped life in Virginia, a "slave society." Even when he excoriated
the institution in his *Notes on Virginia*, he did so in a way that distinguished the
"mass" of virtuous white Virginian farmers from despotic slaveholding planters; his scheme for emancipation and expatriation was predicated on enlightened planters extricating themselves from the institution and eventually
removing—or deporting—black Virginians. Jefferson's idealized nuclear
family, the font of republican values, flourished in independent, slave-free farm
households. Of course, the republican reformer was no prophet: slavery *was*
democratized in republican Virginia, as aspiring farmer-planters eagerly acquired human property.[6] Most important, white Virginians' households contained and governed the growing population of enslaved Virginians. "Family
values" adapted accordingly, as Jefferson's planter-despot was supplanted by
the "benign" patriarch of the extended and inclusive "black-and-white" family.

Jefferson was not oblivious to these developments, though he continued to
promote his hopelessly unrealistic emancipation scheme until his death. He
understood that planters' sons would resist discipline and that the habit of
mastery would be hard to break. Perhaps, he hoped, the ban on bringing personal "servants" to University Grounds would help; perhaps professors—
including many foreigners who did not (at first) own slaves—would set an
inspiring example in their own homes; at the very least, the University could
present a slavery-free facade. "The design for the University of Virginia," Maurie D. McInnis writes, "built on Jefferson's many decades of architectural experiments in a slave society" as "he determined how best to mask slavery by
creating separate private and public zones in buildings and landscapes." But
slaves were ubiquitous and the lines Jefferson sought to inscribe on the geography of the Academical Village proved porous. "Separate zones" could not be
policed as students regularly interacted—and often abused—"the enslaved
who lived and worked around them." Enslaved workers enjoyed the relative
freedom of moving about Grounds and the neighborhood, servicing the informal market for alcohol and other illicit goods. At the same time, however, the
nature of the space meant that hotelkeepers and other legal owners could not
exercise effective discipline over their chattel or protect them from assault and
abuse. Enslaved people at the University "were owned simultaneously by no
one and everyone," diluting the "clear lines of authority" customary on planta-

tions, but reinforcing a broader conception of white supremacy and race privilege.

The irony of slavery at the University is that the ameliorative impulses of enlightened planters enjoyed wider scope on their home plantations. Jefferson may have imagined that his design for the University would promote enlightenment by replicating and improving on the circumstances of his own educational journey. But the "family values" that were so central to his political and educational philosophy meant something vastly different in 1825, when the first students arrived in Charlottesville, than when a much younger Jefferson dreamed of reforming his beloved Commonwealth. In the intervening years, the patriot necessarily adapted to the political and social realities of a society in which the peculiar institution was deeply, inextricably entrenched. The Virginian was bound to overlook what he could not bear to see. The University's design nonetheless testified to his enduring commitment to progress, enlightenment, and republican government. Even as he faced inevitable disappointment in his utterly unrealistic hopes for the rising generation, Jefferson's Academical Village testified to the values he sought to promote throughout his career.

Notes

1. Billy L. Wayson, *Martha Jefferson Randolph: Republican Daughter & Plantation Mistress* (Palmyra, VA: Shortwood Press, 2013).

2. Jefferson to the Trustees of the Lottery of East Tennessee College, May 6, 1810, *PTJRS*, 2:366.

3. *Notes*, Query XIX ("Manufactures"), 165.

4. Ibid., 164–65.

5. Jefferson to William Roscoe, December 27, 1820, *Founders Online*, https://founders.archives.gov/documents/Jefferson/98-01-02-1712.

6. Alan Taylor, *The Internal Enemy: Slavery and War in Virginia, 1772–1832* (New York: W. W. Norton, 2013).

Avoiding "The appearance of dictating to the Assembly"

Thomas Jefferson and the Establishment of the University of Virginia, 1818–1819

ELLEN HICKMAN

IT IS WELL KNOWN that Thomas Jefferson considered the establishment of the University of Virginia to be one of his greatest accomplishments. In designing his own gravestone, he famously listed his role as father of the University along with his authorship of the Declaration of Independence and the Virginia Statute for Religious Freedom, while omitting his service as United States president.[1] Jefferson's leadership in founding the University was rare for his retirement years, which were marked by a desire to avoid public life. While he ultimately wanted his role in the creation of the University to be well known, in the crucial period of 1818 to 1819, for the sake of political expediency Jefferson obscured his efforts to establish his Central College of Charlottesville as the new state university. His method of leadership involved quietly recruiting allies to his cause, drafting a persuasive case for Central College without seeming to advocate strenuously in public for its selection, and presenting a ready-made report and bill that secured his vision. The work of the editorial team in editing volume 13 of the *Papers of Thomas Jefferson: Retirement Series* illuminates Jefferson's undercover labors during the period leading up to the General Assembly's establishment of the Central College as the University of Virginia, and adds new dimensions to some of the most studied documents of that episode by returning to the manuscript originals as well as presenting variant texts.

By 1818 Jefferson had already been working for several years to establish the Central College in Charlottesville and simultaneously to promote the creation of an official state university. Progress was finally made on the latter front in February of 1818 when the Virginia General Assembly approved "An Act appropriating part of the revenue of the Literary Fund, and for other purposes," which authorized the creation of a University of Virginia.[2] Under the provisions of this act, Governor James P. Preston appointed twenty-four commissioners (among them Jefferson and James Madison) who were to meet at a tavern at Rockfish Gap in the Blue Ridge Mountains on August 1, 1818, to craft a report for the General Assembly. In this report they were to select a site for the University as well as offer recommendations on the nature of its buildings, curriculum, organization, and governance. Throughout the months leading up to the meeting of the University of Virginia Commissioners, Jefferson constructed his argument for the selection of Central College as state university and undertook what he described to Madison as the "campaign of Rockfish gap."[3]

Jefferson pursued this Rockfish Gap campaign clandestinely, not wanting his patronage of the Central College to give his political enemies either a partisan reason to reject it as the state university or cause to complain that the proceedings were biased in favor of Charlottesville. But for all that Jefferson wanted to downplay his role in the proceedings, his fellow University Commissioners assumed that he would in fact be taking a strong lead. Friend and fellow commissioner Archibald Stuart wrote Jefferson in May, several months before the Rockfish Gap meeting, that "it is the Gen[l] expectation that you & M[r] Madison will be prepared to submit such a report to our body as we ought to adopt."[4] Jefferson asked Madison to prepare a report for the commissioners to consider, presumably to make it seem that he himself was not dictating the outcome of the proceedings. Madison however refused, and it was left to Jefferson to craft a report that would secure the University for Charlottesville, without presenting this outcome as a foregone conclusion so that either the University Commissioners or the General Assembly would reject it.[5]

Scholars have long known that Jefferson composed the report of the University Commissioners before the actual Rockfish Gap meeting took place, as he enclosed a draft to Madison in a letter of June 28, 1818. Jefferson also invited friendly commissioners Spencer Roane and Littleton W. Tazewell to join him and Madison in secret at Monticello before the commissioners' meeting to discuss what he casually referred to as a "sketch" of a report.[6] But the two surviving drafts that Jefferson prepared (one clean with numbered pages, which was likely that sent to Madison, and one earlier and much more heavily reworked) have largely been ignored. Researchers have concentrated instead on the final report as published in 1818 and later reprintings of the report. In volume 13 of the *Retirement Series*, we have printed a collated version comparing Jefferson's drafts of the report alongside the final manuscript report as adopted by the University Commissioners and submitted to the General Assembly.[7]

Evidence of copying errors by Jefferson in the rougher of the two drafts suggests that there may have been an even earlier manuscript that he built on.[8] Jefferson's process of creating these drafts and the evolution between versions show his strategy for persuading his fellow commissioners to select the Central College for the University, and his efforts to disguise the fact that he was attempting to guide the selection process. Even in his invitation of sympathetic colleagues to discuss the matter before the Rockfish Gap meeting, Jefferson downplayed his involvement. In his June 28 letter asking Roane to come to Monticello before the commissioners' meeting, Jefferson implied that he had not yet begun to write his little "sketch" of a report. In fact, based on his enclosure of the clean draft to Madison on this same date, Jefferson had already produced at least two complete drafts totaling more than thirty manuscript pages.[9]

Some of the most extensive textual changes between Jefferson's drafts of the Rockfish Gap Report and the report as ultimately adopted by the commissioners are in the initial pages of the document. In this section, Jefferson laid out which site had been chosen for the University and describes the recommended buildings for the institution. Although Lexington and Staunton in the Shenandoah Valley were also ostensibly being considered as sites for the University, Jefferson wrote this portion of the report with the assumption that Charlottesville would be chosen. As the report evolved, Jefferson streamlined the case for choosing Central College, eliminating points that were not particularly compelling and simplifying his argument overall.

In all surviving versions of the report (the earliest draft, the clean draft, and the final version as adopted), Jefferson states that the three factors the commissioners considered in making their choice of site were healthiness of location, fertility of surrounding countryside, and centrality of the site to the white population of the state.[10] While Jefferson consistently acknowledged across versions that Charlottesville, Staunton, and Lexington were equally healthy and fertile sites, in his drafts he elaborated on the relative water quality of the locations. According to Jefferson, Charlottesville's water was "pure and free from foreign ingredients" but that of the Shenandoah Valley locations was "distinguished by it's calcareous impregnation" and required a period of adjustment before its "drastic effect" could be tolerated by newcomers.[11] By the time he prepared the final version of the report, Jefferson cut his statements about water quality, simply stating that all sites were equal in healthiness and fertility and that proximity to the center of white population was the only factor to be considered in selecting the site of the University. Jefferson thereby eliminated a weak argument that would have served only to make proponents of Staunton and Lexington defensive and have provided them with a point on which to protest.[12] Similarly, by the time he composed his final version of the report, Jefferson had dropped his explanation that the site selection process did not consider the College of William and Mary or any of several of Virginia's large commercial centers for the state university because these did not meet the criteria of healthiness or centrality.[13] Introducing these other possible sites with advantages not possessed by the Central College could have raised the question as to why the selection process should prize healthiness over resources, or centrality over convenience of transportation.

In refining the report, Jefferson also removed his explanation of how he had concluded that Charlottesville was nearest the geographic center of the white population of Virginia. When he sent his clean draft to Madison in June of 1818, Jefferson enclosed extensive calculations based on the 1810 federal census by which he felt he had proved that Charlottesville was closer to the geographic center of white population than either Staunton or Lexington.[14] As he informed Madison, Jefferson never intended to present these calculations to the commissioners, but in his drafts of the report, he instead included several paragraphs summarizing his reasoning.[15] The final report as adopted by the commissioners stated that "the board, after full enquiry & impartial & mature consideration, are of opinion that the central point of the white population of the state is nearer to the central college, than to either Lexington or Staunton" but offered no evidence in support of this opinion.[16] Jefferson apparently concluded that he could be most convincing in this argument by showing his opponents as little of his methodology as possible. He was ultimately correct on this score; after the report was adopted by the commissioners and submitted to the General Assembly, the issue of how to calculate correctly the centrality of white population was hotly debated. Joseph C. Cabell, Jefferson's ally and agent in the state senate, published Jefferson's calculations anonymously in the *Richmond Enquirer* in the misguided hope of ending the argument.[17] Among other complaints, opponents in the state legislature correctly pointed out that Jefferson's method did not actually calculate white population as it claimed. By subtracting the number of slaves from the overall population as reported in the census, he had calculated centrality of population with free blacks included in the total, which added more population east of the Blue Ridge Mountains and favored Charlottesville over the Shenandoah Valley sites.[18]

Another portion of the Commissioners' Report that Jefferson edited extensively and condensed between drafts is that which recommends a design for the buildings of the University. His trimming here was less a refining of his vision of academic architecture than an attempt to obscure that the report was written with the selection of Central College as a foregone conclusion. Jefferson's earliest draft described in detail the current status of construction at Central College, elaborated his architectural design theories for the college, included his musings on the value of exposing students to classical design, and even began to calculate the number of bricks necessary for each planned building. By his clean draft version, Jefferson had cut this down to an opening assertion that the commissioners agreed that the design plan "which has been adopted by the Visitors of the Central College is well suited to the purpose of the University" followed by a considerably condensed description of the established architectural plan for Central College.[19] In the final report as adopted by the commissioners, Jefferson dropped explicit references to Central College from the report's recommendations for the university buildings, and the report instead succinctly outlines Jefferson's preexisting plans for the grounds of Central College without identifying them as such.[20] Thus Jefferson fulfilled the legislature's command that the report supply advice on buildings without explicitly arguing the merits of Central College. An additional interesting change made to the report's proposed architectural design was the addition by Jefferson of the provision for a room that could be used for religious worship to his later, cleaner draft. This alteration was one of a very few made to this draft by Jefferson late in the process in a different, darker ink than that used for the manuscript and his other revisions to it, suggesting that this change was made around or at the time of the Rockfish Gap meeting, perhaps at the suggestion of the other commissioners.[21]

Once Jefferson's carefully crafted report was approved by his fellow commissioners at the Rockfish Gap meeting and forwarded to the legislature, his next campaign action was to draft a bill by which the General Assembly could enact the report's recommendations and officially declare Central College to be the choice for the state university. As the fight for Central College moved to the legislature, Jefferson was reliant on his agents in Richmond to act on his behalf and to continue to obscure his role. He was kept informed throughout by friends carrying letters and messages back and forth to his most active ally, state senator Cabell. It was Cabell who suggested in mid-November 1818 that it would be best if Jefferson had a bill confirming the findings of the Rockfish Gap report already prepared at the start of the legislative term. Jefferson complied, and in a matter of weeks produced a university bill. Cabell, along with Albemarle County delegates William F. Gordon and Samuel Carr, enlisted Samuel Taylor of Chesterfield to immediately move the Rockfish Gap report to subcommittee in the House of Delegates. Taylor was presumably recruited because his lack of obvious ties to Charlottesville or to Jefferson made him seem disinterested. To further remove evidence of Jefferson's involvement, Cabell had Taylor recopy Jefferson's university bill into his own hand before introducing it to the committee. Even with Jefferson obscuring his role in promoting Central College to this extent, Cabell reported that "[s]ome imprudent friend has suffered it to get out that you are the author of the bill. It has been sneeringly remarked that we have a bill 'ready cut & dry.' I hope the knowledge of the fact will do no injury. An attempt will doubtless be made to give it the appearance of dictating to the Assembly: yet I believe it will not succeed."[22] Despite Cabell's concerns, after a month of legislative wrangling, this bill that Jefferson wrote did in fact pass in the General Assembly with only minor changes, and Central College was made the University of Virginia in January of 1819.

Jefferson was so careful in disguising his labors throughout 1818 on behalf of Central College that even when his influence on the process was frequently suspected and condemned by his opponents, they were unable to prove any overt action on his part. Other than his appearance at the Rockfish Gap meeting, Jefferson conducted his fight for the establishment of the University of Virginia from the privacy of his retirement at Monticello. In response to allegations that Jefferson had influenced the outcome of the Rockfish Gap meeting, one of his fellow commissioners wrote in Jefferson's defense that the former president had only ventured an opinion at the meeting when his vote was called for.[23] While it was understood that Jefferson was strongly in favor of a state university and that his Central College was his choice for it, he surreptitiously promoted his cause in 1818 in a manner that attempted to avoid debate by obscuring his arduous labor on behalf of a University of Virginia in Charlottesville.

Notes

1. Jefferson, Design for Tombstone and Inscription, [before July 4, 1826], Library of Congress, Jefferson Papers.

2. *Acts Passed at a General Assembly of the Commonwealth of Virginia*, [1817–1818 sess.], (Richmond, 1818), 11–15.

3. Jefferson to James Madison, April 11, 1818, *PTJRS*, 12:625.

4. Archibald Stuart to Jefferson, May 30, 1818, *PTJRS*, 13:80.

5. Jefferson to Spencer Roane, June 28, 1818, *PTJRS*, 13:110.

6. Ibid., and Jefferson to Littleton W. Tazewell, June 28, 1818, *PTJRS*, 13:111–12.

7. Jefferson's Draft of the Rockfish Gap Report, [ca. June 28, 1818], *PTJRS*, 13:189–208; Rockfish Gap Report, August 4, 1818, *PTJRS*, 13:209–24.

8. *PTJRS*, 13:204n52.

9. Jefferson to James Madison, June 28, 1818, *PTJRS*, 13:108–9.

10. *PTJRS*, 13:189, 210.

11. *PTJRS*, 13:189-90.

12. *PTJRS*, 13:210.

13. *PTJRS*, 13:189, 210.

14. Jefferson to James Madison, June 28, 1818, *PTJRS*, 13:108–9; Jefferson's Notes on the Geographic Center of Virginia's Population, [before June 28, 1818], *PTJRS*, 13:185–88.

15. *PTJRS*, 13:190–91.

16. *PTJRS*, 13:210.

17. Joseph C. Cabell to Jefferson, December 17, 1818, *PTJRS*, 13:497–98; Jefferson's Notes on the Geographic Center of Virginia's Population, [before June 28, 1818], *PTJRS*, 13:185–88; *Richmond Enquirer*, December 17, 1818.

18. Joseph C. Cabell to Jefferson, December 24, 1818, *PTJRS*, 13:514–16; Joseph C. Cabell to Jefferson, January 18, 1819, *PTJRS*, 13:583–84.

19. *PTJRS*, 13:191.

20. *PTJRS*, 13:210–11.

21. *PTJRS*, 13:191, 203n22.

22. Joseph C. Cabell to Jefferson, December 14, 1818, *PTJRS*, 13:491.

23. John G. Jackson to Joseph C. Cabell, December 13, 1818, Cabell Papers, Albert and Shirley Small Special Collections Library, University of Virginia.

From Academy to Academical Village

Thomas Jefferson's Architectural Designs
for Public Education

JOSEPH MICHAEL LASALA

FOR THOMAS JEFFERSON, the best means of ensuring the survival of the new republic that he and the other Founding Fathers established in 1776 was an educated and well-informed citizenry. "It is an axiom in my mind," he wrote, "that our liberty can never be safe but in the hands of the people themselves, and that too of the people with a certain degree of instruction. This it is the business of the state to effect, and on a general plan."[1] To this end, he championed a system of public education for Virginians, and the crowning achievement of his crusade was the establishment of the University of Virginia and the Academical Village of buildings that he designed to house the institution.

Throughout the decades, Jefferson continued to advocate for numerous proposals and legislative bills for public education, both directly and behind the scenes through political proxies. At one point during his presidency, on hearing that the Virginia legislature was considering the formation of a new university, he wrote to a delegate in the state assembly that "no one can be more rejoiced at the information that the legislature of Virginia are likely at length to institute an University on a liberal plan. [C]onvinced that the people are the only safe depositories of their own liberty, & that they are not safe unless enlightened to a certain degree, I have looked on our present state of liberty as a short-lived possession, unless the mass of the people could be informed to a certain degree. . . ."[2] Jefferson clearly believed that education not only served to improve the individual, it served an important societal and civic function as well, benefiting the nation as a whole, and safeguarding the preservation of its hard-fought freedom.

The one-room schoolhouse at Tuckahoe where Thomas Jefferson first began his studies. (Image courtesy of Tuckahoe Plantation)

Jefferson's own education was typical of eighteenth-century Virginia landed gentry. It began with a private tutor in the one-room schoolhouse at Tuckahoe Plantation, which still stands. Jefferson's parents, Peter and Jane, temporarily relocated their family from Shadwell to Tuckahoe when Thomas was just three years old in order to fulfill the dying wish of the estate's owner, William Randolph, who was Jane's cousin and Peter's close friend. Education was clearly a priority for Randolph, as evidenced by the instructions for education of his son that he left for Peter Jefferson: "Whereas I have appointed by my will that my dear only son Thomas Mann Randolph should have a private education given him in my house at Tuckahoe, my will is that my dear and loving friend Mr. Peter Jefferson do move down with his family to my Tuckahoe house and remain there till my son comes of age with whom my dear son and his sisters shall live."[3]

At the age of five, Thomas Jefferson joined his cousin Thomas Mann Randolph in the Tuckahoe schoolhouse where they received instruction in writing, grammar, and spelling. These "English School" lessons, as Jefferson would later refer to them in his autobiography, lasted for four years. When he was nine, his family returned to their Shadwell homestead, where Thomas enrolled in what he called a "Latin School." Here, he received instruction in the classics, including ancient languages and literature, although the Latin School teacher apparently did not impress his young student. "My teacher mr Douglas a clergyman from Scotland was but a superficial Latinist, less instructed in Greek, but with the rudiments of these languages he taught me French." Following the death of his father in 1757, fourteen-year-old Thomas began studying under the Reverend James Maury, "a correct classical scholar, with whom I continued two years."[4]

In 1760, when he was sixteen, Jefferson entered the College of William and Mary in Williamsburg where he was exposed to the Enlightenment philosophies of one of the few professors there whom he truly admired, William Small, the only nonclergyman on the faculty and a man he would come to consider a father figure. Jefferson would later write that Small was "a man profound in most of the useful branches of science, with a happy talent of communic[atio]n correct & gentlemanly manners, & an enlarged & liberal mind. [H]e, most happily for me, became soon attached to me & made me his daily companion when not engaged in the school; and from his conversation I got my first views of the expansion of science & of the system of things in which we are placed."[5]

After two years at William and Mary, Jefferson began studying law under the tutelage of George Wythe, a local attorney and close friend of William Small. Jefferson later explained that Small "procured for me the patronage of mr Wythe, & both of them, the attentions of Governor Fauquier, the ablest man who ever filled the chair of government here." A favorite rendezvous for Jefferson, Wythe, and Small was the Governor's Palace where, over food and wine, they would discuss science, philosophy, politics, and current events of the day. "[A]t these dinners I have heard more good sense, more rational & philosophical conversations than in all my life besides. [T]hey were truly Attic societies."[6] In addition to the rebuilt Governor's Palace, the George Wythe House still stands in Williamsburg, and visitors can easily envision mentor and protégé spending several hours each day engaged in one-on-one instruction and dialogue in the main rooms of the house.

It is interesting to note that when Jefferson reminisces later in life about his most memorable interactions with his professors and mentors during his college years in Williamsburg, they consistently take place *outside* of the classrooms and lecture halls of William and Mary's main structure, now known as the Wren Building. The lessons and interactions that he recollects most fondly from this time are the ones that take place "when not engaged in the school."

Subsequently, whenever he is asked for advice and design suggestions for a proposed college or university, either for Virginia or outside of the state, Jefferson renounces the familiar William and Mary model of a single, massive, all-purpose academic building then popular with most American universities, and instead recommends a village-like group of small, separate houses where students could meet and converse with their teachers in classroom spaces that are essentially the downstairs parlor in the professor's home—no doubt recalling his time well spent in the parlors and dining rooms of William Small, George Wythe, and Governor Fauquier.

In fact, when describing an ideal university arrangement to the trustees of East Tennessee College, Jefferson suggested that in addition to teaching students in their individual homes, the professors "might be at the head of their table if, as I suppose, it can be reconciled with the necessary economy to dine them in smaller & separate parties rather than in a large & common mess."[7] (At William and Mary, students took communal meals in the Main Building's "great hall.") It is as if Jefferson is attempting to use domestically inspired collegiate spaces to encourage the same kinds of close social interactions and congenial relationships between teacher and student that he himself experienced as a young man in Williamsburg—not in the impersonal classrooms and great hall of the main college building, but in the inviting homes of his instructors and their colleagues. Even the terminology that Jefferson used to describe his conceptual college-town setting has its origins in Williamsburg. When the Virginia capitol was relocated in the 1780s, Jefferson wrote that "the removal of the seat of government to Richmond ... has made of Williamsburgh a mere academical village."[8]

Jefferson's first opportunity to create an architectural design for a college building occurred in 1771 at his own alma mater, which was then in need of additional space. Jefferson had nothing nice to say about the building that housed the College of William and Mary. He described his overall contempt for Williamsburg's architecture: "The College and Hospital are rude, misshapen piles, which, but that they have roofs, would be taken for brick-kilns."[9] It was not only the exterior appearance of the College and its architectural style with which Jefferson was unimpressed, however. He was also highly critical of life inside its walls and how unpleasant and potentially detrimental it was for the students, evidently based on his own prior personal experience. "[M]uch observation & reflection on these [collegiate] institutions have long convinced me that large and crouded buildings in which youths are pent up, are equally unfriendly to health, to study, to manners, morals & order...."[10]

So, when offered the chance to make substantial alterations to this building, how did Jefferson respond?

Ironically, despite his later repeated insistence that a college should not consist of a single, massive, all-purpose building housing all of the school's functions under one roof, Jefferson nevertheless planned to expand the College of William and Mary with a large addition that would more than double the main building's size, as seen on his architectural drawing for the extended floor plan. He no doubt turned to his edition of Palladio's *Four Books of Architecture*, which he first acquired a decade earlier when he was a student at William and Mary, and chose one of the several palazzo forms illustrated within its pages. His design for a quadrangle arrangement of classrooms organized around an open courtyard containing an outdoor yet covered walkway would, decades later, become the genesis of his plan for what would eventually evolve into the University of Virginia. Nevertheless, this grandiose design for the Wren Building addition stands in contradiction to all of Jefferson's later plans and suggestions for higher-level educational institutions where he consistently recommends a much smaller-scale, modular arrangement of buildings that could be constructed incrementally over time as needed. When offering advice for constructing a newly proposed university in 1805, for example, Jefferson wrote that "the greatest danger will be their over-building themselves, by attempting a large house in the beginning, sufficient to contain the whole institution. [L]arge houses are always ugly, inconvenient, exposed to the accident of fire, and bad in cases of infection."[11] So perhaps Jefferson considered it serendipitous that, due to the impending revolution, his substantial addition to the already massive college building at William and Mary was never built.

Jefferson's design for the William and Mary addition was his first and last transgression into the standard American paradigm of a single, all-inclusive building that housed all collegiate functions. From then on, whenever the subject was raised, Jefferson instead proposed his Academical Village concept of a small, separate house for each professor, with his classroom on the ground floor and two rooms above for his living quarters. The students would live side by side with their teachers, in dormitory rooms that were connected to the schoolhouses by a covered walkway, protecting them from the elements as they moved from class to class.

This was not the first time that Jefferson employed the architectural motif of a two-story house flanked by single-story wings topped by a flat roof that served as an upper-level walkway and was supported by a series of brick columns that created a covered, all-weather passage below. We not only see such colonnaded service wings at Jefferson's own Monticello, but he specifically referred to the office wings flanking the President's House in Washington as another precedent: "[T]he dormitories will be covered flat, as the offices of the President's house at Washington was, and will furnish a fine walk from the chambers of the professors."[12] In fact, the striking similarity between the President's House office wings and Jefferson's designs for college dormitories led to the nearly century-long misidentification of one of Jefferson's architectural drawings. The drawing had been cataloged as a circa 1804 study for the colonnades flanking the President's House in Washington,[13] but in fact it turns out to be an 1817 cross-section for the dormitories and covered walkway in Jefferson's University of Virginia design. The drawing once thought to be of the President's House wings aligns exactly with a pair of later drawings detailing the structural components of the flat roof walkway terrace atop the University dormitories—just drawn at a different scale.

Yet another one of Jefferson's architectural drawings for an educational facility had been misidentified for nearly a century, this time as an early floor plan study for a typical pavilion at the University of Virginia. In the left margin of the sheet, Jefferson labeled the subject of the drawing "A Pavilion," so it is easy to see how this original misidentification came about. Previous architectural historians have dated this drawing to 1804–1805, which corresponds to Jefferson's early description of a conceptual university design in a January 1805 letter to state politician Littleton Waller Tazewell in which he recommends individual pavilions as being best suited for such a purpose. What is interesting about this floor plan drawing is that it lacks the covered walkways in front of the pavilion and dormitory rooms, which Jefferson had consistently included in all of his university design proposals. It turns out there is a reason that the covered walkway is missing from this "Pavilion" drawing, and it helps solve a mystery and fill a missing link in Jefferson's educational and architectural legacy.

Jefferson himself best expressed the origin of his idea of public education in Virginia when he reminisced late in his life about the revised code of statutes that he and his law teacher George Wythe, along with Edmund Pendleton, collaborated on between 1776 and 1779. "[N]o body can doubt my zeal for the general instruction of the people," he insisted. "[W]ho first started that idea? I may surely say myself. [T]urn to the bill in the revised code which I drew more than 40. years ago; and before which the idea of a plan for the

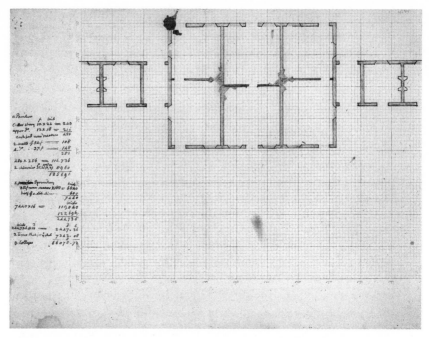

Jefferson's floor plan for a district college, 1817. (Collection of the Massachusetts Historical Society)

education of the people generally had never been suggested in this state."[14] Among the more than 120 pieces of legislation that Jefferson and his colleagues submitted to the Virginia Assembly, it was Bill #79, "A Bill for the More General Diffusion of Knowledge," that Jefferson was referring to here. In its preamble, Jefferson argued that public education was essential to the survival of the newly formed republic as "it becomes expedient for promoting the publick happiness that those persons, whom nature hath endowed with genius and virtue, should be rendered by liberal education worthy to receive, and able to guard the sacred deposit of the rights and liberties of their fellow citizens, and that they should be called to that charge without regard to wealth, birth or other accidental condition or circumstance. . . ."[15]

The bill proposed a three-tier system of public education in Virginia. For the primary level, the state would be divided into districts called "hundreds," each of which would be responsible for erecting and maintaining a schoolhouse where the rudiments of reading, writing, and arithmetic would be taught. At the secondary or "grammar school" level, students would be taught languages, including Latin and Greek, and higher forms of arithmetic. And finally, at the third level, the state university would offer the most advanced course of education and professional instruction. In his autobiography, Jefferson further elaborated on his proposal for a three-tier system of public education and described the various types of school facilities to house each level of instruction.

At the first level, Jefferson used several terms interchangeably in his bills and correspondence to describe the schoolhouses, including primary schools, elementary schools, and ward schools. In each case, however, the physical building was essentially the same: a log or wood-framed one-room schoolhouse, not unlike the one he attended as a young boy at Tuckahoe. Jefferson's proposal for the building and funding of primary-level schools throughout the state was that each district should

> put to their vote whether they will have a school established, and the most central and convenient place for it; get them to meet & build a log schoolhouse, have a roll taken of the children who would attend it, and of those of them able to pay: these would probably be sufficient to support a common teacher, instructing gratis the few unable to pay. [I]f there should be a deficiency, it would require too trifling a contribution from the county to be complained of; and especially as the whole county would participate, where necessary, in the same resource. [S]hould the company, by it's vote, decide that it would have no school, let them remain without one. [T]he advantages of this proceeding would be that it would become the duty of the Wardens elected by the county to take an active part in pressing the introduction of schools, and to look out for tutors.[16]

As for the second tier or general grade of education, Jefferson proposed several grammar schools or district colleges to be dispersed throughout the state. The secondary level of education would include among its subjects Greek, Latin, and higher mathematics. Until recently, it was believed that Jefferson did not produce any drawings for these secondary schoolhouses—at least not according to the major published catalogs of Jefferson's architectural drawings, *Thomas Jefferson Architect* (1916) and *Thomas Jefferson's Architectural Drawings* (1960). The only clues to the architectural layout and design of these secondary schools appeared in Jefferson's written descriptions of the buildings from his aforementioned "A Bill for the More General Diffusion of Knowledge," where he stated that each district within the state should build "a house of brick or stone for the said grammar school, with necessary offices, built on the said lands, which grammar school-house shall contain a room for the school, a hall to dine in, four rooms for a master and usher, and ten or twelve lodging rooms for the scholars."

This grammar school description sounds very similar to the previously discussed "Pavilion" floor plan, which had been identified in the Jefferson drawing catalogs as an early (circa 1804 or 1805) study for a pavilion at the proposed state university. In actuality, however, this drawing is not an early study for a university building. It is the elusive drawing for a regional grammar school or district college at the second level of Jefferson's three-tier system of public education. And now that we know its correct identification, we can also redate it from 1805 to 1817. On October 24, 1817, Jefferson submitted a draft for his latest "Bill for Establishing a System of Public Education," in which he once again proposes three levels of education consisting of elementary schools, district colleges, and a state university. The section of the bill describing the district colleges, of which there were to be nine dispersed throughout the state, contains a description of the school facilities matching this floor plan and cost estimate. Furthermore, in a postscript to the letter accompanying this bill, Jefferson writes, "P.S. I drew a plan of a College and it's dormitories, such as the bill calls for to demonstrate that it will not cost more than the sum allotted."[17]

The October 1817 time frame for this district college drawing is significant because now, instead of being a preliminary architectural study for the third level of education (the university), it instead postdates Jefferson's university building concepts, having been drawn three years after he drew his architectural plans for a typical university pavilion and dormitories in the summer of 1814, which we will soon see. Therefore, it is not early or preliminary at all. On the contrary, it is a mature, fully thought-out design for the second level of public education, complete with detailed calculations for the number of bricks needed to construct each of the nine proposed colleges, and a cost estimate based on these materials. October 1817 was a pivotal moment in the progress of Jefferson's long-standing public education efforts. At the same time that he was drafting plans for second-level district colleges to be built throughout Virginia, he participated in the laying of the cornerstone that marked the start of construction on Central College, an outgrowth of Albemarle Academy, and the seed that he was hoping would germinate to become the University of Virginia, thus completing the third and final level of public education facilities in the state.

Curiously, in his 1779 "A Bill for the more General Diffusion of Knowledge," in which he included a detailed architectural description for the second-level district college buildings, Jefferson did not provide an architectural description of the structure or structures intended to house the state university at the third level of public education. And that is because the state university was already built. At the time he wrote his public education bill, Jefferson naturally assumed that the College of William and Mary, then the preeminent educational institution in Virginia, would be converted into the state university. Jefferson endeavored over the ensuing years to change the curriculum of William and Mary to match the university course descriptions he had written into his bill, replacing several of the ecclesiastical subjects and their instructors with new ones from the third- or professional-level listings. These and other proposals would, if adopted by the Virginia legislature, make William and Mary a true university in Jefferson's eyes, cutting across social and economic barriers to produce an educated elite of the best and brightest minds in the Commonwealth at the public expense. But after years of opposition to these changes, Jefferson finally abandoned his aspirations for William and Mary and began to formulate a plan for a new state university of his own design, both in terms of its curriculum and architecture, and located not in Williamsburg, but more central for Virginia, in the vicinity of his home, Monticello, in Albemarle County.

In the summer of 1814, Jefferson finally had an opportunity to transfer his long-established written concepts for a university into an architectural plan when the trustees of Albemarle Academy asked him to prepare a set of drawings and cost estimates for their proposed facilities. Although Albemarle Academy was chartered as a small, local district school, Jefferson had much grander ambitions in mind for it. He hoped, in fact, to expand the modest scope of this regional school to encompass the functions of his third tier of public education—the state university. Several months earlier, in January of 1814, Jefferson wrote to a longtime friend, "I have long had under contemplation, & been collecting materials for the plan of an university in Virginia ... this would probably absorb the functions of W^m. & Mary college, and transfer them to a healthier and more central position. perhaps to the neighborhood of this place [Monticello]."[18]

We can see further evidence of Jefferson's ulterior motive in his architectural plans for the institution. Instead of one building containing the classroom, offices, and dining hall that we just examined and identified as the plan for a district college, Jefferson instead drew a much larger arrangement of several pavilions, one for each teacher, connected by student dormitory rooms, all fronted by a covered walkway, and surrounding an open square of grass and trees. This precisely matches Jefferson's conceptual plans from his earlier correspondence, where he stated that the best building layout for a university is that of an Academical Village of small, separate houses for each professor,

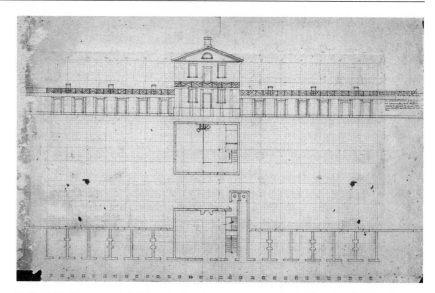

Jefferson's elevation and floor plan for a typical pavilion and dormitories at Albemarle Academy, 1814. (A Calendar of the Jefferson Papers of the University of Virginia, Jefferson Papers, Albert and Shirley Small Special Collections Library, University of Virginia)

with adjacent dormitories for their students, connected around a village green by a covered walkway.

> I consider the common plan, followed in this country, but not in others, of making one large & expensive building as unfortunately erroneous. [I]t is infinitely better to erect a small and separate lodge for each separate professorship, with only a hall below for his class, and two chambers above for himself; joining these lodges by barracks for a certain portion of the students opening into a covered way to give a dry communication between all the schools. [T]he whole of these arranged around an open square of grass & trees would make it, what it should be in fact, an academical village, instead of a large & common den of noise, of filth, & of fetid air. [I]t would afford that quiet retirement so friendly to study, and lessen the dangers of fire, infection & tumult.[19]

Over the next few years, Albemarle Academy evolved into Central College, a name that was deliberately chosen by Jefferson to further boost the establishment's chances of being selected as the site of the University of Virginia on account of its central location within the state. Despite the name change, the building plans and layout for the grounds remained essentially the same.

The one significant update to the design of Central College's buildings was that the once simple and identical pavilions for the professors took on an added educational function as architectural models to inspire and instruct the students who would be taught the fine arts, including architecture, as part of the expanded professional-level curriculum of the school. As a result of this new didactic function for the professors' pavilions, Jefferson sought design ideas from two other architects with whom he worked previously on the public buildings of Washington during his presidency: William Thornton, the architect of the U.S. Capitol, and Benjamin Henry Latrobe, superintendent of public works who oversaw the construction of the Capitol as well as the President's House. Their feedback led to some fortuitous additions and improvements to Jefferson's simple plans for his Academical Village, such as the inclusion of a grand, central building to serve as the focal point of the complex. For this central building, Thornton simply suggested a more elaborate pavilion, differentiated from the other flat-roofed pavilions by a gabled roof forming a pediment, supported by columns of the Corinthian order—the most decorative of the classical orders. Latrobe went a step further and proposed a grand cubical building with a dome, similar in appearance to the Villa Rotonda by Jefferson's favorite Renaissance architect and author, Andrea Palladio. Over time, the model for this central building changed from the cubical Villa Rotonda to the spherical Pantheon, as reinterpreted by Jefferson and Latrobe to serve the functions of an academical building. Jefferson resurrected his own earlier design proposal for the U.S. Capitol in Washington, which consisted of a circular floor plan divided into oval-shaped rooms, and applied these plans to the lower floors of his Rotunda. The top floor consisted of a single circular room housing a library under the dome.

Jefferson incorporated several of Thornton's and Latrobe's suggestions into his plans as his designs for Central College evolved over the following months, and he made further modifications to his original large square ground plan based on the irregular topography of the newly acquired site. The original arrangement of nine identical pavilions around a large open square evolved into a narrow, terraced lawn flanked by ten uniquely designed pavilions demonstrating the proportions and details of neoclassical architecture, and capped off by a great domed Pantheon-inspired structure at the head of this lawn, which served not as a religious temple, but a temple dedicated to education— the University's library. Ultimately, Central College was indeed selected as the site of the University of Virginia, and Jefferson's three-tier public education system was finally realized. "[T]he state in which I live is now engaged in the establishment of an University, in which all the sciences will be cultivated which the circumstances of our country would as yet render useful. [T]his institution will employ the remaining days and faculties of my life, and will be based on the illimitable freedom of the human mind."[20]

Notes

1. Jefferson to George Washington, January 4, 1786, *PTJ*, 9:151.

2. Jefferson to Littleton W. Tazewell, January 5, 1805, *Founders Online*, http://founders.archives.gov/documents/Jefferson/99-01-02-0958.

3. Goochland County Will & Deed Book, No. 5, 73.

4. Jefferson, Autobiography, 6 Jan.–29 July 1821, January 6, 1821, *Founders Online*, http://founders.archives.gov/documents/Jefferson/98-01-02-1756.

5. Ibid.

6. Thomas Jefferson to Louis H. Girardin, January 15, 1815, *PTJRS*, 8:200.

7. Jefferson to the Trustees of the Lottery for East Tennessee College, May 6, 1810, *PTJRS*, 2:365–66.

8. Jefferson to Samuel Henley, October 14, 1785, *PTJ*, 8:635.

9. *Notes*, Query XV, 153 (footnotes omitted).

10. Jefferson to the Trustees of the Lottery for East Tennessee College, May 6, 1810, *PTJRS*, 2:366.

11. Jefferson to Littleton W. Tazewell, January 5, 1805, *Founders Online*, http://founders.archives.gov/documents/Jefferson/99-01-02-0958.

12. Jefferson to Benjamin Henry Latrobe, August 3, 1817, *PTJRS*, 11:587.

13. Fiske Kimball, *Thomas Jefferson Architect* (Boston: Riverside Press, 1916), Drawing K-176; and Frederick Doveton Nichols, *Thomas Jefferson's Architectural Drawings* (Charlottesville: University of Virginia Press, 1961), Drawing N-406.

14. Jefferson to James Breckenridge, February 15, 1821, *Founders Online*, http://founders.archives.gov/documents/Jefferson/98-01-02-1839.

15. "79. A Bill for the More General Diffusion of Knowledge," 1779, *PTJ*, 2:527.

16. Jefferson to Joseph C. Cabell, February 2, 1816, *PTJRS*, 9:436 (footnote omitted). Jefferson's polygraph copy of this letter is slightly different and mentions "log houses for the school and dwelling of the master," therefore suggesting the construction of two adjacent log houses on the elementary school site.

17. Jefferson to Joseph C. Cabell, October 24, 1817, *PTJRS*, 12:134.

18. Jefferson to Thomas Cooper, January 16, 1814, *PTJRS*, 7:127 (footnote omitted).

19. Jefferson to the Trustees of the Lottery for East Tennessee College, May 6, 1810, *PTJRS*, 2:365.

20. Jefferson to Marc Auguste Pictet, December 26, 1820, *Founders Online*, http://founders.archives.gov/documents/Jefferson/98-01-02-1710.

Elevating Jefferson's High-Flying Vision for His Last Delorme Dome Project at the University of Virginia's Rotunda

DOUGLAS J. HARNSBERGER

URING THE last five years of his highly productive eighty-three-year life span, Thomas Jefferson pursued two special architectural objectives that fired his imagination for the University of Virginia's Rotunda. One of these pursuits was realized with the successful construction of the Rotunda's innovative Delorme Dome of 1825. His second pursuit, a daring, if not dangerous, vision to use the Rotunda's Dome Room as an acrobatic kind of planetarium classroom, did not progress past the preliminary conception phase—and all of Western civilization is poorer for its demise.

As the University's chief curriculum planner, Jefferson sought to establish a course of study that embodied his Age of Enlightenment educational ideals. At the top of his list of the necessary scientific disciplines, he called for the exploration of the universe through the study of the mathematical sciences and astronomy. With his goal to establish a state-of-the-art astronomy curriculum at the University, Jefferson envisioned a remarkable boom-lift contraption that would elevate the astronomy professor (the "Operator") to the peak of the Rotunda's Dome Room. Once elevated to the top of the dome's "concave," the professor would be positioned to place by hand small hemispherical orbs representing stars and planet onto an oversized celestial star chart painted onto the dome's interior plaster surface.

As a self-taught architect and builder, Jefferson enjoyed imparting his knowledge of innovative building technologies, no more so than when he tutored other architects and builders on how to employ an ingenious sixteenth-century method of wood-laminated dome construction known as "Delorme's method" after the French Renaissance architect Philibert Delorme.[1] Jefferson's passion for constructing American neoclassical domes using Delorme's technique began with his romantically charged tour of the Halle au Blé in Paris with Maria Cosway in August 1786. The Parisian grain market's spectacular Delorme Dome by architects Legrand and Molinos spanned over 138 feet in diameter and featured radiating bands of glass skylights. Jefferson was delighted by the dome's bedazzling effect and wrote to Madam Cosway in his famous "Head and Heart" dialogue with himself that "it was the most superb thing on earth!"[2] Thus began a four-decade-long obsession for Jefferson to apply Delorme's method for a President's House competition proposal (1792), his rebuilt residence at Monticello (1801), a Navy drydock barrel-vaulted roof proposal (1802), the U.S. Capitol's House of Representatives' ceiling (1804), and with his ultimate Delorme Dome application at the Rotunda (1824). The construction work at the Rotunda culminated with the finish plastering of the Dome Room ceiling, just a few months before Jefferson's death on July 4, 1826.[3]

An Aspiration to Teach Astronomy from the Concave of the Rotunda's Dome Room

In the spring of 1819, Jefferson was focused on developing the new curriculum for his final architectural essay, the University of Virginia (UVA). For the University's centerpiece building, the Rotunda, he envisioned a dynamic use for the second-floor Dome Room as a hemispherical classroom-in-the-round for teaching astronomy. Jefferson considered astronomy to be the "most sublime" of the eight "Natural Philosophies" that he listed in his new University's curriculum.[4] What better way he reasoned to use the "concave of the dome" than to make a gridded celestial blackboard of its smooth plaster surface and transform it into a mechanized kind of planetarium to plot the stars and planets of the Northern Hemisphere's night sky?

In his personal folio "Notes on the University," he wrote, "the plaster surface of the dome would be painted a vivid sky blue, and be arrayed with constellations of gilded stars in the shape of half spheres." Each star would be fixed to the dome's surface by the boom-elevated professor and positioned according to the most accurate celestial coordinates known. A precise grid of longitudinal and latitudinal lines would be drawn across the concave surface of the dome to organize the mapping of the night sky. Jefferson envisioned that the astronomy professor would place hundreds of stars and planets on the oversized hemispherical blackboard as he lectured the students from his elevated saddle, perched thirty feet above the classroom floor. The "concave of the dome" would serve as an enormous astronomical star chart to support the professor's weekly lectures in Celestial Cartography—that is, the plotting of all the known stars and planets in the Northern Hemisphere.[5]

But just how would the astronomy professor elevate above the Dome Room floor to position by hand each of the gilded stars? To achieve such a Peter Pan levitation, Jefferson drew a simple diagram to explain his novel elevating concept. His sketch shows a thirty-five-foot-long oak boom lifted up by rope and pulley to the dome's apex. In the middle of his astronomy classroom description, he inserted an annotated diagram of the "Operator's" hoisting mechanism. It includes a note referencing a "common saddle with stirrups" to be attached at the end of the boom. So where did the idea of employing a horse saddle originate? Perhaps it was derived from his morning horse-riding routine about his Monticello plantation. Jefferson noted that the operator would mount the boom lift on such a saddle and be elevated vertically by a long oak boom lift, via a rope-and-pulley system, up to the full height of the dome, thirty-six feet above the Dome Room floor. The operator would be able to move horizontally as well across the concave surface of the dome with the pulling assistance of several students below, pivoting the boom laterally from a ball-and-socket connection at the other end of the boom in the exact center of the room.

One can imagine, however, how vulnerable the operator would have been, riding a saddle at the end of a boom-lift high above the Dome Room floor. Surely the hoisted professor would have been subjected at some point to the playful, if not hurtful, mischief of the students who were charged with the handling of the ropes and pulleys below, as Alan Taylor's essay in this volume certainly suggests. The Charlottesville cartoon artist Charles Peale produced an amusing illustration in this vein for an article on this subject for the *University of Virginia Magazine*. In the playful cartoon, the stargazer Jefferson appears to be oblivious to the predictable antics of the rope-pulling students below.

Acknowledging Jefferson's serious interest in creating a Dome Room astronomy classroom, why then didn't his boom-lift device proceed to fabrication? And why didn't the concave of the dome receive the gridded map coordinates of the Northern Hemisphere? No one knows why he abandoned the planetarium concept because Jefferson never wrote in his University Notes about what changed his mind to reprogram the Dome Room into a more staid and traditional University Library.

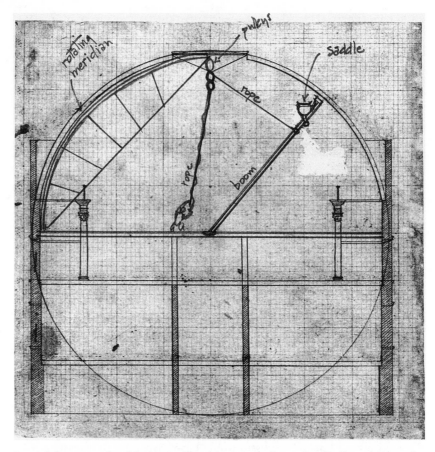

Boom-lift concept sketch by the author, drawn over a facsimile of Jefferson's Rotunda section drawing, 1819. (A Calendar of the Jefferson Papers of the University of Virginia, Jefferson Papers, Albert and Shirley Small Special Collections Library, University of Virginia)

Several practical problems with his boom-lift scheme come to mind that may have prompted his change of thinking:

Perhaps the thirty-foot-long oak boom-and-saddle hoisting mechanism was criticized by others who read his notes (such as the master builders Dinsmore and Neilson) as too unwieldy and dangerous to operate. "Dropping the boom" may be an old theater expression, but its meaning might apply equally well in this case. The loss of control of a massive thirty-foot

"Jefferson Rides the Boom-lift to Map the Stars of the Northern Hemisphere," cartoon by Charles Peale. (Published with the artist's permission; first appeared with the author's article "The Celestial Dome," *University of Virginia Magazine,* Winter 2012)

oak boom, similar in mass to a modern telephone pole, certainly would have had the potential to kill the operator riding the boom, as well as several of the terrified students sitting at their desks below.

Perhaps the concept of lecturing from thirty feet in the air, suspended beneath an oversized celestial blackboard, was unacceptable to the incoming professor of astronomy. How, after all, was the hapless professor supposed to refer to his lecture notes while trying to maintain his balance in the saddle at the end of the precarious boom?

Perhaps the large glass-covered oculus at the apex of the dome was identified as working against the objective of creating a night sky for the desired planetarium function. The oculus feature would also have conflicted with the rope and pulley's centralized location in Jefferson's sketch. How was the proposed pulley to attach at the dome's apex when the glass oculus assumes that central location at the peak of the dome?

Or perhaps, most sensibly, Jefferson simply recognized that the programming priority to locate the University Library within the Rotunda Dome Room outweighed his visionary dream to create an interactive astronomy classroom.

Whatever the actual reason for abandoning his high flying astronomical vision, by the fall of 1819 Jefferson had generated a new floor plan for the Dome Room that now included a classical colonnade supporting a balcony encircling the room, with the label "Library" added in the top right corner. With that pivotal program change for the Dome Room, Jefferson's avant-garde astronomy classroom concept was relegated to a forgotten status in the early architectural history of the University.

During a research fellowship with the International Center for Jefferson Studies in 2014, the author had the privilege of transcribing for the first time Jefferson's two pages of handwritten notes wherein he proposed the Dome Room astronomy classroom for *The Papers of Thomas Jefferson: Retirement Series*. I submitted the transcription of Jefferson's notes along with an interpretive sketch of Jefferson's boom-lift device to Jeff Looney, editor of those *Papers*, and he responded with these insightful comments:

> Jefferson's initial intention to use the concave of the Rotunda Dome to map the northern heavens and teach astronomy grew out of his own abiding interest in astronomy and was central to his grand vision for the theoretical and practical study of natural philosophy at the University of Virginia. The mathematical sciences in general and astronomy in particular were seen by Jefferson and his peers as the culmination in the education of the enlightened man, the most direct way to perceive God through the sublime workings of His unchanging physical laws on an unimaginable grand scale. The placement of a planetarium at the highest point of the university's most imposing building would thus have had immense symbolic significance for Jefferson and for the students at the institution to which he devoted his last years.

Thomas Jefferson as Architect and Builder of the Rotunda's Delorme Dome

Unlabeled and unrecognized by generations of architectural historians, a curious diagram of circles and radiating spokes was drawn by Jefferson, and glued to the top left corner of the title sheet of his "Additional Notes for the Library." In 1824, at the age of eighty-one, Jefferson overcame the pain in his arthritic right hand to draft a framing diagram of the wood-laminated dome for the Rotunda.[6] His line drawing tells us that the Rotunda's Delorme Dome featured 29 primary ribs, 28 secondary ribs, 56 tertiary ribs, and 112 quaternary ribs, for a total of 225 ribs. Such a precise rib count may be extrapolated from his unfinished framing diagram by following the spacing method that Jefferson employed to arrange the 29 primary ribs around the circle. A faint dimension line that he drew in the 12 o'clock sector of the drawing shows us that Jefferson spaced the primary ribs precisely eight feet apart measured along the outside tension ring. An 8-foot spacing module extended around the circumference of a 74-foot diameter produces 29 primary evenly spaced ribs, a curiously irregular number for an architect with Jefferson's mathematical skills. The secondary, tertiary, and quaternary ribs that followed were spaced evenly within 4-foot, 2-foot, and 1-foot spacing modules. We can imagine that Jefferson's trusted master builders, James Dinsmore and John Neilson, were tasked to prepare a detailed lumber "take-off" from Jefferson's framing diagram. Presumably the craftsmen were advised verbally by the architect that the "circle and spokes" framing diagram was drawn at a scale of 1 inch equals 20 feet, a standard engineer's scale. When the author placed a $1'' = 20'$ scale across the middle of Jefferson's diagram, the oculus ring in the middle dimensions measured precisely 17 feet in diameter and the diameter of the dome also scaled correctly at 74 feet. Thus, this unassuming, little line drawing is key to understanding how Jefferson's Delorme Dome framing project was conceived by Jefferson and interpreted in the field by Dinsmore and Neilson in the spring of 1825. The sketch is in fact a valuable construction drawing that was intended to convey crucial structural information to the dome's builders.

Jefferson also wrote a brief handwritten specification to describe other construction details of the dome. It included the finished dimensions of the laminated ribs, oculus, and tension rings, and a description of the purlin ties that provided lateral rigidity to the dome assembly. These specifications were conveyed with shorthand brevity, but they provide essential construction information that the builders needed to assemble the tension ring at the base, followed by the radial ribs, then the cross-purlins, and finally the oculus's compression ring at the peak of the dome. Jefferson's Rotunda Delorme Dome specification states:

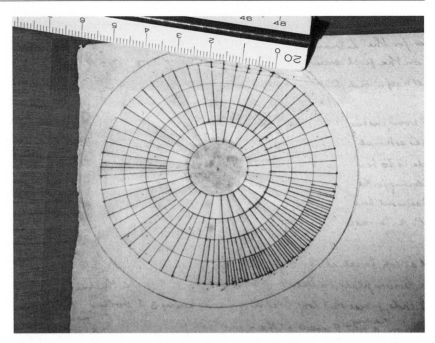

Jefferson's Rotunda Delorme Dome Framing Plan Sketch affixed with red wax to his memorandum titled "Additional Notes for the Library," 1824. (A Calendar of the Jefferson Papers of the University of Virginia, Jefferson Papers, Albert and Shirley Small Special Collections Library, University of Virginia)

> On the top of the wall lay a curbed plate, *in Delorme's manner*, consisting of 4 thicknesses of 3 I. each, 22 I. wide, pieces 12 f. long, breaking joints every 3 f. bolted through with bolts of iron having a nut and screw at their end.
> On this curved plate the ribs of the roof are to rest. The ribs are to be 4 thicknesses of 1 I. plank, in pieces 4 f. long breaking joints at every foot. They are to be 18 I. wide, which leaves 4 I. of the plate for the attic uprights to rest on. The ribs are to be keyed together by cross boards at proper intervals for the ribs to head in as they shorten. The curb of the skylights to be made also in Delorme's way, but vertically.[7]

By combining these brief specifications with the Delorme rib-framing information conveyed in Jefferson's "wheel and spokes" diagram, the author realized that it would be feasible to create a set of contemporary construction drawings to describe, with reasonable accuracy, the original Delorme Dome framing assembly. Because Jefferson's 1825 Delorme structure perished in the

Rotunda's Great Fire of 1895 and was replaced by architect Stanford White's Guastavino tile dome in 1903, the physical evidence of the Delorme construction was destroyed. So not since 1825, almost two hundred years ago, has Jefferson's Delorme Dome framing been exposed to view.

With the bicentennial of the Rotunda's construction approaching, the author suggested to his colleague professor Ben Hays (who teaches "The History of American Building Technology" within the School of Architecture at the University of Virginia) that they collaborate on a class project to have the students construct a one-third full-size scale model of the Rotunda Delorme Dome. The framing structure would be twenty-five feet in diameter and be constructed of authentic materials; that is, with radial segments of white oak planks, clinched together with replica iron nails to form the laminated ribs, base tension ring and oculus ring. The project was financially supported through the generosity of the UVA Bicentennial Committee and a private sponsor, Castleton Farms, in Rappahannock County, Virginia.

In keeping with the course's theme, to explore building technologies both old and new, the students were encouraged to use a state-of-the-art cutting tool, a computer-directed CNC (computer numerical control) router, to produce the eight hundred pieces of radial rib components. Hand cutting the components with scroll saws, as was done originally, would have been prohibitively time consuming. During the final weeks of class in May 2018, the Delorme "Half Dome" Structure was erected on the North Terrace of the Architecture School. After graduation ceremonies on the Lawn were concluded, the Bicentennial Committee granted special permission to move the Delorme Structure to the south end of the Lawn to showcase its sculptural form in front of Cabell Hall for the month of June. Before the resodding of the south end of the Lawn in the first week of July, the Delorme Half Dome was disassembled a second time and trucked to Castleton Farms in Rappahannock County, where it awaits its next manifestation as an outdoor amphitheater for weddings and special occasions.

In her novel, *A Winter in Washington*, author Margaret Bayard Smith reports Jefferson's remark, "Architecture is my delight, and putting up and pulling down, one of my favorite amusements."[8] The statement captures Jefferson's lifelong pursuit with "putting up and pulling down" his many neoclassical essays in the Italian Palladian manner and, in this case, in the French Delorme manner. Owing to his meticulous Delorme Dome framing plan sketch and the written specifications that he left for us to decipher in his "Notes for the

A one-third-scale framing model of Jefferson's Rotunda Delorme Dome, by the University of Virginia School of Architecture's American Building Technology class, spring 2018. (Image courtesy of Dan Addison, University of Virginia)

Library," Jefferson's last application of Delorme's method at the Rotunda is accessible again for future architectural historians to further analyze—and perhaps also for future neoclassical Delorme Dome builders to emulate with their own dome creations à la Delorme.

Notes

1. Philibert Delorme, *Le Nouvelle Inventions Pour Bien Bastir* (1561) (New inventions for building well). Jefferson purchased a copy of Delorme's treatise in Paris while serving as Minister to France in the fall of 1786.

2. Jefferson to Maria Cosway, October 12, 1786, "The Dialogue between Head and Heart," *PTJ*, 10:445.

3. E.g., Jefferson to Benjamin H. Latrobe, November 2, 1802, *PTJ*, 38:619, recommending the use of Delorme's method for the barrel-vaulted roof on the Navy drydock proposal: "[A] roof can be thrown, in the manner of the Halle au Blé at Paris." Later, in 1814, Latrobe employed the French vaulting system to construct the exterior dome of the Baltimore Cathedral.

4. Jefferson to Nathaniel Bowditch, May 2, 1815, *PTJRS*, 8:455 ("most sublime").

5. Thomas Jefferson Academical Village, Object #48, "University of Virginia" Specification Book, dated July 18, 1819, Iron gall ink on wave paper, N-318, Special Collections Department, Manuscripts Division, University of Virginia.

6. Thomas Jefferson Academical Village, "Additional Notes for the Library" (1824), Iron gall on wave paper, N-332, Special Collections Department, Manuscripts Division, University of Virginia.

7. Ibid.

8. Margaret Bayard Smith, *A Winter in Washington*, vol. 2 (New York: E. Bliss and E. White, 1824), 261.

The Liberty and Tyranny of Jefferson's Academical Village

MAURIE D. McINNIS

W HEN WHITE SUPREMACISTS gathered in Charlottesville on August 11 and 12, 2017, many asked, "Why here?" Surprising and troubling as that decision might have been to many current residents of today's progressive Charlottesville, there are many reasons why this city was such a resonant choice for Richard Spencer. Like many cities in the South, Charlottesville has a long history of racial oppression. As one of the cities to enact "massive resistance" by closing the public schools and one of the last to integrate its school system in the 1950s, Charlottesville was a bastion of Jim Crow politics and racial attitudes. Many of today's residents believed that the massive monument to Robert E. Lee on a central square in downtown Charlottesville elevated and perhaps celebrated that history. Hence their conversation about removing it from the city center. That clash of present and past, that clash of today's progressive definition of a racially inclusive liberty with the past's celebration of racial tyranny, is what made Charlottesville such a perfect symbolic site for Spencer and today's neo-Nazis and white supremacists. This tension is not just about present and past, but instead is a tension that has existed at the city's most prominent institution—the University of Virginia—from its very inception.

In July 1817, Thomas Jefferson stood in a field about a mile from the Albemarle County courthouse to block out the location of the buildings he planned to erect for Central College. Having recently purchased land from John Perry, the seventy-four-year-old Jefferson used his theodolite to fix the center of the northern square, "the point destined for some principal building."[1] Today at the University of Virginia, the moment when the institution's physical presence first took shape is often presented as particularly prescient. At the University's Darden Graduate School of Business, a sculpture depicts the solitary genius of Jefferson, alone in a field, dreaming the University into existence.

Jefferson had been thinking about the importance of education in the new nation for decades; he had even sponsored a bill in Virginia, which did not pass, for expansive primary and secondary education for all white male citizens as early as 1779, a fairly radical concept in its time. He wrote to James Madison, "Above all things I hope the education of the common people will be attended to; convinced that on their good sense we may rely with the most security for the preservation of a due degree of liberty."[2] He was worried that those "entrusted with power have, in time, . . . perverted it into tyranny." Thus, to preserve liberty, to protect against tyranny, he proposed a comprehensive system of education. He wrote, "[T]he most effectual means of preventing . . . [tyranny] would be, to illuminate, . . . the minds of the people at large . . . ."[3]

Jefferson's plans for Central College, later the University of Virginia, were radical for the time. He had spent a lifetime musing about the meaning of liberty. And a lifetime wondering how best to preserve it for future generations. Rather than narrowly prepare students for the study of law or to be clergy as at most universities, he wanted students to have a broad and liberal education. As he wrote his friend, "[E]nlighten the people generally, and tyranny and oppressions of body & mind will vanish like evil spirits at the dawn of day. . . . [T]he diffusion of kno[w]le[d]ge among the people is to be the instrument by which it is to be effected."[4]

As Jefferson stood on that field near to where the conference on the founding of the University of Virginia was held, he was not alone on that day, nor was he alone as the work of constructing the University became a reality. From its beginning through the end of the Civil War, the University of Virginia was the work of many individuals, including hundreds of enslaved laborers. Jefferson's University, from its very beginning, was built on the tyranny of slavery. It began on that July day when Jefferson marked off that "old field"; accompanying Jefferson was his overseer, Edmund Bacon, an Irish builder named James Dinsmore, and "ten hands," a nineteenth-century term used to indicate enslaved laborers. Together the group used twine, shingles, and pegs to mark off the "foundations of the University." After marking it off, Jefferson "set the men at work."[5]

From constructing and maintaining the buildings to feeding and caring for the faculty and students, enslaved people brought into existence and later sustained the institution. Additionally, and more abstractly, it was the state's slave-based economy that provided the wealth that made it possible for most of the students of the University to attend (a vast majority of the students came from the state's and the region's slaveholding families). The University's history was thus tied inextricably to the South. Many of its alumni became the South's ruling class. They were important southern politicians and intellectual leaders; they were congressmen and governors; they were leading voices in the proslavery movement and soldiers in the Confederate Army.

Learning this history and telling its stories has been a collective project. It has been available all the time, but it was not discussed, sitting in the vaults of the Albert and Shirley Small Special Collections Library at the University of Virginia. The Library has been a great partner on the project we began in 2013 to digitize all the University's early archives. Over the years, dozens of students have contributed to this project by transcribing the University's archival materials and creating XML tags that make them easily searchable. The students who have worked on this project have also contributed by writing essays and conducting additional research, allowing the threads of evidence to be woven together into a richer and fuller story. This has allowed us to piece together the clues hidden in phrases like "hands" and "set at work."[6]

This is work that has been ongoing for years, but now has a new urgency. What we all need to address, what August 11, 2017, calls upon each one of us to confront, is the central paradox at the heart of the University of Virginia, in fact, the central paradox of the nation, the unresolved paradox of American liberty. How is it that the nation that defined the natural rights of humankind did so within a system that denied those same rights to others based on the color of their skin? And what does it mean to have a public university founded to ensure liberty and protect against tyranny that was from its inception built upon the stolen liberty and oppression of those enslaved?

In its very inception, even in Jefferson's own imagining of what the University of Virginia could be, he understood it to be an institution with slavery at its core, both in how it functioned and what its purpose was. He believed that a southern institution was necessary to protect the sons of the South from abolitionist teachings in the North. Jefferson wrote to his friend James Breckinridge and expressed his concern with sending the youth of Virginia to be educated in the North, a place "against us in position and principle." He worried that in northern institutions young Virginians might imbibe "opinions and principles in discord with those of their own country. [T]his canker is eating on the vitals of our existence, and if not arrested at once will be beyond remedy."[7] In other words, Jefferson believed it was important to educate Virginians and other southerners in an institution that understood and ultimately supported slavery. He had never known life without slavery, and the educational institution he designed in the last decade of his life had slavery at its core. The tyranny of slavery remained essential to the University of Virginia for the first fifty years of its history until the end of the Civil War brought freedom to the people who lived and labored there.

The design for the University of Virginia built on Jefferson's many decades of architectural experiments in a slave society. In these, he determined how best to mask slavery by creating separate private and public zones in buildings and landscapes. For example, just as he took office as the governor of Virginia in 1779, Jefferson began a series of sketches for the remodeling of the Governor's Palace in Williamsburg. Jefferson's unbuilt designs included the insertion of a service passage that would have allowed for the movement of enslaved domestics into and through the governor's residence without their having to use the main entrances or pass through the public entertaining rooms.[8]

When he redesigned Monticello after his return from France in 1796, he made similar alterations. These are most obvious in the dining room where he installed a number of devices that allowed him to diminish the number of enslaved attendants necessary to wait on table. He installed shelves mounted on a revolving door, so that food could be placed there and then brought into the room either by a trusted enslaved servant or a family member. He also used standing carts, called dumbwaiters, to receive dirty dishes, again diminishing the number of enslaved workers necessary for serving meals. The purpose of these devices was not lost on Margaret Bayard Smith, who visited Monticello in 1809. She noted that when Jefferson wished to "enjoy a free and unrestricted flow of conversation," he placed a dumbwaiter near every diner, "so as to make the attendance of servants entirely unnecessary, believing as he did, that much of the domestic and even public discord was produced by the mutilated and misconstructed repetition of free conversation at dinner tables, by these mute but not inattentive listeners."[9]

Importantly for his later work at the University, Jefferson also manipulated Monticello's landscape in such a way that it masked the visibility of the labor performed by his enslaved workforce. Famously, his entire row of domestic service spaces, including kitchens, smokehouses, stables, and some quarters, were buried in the embankment, below the level of the main floor of the house. As a result, these spaces were entirely invisible from the pleasure gardens

above where Jefferson entertained his guests. Among those rooms in the basement may be the one in which Sally Hemings lived, nearby but also hidden
away. Additionally, the design for the house clearly demarcated distinct zones,
public, private, and enslaved. The entry hall, parlor, and dining rooms were
the public rooms of the house where Jefferson received visitors. These were
aligned along one axis of the house, and along the other were the private rooms,
including his suite of rooms referred to by one of his grandchildren as the "sanctum santorum." In these wings were a transverse hallway, generally not visible
from the public rooms, where the enslaved could move in order to do the work
expected of them. These hallways connected to the stairs that led down to the
service level where the kitchens, storerooms, stables, and other service rooms
were located. In this design, the work of the enslaved was largely hidden from
the regular daily activities of Jefferson's family and guests.

When Jefferson approached his design for the Academical Village, he employed a similar strategy, manipulating both the architecture and the topography in order to create separate zones for free and enslaved. Like the lawn at
Monticello, the Lawn at the University of Virginia completely masks the
labor that took place behind its facade. The front faces of the buildings on
the Lawn were primarily intended for faculty and students. Since the earliest depictions, this view has dominated the way the University has been
represented, showing the University as merely a series of building facades,
pavilions marching up the terraces to the Rotunda at the northern end.
These images were generally unpopulated, representing the University as an
architectural abstraction, an educational ideal largely devoid of the people
who inhabited it.

Behind those pavilions were large spaces that are today referred to as gardens. In the earliest plan of the University (often called the Maverick Plan),
created before the University was completed, these spaces are blank. What we
today call gardens were instead work yards where enslaved laborers were expected to live and labor for the faculty and students at the University. In these
spaces enslaved African Americans grew food and prepared it, raised and butch-
ered animals, washed laundry, chopped wood, and struggled to build lives and
families. Today they are filled with geometric walkways and ornamental trees
and shrubs from the mid-twentieth-century design of the Garden Club of
Virginia. From the beginning, Jefferson understood these areas as he understood plantations: they were the necessary work zones for domestic life where
the professors and hotelkeepers would add more buildings because, as he
noted, "a smokehouse is indispensable to a Virginia family."[10] With time, dozens

of buildings were added to the gardens: slave quarters, cook and wash kitchens, smokehouses, woodsheds, and privies, among others.

For the first fifty years of the University's history, three groups of people were living there: faculty and hotelkeepers (and their families), students, and enslaved workers. The number of students grew steadily over the period from 1825 to the beginning of the Civil War, with a marked increase beginning around 1850, from about 120 in its first year to about 600 just before the Civil War. The number of faculty also grew from the original 8 to 17 in 1860. Furthermore, about 100 to 150 enslaved people were owned by faculty and hotelkeepers who lived in the Academical Village.

As at many other southern universities, students were not permitted to bring their own enslaved servants with them. This rule appeared alongside many others in the very first publication of the University's rules called the *Enactments*. The Board of Visitors, with Jefferson as it rector, passed the following regulation months before the University had any faculty or students, "No Student shall, within the precincts of the University . . . keep a servant."[11] That rule remained in place until the end of the Civil War.

Revealing the complexity of his relationship with slavery, Jefferson had written about the corrupting influence of slavery on the morals of southerners even as he wanted to remove southerners from northern colleges that critiqued the institution. A painter in the early nineteenth century captured poignantly the violence that the enslaved faced on a daily basis. On the back of a portrait of an unknown individual, the artist created a dual image with the words "Virginian Luxuries," at the bottom. This chilling image captured the depravity that Jefferson had warned about decades earlier in his *Notes on the State of Virginia* when he wrote of the "unremitting despotism" of slavery and noted how "[t]he parent storms, the child looks on, catches the lineaments of wrath, puts on the same airs in the circle of smaller slaves, gives a loose to his worst of passions, and thus nursed, educated, and daily exercised in tyranny, cannot but be stamped by it with odious peculiarities. The man must be a prodigy who can retain his manners and morals undepraved by such circumstances."[12] Many of the students at the University had clearly been nursed and educated in the exercise of tyranny.

Whatever the impetus for the rule that forbade personal servants, it did not remove students from a position of mastery. Most of the students came from the South's planter class. They were accustomed to the relationship of master and servant, and it was a defining feature of life in the Academical

The corrupting influence of slavery. ("Virginian Luxuries," unidentified artist, probably New England, ca. 1825, oil on canvas, 1993.100.1, T1994-121, The Colonial Williamsburg Foundation, museum purchase)

Village.[13] At the University, they found themselves at the center of the intellectual debates about the place of slavery in southern society. As the decades progressed, slavery became the nation's most pressing political issue, and the University's faculty became some of the nation's leading proslavery voices.[14] In both their classrooms and their social clubs, students at the University were surrounded by conversations that only cemented the notions of mastery they had been taught at home. The students at the University of Virginia acted as if they were master of any and all enslaved in the Academical Village. The disciplinary decisions made by the faculty only reinforced the students in their understanding of their own place in the master class.

Jefferson's architectural plan had created distinct zones for the students and for the enslaved. The enslaved were to live and work in the basements and in the work yards where students were to have little reason to venture. Students were to spend their time in their dormitory rooms and in classrooms and the library, places where the enslaved were to have little reason to venture. The lived reality contrasted sharply. Instead of separate zones, there were frequent daily interactions between the students and the enslaved who lived and worked around them. The high walls of the gardens would have limited the ability of the enslaved to see beyond; the walls were intended to be barriers, to separate people owned by one faculty member or hotelkeeper from another and make it easier for their owners to keep an eye on them and monitor their whereabouts. But they did not function so in reality. Instead, work at the University meant that the enslaved moved freely in and around the University precincts as they conducted the daily business of running the school. They moved from work yard to work yard, from hotel to student rooms, from University to town.

Jefferson's design, in theory, was intended to make it easy for the professor or the hotelkeeper to watch the enslaved working in the gardens from the back windows of the pavilions or the hotels. In reality, however, outbuildings and walls blocked sightlines. The alleyways were virtually impossible to monitor. The dark of night provided additional cover. Enslaved workers knew that they could use that invisibility to their advantage. Even though they were owned by either hotelkeepers or the faculty, their jobs meant that they were most often away from the watchful eye of their owner.

The many duties performed by enslaved people that required moving around the University and back and forth from town—obtaining and preparing food, chopping and hauling wood, carrying supplies to students' rooms, running errands for students, to name only a few—meant that the usual forms of surveillance present in a slave society largely broke down. The enslaved were able to use their ability to move about in places where they could not be observed and the fact that their duties meant they were expected to be in many different places as cover to assert some control in their own lives.

Simultaneously, however, it also meant that they were subject to the commands of everyone. Despite the ability to assert some control over their movement and their lives, the enslaved in the Academical Village lived under the constant threat of violence, women and girls especially. As most of the young men were of the planter class, many were used to having a personal servant. For some of the students, they believed that they had the right to assert white mastery over any enslaved individual. In their letters and diaries, the students wrote of the men who tended their rooms possessively. Charles Ellis, who was a student from 1835 to 1836, wrote of "my servant" waking him in the morning and of "Albert, our servant," arranging his room. Such possessiveness of the enslaved people owned by others only contributed to the feeling held by many students that they had a right to treat the people working in the Academical Village as their own property.[15] At times, the enslaved were in jeopardy because of this ambiguity. Would they rather be punished by the faculty or hotelkeepers for doing the things students wanted, or the students for not doing so?

At other times, the enslaved learned how to use this ambiguity to their own advantage. The enslaved who worked in the Academical Village learned quickly how to exploit their relative freedom to move in and out and about the University without close supervision. Many used the misbehavior of the students to their own advantage, engaging in a variety of entrepreneurial activities that gave them access to cash. Perhaps most commonly, they profited from the students' prohibited behaviors, getting them alcohol and helping them participate in their favorite pastimes, such as gambling on card playing and cockfighting. This was a constantly vexing problem for the faculty, who tried again and again to control the students' access to alcohol and illicit activities.

Men were assigned to wait on students in their dormitories; many enslaved women worked at the University as well. Their duties often centered around food preparation and laundry, or working as domestic servants for the faculty. Even though their duties did not normally have them working directly with students, their presence in the Academical Village made them particularly vulnerable, especially to sexual violence. In one instance, Gessner Harrison, who was chairman of the faculty at the time, complained to the faculty about several students. Upon returning from Fitch's tavern in Charlottesville after midnight, their "riotous" behavior had awakened the professor when he heard a group of students "knocking at his cellar door & heard indecent propositions made to a female servant." Each of the students was called in to testify before the faculty. The faculty determined to dismiss one student, not because of his actions that night, but because he was frequently drunk. At the same time, they only admonished another for his drinking and "indecent conduct in endeavouring to get access to a female servant in a pavilion of one of the professors."[16]

Women were vulnerable throughout the Academical Village, especially so at night when both students and enslaved knew how to use the cover of darkness to obscure their movements and activities. Standing one night around a pump for water, several women were treated with "rudeness and indecency" by a group of students. We have no way of knowing what behaviors are hidden by those words, as the faculty often used euphemistic terminology when discussing matters of a sexual nature. In another instance, G. Tucker broke into Dr. Patterson's pavilion (Pavilion V) in pursuit of an unnamed woman owned by Patterson. The incident was described only as an "outrage." Clearly it was a significant assault, as the chairman expressed "abhorrence at his conduct."[17]

In another instance, the faculty were more explicit in describing the action of the students, clearly labeling it "a violent outrage (a rape)." The victim was described as a "small negro girl, a slave about 12 years old." The attack took place west of the University, near boardinghouses operated by Colonel Johnson and Mr. Leake, near the University cemetery. The rape was committed by three University students. They were discovered by three other students who "interfered to prevent it." In this instance, the students reported the actions of their classmates to the authorities, and the faculty voted to expel them from the University.[18]

The vulnerability of women was twofold, not only in the actions themselves but also in the fact that in many cases the faculty often did nothing. In Harrison's complaint, because "there was no evidence but that of a slave," and because the "offence occurred in the dark," and the students denied involvement, the faculty decided not to do anything.[19] In the second incident, when they broke into Patterson's pavilion, the punishment was light. The student was expected to apologize to Dr. Patterson and his family. The chairman reported that the student "did not seem to be much impressed with the immorality of his conduct." But in response the chairman merely "read him a severe moral lecture, & reprimanded him in the strongest terms."[20] In other words, students knew well that they were rarely held accountable for their behavior.

One of the most shocking incidents of violence occurred when student Nathan B. Noland savagely beat a ten-year-old girl in 1856. History has not recorded her name, or what happened to her afterward. The girl was owned by a female relative of a Lucy Terrell who operated a boardinghouse only a few hundred yards away from the Academical Village near the present-day St. Paul's Church. On the day of the attack, the young girl was at Terrell's boardinghouse; she had heard a knock on the back door and someone calling her name. Awaiting her on the other side of the door was a student who boarded at the house, a student she had encountered earlier that afternoon as she was walking through the University. When she came to the door, the student grabbed her, pulled her out of the house, threw her to the ground, and mercilessly beat and kicked her; she curled into a ball, crying out loudly. The pain was so great, she passed out.[21]

What we know of this event is what was recorded by the white authorities, in this case what was recorded by the faculty who questioned the student.[22] The day after he had beaten the young girl, Noland was summoned by the faculty to answer their questions. According to the student's testimony, he encountered the young girl wandering through the University. The faculty asked Noland why he had beaten her, leaving her "for a time insensible, and to require the attendance of a Physician afterwards." In Noland's testimony, he claimed that she had spoken to him with insolence.

The beating this young girl received was one of many acts of violence perpetrated by students on the enslaved people who lived and worked in and around the University. Noland's testimony chillingly revealed the ever-present danger that all enslaved people faced, a danger heightened in the University setting. Noland told the faculty "whenever a servant is insolent to him, he will take upon himself the right of punishing without the consent of the master." The result of this attitude was that the enslaved who lived and worked around the University had not one master but hundreds, all of whom were steeped in the pervasive proslavery thought that perpetuated the notion of a master class and was promulgated at the University. It meant that the enslaved people were daily subject to the arbitrary actions of faculty, hotelkeepers, and students, and the commands of these different groups were frequently contradictory, making navigating daily life fraught with peril for those enslaved at the University of Virginia.

Such accounts reveal important aspects of the racial attitudes that enabled some students to act with such inhumanity. Of the many cases captured in the faculty minutes, Noland's attitudes are particularly chilling and spelled out in great detail. The faculty was quite taken by his assertion that he would punish the human property of another. They asked him, "Do you mean to assert the right to exercise your own will, . . . in the infliction of punishment on a servant of another person?" In the questioning that followed, he said that he could not promise that he would not do so again, only that he would try to restrain himself "not to whip a servant so severely as I did in this case, but no further." The faculty decided to expel Noland "in view of the danger to the peace of Society & the good order of the University." The latter is important to note, because their concern about the "peace of Society" was not a concern that he had severely beaten a child, but that he had beaten a person who belonged to another owner and that he said he would do so again. The "good order" they wished to preserve was a complicated series of layers of white authority.

The faculty, through the enactments, had authority over the Academical Village, this included the students, hotelkeepers, and the enslaved no matter who owned them. In addition to the usual authority that faculty had over the people they personally owned, they also exercised authority over the enslaved owned by others, especially those owned by the hotelkeepers, both in specifying their expectations for their labor and in meting out punishments. In addition, the faculty also granted the hotelkeepers certain authority over the students, expecting them to act as agents of the faculty, although many students questioned that authority. Noland's beating of the young girl threatened to undermine the authority of hotelkeepers to supervise students and manage the enslaved who worked for them. Additionally, Noland's actions threatened more broadly the structure of southern slave society that reserved to the owner the right to punish.

The faculty's decision to expel Noland did not stand. The following day they met again. Before them was a letter written by the student. In it, Noland apologized to the owner of the girl, the other residents of the boardinghouse, and the college authorities. He admitted that it was wrong to "inflict punishment upon a servant belonging to another," but said he believed that "the correction of a servant for impertinence, . . . is not only tolerated by society, but . . . may be defended on the ground of the necessity of maintaining the due subordination in this class of persons."[23] Defending his actions by saying it was "tolerated by society" and that it was a "necessity" to maintain the racial order, was apparently persuasive to the faculty and "in view of the contrition expressed," they rescinded their decision to expel him. The faculty's decision to allow Noland to continue at the University reveals the overriding racial sentiment. Maintaining the racial order was paramount.

The decision of the faculty speaks to the violence that upheld the system of slavery and that generally went unquestioned. Noland's apology was not to the girl, but to the owner of the girl. His defense was rooted in the kinds of conversations that were part of campus life, conversations that should be chilling in light of the events of August 11, 2017. In the debating societies and in the school's literary magazines, students argued for a natural hierarchy; they argued for the rightness of a master class based on a racial hierarchy. Noland presented his defense to a group of faculty, several of whom were leading intellectuals in the proslavery movement. They likely agreed with many of his assertions, especially the assertion of "the necessity of maintaining the due subordination in this class of persons." What Noland maintained followed their own arguments for the rightness of a natural hierarchy based on chattel slavery for those of African descent. To them, if there was a crime in this savage beating, it was a crime against the owner.

The enslaved who lived and worked at the University of Virginia found themselves in an unusual situation. Their life differed in many important ways from that on a plantation; many of them likely had lived on one prior to coming to the University. Now instead of clear lines of authority, the owner and the enslaved, they encountered a much more complicated social order. The authority of their owner was diluted by their ability to move around and engage in activities with a much larger enslaved community, both those in the Academical Village and those in Charlottesville. But they also had hundreds of others—faculty, hotelkeepers, and students—who acted in many instances as if they were the owners. So their situation was that they were owned simultaneously by no one and everyone. They used this ambiguity to carve out more freedoms for themselves, to engage in entrepreneurial activities, and to build families. Nevertheless, the prevailing ideology among the students, faculty, and hotelkeepers was that all of the enslaved were property; accordingly, all of the white people at the University held certain rights of mastery over the enslaved, even if they did not own them. This ambiguity of authority meant that the enslaved were increasingly vulnerable to physical violence, and in the violent culture of nineteenth-century student life, that violence was often enacted upon them. That was the tyranny of the Academical Village.

For too long, the University of Virginia has been silent about these stories, but things have begun to change. Thanks to the work of many including JUEL (Jefferson's University—the Early Life), the President's Commission on Slavery and the University, and the student members of the Memorial for Enslaved Laborers, the University's bicentennial celebrations have been very different from those of the sesquicentennial. That earlier celebration, with its mythologizing and worshipping of Jefferson, aligned with the racial attitudes of 1969. The University of Virginia had only recently integrated its undergraduate population; it was one of the last southern universities to do so. The current bicentennial celebrations are decidedly different. Nevertheless, there is so much more work to be done. In addition to bringing this history out of the archives and into the public consciousness, the University also needs to grapple with the implications of this history. For too long, the University was a place where a racial hierarchy was asserted and young men were trained to be part of a white master class, not just during the period of slavery, but long afterward. We have to acknowledge the tyranny of these beliefs that held millions in bondage and led to a Civil War, followed by disenfranchisement and segregation enshrined in law. The appearance on August 11 of neo-Nazis and other white supremacist groups on campus should be chilling to everyone. They are showing up elsewhere on college campuses; they will return to Charlottesville. All of this should remind the University community of the urgency to work together to acknowledge and understand the tyranny of the Academical Village. All of this should remind us of the urgency of the University of Virginia defining its purpose in its third century. It has, until now, fallen short on its mission to "enlighten the people generally." We must all ask ourselves: What does the University of Virginia need to do to come closer to the promise of liberty, to vanish the "evil spirits" of tyranny and oppression?

Notes

1. Jefferson, "Notes on the Siting of Central College," July 18, 1817, *PTJRS*, 11:544.

2. Jefferson to James Madison, December 20, 1787, *Founders Online*, https://founders
.archives.gov/documents/Jefferson/01-12-02-0454.

3. *A Bill for the More General Diffusion of Knowledge*, 1779, *PTJ*, 2:526.

4. Jefferson to [Pierre] Samuel du Pont de Nemours, April 24, 1816, *PTJRS*, 9:701.

5. Edmund Bacon, "Jefferson at Monticello: The Private Life of Thomas Jefferson," in *Jefferson at Monticello: Recollections of a Monticello Slave and of a Monticello Overseer*, ed. James A. Bear Jr. (Charlottesville: University of Virginia Press, 1967), 32–33.

6. This essay is drawn from a more expansive volume, Maurie D. McInnis and Louis P. Nelson, eds., *Educated in Tyranny: Slavery at Thomas Jefferson's University* (Charlottesville: University of Virginia Press, forthcoming). For access to University of Virginia's archival records, see "Jefferson's University—The Early Life" project, http://juel.virginia.edu.

7. Jefferson to James Breckenridge, February 15, 1821, *Founders Online*, https://founders.archives.gov/documents/Jefferson/98-01-02-1839.

8. Mark Wenger, "Jefferson's Designs for Remodeling the Governor's Palace," *Winterthur Portfolio* 32, no. 4 (Winter 1997): 223–42.

9. Margaret Bayard Smith, *The First Forty Years of Washington Society: Portrayed by the Family Letters of Mrs. Samuel Harrison Smith (Margaret Bayard) from the Collection of Her Grandson, J. Henley Smith*, ed. Gaillard S. Hunt (New York: Scribner, 1906), 387–88.

10. Jefferson to Arthur Brockenbrough, November 12, 1825, *Founders Online*, https://founders.archives.gov/documents/Jefferson/98-01-02-5656.

11. Meeting Minutes of the University of Virginia Board of Visitors, October 4, 1824, *Founders Online*, https://founders.archives.gov/documents/Jefferson/98-01-02-4598.

12. *Notes*, Query XVIII, 162.

13. See also Jennings L. Wagoner Jr. "Honor and Dishonor at Mr. Jefferson's University: The Antebellum Years," *History of Education Quarterly* 26, no. 2 (Summer 1986): 155–79.

14. The development of proslavery thought at the University of Virginia is discussed in Thomas L. Howard III and Alfred Brophy, "Proslavery Thought," in McInnis and Nelson, *Educated in Tyranny*.

15. Chairman's Journals, RG-19/1/2.041, Albert and Shirley Small Special Collections Library, University of Virginia, Charlottesville (hereafter U.Va.), vol. 5, 1833 August–1835 June, February 17, 1834.

16. Chairman's Journals, RG-19/1/2.041, U.Va., vol. 1, 1825–1830 July, June 25, 1829.

17. Ibid., February 5, 1830.

18. Chairman's Journals, RG-19/1/2.041, U.Va., April 24, 1850.

19. Chairman's Journals, RG-19/1/2.041, U.Va., vol. 1, 1825–1830 July, November 8, 1830.

20. Ibid., February 5, 1830.

21. The account of the girl's beating is recorded in University of Virginia General Faculty Minutes, RG-19/1/1.461, U.Va., vol. 7, May 2 and 3, 1856, 475–78. Quotations here and in subsequent paragraphs are from this source.

22. In many ways the faculty served as a judicial authority. The chairman of the faculty often investigated a complaint. That was commonly followed by a meeting of the faculty who heard testimony from individuals and made disciplinary decisions. Their authority extended over students, hotelkeepers, and the enslaved.

23. Ibid.

JEFFERSON'S MIND FOR THE UNIVERSITY

While Jefferson's role in the architectural design of the University is better known, he was no less concerned with what would happen in University classrooms after faculty and students arrived in Charlottesville. Jefferson's educational vision depended on the careful preparation of the curriculum and choice of professors. Even the purchase of books for the University and their arrangement on the library shelves did not escape his careful planning. Unstinting in his efforts in spite of his age, the first rector devoted himself to fulfilling his own broad educational vision. Innovation would define the curriculum at Mr. Jefferson's University, excellence the faculty, breadth the library.

While other American colleges in the early nineteenth century required students to follow a prescribed course of study, drawing on his own, insatiable appetite for virtually every possible subject of inquiry, Jefferson's new university would permit students to pursue an elective course of classes suited to their own interests. This novelty certainly appealed to prospective students, but it also encouraged professors to pursue advanced study in their respective fields and thus to establish the University as a preeminent place of learning. Inspired by the finest faculty, engaged students would promote the development and diffusion of human knowledge. As they formed strong attachments with each other and across the generations, students and teachers would live the Enlightenment.

The disciplines of law and politics ("moral philosophy"), the two positions that Jefferson insisted not be filled by foreign-born professors, posed a special problem. Having lived through what he saw as the political and legal heresies of the 1790s—what he termed the "reign of witches"—and fearing what the Missouri Crisis of 1820 portended for the future of a deeply divided union, Jefferson was more cautious about potentially dangerous innovation in legal and political fields. After all, "The University's" law students, disproportionately drawn from the Commonwealth and its southern neighbors, were supposed to play a prominent role in protecting republicanism in their states against perceived encroachments by the federal government. This made designing their education all the more critical. Jefferson and his fellow board member James Madison generated a list of appropriate books for the study of law and moral philosophy that made their political preferences clear. Unlike other areas of study, the search for professors of law and moral philosophy would focus on finding the ablest advocate of Democratic-Republican orthodoxy, not simply on recruiting the "best and the brightest." In these fields, any member of the faculty must be a true Whig/Republican; a New England Federalist (or even a "Richmond lawyer"—the state capital was a suspected cesspool of Federalists) would not do. Further complicating his efforts to fill the law professorship, Jefferson insisted that the incumbent dedicate himself entirely to the University, forgoing any legal practice on the side, as was common for professional faculty at other schools. This was essential if the University was to provide the type of academic community that Jefferson had cherished in his own education. (This requirement also posed a problem in the search for the professor of medicine.) Finally, after multiple failed offers, the University hired John T. Lomax, a noted lawyer from Fredericksburg, and George Tucker, a Democrat congressman from Virginia.

Even in the study of medicine, where a skeptical Jefferson thought quackery and superstition still reigned, he sought to institute the best possible practical curriculum on a solid scientific foundation. Jefferson was justifiably suspicious of the education doctors received in the early nineteenth century, Robert S. Gibson explains, and of the "fanciful theories" that masqueraded as medical knowledge. Building upon studies in chemistry and biology, and grounded in empiricism, a more systematic form of medical education was necessary. The Anatomical Theatre, designed by Jefferson and completed in 1827, would be an important part of that education (as would the necessary practical experience that young graduates would gain working with sick patients after they left Charlottesville). In many respects, Gibson explains, Jefferson's innovative plans for his medical school presaged the fundamental reforms to medical education that overtook the profession only seventy-five years after the University opened.

Jefferson's Anatomical Theatre supported a practical medical education. (University of Virginia prints and photographs file, accession no. RG-30/1/10.011, Prints 07390, Albert and Shirley Small Special Collections Library, University of Virginia)

Of necessity, such a forward-looking curriculum required the best faculty. This would prove to be one of Jefferson's greatest challenges. Thomas Cooper, the first faculty member he hired, faced vocal and damning opposition because of his unorthodox religious views. To protect state funding for the University, Jefferson capitulated to the criticism and dismissed Cooper with a handsome financial settlement, although he never taught a single class. As buildings were completed and the opening of the University began to come into sight, Jefferson sought first to fill his faculty in the United States, turning to New England where higher education was much better established. But few educated northerners wanted to risk the travails of what seemed to be a backwater, southern village. In the face of strong criticism, but undeterred, Jefferson sent Francis Gilmer to England in 1824 on a confidential mission to find faculty for the school's imminent opening. When six of the eight new faculty seats were filled with foreigners, northern critics quipped that Jefferson might as well have decided that the buildings "should not be built with American bricks and have sent to Europe for them."[1]

The buildings, faculty, and curriculum were not the end of the matter in creating the Academical Village. With his manic interest in books, Jefferson's careful design of the University library—down to elaborating a schema for cataloging books and rules for students' access to and borrowing of them—would occupy an extraordinary amount of time.

Books took center stage in Jefferson's Enlightenment philosophy and would have a similar role in his Enlightenment university. If each generation had an obligation to make progress in human affairs and science, the retention of past knowledge, as a foundation and baseline, was essential. By transmitting knowledge across generations, books enabled Enlightenment and progress. More than that, Juretta Jordan Heckscher explains, books were for Jefferson "at all times his chosen companions," to use his granddaughter Ellen's words, and "tools of sociability and community." Projecting on his envisioned students his own studious, bibliophile character, he saw the library as the very center of the University. The opportunity to draw up a comprehensive list of books to be acquired for the University was undoubtedly a gratifying task, the capstone of his great educational enterprise.

Yet drawing up a list of necessary and hoped-for acquisitions was not the end of the bibliophile's heroic efforts. He also wanted to advise (and control) the cataloging, shelf placement, and regulations for access to the collection. Only after an appeal from the University's first librarian, notes Endrina Tay, did Jefferson permit a limited relaxation of the rule that required students to have faculty permission to borrow a book, although he relented only while insisting that the librarian must be able to locate every book at any time, a misplaced book being "lost" to the University.

Jefferson was fond of invoking the maxim that "the earth belongs . . . to the living"; control from the grave was ill advised and, without the complicity of

The Rotunda library was the heart of Jefferson's Enlightenment university. (Interior of Library, University of Virginia, ca. 1898, LC-DIG-ds-06610, Library of Congress, Prints and Photographs Division)

the living generation, a logical impossibility. Alas, the same held true for university rectors. It was not long after Jefferson's death before some of his careful plans for curriculum and operations at the University of Virginia were amended or ignored—with all due respect, of course, for his ongoing, undying influence.

Despite Jefferson's great care in selecting the best (appropriate) professor and recommending the best texts for the study of law, students generally preferred the more easily digested Blackstone (in spite of what Jefferson saw as the author's monarchical tendencies) to the much more difficult, if not indigestible, Coke (the purer font of republican jurisprudence)—students in the nineteenth century were not so very different from their counterparts in the twenty-first. By the 1830s, James P. Ambuske and Randall Flaherty have discovered, even the faculty found it more convenient to start with Blackstone as they laid a foundation for studying the common law, Jefferson's misgivings notwithstanding.

Demanding a separation of church and state, Jefferson did not plan for a chapel at the state university; University of Virginia's chapel was dedicated in 1890. (Image courtesy of Sue Kell, University of Virginia)

The devolution from Jefferson's design was even more evident in the area of religion, as Cameron Addis shows. Jefferson sought to limit the influence of religion at his University for two reasons. First, he feared the corrupt influence of privileged elites, the backward-looking "kings, nobles, and priests" who had always been dedicated to shoring up their own power at the expense of free thought and innovation. While other American colleges were still subject to clerical influence if not control, students at the University of Virginia would be free to search for new knowledge and truth. Second, Jefferson was deeply conscious that the University would be state-created and state-controlled and that a clear separation between "church" and University was therefore imperative. Jefferson became the target of scathing criticism because of the University's irreligiosity and supposed hostility to Christian orthodoxy. Speaking to Jefferson's influence, one Presbyterian minister quipped that "[w]hen Satan promised all the kingdoms of the world to Christ he laid his thumb on Charlottesville and whispered, 'Except this place, which I reserve for my own especial use.'" Thomas

Cooper was a casualty of Christian backlash, but otherwise Jefferson stood firm: there would be no professor of divinity and no dedicated chapel. While in his effort to obtain funding he had assured Virginia's legislature that religious services might be held in the Rotunda (subject to "impartial regulations"), in spite of multiple requests, this did not happen while he lived. Yet within a few years of his death, the religious regime at the University—like so much else— began to change. Revivalism—driven by the free market of religion that sepa- ration of church and state encouraged—transformed life on Grounds, Addis shows; a chaplain was hired, and a spacious new chapel was dedicated in 1890. Jefferson's influence, though, was not entirely forgotten: the University's chap- lain was paid only through the voluntary contributions of faculty and students, and the chapel has always been pointedly nondenominational.

Were Jefferson to visit the University today, much would be unrecognizable to the old sage. He would certainly recognize the Lawn, and perhaps that makes his association with the architecture so easily understood. Yet, given the chance to ask about "his" University, he undoubtedly would turn with astonishment— and, perhaps, gratification—to multiple curriculums, a diverse population of students, faculty, and staff, and vast library collections that bear only the faint- est resemblance to his original vision. All of which is a reminder that without the students and professors, the classes and library, the learned old and the dis- covered new, the University of Virginia would have been, and would be today, only an architecturally interesting assemblage of bricks and columns.

Note

1. *National Advocate* (New York), December 29, 1824.

Medical Education in the Nineteenth Century
Jefferson and Flexner Revisited

ROBERT S. GIBSON

Abraham Flexner, His Report and Its Aftermath

Medical education in nineteenth-century America was exceedingly superficial and brief. Charles Eliot, the president of Harvard College, wrote in his annual reports: "The ignorance and general incompetency of the average graduate of American Medical Schools, at the time when he receives the degree which turns him loose upon the community, is something horrible to contemplate.... The whole system of medical education in this country needs thorough reformation."[1] Some characterized it as "a national scandal," and virtually all agreed that the systemic deficiencies led to an enormous overproduction of poorly trained medical practitioners, even from the long-established northeastern medical schools.[2] Many factors fostered and sustained this abomination, including the absence of effective licensing laws and protective boards at the state and national levels, the inability or lack of interest of colleges and universities to establish and enforce high academic standards for medical students and professors, the unbridled pecuniary interests that dominated the medical profession throughout most of the nineteenth century, and a general lack of public outcry. Growing from the nation's burgeoning laissez-faire capitalistic attitude spawned by the political forces of Jacksonian democracy, the whole field of medicine was thrown open to all sorts of practitioners and entrepreneurs who established schools as moneymaking ventures rather than as university-based academic enterprises intent on serving the public.

It was not until the first decade of the twentieth century that several groups of academically minded medical educators came together in unity of purpose and began to openly advocate for meaningful reform.[3] This call to action resulted in the famous Flexner Report published in 1910 by the Carnegie Foundation.[4] Unlike previous reform attempts,[5] the Report galvanized public and professional sentiment, led to much-needed reform, and eventually gave rise to the system of modern medical education that we know today.[6] Indeed, the breakthrough change triggered by the Flexner Report is considered one of the most momentous events in the history of medical education in North America.[7]

The Flexner Report was the first successful large-scale effort to standardize and elevate medical education and scholarship in the United States and Canada. In 1908 the Carnegie Foundation for the Advancement of Teaching hired Abraham Flexner, a nonphysician professional educator,[8] to undertake a survey of all existing medical schools in North America. To prepare for this daunting task, Flexner carefully studied the history of medical education, particularly the preeminent German system that emphasized laboratory research,[9] and spent many days at the Johns Hopkins University School of Medicine and the Rockefeller Institute for Medical Research envisioning the ideal medical school model. He then visited and personally examined every one of the 155 schools (147 in America and 8 in Canada) in the next 18 months, evaluating their organizational structure, their policies related to administrative oversight and public accountability, admission and graduation requirements, and curricular content. In addition, he assessed the size and education of the faculties; the availability of library, laboratory, and clinical facilities; their funding resources, and the congruence between the school's catalog and actual operations. Flexner also recorded ratios of practicing physicians for different states and provinces.[10]

Flexner produced an extraordinarily detailed report that some have called "a classic in muckraking journalism."[11] This is because the author, with unrestrained candor, severely criticized the vast majority of schools for their backwardness and disarray, and loose and lax systems that were devoid of any commitment to standards of academic excellence or goals beyond that of financial gain for the faculty. Moreover, in some cases he recommended their immediate extinction! As a result, after the Report was published, many of the weaker schools closed voluntarily or were shut down, and the remainder were either merged with stronger programs or reformed to conform to the Flexnerian model.[12]

The Flexnerian model rejected institutional diversity and sought to purify and homogenize medical education.[13] There was no room in Flexner's system for practical, nonresearch schools, even if they happened to provide respectable teaching, or for any of the sectarian schools. The only acceptable system was in essence an uncommonly exclusive, university-based academic medicine model, patterned after the Johns Hopkins School—the "one shining star" that fulfilled all of his essential criteria. That model had several characteristics, as outlined below.

First, Flexner advocated that all medical schools be "properly" positioned within full-fledged, research-oriented universities.[14] The university and its medical school should not be geographically separated. Ideally, the medical school should be located in a sizable city, in which patients with a variety of illnesses could easily be found. The employed staff were to adhere strictly to the protocols of mainstream science and research. According to Flexner, only scientifically sound medical concepts and practice principles were to be taught. Sectarian schools that promoted osteopathic, homeopathic, chiropractic, and various other "eclectic" philosophies were all discredited.[15]

Second, the constituency of medical school faculty was to be limited. There could be no part-time practitioner-teachers. Instead, the physician educators and scientists of the medical school must be well-trained, full-time employees on salary, devoted to teaching and a research agenda, with little or no fee-based compensation for any outside clinical practice.[16] Flexner called this the "full-time" plan, and he considered it fundamental to his model. It was, perhaps, his most important recommendation. Although faculty members were permitted to participate in some charity care, the transmission of existing scientific knowledge and, importantly, the creation and advancement of new knowledge were to be the focus of the academic physician's life.

Third, medical schools were to admit only academically qualified students.[17] This meant students who had at least two years of science-based collegiate education with preference given to those with an undergraduate degree.[18] In Flexner's words, "The privileges of the medical school can no longer be open to the casual stroller from the highway. It is necessary to install a doorkeeper who will, by critical scrutiny, ascertain the fitness of the applicant" to meet the demands of a long and arduous curriculum.[19]

Fourth, medical schools were to have spacious, well-stocked laboratories for hands-on anatomical dissection, for physiological and chemical experiments, and for microscopic specimen examinations. These facilities were to be readily accessible, equipped with the latest devices, and maintained in excellent working order.

Fifth, the medical curriculum was to be rooted in science, lengthened to four years, sequenced in an educationally sound order, and made more rigorous with proof of learning before advancement to the next stage of study. The first two years were to focus on foundational principles in the "basic science" disciplines of anatomy, physiology, pathology, biochemistry, bacteriology, microbiology, and pharmacology. Formal instruction in the classroom was to be combined with hands-on experience in well-equipped laboratories in a way that promoted active learning. The third and fourth years were to be devoted to the practical application of scientific principles and clinical skill development. During each clinical clerkship, medical students must themselves interview and examine a considerable number of patients with varied illnesses and perform appropriate diagnostic procedures under the supervision of a qualified faculty member. Ideally, the teaching hospital, outpatient clinics, and laboratory venues of instruction should be "under complete educational control" by the parent university.[20]

Sixth, medical school faculty were to recognize that students need abundant time to learn—to think, wonder, digest, and reflect. According to Flexner, "absurd overcrowding" of the curriculum was to be avoided.[21] The subjugation of students to "interminable lectures and recitations" every day must stop!

Seventh, in addition to scientific knowledge, Flexner recommended that students be taught intellectual discipline, critical thinking and communication skills, and habits of lifelong learning. Student experiences were to embrace principles that promoted concepts of health and prevention of disease for the larger good, rather than merely focusing on curing individuals. "Directly or indirectly, disease has been found to depend largely on an unpropitious environment. A bad water supply, defective drainage, impure food, unfavorable occupational surroundings are matters, all of them for social regulation." It is thus important for physicians to have "an exalted conception of their own duty to promote social conditions that conduce to physical well-being."[22]

Eighth, Flexner mandated state oversight of the training of physicians through protective boards,[23] and a process that promoted public accountability. Medical schools were to be created only with the permission of the state government. Moreover, the size of any such school was to be subject to state regulations. Flexner, along with the Carnegie Foundation, held that "all colleges and universities, whether supported by taxation or private endowment," were public service corporations, and that "the public is entitled to know the facts, concerning their administration and development, whether those facts pertain to the financial or educational side."[24]

Ninth, the curriculum, pedagogical practices, and facilities of medical schools were not to be viewed as forever inviolate. Administrators were to embrace the concept of evolutionary change to address such things as growth in knowledge (especially new scientific discoveries linked to disease etiology and/or treatment), technological advances, changes in public health policy, including accreditation standards, and/or new competency requirements. Flexner was quite clear that his blueprint for reform should not be viewed as a final document. Rather, he saw it as dealing with the present and the near future only, a generation at most.[25]

Tenth, deans and others involved in the educational enterprise were to recognize that modern medical education would be expensive. As such, it would require support from the parent university and from external sources such as the state, foundation grants, and individual philanthropy. Flexner anticipated that with fewer schools (he proposed a reduction from 155 to 31), the task of raising money for modern, well-equipped laboratories, teaching hospitals, and competitive salaries for the full-time faculties would not be "impossibly formidable."[26]

The timing of the Flexner Report was fortuitous. It was published during the Progressive Era's emerging consensus in favor of raising standards for the traditional professions, and at a time when the public was ready for change. In addition, a number of specific factors aided its acceptance and fueled the momentum of the medical reform movement. These included:

The Flexner Report was evaluative, rather than simply exhortative, and it exposed each school's deficiencies to public and professional scrutiny. It was conducted and composed with literary and rhetorical precision by a nonphysician professional educator with strong backing from respected organizations such as the Carnegie Foundation and Rockefeller Institute for Medical Research that were well-endowed and largely independent of physician groups intent on pushing a political agenda for personal gain. The Carnegie name likely opened a good many doors that otherwise would have remained closed to Flexner's examination.[27] Moreover, Flexner was very probably the only man who had inspected all 155 medical schools in North America, and this gave his report substantial authority.

Flexner, through the popular press, made the public aware that proper medical training made a difference to patients and society—that modern medicine worked and that experimental research offered the hope of even greater achievements.[28] Moreover, he deftly used rhetorical devices, notably industrial and economic language, to win over reform-minded progressives and financiers who were outside of the medical establishment.[29]

There was a willingness to support basic research in America that had been spurred by the impressive practical successes of German science. Also, scientific discoveries in America and Europe relating to infectious disease led to the introduction of clinical laboratories to improve diagnostic certainty and management, and the need for physicians to be trained in lab techniques.

The United States was in the midst of a major shift in medical care from the home to the hospital for acutely ill patients. The increased importance of hospitals as a safe and effective venue of care meant greater availability of sites for clinical and laboratory instruction.[30]

A powerful incentive arose from the interaction of professional self-regulating activities (e.g., the accreditation of medical schools by organizations such as the Council on Medical Education of the AMA and the AAMC) and the licensing laws and requirements that were imposed by the states. The latter was a particularly important factor in the closing of many of the "factories making ignorant doctors."[31]

Philanthropy drove reforms stimulated by the Report. The Rockefeller Foundation, through its General Education Board, was quick to assume a role of benefactor in efforts to restructure medical education. In 1913 Flexner was recruited to help the board in its decisions. He was instrumental in securing $50 million from John D. Rockefeller Sr. and raising large sums from other benefactors. From 1913 to 1928, the board deferred to Flexner on almost all matters relating to medical education and the granting or denial of Rockefeller Foundation awards. It is noteworthy that the original $50 million investment was increased twelvefold to $600 million and most of what was distributed was given to medical schools deemed worthy of developing.[32]

In some cases, economic exigencies contributed to school closures. As pointed out by Paul Starr in his highly acclaimed work, *The Social Transformation of American Medicine*, "proprietary medical colleges faced a Hobson's choice. If they ignored the new standards for medical education, their diplomas would cease to be recognized by state licensing boards and students would lose any incentive to enroll. If, on the other hand, they tried to comply with the standards, they would be rewarded with fewer students and higher costs because of the more stringent preliminary requirements, longer periods of training, and more expensive facilities and equipment."[33]

Compounding this "take it or leave it" circumstance, philanthropic rescue was almost always out of reach for the proprietary schools.[34]

One of the unfortunate consequences of Flexner's advocacy of university-based medical education was that medical education became much more expensive, putting such education out of reach for all but upper-class white males.[35] Some of the small "proprietary" schools Flexner condemned, while scientifically weak, did admit women, African Americans, and students of limited means. These students could not afford six to eight years of university education and were often simply denied admission to medical schools affiliated with universities. At the same time, the Report tended to delegitimize existing women doctors and doctors of color. Of the seven schools that were dedicated primarily to the training of women in the early twentieth century, six were closed by 1930; only the Women's Medical College of Pennsylvania remained open.[36] Similarly, five of the seven historically black medical schools closed in the wake of Flexner-era reforms; Meharry in Nashville and Howard in Washington, DC, were the only survivors.[37]

In recent years, some historians have acknowledged that there were five major parties that contributed significantly to medical education reform. Among these were the universities themselves, the AMA and AAMC, state licensing boards, and a small cadre of reform-minded academics that included Abraham Flexner. But is this a complete inventory? Were there others, particularly from the antebellum South, whose vocal advocacy and intentional exertions merit recognition?

Thomas Jefferson and His Contributions to Medical Education in Antebellum America

As Jefferson wrote to Dr. Charles Everette, a graduate of the University of Pennsylvania, in 1795, "Whenever I see three physicians together, I look up to the sky to discover whether there' a turkey buzzard in the neighborhood."[38] In his time, Thomas Jefferson railed against doctors with the same sarcasm and skepticism that Cicero heaped on the profession of augurs.[39] He did so because of his belief that medical science was "the most important of all others" since, in the final analysis, health, happiness, and life itself depends on it, and because medicine, when practiced as a scientific discipline, affords the greatest opportunity and widest scope for the exercise of humanity.[40] Jefferson also saw that of all the sciences, medicine was the one most in need of reform. In a lengthy 1807 letter to his good friend, Dr. Caspar Wistar of the University of Pennsylvania, Jefferson showed an amazing grasp of the state of medicine in late eighteenth- and early nineteenth-century America, including its deficiencies and the possibilities for future improvement.[41] In this writing and others, he admonished physicians for their allegiance to an unscientific assemblage of overly simplistic theories about the cause, seat, and cure of disease; for their puerile observations and deceptive remedies that were often shrouded in language of concealment and obfuscation; and for promoting a degree of heroic intervention that was often more ruinous of health than restorative.[42]

Jefferson firmly believed in the ancient doctrine, *vis medicatrix naturae*, literally meaning the healing power of nature.[43] In his 1807 letter to Wistar, Jefferson contended that because there were many morbid conditions about which little was known, physicians could rarely establish a definite cause of disease, and "to an unknown disease there cannot be a known remedy." He urged therefore that "having been so often a witness to the salutary efforts which nature makes to reestablish the disordered functions, he [the physician] should rather trust to their actions [actions of nature] than hazard the interruption of that, and a greater derangement of the system, by *conjectural experiments* on a machine so complicated, & so unknown, as the human body, & a subject so sacred as human life. [O]r, if the appearance of doing something be necessary to keep alive the hopes & spirits of the patient, it should be of the most innocent character."[44]

Being a staunch supporter of the scientific method, Jefferson was particularly opposed to physicians who allowed their "fanciful theories" to outrun their facts. He distrusted orthodox medical practice, which he considered subject to whim, and preferred a simple statement of ignorance when facts were insufficient. This is well illustrated in his *Notes on the State of Virginia,*where he wrote, "Ignorance is preferable to error; and he is less remote from the truth who believes nothing, than he who believes what is wrong."[45] In his admonishment, Jefferson went on to say:

> I have lived myself to see the disciples of Hoffman, Boerhave, Staahl, Cullen,
> Brown succeed one another like the shifting figures of a magic lanthern, & their
> fancies [theories of disease], like the dresses of the annual Doll-babies from
> Paris becoming, from their novelty, the vogue of the day, and yielding to the
> next novelty their ephemeral favor. [T]he patient treated on the fashionable
> theory sometimes gets well in spite of the medicine. . . . [I]t is in this part of

medicine that I wish to see a reform, an abandonment of hypothesis for sober facts, the first degree of value set on clinical observation, and the lowest on visionary theories. . . . [T]he only sure foundations of medicine are an intimate knowledge of the human body, and observations on the effects of medicinal substances on that.[46]

Jefferson was aware that improper treatment could produce iatrogenic problems and clearly believed that more harm than good could be done by overly aggressive physicians.[47] Moreover, he asserted that had physicians left their patients to nature, instead of bleeding them and prescribing excessive doses of drugs of unproven benefit, more lives would be saved. He expressed this by saying:

[T]he adventurous physician goes on, & substitutes presumption for knolege. [F]rom the scanty field of what is known, he launches into the boundless region of what is unknown. . . . I believe we may safely affirm, that the inexperienced & presumptuous band of Medical tyros let loose upon the world, destroys more of human life in one year, than all the Robin hoods, Cartouches, & Macheaths do in a century. . . . I would wish the young practitioner especially to have deeply impressed on his mind the real limits of his art, & when the state of his patient gets beyond these, his office is to be a watchful, but quiet spectator of the operations of nature, giving them fair play by a well-regulated regimen, & by all the aid they can derive from the excitement of good spirits & hope in the patient.[48]

Jefferson exhibited strong antagonism to any instruction in unproven medical theory, which he characterized as "the Charlatanerie of the body, as the other [theology] is of the mind."[49] Facts, he said, must displace "fanciful theory" and in the absence of facts, "the judicious, the moral, the humane physician should stop."[50] This last admonition reveals Jefferson's belief in one of the most enduring principles of Hippocratic medicine—the principle of "Primum non nocere," or "First do no harm." To this, however, Jefferson added the importance of affectionate optimism. Indeed, the state of medicine in his time was such that the best medicine available was often the healer's empathic vigilance and comfort and his hopefulness in the recuperative power of nature.[51]

During Jefferson's lifetime, and well into the nineteenth century, doctors emphasized the primacy of intrusive medical treatment, often to the exclusion or subordination of scientifically obtained findings.[52] Many orthodox physicians feared being dismissed as "inert" practitioners; the imperative to intervene usually in a "heroic manner" was crucial to their professional image, standing, and income. Such physicians held inflated beliefs about the efficacy of their remedies, ignoring the healing powers of nature. They denounced "expectant methods of treatment," implying that nonintervention was an immoral abrogation of professional responsibility. Many physicians feared that a "scientific emphasis," understood as a desire to locate the cause and seat of disease rather than combating it, could "corrupt" the practitioner's duty to "cure" disease and affliction. Above all else, prescribing "active and intrusive" measures (e.g., blistering, copious bloodletting, and toxic purgatives) to "subdue" all symptoms was fundamental to "proper" medical practice. The 1799 death of George Washington is one of the best-known examples of a patient finished off by the misguided heroics of eighteenth-century medicine. During Washington's final twelve hours of life, three physicians engaged in an unrelenting battle to subdue his "massively inflamed throat."[53] They bled him four times, removing more than 80 ounces of blood (2.37 liters or 40 percent of his total blood volume), "painfully blistered" his throat, feet, legs, and arms with a "Spanish fly," and administered three powerful purgatives that included mercurous chloride (calomel) and antimony tartrate, which was "guaranteed to make the former president vomit with a vengeance." These interventions surely exacerbated Washington's excruciating sense of suffocation due to the escalating nature of his ever-advancing throat and laryngeal edema.[54]

Unfortunately, Jefferson's admonitions against nonscientific medical treatment, especially bloodletting, had little impact outside of Charlottesville. Leading medical men and medical schools in America and Europe continued to push the use of radical treatments, using ingenious arguments to justify their use; and in another symbolic indication of its popularity, the *Lancet*, founded in 1823 became "the Hector of English orthodox medical journals,"[55] despite the fact that Pierre Charles Alexandre Louis in 1835 had by all reasonable accounts "dealt the deathblow to bleeding" when, by means of medical statistics, he proved it worthless in pneumonia.[56] Even William Osler (1849–1919) of the Johns Hopkins School of Medicine in his many editions of *Principles and Practice of Medicine* (1892, 8th ed., 1912) advocated bleeding as "a good practice" for more than a few afflictions if used early in the course of illness.[57]

Jefferson's criticism of eighteenth- and nineteenth-century medicine extended to institutional care.[58] In 1800, there were only two general hospitals in the United States—one in Philadelphia and another in New York—and these "novel institutions played only a minor role in the provision of medical care."[59] The great majority of in-patient beds were provided in almshouses that also served as workhouses. Jefferson considered these institutions to be instruments of human degradation and indignity. He viewed the almshouse ward as a death trap rather than a place of healing, "where the sick, the dying and the dead are crammed together, in the same rooms, and often in the same beds."[60] As late as 1824, Jefferson lamented: "I will ask how many families in Richmond would send their husbands, wives or children to a hospital, in sickness? to be attended by nurses hardened by habit against the feelings of pity, to lie in public rooms, harrassed by the cries and sufferings of disease under every form, alarmed by the groans of the dying, exposed as a corpse, to be lectured over by a clinical professor, to be crouded and handled by his students to hear their case learnedly explained to them, it's threatening symptoms developed, and it's probable termination foreboded?"[61]

Like his friend of more than thirty years, Dr. Pierre Samuel du Pont de Nemours, Jefferson favored dehospitalization of disease and poverty.[62] In his *Notes on the State of Virginia*, he described the parish relief system of his native state as the most effective, inexpensive, and compassionate scheme of self-help and medical assistance at home, and one that probably promised greater therapeutic success free from cross-infection. Both men believed that the "natural domestic environment" combined with kind nursing not only fortified familial and social relationships but also saved a much greater proportion of citizens from abuse. Removal of the sick or downtrodden to a hospital, they asserted, creates a form of double liability. On the one hand, it deprived the sick of a better chance of recovery through therapeutic ministration of family and neighbors. On the other, the vastly greater mortality of almshouse wards threatened permanent loss of income and the viability of the family itself.

According to historian Courtney R. Hall, there were two characteristics of Jefferson's thinking that led him to sharply criticize the medical customs and practices of his time.[63] The first of these was his firm belief in observation, measurement, and experiment as the sine qua non conditions for any scientific inquiry. This was illustrated in his many careful agricultural and mechanical experiments, his fieldwork in paleontology, his elaborate arrangement of tabular data regarding weather and climate, and his own experimentation with the smallpox vaccine. The second trait was his utilitarian attitude. Jefferson was a true pragmatist whose chief interest was in adapting the revelation of science to human need. To be worthy of man's consideration, Jefferson believed that science in all of its branches should contribute positively to human welfare, and he demonstrated this in action. These basic criteria, the first a description of his scientific method, and the second a definition of what to him was the true objective of all science, suggest his remarkable insight as a scientist and free-thinking secular humanist. Jefferson assumed that medical therapeutics, to be helpful, must square with these basic criteria. He openly and harshly discounted "visionary theories" or empty hypotheses in the absence of "sober facts"—facts derived from a systematic investigation of phenomena intended to add to the sum total of verifiable knowledge through observation, experiment, and clear reasoning. He approved heartily of remedial activities that medical science had proven beneficial. He never tired of praising the work of John Coakley Lettsom, Edward Jenner, Benjamin Waterhouse, and others who had taken part in the international vaccination effort, and was quite proud of his own part in the American phase of smallpox control through effective vaccine production and administration. To Jenner's nephew he wrote in 1806, with characteristic sweep, "Medecine has never before produced any single improvement of such utility" as Edward Jenner's achievement.[64] In another passage that further illustrates Jefferson's belief in the importance of bringing new knowledge to the bedside of the sick, he wrote, "Harvey's discovery of the circulation of the blood was a beautiful addition to our knowledge of the animal economy. but on review of the practice of medicine before & since that epoch, I do not see any great amelioration which has been derived from that discovery."[65]

Jefferson urged that the medical profession needed to move upward on the scale of good. In advocating for change, he recognized that any beneficial transformation would depend, first and foremost, on the steadfast character and virtue of physicians, individually and collectively. To Jefferson, an important step in demonstrating to the public a willingness to change was a repudiation of speculative theories in favor of scientific evidence as the only means whereby medicine might be elevated to a rank among the exact sciences. He also recognized that another, perhaps more important, step was necessary—that the entire business of medical education must be reformed.

The School of Medicine at the University of Virginia was Jefferson's most concrete contribution to the advance of medical education, and it epitomized his interest in providing the new republic with an enlightened corps of physicians broadly educated in both medical science and the humanities. When considered in the context of early nineteenth-century America, some, if not all, of his visionary concepts represented the best and most innovative ideas of his time, and Jefferson's insightful organizational plan for academic medicine was remarkably similar to that described in Flexner's 1910 Report. Most significantly, his plan advocated the purest, most rigorous academic model for medical education—a school with a socially responsible agenda that was genuinely articulated with a "modern" university, replete with students willing to meet the demands of a long, arduous curriculum that emphasized the preclinical sciences and proof of learning by rigorous examination. It would also have a full-time faculty, all scholars of the first order who maintained an unequivocal and conscientious commitment to the discovery, aggregation, and dissemination of medical knowledge for public benefit.

Jefferson realized that medical education was much better organized and conducted in European schools (especially in London, Edinburgh, and Paris) than in America. However, he surmised that the educational and professional problems peculiar to the special conditions of the new republic of America would not be satisfactorily solved by the transplantation of a foreign system.[66]

So what actions illustrate how far-reaching Jefferson was in his academic thinking, the issues he chose to address, the goals he set, and the solutions he proposed?

University-Based Model

First and foremost, Jefferson addressed the *educational environment* and chose to create a medical school that was an integral part of a genuine university from its inception, "where every branch of science ... should be taught in it's highest degree" and "with more minuteness and detail than was within the scope of the General [collegiate] schools."[67] To Jefferson, the proper place for the study of medicine was of fundamental importance.[68] He deplored the inadequacy of the apprenticeship and independent "for profit" medical school models. Moreover, he seemed to recognize that even the "best" medical schools in America (e.g., those loosely aligned with Harvard, Yale, Columbia, and the University of Pennsylvania) had no credible relationship with their colleges except in using the authority granted to them to award medical degrees. These schools were physically separate and administratively autonomous.[69]

Unlike conditions at other American medical schools, all branches of useful knowledge were brought together at the University of Virginia, where interdisciplinary curricular arrangements were encouraged so students would have ample opportunity to become broadly educated in multiple domains of knowledge.[70] Also, Jefferson recognized the value of intimacy that derived from frequent interaction between pupil and teacher, and he ensured a truly immersive experience by locating all professors and students on the main grounds in close proximity to one another. His design called for a series of pavilions, one for each of the eight original academic schools that included Medicine, Chemistry and Botany, Physics and Astronomy, Mathematics, Law, Moral Philosophy, and both Ancient and Modern Languages. Room assignments were arranged so that students of a particular school would be located adjacent to their professor's pavilion.[71]

The focal point of Jefferson's University was the Rotunda, containing a library where up to seven thousand books would be cataloged in a manner that afforded students and professors ease of use. This by itself was revolutionary, since as pointed out in the Flexner Report, a well-stocked library was not an important feature of most medical schools in nineteenth-century America.[72]

Kenneth Ludmerer, an eminent medical historian and practitioner, suggests that the movement of medical education into the modern American university was a pivotal event in the rise of academic medicine and the development of biomedical research in America.[73] Most historians assert this did not occur until the last few decades of the nineteenth century. Although Daniel Coit Gillman, William Welch, and others who helped create the Johns Hopkins School of Medicine in 1893 deserve considerable credit in advancing medical education and scholarship, it can be argued that Jefferson was the first to promote the notion that advanced learning is profoundly influenced by the institutional framework where instruction occurs; that learning to heal, like every other professional discipline, is best built on a foundation of science; and that the foundation of science is best created and perpetuated by being strongly positioned in a genuine university setting.

Full-Time Faculty: All Eminently Qualified

The second innovation that Jefferson first instituted at the University of Virginia focused on the *competency requirements for medical faculty and their commitment to academic work.*[74] Throughout most of the nineteenth century, medical schools relied exclusively on part-time practitioner-teachers whose principal source of income came from large private practices, supplemented by lecture and graduation fees, and from apprentices who, in some instances, were also students at their respective medical schools. The majority of these practitioner-teachers had neither time for nor interest in advancing scientific knowledge, publishing scholarly work, or seeing that the results of their investigations were applied for public benefit.[75]

At the University of Virginia, the competency requirements for all professors, medical and nonmedical, were the same and comprised more than the potential for eminence in their respective field of learning.[76] To Jefferson, the essential qualifications included: a broad education and culture combined with deep knowledge of one's specialty; an ability to communicate and effectively teach the specialty; industry and integrity in one's field of scholarship; sobriety; an accommodating and peaceful temper; and an unwavering commitment to innovation, collaboration, and service to society. When identifying the primary dictum that was to guide the University of Virginia's Board of Visitors in making each appointment, Jefferson said, "the only question . . . we can ever ask ourselves, as to any candidate, will be, Is he the most highly qualified?" We cannot "indulg[e] motives of favoritism and nepotism" if we expect to "give to our institution splendor and preeminence over all it's sister-seminaries."[77]

Jefferson made it clear that if the field of medicine was to advance, colleges and universities needed to embrace the concept of total devotion to academic work.[78] To Jefferson, this meant hiring full-time salaried instructors and greatly restricting their private practice so that they would have sufficient time to teach and mentor their students, enforce moral and academic discipline across University grounds, and produce and disseminate new knowledge of practical value. When Jefferson, as rector of the Board of Visitors, appointed the first full-time salaried professor of medicine in America, he sought to create a new breed of academically minded educators, men who valued intellectual distinction and integrity more than monetary reward.[79]

A full-time salaried teaching staff, first instituted at Virginia, is now widely regarded as a prerequisite for accreditation by national licensing agencies. As Ludmerer points out, however, this concept was very slow to be adopted in American medical schools. "In the 1870s and 1880s, a few full-time teaching and research positions began to appear, particularly at pioneering medical schools like Harvard and Michigan." He goes on to say, "By 1910, 613 full-time salaried instructors could be found in the 131 medical schools then existing, noting that these full-time salaried instructors were primarily in the laboratory [not clinical] departments."[80] This is another example that fails to acknowledge a "first" of the University of Virginia.

Length and Pace of Academic Terms

A third noteworthy difference between medical education in Charlottesville and the great mass of other American schools pertains to the *length and pace of each academic session*. It was by design the same length as those of all other University departments. In the early years, terms were set at ten and a half months with a mere six weeks off for vacation.[81] At all other contemporary medical schools in America, including the long-established northeastern schools, classroom instruction commenced in November and concluded in January or February, a total of only three or four months.[82]

Unlike most educators of the time, Jefferson believed that all students needed abundant time to review and assimilate material imparted by lecture, to engage in private reading and laboratory work, to buttress their understanding through dialogue and debate with peers and professors, and for physical exercise. When Jefferson inaugurated the 10+ month term, he asserted, "time & experience as well as science are necessary to make a skilful physician" and if pushed too hard, not giving learners time for every step, "they baulk & the machine retrogrades."[83] In another passage that illustrates his appreciation of the irreducible element of time, Jefferson wrote, the proper character of a school is one where what is learned is "learned thoroughly, and [so are] the principles on which it is founded."[84]

In the early years at the University of Virginia, the medical school offered only two lectures per day, on Tuesday, Thursday, and Saturday, each about ninety minutes long, and this plan, it was declared, afforded students ample time for gradually acquiring and thereby digesting the information conveyed by oral instruction. In the University catalogs of the 1830s, this lecture schedule was prominently featured and held up as a distinct advantage over the plan of the large city schools where attendance at six or seven lectures in rapid succession, every day, resulted in "confusion of thought and fatigue of mind."[85]

Foundational Learning in Basic Science and Developmental History

Jefferson was probably one of the very first Americans to understand the importance of *preclinical training in the basic medical sciences*, meaning that the scientific aspects of courses in anatomy, human physiology in health and disease, pathology, chemistry and pharmacology (often called materia medica and pharmacy) would precede the study of the practice of medicine and surgery.[86] Like Flexner, Jefferson understood the value of practical bedside experience but thought it an unprofitable use of time for first-year and even some second-year students. Only when well versed in the principles of scientific inquiry and basic knowledge was the student ready to benefit from clinical instruction, and not before. This policy of first instructing students in the fundamental branches of medical science before directing them to its practical application was an innovation not followed in other schools.

Since there was no hospital in Charlottesville or any desire to build one, and little opportunity for students to observe sickness at the domestic bedside, Jefferson anticipated that young medical graduates of the University of Virginia would have to find their own ways of gaining advanced practical experience before they could reasonably expect to build a practice of citizens able to pay for a doctor's services. He regarded this form of postgraduate professional development, even for physicians bound for rural practice, as a necessary step to ensure competent patient care.[87] In one of the last letters he wrote before his death, he said, "[B]ut consider that we do not expect our schools [at the University of Virginia] to turn out their Alumni already enthroned on the pinnacles of their respective sciences; but only so far advanced in each as to be able to pursue them by themselves and to become Newtons and Laplaces by energies and perseverances to be continued thro life."[88] This passage suggests that in Jefferson's mind, "learning to heal" was indeed a life-long process that only begins with what one is taught in medical school. It is of interest that Jefferson recognized the deficient opportunities for clinical training at his University and suggested a solution when he wrote,

> I have always had Norfolk in view for this purpose. [T]he climate, and Pontine country around Norfolk render it truly sickly in itself. [I]t is moreover the rendezvous not only of the shipping of commerce, but of the vessels of the public navy. [T]he U.S. have there a hospital already established, and supplied with subjects from these local circumstances. I had thought, and have mentioned to yourself and our colleagues, that when our Medical school has gotten under way, we should propose to the federal government the association with that establishment, and at our own expense, of the *Clinical branch of our Medical school*, so that our Students, after qualifying themselves with the other branches of the Science here, might complete their course of preparation by attending clinical lectures for 6. or 12. months at Norfolk.[89]

Jefferson was familiar with the marine hospital system in his state and elsewhere, and he recognized its potential for postgraduate teaching.[90] In October 1780, when he was governor, the Commonwealth of Virginia enacted a first-of-its-kind law to help pay hospital expenses for ill seamen and marines in the state, and by a subsequent act in 1788, built the first hospital dedicated to the care of men who made their living at sea. This state-sponsored hospital was located in the port city of Norfolk and was sold to the federal government in 1801, three years after President John Adams signed into law a congressional act that created the Marine Hospital Fund that eventually morphed into the U.S. Public Health Service. During Jefferson's presidency, the fund was used to establish federally run treatment facilities in Norfolk, New Orleans, and

Boston.[91] Dr. Benjamin Waterhouse was appointed director of the Boston Marine hospital by Jefferson, and during his tenure, he "established a system of student internships and in effect turned the Boston Marine hospital into the country's first teaching hospital."[92]

In line with Jefferson's broad concept of education, the University of Virginia was quite probably the first school in the United States to include a series of formal lectures on the history of medicine, with explanations of its successive theories and practice principles from Hippocrates to the present, within a medical school curriculum.[93] Rather than focusing on the "novelty of the day," Jefferson insisted that to be effective in any academic sphere one must be equipped with sound knowledge of the developmental background of the field. It was his belief that the curriculum, in blending the best ideas of the ancients with the more insightful perspectives set forth by the moderns, would not only enlighten but inspire youthful matriculates. It would also serve as a "moral exercise,"[94] by revealing examples of aggressive and abusive behavior of men, institutions, and nations. Indeed, by informing students of the past, history would "qualify them as judges of the actions and designs of men" and thus "enable them to know ambition under every disguise it may assume; and knowing it, to defeat its views."[95] According to Jock Murray, the series of lectures on medical history were based mostly on John Friend's *History of Physick* and the highly regarded works of Kurt Joachim Sprengel of the University of Halle.[96]

The medical school of the University also offered a course on the general principles of medical jurisprudence or forensic medicine—the application, in other words, of medical science to legislative and judicial inquiries.[97] This was an innovation that few schools offered in early nineteenth-century America, and not surprisingly, it attracted many students from the School of Law.

Proof of Learning by Rigorous Examination

Jefferson further demonstrated his visionary thinking when he disavowed time or money alone as an element in securing the doctor of medicine degree, and made knowledge and the ability to communicate it the primary criteria.[98] Instruction in the science of medicine would be conveyed partly by courses of lectures and anatomical demonstrations and partly by the study of approved textbooks, and in all cases, *the assiduity of each student would be tested by a rigorous system of oral, written, and public examinations.* For example, immediately before each lecture, students in all scientific departments were tested on the preceding lecture and any assigned reading. This practice of daily exams, which was one of many extraordinary features in the organization of the University of Virginia, enabled the professor to explain parts of the material that were imperfectly understood by the class, fill in the vacant gaps, and weed out those incorrigibles who failed to show a satisfactory scale of preparation throughout the year. The student could thus obtain a valuable means of retaining correct information, while experiencing an incidental advantage in familiarizing him with the mode of trial to which he would be subjected in his final examination for graduation.[99]

From the start, there were two "general examinations" in the medical school—an "intermediate" (midterm) and a final exam. The final exam was partly oral but mostly written and subjected students to "searching interrogations" on the details in all aspects of the topics covered in each of the seven courses of lectures, textbook assignments, and experiential demonstrations in anatomy, chemistry, and pharmacy.[100] It was patterned after the Oxford system, and administered and graded by a "Committee of Professors" constituted to include medical and nonmedical faculty, with the written English taken into account as a specific condition of the coveted MD degree. According to Dr. Robley Dunglison, the first medical professor hired by Jefferson, the Virginia plan comprised eight elements:[101]

(1) The Chairman of the Faculty shall appoint for the examination of each school, a committee consisting of the professor of that school, and two other professors; (2) The professor shall prepare, in writing, a series of questions to be proposed to his class, at the examination, and to these questions he shall affix numerical values, according to the estimate he shall form of their relative difficulty, the highest number being 100; (3) The times of the examination for each school shall be chosen by the Chairman; (4) At the appointed hour, the students of the class to be examined shall take their places in the lecture room [elliptical room of the Rotunda], provided with pens, ink and paper. The written questions shall then, for the first time, be presented to them, and they shall be required to give the answers in writing with their names subscribed; (5) A majority of the committee shall always be present during the examination; and they shall see that the students keep perfect silence, do not leave their seats, and have no communication with one another or with other persons. When in the judgment of the committee, sufficient time has been allowed for preparing the answers, the examination shall be closed, and the papers handed in; (6) The professor shall then carefully examine and compare the answers, and shall prepare a report, in which he shall mark, numerically, the value which he attaches to each; the highest number for any answer being that which had

been fixed upon the value of the corresponding question; (7) The report shall be submitted to the committee, and if approved by them, shall be laid before the [entire] faculty [medical and nonmedical], together with all the papers connected with it, which are to be preserved in the archives of the University; and (8) The students shall be arranged into three separate divisions, according to the merit of their examinations as determined by the following method. The numerical score attached to all questions are to be added together, and also the values of all answers given by each student. If the last number [student's number] exceed three-fourth of the first, the student shall be ranked in the first division; if it be less than three-fourth, and more than one-fourth, in the second [division]; and if less than one-fourth, in the third.

Only those who scored in the top quartile and passed a Latin exam were granted the MD degree.[102] This later requirement was very unusual; its purpose was stated in 1824:

No diploma shall be given to anyone who has not passed an examination in the Latin language as shall have proven him able to read the highest classics in that language with ease, thorough understanding and just quality; and if he be also proficient in the Greek, let that, too, be stated in his diploma. The intention being that the reputation of the University shall not be committed but to those who, to an eminence is some one or more of the sciences taught in it, add a proficiency in these languages which constitute the basis of good education, and are indispensable to fill up the character of a well-educated man.[103]

The academic demands of the University led one student to say, "I think it is the last place in the world for a lazy man to try to enjoy himself."[104] In the awarding of the MD degree, no school in America required more than the University of Virginia. It had the highest standards of scientific and literary scholarship—standards that were not surrendered even in the darkest days of the school's need.[105] Noteworthy is the fact that only 14 percent of medical school matriculates at the University of Virginia received an MD degree between 1828 and 1861.[106]

In contrast to the University of Virginia, at other contemporary medical schools there was no proof of proficiency by written examination. When an exam was given, it was oral in system and farcical in form.[107] To graduate, a student merely had to answer a brief set of perfunctory oral questions, and pay all lecture and graduations fees to their practitioner-teachers.[108] Some schools also required that students write a thesis on a medical topic of their choice.

Virtually every school in Jefferson's time awarded honorary degrees, a practice that Jefferson strongly opposed. In his mind, a degree without proof of learning by "rigorous examination" would seriously compromise the reputation of "his institution." At the University of Virginia, the granting of degrees would be "based solely on merit which had been laboriously acquired and exhibited in the classroom." According to historian Phillip A. Bruce, "Jefferson's distrustful attitude towards honorary degrees was characteristic of a man who had struck fiercely at all artificial distinctions, and who was suspicious of man's disposition to create them where they did not exist."[109] Jefferson's policy was an unprecedented academic virtue in his time, and to this day, only a few institutions of higher education have adopted and sustained it since their inception.[110] In 1850, honorary MD degrees from American medical schools had become so common that the American Medical Association recommended that the practice be severely restricted.[111]

State Oversight

Jefferson opposed unregulated proprietary medical education and instead promoted *state support and oversight of the training of physicians*.[112] He was instrumental in securing an annual appropriation from the state to fund the teaching and scholarly work of the professors. In return, he maintained that the University and its medical school had a fiduciary responsibility to protect and promote the public's trust by "training more able physicians" to serve the citizens of the Commonwealth,[113] and he pledged his support for an annual institutional assessment and accountability through full public disclosure. As the University's rector, Jefferson demonstrated this commitment by creating a culture whereby the "University should in all things, & at all times be subject to the controul of the [state] legislature."[114] Let others be the judge, Jefferson proclaimed, of whether "the institution of my native state" is fulfilling its public purpose in reaching upward and outward and providing those destined for the learned professions ample opportunity to pursue their education "with more minuteness and detail than was within the scope of the General schools."[115]

In nineteenth-century America, the concept of public disclosure was for the most part ignored by medical schools and the profession at large.[116] The vast majority of the schools were autonomous silos, accountable to no one except the physician owners who sometimes had serious conflicts of interest, and had no publicly advantageous agenda for either increasing scientific knowledge or improving its application throughout their state or locality.[117] Medical schools, with few exceptions, not only questioned but openly resisted the right of any other agency to collect and publish the facts concerning their operations. This dynamic did not exist in Charlottesville.

Professionalism

Another aspect of Jefferson's plan included *concepts germane to medical professionalism*. Instilling moral values and habits of virtuous behavior, Jefferson declared, was among the most important goals of education.[118] Although Jefferson's philosophy was rooted in the cardinal and transcendent virtues, he placed particular emphasis on honor, duty to others, and responsibility as quintessential in the training and maturation of physicians. At the University of Virginia, before a student could qualify as a candidate for the MD degree, he had to demonstrate high moral character, determined by the faculty through observation inside and outside the classroom.

Jefferson believed that science alone was an inadequate basis for professional practice. Physicians must possess a core of humanistic and ethical values that included allegiance to the do-no-harm principle, therapeutic restraint when evidence of benefit is lacking, and affectionate optimism. He urged physicians to explore a broader meaning of competence, one combining science with compassion, acting honestly and benevolently to all with the purest integrity, always showing regard for the welfare of individuals and society, and having a desire to serve others in an altruistic way. Jefferson's plan promoted truth telling within and between the student bodies in all academic schools, when he decreed that "every one is bound to bear witness where wrong has been done, . . ." "When testimony is required from a Student, it shall be voluntary, and not on oath. and the obligation to give it shall be left to his own sense of right."[119]

Jefferson's rhetoric reflected several modern-day precepts of professionalism: the demonstration by examination of expert knowledge and communication skills, the importance of self-awareness and its associated mental power and self-control, as embodied in Luke's "physician heal thyself," a commitment to science or evidence-based practice and lifelong learning, a willingness to admit one's limitations, a commitment to social reform through public health initiatives, and professional self-regulation, rather than intrusion by the federal government.

Concluding Comments

Jefferson aimed to modernize an anachronistic system of medical education in America, and his plan was a legitimate response to the pressing problem of his time—ensuring that everyone who practiced medicine be thoroughly trained in medical science. The revolutionary model he proposed for the University of Virginia was at first viewed as an experiment, and one deemed unlikely to succeed by his critics.[120] In the planning of the medical school in Charlottesville, Jefferson's wisdom was not widely recognized because of the chaos, acrimony, and mercenary interests that characterized the medical profession in the nineteenth century. Moreover, he was a lone voice in a wilderness—a reform-minded activist with little or no support outside of Charlottesville.

Jefferson's plan presaged the Flexner Report in seven important ways: (1) it recognized the importance of place, people, and purpose by advocating the most rigorous academic model for medical education—a university-based school replete with students who were obliged to meet the demands of a long arduous curriculum and a full-time faculty, all scholars of the first order, who maintained an unambiguous commitment to the discovery, aggregation, and dissemination of medical knowledge for public benefit; (2) it recommended the medical school be founded on the then-unique idea of providing a thorough scientific education before clinical instruction (preclinical basic science teaching); (3) it advocated giving medical students time to learn by avoiding "absurd overcrowding" of the curriculum; (4) it promoted and enforced strict educational requirements for the medical school, including a rigorous system of oral, written, and public examinations, as a prerequisite to the granting of the MD degree; (5) it supported state oversight of the training of physicians, and a commitment to full public disclosure by university officials; (6) it endorsed clinical instruction in a hospital or dispensary, supervised by the faculty of an academic medical school that was genuinely articulated with a University; and (7) it promoted a broad cultural and philosophical education, and concepts germane to medical professionalism.

Jefferson and Flexner were alike in many of their philosophical precepts—that science without humanism is a social sin just as politics is when practiced without principles;[121] that formal analytical reasoning, the kind of thinking integral to the natural sciences, should hold pride of place in the intellectual training of physicians, and that every man owes a duty to his profession and society, and in no profession is the obligation more clear than in medicine. Both men were champions of scientific excellence and archenemies of mediocrity, and they defended their country against the mediocrity of ideas, morality, and actions. And both had the foresight to recognize the concept of generational independence—that their blueprints for reform would not be final, that it only "deals with the present and near future, a generation at most."[122] Jefferson and his University, as well as Flexner, were less bold and progressive than we today might demand; they were limited by their own and society's assumptions, with respect to their views on the education of women, African Americans, and the poor. Thus, both men failed a critical test of commitment to equality of opportunity.

The author recognizes that this historiographic work is incomplete. To legitimately prove the supposition that Jefferson's University plan was a worthy forerunner of the modern medical school model, so well described in the 1910 Flexner Report, much more information, historical statistics, and analytical interpretation from a wider variety of archival sources are needed. This important next step can be accomplished by completing an in-depth institutional history of Jefferson's school of medicine and comparing its evolution with other schools that were in operation in 1825.[123]

Notes

The research for this essay has been supported by a grant of admission to various archives, including those of the University of Virginia, the International Center for Jefferson Studies, and the College of Physicians of Philadelphia. The author would also like to acknowledge Andrew O'Shaughnessy, Saunders Director of the Robert H. Smith International Center for Jefferson Studies, and James B. Murray, vice rector of the University of Virginia, for their encouragement and generous time in reviewing many of the ideas related to this ongoing project, and Nicole Schroder, PhD candidate in history, University of Virginia, for her assistance in locating primary source material.

1. Charles Eliot, *Annual Report of the President of Harvard College* (1871–1872), 25–26, and (1869–1870), 18.

2. The most recent and esteemed scholarship on the history of American medical education is the three-volume work by Kenneth M. Ludmerer, *Learning to Heal* (New York: Basic Books, 1985), *Time to Heal* (New York: Oxford University Press, 1999), and *Let Me Heal* (New York: Oxford University Press, 2015). Earlier sources include: Robley Dunglison, *The Medical Student: Aids to the Study of Medicine* (Philadelphia: Carey, Lea & Blanchard, 1837 and 1844); Nathan S. Davis, *History of Medical Education and Institutions from the First Settlements of the British Colonies to the Year 1850* (Chicago: S. C. Griggs and Co., 1851); Henry J. Bigelow, *Medical Education in America: Annual Address read before the Massachusetts Medical Society, June, 7, 1871* (Cambridge: Welch, Bigelow and Co., 1871); John S. Billings, *Ideals of Medical Education: The Address in Medicine*, reprinted in the *New Englander* and *Yale University Review* (August 1891); William F. Norwood, *Medical Education in the United States before the Civil War* (Philadelphia: University

of Pennsylvania Press, 1944); Edward C. Atwater, "Financial Subsidies for American Medical Education before 1940" (MA thesis, Johns Hopkins University, 1974); and William G. Rothstein, *American Medical Schools and the Practice of Medicine* (New York: Oxford University Press, 1987).

3. The principal organizations arguing for reform were the Association of American Medical Colleges (AAMC), founded in 1876; the Council on Medical Education (CME) of the American Medical Association (AMA), founded in 1905, and the Federation of University Medical Schools, founded in 1908. The organization that provided the stimulus for meaningful reform was the Carnegie Foundation for the Advancement of Teaching (CFAT), founded in 1905 under the leadership of its president, Henry S. Pritchett.

4. Abraham Flexner, *Medical Education in the United States and Canada* (New York: Carnegie Foundation for the Advancement of Teaching, 1910) (hereinafter Flexner Report).

5. From its inception in 1846 until the end of the century, the AMA battled for reform with little visible effect, in part because of disabling internecine squabbles. Lacking any legal license, the reform-minded members of the AMA sought to work by moral suasion alone. One example is the AMA report calling for reform written by Dr. James Lawrence Cabell of the University of Virginia. See Transactions of the American Medical Association (1854): 7:53–81.

6. The Flexner Report was not an entirely original document; most of the ideas had been articulated by academically minded medical educators since the 1870s. This was especially true for an enlightened group of new university presidents, all with a cogent reform agenda—Charles W. Eliot of Harvard (term 1869–1909), Andrew Dickson White of Cornell (term 1866–1885), James Burrill Angell of Michigan (term 1871–1909), and Daniel Coit Gillman of Johns Hopkins University (term 1876–1901). In addition, the four founding physicians of the Johns Hopkins School of Medicine—pathologist William H. Welch (1850–1934), surgeon William S. Halsted (1852–1922), internist William Osler (1849–1919), and gynecologist Howard Kelly (1858–1943)—deserve considerable credit in elevating medical education and scholarship in America. Also, the unpublished 1905 report by the Council on Medical Education of the AMA, compiled after an inspection of 162 American medical schools, includes many conclusions similar to those in the 1910 Flexner Report.

7. The 346-page Flexner Report has been called the "most influential of all" in medical education and was sufficiently momentous to be included in a 1974 issue of *Daedalus* entitled "Twentieth Century Classics Revisited." Carleton B. Chapman, "The Flexner Report by Abraham Flexner," *Daedalus* (1974): 103, 105–17.

8. Abraham Flexner (1866–1959) received an AB in Classics from Johns Hopkins in 1886, after which he founded a private high school in Louisville. In 1905, he closed his school to pursue graduate work at Harvard where he studied science under George H. Parker at the Agassiz Museum, psychology under Hugo Munsterberg, Edwin Holt, and Robert Yerkes, and philosophy under Josiah Royce. He then studied brain anatomy under his brother Simon Flexner at the Rockefeller Institute for Medical Research in New York. In 1907–1908, he studied higher education under Friedrich Paulson at the University of Berlin and wrote his first book, *The American College: A Criticism*. On returning to the United States, he served as a staff member of the Carnegie Foundation

(1908–1912) and as secretary of the General Education Board of the Rockefeller Foundation (1913–1928). Flexner was also a founder and first director of a "scholar's utopia"—the Institute for Advanced Study at Princeton University (1930–1939)—which brought together some of the greatest minds in history, including Albert Einstein, to collaborate on intellectual discovery and research. Some of his often-overlooked publications included: *Medical Education in Europe: A Report to the Carnegie Foundation* (1912), *A Modern School* (1916), *Daniel Coit Gillman: Creator of the American Type of University* (1946), and *Funds and Foundations: Their Policies Past and Present* (1956). Franklin Parker, "Abraham Flexner, 1866–1959," *History of Education Quarterly* 2, no. 4 (1962): 199–209.

9. Flexner specifically identified Theodore Billroth's book, *Medical Education in the German Universities* (1876), as his major primer. Other authorities cited in his Report included: John Dewey (1859–1952, PhD Johns Hopkins 1884), Wilhelm Lexis (1837–1914, PhD University of Bonn, 1859), Friedrich Paulsen (1846–1908, PhD University of Berlin, 1871), Adolf von Strumpell (1853–1925, MD University of Leipzig, 1875), Nathan S. Davis (1817–1904, MD College of Physicians and Surgeons of Western District of NY, 1837), Henry J. Bigelow (1818–1890, MD Harvard, 1841), William W. Keen (1837–1932, MD Jefferson Medical College, 1862), John S. Billings (1838–1913, MD Cincinnati Medical College of Ohio, 1860), William Pepper (1843–1898, MD University of Pennsylvania, 1864), William Osler (1849–1919, MD McGill University Faculty of Medicine, 1872), William Welch (1850–1934, MD Columbia College of Physicians and Surgeons, 1875), Christian A. Herter (1865–1910, MD Columbia College of Physicians and Surgeons, 1880), Graham Lusk (1866–1932, PhD University of Munich, 1891), Edwin O. Jordan (1866–1936, PhD MIT, 1888), and Francis R. Packard (1870–1950, MD, University of Pennsylvania, 1892).

10. Flexner found that "[i]n the entire United States, there is already on average one doctor for every 568 persons, that in our large cities there is frequently one doctor for every 400 or less, that many small towns with less than 200 inhabitants each have two or three physicians." By comparison, the ratio of physicians to general population was approximately 1:1,500 in Germany and 1:1,030 in Canada. See Flexner Report, 14–17, and Douglas Page, "The Flexner Report: 100 Years Later," *International Journal of Medical Education* (2010): 74.

11. Ludmerer, *Learning to Heal*, 166–90.

12. Flexner's plan called for a drastic reduction in the number of medical schools—elimination of all but 31 of the 155 surveyed schools—and a > 50 percent decrease in the annual output of MD graduates. His calculations indicated that if each of the 31 surviving medical schools graduated 70 doctors per year, the country's need would be easily met. See Flexner Report, 146.

13. Ludmerer, *Learning to Heal*, 187.

14. Flexner Report, 143, and Ludmerer, *Learning to Heal*, 167.

15. A total of 32 "medical sectarian" institutions were reported on, all located in the United States. There were 8 osteopathic, 15 homeopathic, 1 chiropractic, and 8 eclectic schools. See Flexner Report, 156–66, 172–73.

16. The Johns Hopkins School of Medicine did not strictly enforce this requirement, as heads of the clinical departments were permitted to supplement their incomes with revenue from their private practices.

17. Flexner Report, 26, 61.

18. Ibid., 26. A two-year minimum was recommended because the three crucial preparatory courses of chemistry, biology and botany, and physics "cannot be carried through in a briefer period."

19. Ibid., 22

20. Ibid., xi.

21. Ibid., 76–77.

22. Ibid., 26, 67–68.

23. Ibid., 19, 167, 171

24. Ibid., ix.

25. Ibid., 143.

26. Ibid., 102.

27. With the Carnegie name inspiring visions of philanthropic largesse and a prominent medical journal linking the inspections to inclusion in the free retirement plan that the foundation was creating for professors (now known as TIAA/CREF), Flexner had little difficulty gaining access to medical schools. Paul Starr, *The Social Transformation of American Medicine* (New York: Basic Books, 1982), 119; JAMA, "Editorial: The Influence of the Carnegie Foundation on Medical Education Reform," *Journal of the American Medical Association*, 53 (1909): 559–60; and Robert M. Lester, *Forty Years of Carnegie Giving* (New York: Charles Scribner's Sons, 1941), 45, 153.

28. When Professor Lawrence Henderson of Harvard identified the period 1910–1912 as the Great Divide in United States medical care—when "for the first time in human history, a random patient with a random disease consulting a doctor chosen at random stood better than a 50-50 chance of benefiting from the encounter"—his sharply turned phrase heralded the changing public attitude toward the value of medical care. Herman Somers and Anne Somers, *Doctors, Patients, & Health Insurance* (Washington, DC: Brookings Institution, 1961), 136–37.

29. Flexner Report, 14, 16.

30. In the aftermath of the Flexner Report, a further movement toward standardization and accreditation came in 1913 when the American College of Surgeons (ACS) was founded. For a hospital to gain the prestigious accreditation of the ACS, it had to meet a rigorous set of standards relating to the professional staff, record keeping, and diagnostic and therapeutic facilities. Of 692 large hospitals examined in 1918, only 13 percent were approved and placed on a published list, signifying a safe and scientifically efficient organization. By 1932, 93 percent of the 1,600 hospitals examined met ACS requirements. See Richard H. Shryock, *The Development of Modern Medicine* (Madison: University of Wisconsin Press, 1979), 348.

31. "Factories for the Making of Ignorant Doctors," *New York Times*, July 24, 1910.

32. Abraham Flexner, *Funds and Foundations: Their Policies Past and Present* (New York: Harper, 1952): 52.

33. Starr, *Social Transformation*, 119.

34. Soma Hewa, "Rockefeller Philanthropy and the Flexner Report on Medical Education in the United States," *International Journal of Sociology and Social Science* 22 (2002): 1–47.

35. Hans Bear, "The American Dominative Medical System as a Reflection of Social Relations in the Larger Society," *Social Science and Medicine* 28 (1989): 1106.

36. The proportion of women who graduated from medical schools decreased to an all-time low after the Flexner Report was published (2.9 percent in 1915), and the proportion remained < 5 percent until the 1970s, when social forces challenged and broke down the barriers that prevented women from studying medicine. See Gerald E. Markowitz and David K. Rogers, "Doctors in Crisis: A Study of the Use of Medical Education Reform to Establish Modern Professional Elitism in Medicine," *American Quarterly* 25, no. 1 (1973): 83–107; Shari L. Barkin et al., "Unintended Consequences of the Flexner Report: Women in Pediatrics," *Pediatrics* 120 (2010): 1055–57; Mary R. Walsh, *Doctors Needed: No Women Need Apply—Sexual Barriers in the Medical Profession, 1835–1975* (New Haven, CT: Yale University Press, 1977), 176–93; and Ellen S. More, *Restoring the Balance: Women Physicians and the Profession of Medicine, 1850–1995* (Cambridge, MA: Harvard University Press, 1999).

37. Flexner was matter-of-fact in explaining that five of the seven black schools be closed, claiming only Howard and Meharry were "worth developing." Of note, Flexner secured funding from Rockefeller and Carnegie to save these two schools. See Flexner Report, 181; and Todd Savitt, "Abraham Flexner and the Black Medical Schools," in *Beyond Flexner: Medical Education in the Twentieth Century*, ed. B. Barzansky and N. Gevitz (New York: Greenwood Press, 1992), 65–81.

38. Samuel X. Radbill, "The Autobiographical Ana of Robley Dunglison," *Transactions of the American Philosopical Society* 53 (1963): 26. Robley Dunglison (1798–1869) became Jefferson's personal physician in 1825. In his *Personal Memoranda*, Dunglison recalled this comment made by Jefferson while in the presence of Dr. Everette, and he claimed that it "illustrated Mr. Jefferson's attitude towards physicians." Sarah N. Randolph, *The Domestic Life of Thomas Jefferson* (New York: Harper & Brothers, 1871), 394–95. Charles Everette (d. 1848) practiced medicine in Charlottesville as early as 1798. PTJ, 3:196.

39. Martin Clagett, *Scientific Jefferson Revealed* (Charlottesville: University of Virginia Press, 2009), 54.

40. On the importance of health and medical science, see Jefferson to Dr. Thomas Cooper, January 16, August 25, and October 7, 1814, PTJRS, 7:124–31, 606–7, and 8:12–13; to Peter Carr, August 19, 1785, and August 10, 1787, PTJ, 8:405–8 and 12:14–19; to Thomas Mann Randolph, November 25, 1785, August 27, 1786, and July 6, 1787, PTJ, 9:59–60, 10:305–9, and 11:556–59; and to John Adams, July 5, 1814, PTJRS, 7:451–55. See also Courtney R. Hall, "Jefferson on the Medical Theory and Practice of his Day," *Bulletin of the History of Medicine* 31 (1957): 235–45, and Jock Murray, "Thomas Jefferson and Medicine," *Journal of Medical Biography* 5 (1997): 146–57.

41. Jefferson to Caspar Wistar, June 21, 1807, *Founders Online*, https://founders .archives.gov/documents/Jefferson/99-01-02-5789. This frequently quoted letter is the longest and most detailed of Jefferson's criticism of the medical profession.

42. Jefferson to William Green Munford, June 18, 1799, PTJ, 31:126–30; to John Crawford, January 2, 1812, PTJRS, 4:394–95; to Ezra Sargeant, February 3, 1812, PTJRS, 4:477; to William Short, October 31, 1819, *Founders Online*, https://founders.archives.gov /documents/Jefferson/98-01-02-0850; and to Robley Dunglison, November 26, 1825,

Founders Online, https://founders.archives.gov/documents/Jefferson/98-01-02-5687. In the letter to Dunglison, Jefferson wrote, "[T]ime & experience as well as science are necessary to make a skilful physician, and Nature is preferable to an unskilful one." See also J. S. Spratt, "Thomas Jefferson: The Scholarly Politician and His Influence of Medicine," *Southern Medical Journal* 69 (1976): 660–66.

43. The precept underlying the phrase "vis medicatrix naturae" was that nature, if left alone, would restore natural balance that had been undone by disease. Doctors, Jefferson believed, interfered with this restorative process, and that their slavish devotion to purging, harsh emetics, and bleeding served only to torment the patient. See Jefferson to Thomas Mann Randolph, January 18, 1796, *PTJ*, 28:579–80; to Martha Jefferson Randolph, May 31, 1798, *PTJ*, 30:381, and to Gideon Granger, January 24, 1810, *PTJRS*, 2:178–80; and Harry Bloch, "Thomas Jefferson 1743 to 1826: Thoughts on Medicine, Child Care and Welfare," *New York State Journal of Medicine* 72 (1972): 3030.

44. Jefferson to Caspar Wistar, June 21, 1807, *Founders Online*, https://founders .archives.gov/documents/Jefferson/99-01-02-5789.

45. *Notes*, Query VI, 33 (footnote omitted). See also Jefferson to the Reverend James Madison, July 19, 1788, *PTJ*, 13:379–83, in which Jefferson wrote on false speculations: "It is always better to have no ideas than false ones; to believe nothing, than to believe what is wrong"; and Jefferson to William Green Munford, June 18, 1799, *PTJ*, 31:127–28, in which he says, "[T]he state of medecine is worse than that of total ignorance. could we divest ourselves of every thing we suppose we know in it, we should start from a higher ground & with fairer prospects . . . of the diseases of doubtful form, physicians have ever had a false knowlege, worse than ignorance."

46. Jefferson to Caspar Wistar, June 21, 1807, *Founders Online*, https://founders .archives.gov/documents/Jefferson/99-01-02-5789.

47. Unlike many other Founding Fathers, Jefferson was strongly opposed to just about every aggressively intrusive intervention, whether it be heroic depletive or stimulant treatment, and he himself avoided almost all forms of it throughout his life. His disdain for violent bleeding and purging not only extended to his family, but he forbade his plantation overseers from having it performed on his slaves. He informed his managers to "never bleed a negro," that physicians should only be called sparingly because "in most other cases [other than pleurisy, malaria, and dysentery] they oftener do harm than good." He further advised to treat the ill slave with "a lighter diet and kind attention . . ." and to administer salts since they are "salutary in almost all cases, & hurtful in none." See *Thomas Jefferson's Garden Book*, ed. Edwin M. Betts (Philadelphia: American Philosophical Society, 1944), entries for May 22, 1773, and December 1811, 41 and 467. In a letter from Ellen W. Randolph (Coolidge) to Martha Jefferson Randolph, July 28, 1819, *PTJRS*, 14:565, there is mention of one instance where a plantation slave (named Burwell Colbert) was bled after many less intrusive interventions had failed to relieve an intestinal obstruction.

48. Jefferson to Caspar Wistar, June 21, 1807, *Founders Online*, https://founders .archives.gov/documents/Jefferson/99-01-02-5789.

49. Jefferson to Thomas Cooper, October 7, 1814, *PTJRS*, 8:12–13. Jefferson to William Green Munford, June 18, 1799, *PTJ*, 31:126–30. Also Daniel J. Boorstin, *The Lost World of Thomas Jefferson* (New York: Henry Holt, 1948), 134.

50. Jefferson to Caspar Wistar, June 21, 1807, *Founders Online*, https://founders .archives.gov/documents/Jefferson/99-01-02-5789.

51. Throughout most of the nineteenth century, the majority of Americans considered a visit to a doctor as a toss-up if they would emerge better or worse for the effort. Christopher Jencks and David Riesman, *The Academic Revolution* (New York: Doubleday, 1968).

52. John Harley Warner, *The Therapeutic Perspective: Medical Practice, Knowledge and Identity in America* (Cambridge, MA: Harvard University Press, 1986), and *Against the Spirit of System: The French Impulse in Nineteenth Century American Medicine* (Princeton, NJ: Princeton University Press, 1998).

53. All three physicians were graduates of reputable medical schools: Dr. James Craik (1727–1814), University of Edinburgh; Dr. Gustavas Richard Brown (1747–1804), University of Edinburgh; and Dr. Elisha C. Dick (1762–1825), University of Pennsylvania.

54. Howard Markel, "Dec. 14, 1799: The Excruciating Final Hours of President George Washington," *PBS NewsHour*, December 14, 2014.

55. John S. Haller Jr., *American Medicine in Transition, 1840–1910* (Urbana: University of Illinois Press, 1981), 36.

56. Alfredo Morabia, "Louis and the Birth of Clinical Epidemiology," *Journal of Clinical Epidemiology* 49 (1996): 1327–33; A. Morabia, "Pierre-Charles-Alexandre and the Evaluation of Bloodletting," *Journal of the Royal Society of Medicine* 99, no. 3 (2006): 158–60, and D. P. Thomas, "The Demise of Bloodletting," *Journal of the Royal College of Physicians of Edinburgh* 44 (2014): 72–77. In a follow-up study, "Observations on the Restorative Treatment of Pneumonia," *British Medical Journal* (1866): 627–30, John Hughes Bennett provided additional evidence that reinforced Louis's findings, and concluded that "supporting and restoring the nutritive powers of the system, and avoiding all weakening remedies (poor diet, bleeding, tartar emetics, narcotics, etc.) ought to constitute the practice in pneumonia."

57. In the inaugural edition of this textbook in 1892, Osler on page 530 wrote, "[d]uring the first five decades of this century the profession bled too much, but during the last decades we have certainly bled too little. Pneumonia is one of the diseases in which a timely venesection may save life. To be of service it should be done early . . . the abstraction from twenty to thirty ounces of blood is in every way beneficial." In his 1902 edition, Osler recommended bloodletting in pneumonia (135), yellow fever (189), sun stroke (398), emphysema (659), heart disease and arteriosclerosis (731, 775), and cerebral hemorrhage (1012).

58. Jefferson's critical attitude toward hospital-based care in eighteenth-century America may have been partially shaped by his experience in Paris while serving as minister to France from 1785 to 1789. He gained firsthand knowledge of the d'Hotel-Dieu in Paris, an ancient municipal hospital with a deplorably high mortality rate—so high that the hospital was known as "the gateway to death," "the antechamber to the mortuary," or "Hotel-Mort."

59. Charles E. Rosenberg, *The Care of Strangers: The Rise of America's Hospital System* (New York: Basic Books, 1987).

60. *Notes*, Query XIV, 134.

61. Jefferson to Joseph C. Cabell, May 16, 1824, *Founders Online*, https://founders.archives.gov/documents/Jefferson/98-01-02-4271.

62. The views of Jefferson and Du Pont on social welfare and the treatment of the sick and poor were remarkably similar and are revealed by comparing their writings, especially Jefferson's *Notes*, Query XIV, 133–34, and de Nemours's *Ideas on the Nature, Form and Extent of Assistance to Give the Sick Poor in a Large City* that was published in 1786 at the behest of the Paris Academy of Science. On November 5, 1787, *PTJ*, 12:325–27, du Pont sent Jefferson a copy of his paper and wrote, "I congratulate myself for having confirmed several principles which I found in your Notes on Virginia" (translated).

63. Courtney R. Hall, "Jefferson on the Medical Theory and Practice of His Day," *Bulletin of the History of Medicine* I, no. 3 (1957): 235–45.

64. Jefferson to Reverend Dr. G. C. Jenner, May 14, 1806, *Founders Online*, https://founders.archives.gov/documents/Jefferson/99-01-02-3718.

65. Ibid. See also Jefferson to Judge Thomas Cooper, August 6, 1810, *PTJRS*, 2:667–68.

66. Roy J. Honeywell, *The Educational Work of Thomas Jefferson* (Cambridge, MA: Harvard University Press, 1931), 54–66. See, e.g., Jefferson to Chevalier Quesney de Beaurepaire, January 6, 1788, *PTJ*, 12:499–500; to Francois D'Ivernois, February 6, 1795, *PTJ*, 28:262–63; to John Adams, February 6, 1795, *PTJ*, 28:261–62; to Marc Auguste Pictet, February 5, 1803, *PTJ*, 39:456–57; and to Peter Carr, September 7, 1814, *PTJRS*, 7:636–42.

67. In "The Literary Foundation of the University of Virginia" letter to Peter Carr, September 7, 1814, *PTJRS*, 7:636–42, Jefferson articulated his vision for a capstone university that encompassed "professional schools." While Jefferson saw a need for some education in basic anatomy and the theory of medicine for all collegiate students, he clearly expected those pursuing a career in medical practice to be thoroughly trained in all medical sciences, including morbid anatomy, physiology, pathology, chemistry, materia medica and pharmacy, principles of surgery, and the history of the theories and practice of medicine. In earlier letters to Joseph Priestley, January 18, 1800, *PTJ*, 31:319–23, and to du Pont de Nemours, April 12, 1800, *PTJ*, 31:495–96, Jefferson revealed his advanced ideas about the character and function of a modern university. See also later letters to Littleton Walker Tazewell, January 5, 1805, *Founders Online*, https://founders.archives.gov/documents/Jefferson/99-01-02-0958; to José Corrêa da Serra, October 24, 1820, *Founders Online*, https://founders.archives.gov/documents/Jefferson/98-01-02-1608; to Judge Spencer Roane, March 9, 1821, *Founders Online*, https://founders.archives.gov/documents/Jefferson/98-01-02-1900; and to Edward Livingstone, March 25, 1825, *Founders Online*, https://founders.archives.gov/documents/Jefferson/98-01-02-5077. The academic structure of the University of Virginia is well described in the Minutes of the Board of Visitor's Meeting of October 4–5, 1824, *Founders Online*, https://founders.archives.gov/documents/Jefferson/98-01-02-4598.

68. Jefferson's emphasis on the importance of the environment of learning for professional training presaged the eloquent argument of Cardinal John Henry Newman in his classic book, *The Idea of a University* (London: Longmans, Green and Co., 1852).

69. Virtually every medical school in early to mid-nineteenth-century America was a "closed corporation" administered and controlled entirely by the physician owners—a

situation that was akin to "an *imperium in imperio*" (an empire within an empire) with college and university functionaries assuming little or no control over such matters as the medical curriculum, qualifications and instructional rigor of the teachers, proof of learning by students, and the collection of fees. Medical schools were "essentially private ventures, money making in spirit and object." See Flexner Report, vii, 7, 8, and 12; Ludmerer, *Learning to Heal*, 14–15; and Rothstein, *American Medical Schools*, 29.

70. The lecture schedule and tuition fee system encouraged students to take up studies in three schools. In the Regulations Adopted by the Board of Visitors of the University of Virginia, April 7, 1824, the graduated fees were described: if the student attends one school, he is required to pay $50; if two, $30 each; and if three or more, $25 each. The lecture schedule for all eight schools was set up so there would be no conflicts. In the Regulations Adopted on October 4, 1824, it was stated, "No two of them shall be holden at the same time."

71. Academic instruction occurred on the first floor of each pavilion. The second-floor apartments housed the professor and his family. In 1827, a three-story building, the Anatomical Hall, was completed and dedicated to medical instruction.

72. Flexner Report, 82.

73. Ludmerer, *Learning to Heal*, 5, 38–43. This work by Ludmerer, although widely acclaimed, is for the most part a sectional history that focused on northeastern schools (e.g., Penn, Harvard, Columbia, etc.), Michigan, and Johns Hopkins, and largely ignored southern schools.

74. No educator in America realized more fully than Jefferson that his often-repeated purpose of the University—to teach "all the branches of science useful to us, and ... in their highest degree"—could be fulfilled only by the work of a superior faculty, "either the ablest which America or Europe can furnish, or none at all." Jefferson to Dr. Thomas Cooper, January 16, 1814, *PTJRS*, 7:124–31 and 606–07, Jefferson to William Short, October 31, 1819, *Founders Online*, https://founders.archives.gov/documents/Jefferson/98-01-02-0850. See also Jefferson to Dr. Thomas Cooper, August 25, 1814, *PTJRS*, 7:606–07, and to Joseph C Cabell, February 3, 1824, *Founders Online*, https://founders.archives.gov/documents/Jefferson/98-01-02-4018; and Honeywell, *Educational Work of Thomas Jefferson*, 88–105.

75. An excellent example of the antipathy toward research involved Dr. Silas Weir Mitchell (1829–1914) who, after studying at the University of Pennsylvania (collegiate department), received his MD degree from Jefferson Medical College of Philadelphia in 1850. He then studied physiology in Paris under Claude Bernard, and set up a private physiology laboratory in Philadelphia, where he quickly established his prowess in experimental research. Despite these accomplishments that garnered him international celebrity, he suffered great disappointment when he was twice denied a professorship at the University of Pennsylvania (1863) and his alma mater (1868). Simply stated, Mitchell's interest and expertise in physiological research, rather than clinical practice, was a major impediment to his appointment at two medical schools in the 1860s. Of note, Mitchell came to be known as the most distinguished American physiologist in the period before the establishment of university laboratories at Johns Hopkins and Harvard, and was cofounder the American Physiological Society in 1887 where he sought to facilitate the careers of young scientific physicians. He also served as president of the Asso-

ciation of American Physicians (1887) and the American Neurological Association (1908–1909), and is considered to be the father of neurology in America. See Ludmerer, *Learning to Heal*, 25; W. Bruce Fye, "S. Weir Mitchell, Philadelphia's Lost Physiologist," *Bulletin of the History of Medicine* 57, no. 2 (1983): 188–202; and Anna R. Burr, *S. Weir Mitchell: His Life and Letters* (New York: Duffield, 1929), 129.

76. Jefferson's expectations of his inaugural professoriate is amply described in letters he wrote to: Dr. Joseph Priestley, January 18, 1800, *PTJ*, 31:319–23; Richard Rush, April 26, 1824, *Founders Online*, https://founders.archives.gov/documents/Jefferson/98-01-02-4218; Peter Carr, September 7, 1814, *PTJRS*, 7:636–42; William Short, October 31, 1819, *Founders Online*, https://founders.archives.gov/documents/Jefferson/98-01-02-0850; John Adams, July 9, 1819, *Founders Online*, https://founders.archives.gov/documents/Adams/99-02-02-7176; Joseph C. Cabell, February 3, 1824, *Founders Online*, https://founders.archives.gov/documents/Jefferson/98-01-02-4018; and Dugald Stewart, April 26, 1824, *Founders Online*, https://founders.archives.gov/documents/Jefferson/98-01-02-4219. See also Herbert B. Adams, *Thomas Jefferson and the University of Virginia*, U.S. Bureau of Education Circular of Information, No. 1 (1888): 109–12.

77. Jefferson to Joseph C. Cabell, February 3, 1824, *Founders Online*, https://founders.archives.gov/documents/Jefferson/98-01-02-4018. Jefferson specifically mentioned the College of Philadelphia and Edinburgh University, which had "lost it's character of primacy by indulging motives of favoritism and nepotism, and by conferring appointments as if the professorships were entrusted to them as provisions for their friends." Jefferson goes on to propose *Detur digniori* (let it be given to the more worthy) as the sacred motto that he and the Board of Visitors should subscribe to in the selection of professors.

78. The concept of total devotion to academic life was first expressed in a letter to Joseph Priestley, January 18, 1800, *PTJ*, 31:319–23: "[W]e should propose that the professors follow no other calling, so that their whole time may be given to their academic functions." In the same letter, Jefferson announced his interest in recruiting European scholars if no one in America could be found who was able to meet his stringent standards. When the Board of Visitors hired Robley Dunglison from England as chair of the Medical Department, Jefferson was severely criticized in northern newspapers and medical journals. The most hurtful animus came from Dr. Nathaniel Chapman, of the University of Pennsylvania and editor in chief of the most prominent medical journal in America.

79. The resolution to restrict clinical practice was first adopted by the Board of Visitors on April 7, 1824, and was restated and passed on March 5, 1825, and October 3, 1825. This restrictive policy proved to be a significant recruitment barrier, although one that was effectively overcome. In a letter to Jefferson, dated August 27, 1824, Francis Walker Gilmer, who had been sent to Britain to recruit faculty for the University of Virginia, wrote from London, "I have had more persons recommended for anatomy [and medicine] than for any other place; but immediately they find they will not be allowed to practice medicine &c. abroad, they decline proceeding farther. That I fear will prove an insurmountable obstacle to us in this department." *Founders Online*, https://founders.archives.gov/documents/Jefferson/98-01-02-4493. Also William P. Trent, "English Culture in Virginia: A Study of the Gilmer Letters," in *Johns Hopkins University Studies in Historical and Political Science*, ed. Herbert B. Adams (Baltimore: N. Murray, 1889), 94.

80. Ludmerer, *Learning to Heal*, 125.

81. Regulations adopted by the Board of Visitors of the University of Virginia, October 3–5, 1824. The length of each academic session at Virginia was far greater than at many European universities, and it was, at least initially, a recruitment barrier at the University of Virginia.

82. It has often been said that these dates were chosen to avoid conflicts with seedtime and harvest, and because it was easier to preserve cadavers in the wintertime. By 1850, terms had been lengthened at some of the thirty-six medical schools then in existence; however, the vast majority (72 percent) were eighteen weeks or less, two were five months (University of Pennsylvania, Columbia College of Physicians and Surgeons of New York), and two were longer (seven months at Michigan and ten months at Virginia). See Davis, *History of Medical Education*, 135.

83. Jefferson to Dr. Robley Dunglison, November 26, 1825, *Founders Online*, https://founders.archives.gov/documents/Jefferson/98-01-02-5687, and to Joel Barlow, December 10, 1807, *Founders Online*, https://founders.archives.gov/documents/Jefferson/99-01-02-6952. In a letter to Elizabeth Trist, November 23, 1816, *PTJRS*, 10:545–46, discussing collegiate education generally, Jefferson said, "as far as I am acquainted with the colleges and academies of the US . . . I have found their method of instruction very superficial & imperfect, carrying their pupils over the ground like racehorses, to please their parents and draw custom to their school." Jefferson's comments to Trist singled out Princeton.

84. Jefferson to Elizabeth Trist, November 23, 1816, *PTJRS*, 10:545–46.

85. Philip A. Bruce, *History of the University of Virginia, 1819–1919* (New York: Macmillan Co., 1922), 2:115, and Ludmerer, *Learning to Heal*, 12.

86. Andrew J. Hart, "Thomas Jefferson's Influence on the Foundations of Medical Instruction at the University of Virginia," *Annuals of Medical History* 10 (1938): 56, and Murray, "Thomas Jefferson and Medicine," 152.

87. "Rockfish Gap Report of the University of Virginia Commissioners," August 4, 1818, *PTJRS*, 13:217. Several letters from Jefferson reveal his belief that "experience alone brings skill," that "all theory must yield to experience," and "a little experience is worth a great deal of reading." Jefferson to William H. Crawford, February 14, 1815, *PTJRS*, 8:258–60; to James Maury, June 16, 1815, *PTJRS*, 8:542–45; to Mary Jefferson Eppes, October 26, 1801, *PTJ*, 35:510–11. Also to George Fleming, December 29, 1815, *PTJRS*, 9:302–4.

88. Jefferson to Dr. John Patten Emmet, May 2, 1826, *Founders Online*, https://founders.archives.gov/documents/Jefferson/98-01-02-6087. Emmet was among the eight original faculty members at the University. He received his MD from Columbia College of Physicians and Surgeons of New York in 1822 and taught chemistry, botany, materia medica, and pharmacy between 1825 and 1842. He, along with his colleague, Dr. Robley Dunglison, was instrumental in clarifying the physiological basis of digestion while teaching at the University of Virginia.

89. Jefferson to Joseph C. Cabell, May 16, 1824, *Founders Online*, https://founders.archives.gov/documents/Jefferson/98-01-02-4271 (emphasis added). Although the medical school of the University of Virginia would come under attack for its "wholly inade-

quate clinical facilities," this criticism, often self-serving and at times vicious, is somewhat unfounded. In the vast majority of early nineteenth-century-American medical schools, instruction was almost entirely didactic. Very few schools offered any meaningful clinical experience and the inevitable outcome was that students would graduate "without ever having attended a delivery, without witnessing an operation, and often without having examined a patient." Ludmerer, *Learning to Heal*, 12–13. See also Rothstein, *American Medical Schools*, 34.

90. Ralph C. Williams, *The United States Public Health Service, 1798–1950* (Washington, DC, 1951), 27, 40, and 69–70. See also W. E. Rooney, "Thomas Jefferson and the New Orleans Marine Hospital," *Journal of Southern History* 22, no. 2 (1956): 167–82.

91. During Jefferson's presidency, it has been estimated that 57,287 seamen received treatment at government-owned Marine hospitals. Williams, *United States Public Health Service*, 40.

92. C. Edward Koop, "Remarks to the Students and Faculty of the George Washington University School of Medicine," Washington, DC, April 23, 1986.

93. This series of lectures entitled *The History of the Progress and Theories of Medicine* was one of seven courses that made up the inaugural medical school curriculum at the University of Virginia. These lectures given by Robley Dunglison were published posthumously in 1872 by his son, Richard Dunglison, MD. See Robley Dunglison, *History of Medicine from the Earliest Ages to Commencement of the Nineteenth Century* (Philadelphia: Lindsay and Blakiston, 1872), and Wilhelm Moll, "University of Virginia's 'Firsts' in the History of Medical Education," *Virginia Medical Monthly* 95 (1968): 158–61.

94. Jefferson to Robert Skipwith, August 3, 1771, *PTJ*, 1:77.

95. *Notes*, Query XIV, 148.

96. Murray, "Thomas Jefferson and Medicine," 153. The *History of Physick* was published in two volumes in 1725 and gained Friend the reputation as the first English medical historian. In Hermann F. Kilian's survey of German universities of 1828, Kurt Sprengel was viewed as the finest, most learned and erudite professor in Germany, a keen classical scholar who was an outspoken critic of speculative medical theories. His "pragmatic" *History of Medicine*, published in 1800, was written to present the medical past with all its errors and pitfalls, in the hope that these aberrations would provide valuable lessons and reveal the basic truths on which a more rational medicine could be developed. His writing deemphasized the strictly biographical aspects, stressing instead the connections between medicine and contemporary cultural and philosophical forces.

97. To help medical and law students in their study of medical jurisprudence, the University published the course syllabus in 1827, nine years before publication of Traill's *Outlines of a Course of Lectures on Medical Jurisprudence*. See Radbill, "Autobiographical Ana of Robley Dunglison," 36, 58, 137, 196.

98. In contrast to conditions at other medical schools, particularly the proprietary for-profit schools, professors at the University of Virginia were expected to protect the sanctity of the coveted MD degree. Jefferson knew that the possession of a diploma from most medical schools in America was not proof of merit, and he took steps to avoid this circumstance at his University. This was accomplished, in part, by enforcing strict

attendance requirements, maintaining detailed class participation records for each student, and regularly reporting results to the chairman of the faculty. Any student who neglected his responsibility to attend each and every class, actively participate in all didactic and experiential exercises, and demonstrate a satisfactory "scale of preparation" throughout the ten-month-long academic term would be subject to censure, including summary suspension from the school. Regulations Adopted by the Board of Visitors of the University of Virginia, October 3–4, 1824. See also Bruce, *History*, 2:132; Ludmerer, *Learning to Heal*, 3, 12; and Rothstein, *American Medical Schools*, 32.

99. Professors were expected to recapitulate the main points at the end of each lecture and encourage their students during their evening study to buttress their understanding through independent investigation of textbook material, some of which required visits to the library. Bruce, *History*, 2:129, and Robley Dunglison, "College Instruction and Discipline," *American Quarterly Review* XVIII (1831): 310.

100. While it is not well known, Jefferson was instrumental in the design and construction of a spacious Anatomical Hall, a chemistry laboratory, and a small dispensary attached to the Anatomical Hall where students had an opportunity to examine ambulatory patients and learn the scientific methods of pharmaceutical compounding, of "bringing together ingredients to make pills and potions." Jefferson's design for the Anatomical Hall had many features similar to the work of Vidus Vidius (Latinized name for Guido Guidi). In particular, Jefferson's design was of octagonal shape and there was much emphasis on strong lighting. See D. Puzio, "The Anatomical Theatre (1825–1939)," *Juel* (June 8, 2015), http://juel.iath.virginia.edu/node/242.

101. Dunglison, "College Instruction," 312–13.

102. Each medical student ranked in the top quartile also had to be declared eminent by the Committee of Professors. Other factors woven into this included students' performance in the classroom throughout their careers at the University, a satisfactory grade on both the Latin and English exams, and recognition that they were honorable men of high moral achievement. If all these conditions were met, the name of the student was presented to the Board of Visitors for a final decision.

103. Regulations Adopted by the Board of Visitors of the University of Virginia, April 7, 1824. This requirement was later substituted with an English composition exam.

104. Charles C. Wall, "Students and Student Life at the University of Virginia: 1825–1861" (PhD diss., University of Virginia, 1978), 57.

105. Paul B. Barringer, "A History of the Medical Department of the University of Virginia: It System of Education, and its Results. An Address delivered before the Students and Alumni," October 25, 1887.

106. It was not until 1828 that the University graduated its first class of medicine. All told, that year there were only three students who met all of the necessary criteria for the MD degree; these students had studied an average of thirty-three months and received certificates of proficiency in four different academic departments.

107. Farcical in that the exams were held in private and included "a brief set of casual perfunctory oral questions," and the system "utterly forbade the conscientious elimination of the incompetent and unfit." See Ludmerer, *Learning to Heal*, 3, 12; and Flexner Report, 7, 10. For a further description of the farcical form of exams at most American

schools, and how different were the examinations in the medical school at the University of Virginia, see Dunglison, "College Instruction," 306, 309–13.

108. Bigelow, *Medical Education*, 79; Warner, *Against the Spirit of System*, 19, and Ludmerer, *Learning to Heal*, 3, 12.

109. Bruce, *History*, 2:135–37.

110. The practice of granting honorary degrees dated back to the Middle Ages; the earliest honorary degree on record was awarded to Lionel Woodville by the University of Oxford. When one examines the history of colleges and universities in America, it is clear the vast majority have granted honorary degrees. The very few who have rejected this practice as a matter of policy since their inception include the University of Virginia, Massachusetts Institute of Technology (MIT), Stanford, Cornell, and Rice University. Of note, William Barton Rogers (1804–1882) was a geologist, physicist, and educator at the University of Virginia from 1835 to 1853; in 1861, he founded MIT, where he implemented several of Jefferson's ideas, including the elective system and his policy of no honorary degrees.

111. Norwood, *Medical Education*, 33.

112. William B. Bean, "Jefferson's Influence on American Medical Education," *Virginia Medical Monthly* 87 (1960): 670; and Murray, "Thomas Jefferson and Medicine," 151. See also Jefferson to Henry Dearborn, June 22, 1807, *Founders Online*, https://founders.archives.gov/documents/Jefferson/99-01-02-5793; to Peter Carr, September 7, 1814, *PTJRS*, 7:636–42; and a letter from N. H. R. Dawson, Commissioner of the Bureau of Education, to the Honorable Secretary of the Interior, December 9, 1887, as cited in Herbert B. Adams, *Thomas Jefferson and the University of Virginia*, U.S. Bureau of Education Circular of Information No. 1 (1888): 9–13. The University of Virginia was not the first state-supported public university founded in America. In terms of chronology, Virginia, chartered in 1819, was a later creation than the state "universities" of Georgia (1785), North Carolina (1789), Vermont (1791), Tennessee (1794), South Carolina (1801), and Ohio (1804). But Virginia, although later in terms of founding, was truly in advance of the others in its institutional characteristics that gave it a distinctively university flavor and was the first and only one that offered rigorous instruction in the medical sciences from its inception.

113. Bean, "Jefferson's Influence," 670, and Murray, "Thomas Jefferson and Medicine," 151.

114. Rockfish Gap Report, August 4, 1818, *PTJRS*, 13:221.

115. Jefferson to: Destutt de Tracy, December 26, 1820, *Founders Online*, https://founders.archives.gov/documents/Jefferson/98-01-02-1704; Peter Carr, September 7, 1814, *PTJRS*, 7:636–42. Also Jefferson to: Joseph Priestley, January 18, 1800, *PTJ*, 31:319–23; John Adams, June 15, 1813, *PTJ*, 6:193–95.

116. It has been argued that medical schools have a greater fiduciary responsibility than any other school within an institution of higher education. In addressing this question, Flexner wrote, "In no other situation does education more closely touch the individual and society than the quality of medical training. Not only the personal well-being of each citizen, but national, state, and municipal sanitation, rests upon the quality [and completeness] of training that the medical graduate has received." Flexner Report, xv.

117. Rothstein, *American Medical Schools*, 31–32.

118. Rockfish Gap Report, August 4, 1818, *PTJRS*, 13:179, et seq.

119. Meeting Minutes of the University of Virginia Board of Visitors, March 4–5, 1825, *Founders Online*, https://founders.archives.gov/documents/Jefferson/98-01-02-5019; Meeting Minutes of the University of Virginia Board of Visitors, October 4–5, 1824, https://rotunda.upress.virginia.edu/founders/default.xqy?keys=FOEA-print-04-02-02 -4598.

120. As one example, in a letter to Jefferson, May 26, 1817, *PTJRS*, 11:382–85, John Adams wrote about the "noble triumvirate" of Jefferson, Madison, and Monroe, and its value in fostering the creation of the University, that "the World will expect Something very great and very new." To this, he added his grim prophecy that "if it contains anything quite original, and very excellent, I fear the prejudices too deeply rooted to Suffer it to last long, though it may be accepted at first. It will not always have three Such colossal reputations to Support it."

121. Flexner and Jefferson believed that true wisdom requires practice saturated with humanistic principles. See Flexner Report, 26; letter from Abraham Flexner to Simon Flexner, May 18, 1925, in Simon Flexner papers (in the archives of the American Philosophical Society, Philadelphia); Abraham Flexner, *Medical Education: A Comprehensive Study* (New York: Macmillan, 1925), 18; Abraham Flexner, "The problem of College Pedagogy," *Atlantic Monthly* 103 (1909): 838–44; and Jean M. Yarbrough, *American Virtues: Thomas Jefferson on the Character of Free People* (Lawrence: University Press of Kansas, 1998).

122. Flexner Report, 143. Much like Flexner, Jefferson, reflecting Enlightenment ideals, viewed science as progressive, always moving forward, with no ceiling on discovery. In his 1818 *Report of the Commissioners*, when contemplating the evolutionary nature of knowledge, Jefferson wrote, "and it cannot be but that each generation succeeding to the knowledge acquired by all those who preceded it, adding to it their own acquisitions & discoveries, and handing the mass down for successive & constant accumulation, must advance the knowledge & well-being of mankind: not infinitely, as some have said, but indefinitely, and to a term which no one can fix and foresee." Rockfish Gap Report, August 4, 1818, *PTJRS*, 13:213. And in a letter to Samuel Kercheval, July 12, 1816, *PTJRS*, 10:222–28, Jefferson wrote, "[L]aws and institutions must go hand in hand with the progress of the human mind . . . institutions must advance also, and keep pace with the times . . . and [no] civilised society [should] remain ever under the regimen of their barbarous ancestors." See also Jefferson to James Madison, September 6, 1789, in which Jefferson said, "[T]he earth belongs in usufruct to the living," *PTJ*, 12:382–88; to John Vaughan, February 5, 1815, *PTJRS*, 8:247–48; to John Adams, August 1, 1816, *PTJRS*, 10:284–86; and to Spencer Roane, March 9, 1821, *Founders Online*, https://founders .archives.gov/documents/Jefferson/98-01-02-1900.

123. The University of Virginia with its School of Medicine was chartered on January 25, 1819, but did not begin classroom instruction until March 1825. On this date, the following medical schools were in operation, listed from oldest to newest: University of Pennsylvania, College of Physicians and Surgeons of Columbia University, Harvard University, Dartmouth College, University of Maryland, Yale University,

Brown University, College of Physicians and Surgeons of the Western District of New York (extinct, 1840), Medical Department of Transylvania University (extinct, 1859), Castleton Medical Academy of Vermont (extinct, 1861), Medical College of Ohio, Medical School of Maine of Bowdoin Coll. (extinct, 1921), University of Vermont, Berkshire Medical Institution of Massachusetts (extinct,1867), and the Medical College of South Carolina.

"At All Times His Chosen Companions"

Some Notes on What Books Meant to Thomas Jefferson

JURRETTA JORDAN HECKSCHER

THOMAS JEFFERSON's granddaughter Ellen Randolph Coolidge was in many respects his most kindred spirit in his immediate family, the one whose acuity of intellect and subtlety of reflection most closely mirrored his own. She loved him deeply, and allowed him to inhabit her inner world so completely that in her later years, as she once wrote, when she dreamed, it was most often of him.[1] It is significant, then, that when she began to describe him as she best remembered him—in the years of his retirement—she thought of him first with books. "He seemed to return to private life with great satisfaction," she recalled. "[H]is love of reading alone would have made leisure and retirement delightful to him. Books were at all times his chosen companions. . . ."[2]

"Books were at all times his chosen companions." Among the millions of words that have been written about Thomas Jefferson and books, these may be among the most suggestive, not for what they say about Jefferson's intellectual life, but for what else they invite us to discover about how this man who could not live without books chose to live with them. For Thomas Jefferson, books were literal companions, a near-constant physical presence that he sought to fit to his bodily needs. They were also constant instruments of human companionship, purposefully directed toward nurturing those personal relationships that most deeply nourished his own soul. And throughout his life, he used books to order the experience of time, intimately integrating both the rhythms of the day and the seasons of life into the pursuit of knowledge and wisdom, delight and consolation.

Let us look more closely at what books meant to Jefferson in each of these ways, all of which give context to his design for his University's curriculum and library.

"Turning Over Every Book with My Own Hands": Books as Physical Objects

When Jefferson offered to sell his Monticello Library to Congress to replace the library the British had burned during the War of 1812, he described its creation in terms of his body and its gestures: "[W]hile residing in Paris I devoted every afternoon I was disengaged, for a summer or two, in examining all the principal bookstores, turning over every book with my own hands, and putting by every thing which related to America, and indeed whatever was rare & valuable in every science."[3] Although he was known to praise a bookseller's "tasty" bindings, he had little interest in books as aesthetic objects. They were instruments to be used—by the mind, but also by the body: to be lifted, and held, and handled, and carried, and scrutinized by eye for hours on end.[4] And in that respect, their physical identity mattered greatly. "I disclaim all pompous editions and all typographical luxury," he wrote to a favorite English book dealer, "but I like a fine white paper, neat type, and neat binding. . . ." And in matters of size, his preferences were unequivocal: "When I do not name the edition," he instructed, "never send a folio or quarto if there exists an 8vo. or smaller edition. I like books of a handy size."[5] When he traveled, he traveled with books, a fact that after 1786 combined with his partially crippled wrist to render his preference for octavos and duodecimos inveterate. Eventually, he had what was in effect a traveling library of these "petit format" editions, which he brought to his vacation home at Poplar Forest.[6] That many such books were pirated Dublin editions printed beyond the reach of English copyright law concerned him not at all.[7]

Jefferson's physical respect for books is manifest not only in the great care he took to arrange and house the volumes he owned, but in the restraint he exercised in marking them. Although he occasionally wrote brief notes in them, typically in cross-reference or correction, most of his books are marked only by his personal sign of ownership: a "T" in front of the letter "I" (which also stood for "J") identifying the book's ninth group of pages: TI for TJ, Thomas Jefferson; and where there was a nineteenth such gathering, a handwritten "I" after its letter "T."[8] Yet when he felt it necessary for physical comfort or intellectual convenience, he quite literally cut books down to size. As Millicent Sowerby wrote, numerous publications "issued as quartos or folios but destined by him to be bound in octavo volumes, had . . . their margins . . . cut to the quick if necessary and the leaves folded to fit into the smaller covers." Likewise, "[b]inders were instructed to divide volumes into two parts if too large for Jefferson to hold comfortably, and to bind the two parts separately."[9] Books were his chosen companions, but he was willing to force them to his needs.

Sowerby's words remind us that Jefferson not only wrote books for publication—the *Notes on Virginia*, the *Manual of Parliamentary Practice*, three translations of French philosophy, and a volume of legal argument—he also *made* books, in a most physical sense.[10] The best known is his *Life and Morals of Jesus of Nazareth*, those portions of the Gospels that he could accept in old age, cut from printed Bibles in four languages, pasted to create parallel texts, and bound. Yet there were several others: his so-called Literary Commonplace Book, literary and philosophical passages he transcribed throughout his early life and later culled and bound; similar Legal and Equity Commonplace Books, for his study of the law; and several volumes of poetry and other texts clipped from newspapers, pasted on scrap paper and assembled for his granddaughters in his presidential years. He tore apart books of Latin and Greek literature to rebind them interleaved with modern translations; he bound together scores of political pamphlets to create volumes of the history he and his peers had made; and in retirement, he gleefully showed friends tales of royal scandal, bound to make a single work on the turpitude of kings.[11] In a culture where private manuscripts differed from printed publications across a continuum of forms, and most printed books were purchased unbound, Jefferson's physical interventions were less idiosyncratic than they would be today.[12] Together, they disclose how deeply books companioned the whole of his life, from his youthful search for meaning, to his professional training, to his years of political combat and the balms for it he found in family and the arts, to his lifelong quest for a religion equal to the power of his mind and the demands of his heart.

Not long before his marriage, when Monticello was still but modestly habitable, Jefferson invited a friend to come there and "reach your hand to a library formed on a more extensive plan."[13] He could never imagine living where his books were not in easy reach, and when his house grew big, he chose to live in the midst of his library. That spatial intimacy was matched by furniture, including a revolving armchair that allowed him to direct his attention simultaneously to the contents of several books.[14] Isaac Granger Jefferson, Monticello's enslaved blacksmith, described the practice that such a piece was meant to serve: "Old master had abundance of books: sometimes would have twenty of 'em down on the floor at once: read fust one, then tother."[15] It has been said that "Jefferson interacted with his books as if in an intellectual dialogue"—but in fact, it was often less a dialogue than a consort of voices, like the chamber music in which he took such deep delight.[16]

"So Much Indebted to Your Friendship":
Books as Instruments of Sociability

We may think of him thus, alone with his books—and so he often was. Yet it is striking how assiduously he used them to elicit human companionship, across the whole arc of his life. Books were to Thomas Jefferson powerful tools of sociability and community, surpassing the constraints of space and time.

That fact cannot be properly understood without bearing in mind another: that most members of Jefferson's home communities at Monticello and Poplar Forest—those whose labor made possible all his life in books—were barred from access to books by an illiteracy that carried the weight of pervasive custom, though not of explicit law at that time. Jefferson did nothing to prevent resourceful individuals from learning how to read, but he also made no move to extend literacy to their communities at large.[17] Thus, fundamentally, Monticello was an African American village, most of whose members lived at the foot of the continent's greatest library—and were effectively forbidden its use. Only against that background can this be understood: that Jefferson used books to deepen his companionship with most, if not all, of those who mattered to him most—and thus even the most benign construction of his relationship with Sally Hemings must confront the limits of possibility that her illiteracy represents. Against this background, too, their son Madison Hemings's statement of literacy in late middle age—"I learned to read by inducing the white children [Jefferson's grandchildren] to teach me the letters and something more; what else I know of books I have picked up here and there till now I can read and write"—acquires a poignant eloquence, implicating the primal tragedy that shaped his and his siblings' lives.[18]

For a host of more fortunate others, companionship with Jefferson through books stemmed from his earliest years. As boys, so family tradition recorded, he and his dear friend Dabney Carr would "go with their books to the well-wooded sides of Monticello, and there pursue their studies beneath the shade of a favorite oak."[19] Carr died all too young, but the pattern their friendship discovered persisted through Jefferson's life. Its richest culmination came toward life's close, when he and John Adams healed their friendship through letters, and then made their letters a ceaseless symposium on what they found in books.[20]

One can sometimes locate the start of a Jefferson friendship in the sharing of a book. The best-known example was an evening at Monticello in the waning months of the Revolution when the host and his French visitor "happened to speak of the poetry of Ossian. It was a spark of electricity which passed rapidly from one to the other," this guest remembered; "we recalled the passages of those sublime poems which had particularly struck us, and we recited them. . . . Soon the book . . . was brought forth and placed beside the bowl of punch. And, before we realized it, book and bowl carried us far into the night."[21]

As Jefferson's fame grew, so did his public image as a man of books. Many authors shared their own books with him in hopes of a profitable endorsement—a request that he rarely indulged. "I thank you for the pamphlets you have been so kind as to send me," he told one such applicant in 1825, "but I cannot comply with your request to give my opinion of them. [A]gainst this I have been obliged to protest in every case. I should otherwise, for the last 20. years, have been constantly employed in the trade of a Reviewer of books, for which I have neither taste, talent nor time. . . . no mail comes without bringing me more than I could review before the arrival of the next."[22]

To expose his frank opinions of some books, he had painfully learned, was in fact to risk real damage to the bonds of friendship. Early in 1791, he received a copy of the first part of Thomas Paine's *The Rights of Man*. Forwarding it to a printer at the request of his friend John Beckley, Jefferson also sent a laudatory cover note with an indiscreet comment about "political heresies," by which he unmistakably meant recent writings by John Adams. To his great dismay, the printer included his words in the reprint of Paine's text, leaving Adams in no doubt about what Jefferson had meant. The episode was a milestone on their road to alienation.[23]

Far more valued than books sent in attempts to borrow his prestige were the many he received from scientific, literary, and political luminaries who sought his opinions as an intellectual peer. These opportunities Jefferson cherished, and whether or not the writer was a personal friend already, they often occasioned an exchange of ideas that nurtured ties of friendship and respect. Among these correspondents were men—and a few women—such as Joel Barlow, Pierre Samuel du Pont de Nemours, Joseph Priestley, Mercy Otis Warren, Benjamin Waterhouse, and Frances Wright.[24]

One gift of this sort exemplifies the way that Jefferson used books to extend and strengthen the bonds of sociability. In 1807 his friend the French writer and *salonnière* Madame de Staël sent him a copy of her novel *Corinne*. Later that year, Jefferson loaned it to Lord David Erskine, the British minister in Washington, and Sir Augustus John Foster, secretary to the British Legation. Erskine returned the book a few weeks later, apparently so that Jefferson could lend it to the wife of his friend William Thornton, the architect of the U.S.

Capitol.[25] De Staël's gift to Jefferson had become, in his hands, a gift to at least three others.

Jefferson's library may have been, as another friend said, his private inner sanctum, but he took pride in displaying it to friends and acquaintances and was consistently generous in lending his books, fully recognizing that they might never be returned.[26] In a memorandum concerning his library in the summer of 1773, he duly noted that forty-two volumes were at that time "Lent out."[27] As he implored a young man in 1790, "[t]he losses I have sustained by lending my books will be my apology to you for asking your particular attention to the replacing them in the presses as fast as you finish them, and not to lend them to any body else . . . ." Still, a quarter century later, as he prepared his library for Congress, he had to retrieve volumes from as far afield as Richmond, Philadelphia, and Washington itself.[28]

Throughout his life, Jefferson also bought books for other people, either at their request or on his own initiative. He enlisted a host of European friends and acquaintances to help him build his incomparable collection, yet the number of book-acquisition tasks he undertook for others greatly exceeded his own requests.[29] One such task changed the course of history. "I have had leisure to review the literary cargo for which I am so much indebted to your friendship," James Madison wrote him in 1786. "The collection is perfectly to my mind." When Madison went to Philadelphia the following year, those books had shaped his constitutional thought.[30]

And within the circle of his acknowledged family, Jefferson made the sharing of books both an intergenerational responsibility and an enactment of love. "Inform me what books you read," he enjoined his young daughter in his first letter to her; and his granddaughter recalled that "[h]e interested himself in all we . . . read," advising his grandchildren on what to read, questioning them about their reading, and sometimes "read[ing] aloud to us from his own book, some passage which had struck him." When political commitments drew him from home, another grandchild remembered, "[w]henever an opportunity occurred, he sent us books." And when five-year-old Ellen learned how to read, her grandfather expressed his delight by sending her "two little books . . . and if you continue to learn as fast," he assured her, "you will become a learned lady and publish books yourself."[31]

The financial catastrophe that followed Jefferson's death required even his books to be sold for his debts. His family's urgent efforts to purchase them back suggest how precious they had become as tokens of him. As one grandson-in-law implored another, sounding a frantic note, "I beg you to interest your-self in my behalf in relation to the books; remember that his library will not be sold again, and that all the memorials of T. J. for myself and children, and friends, must be secured now!—this is the last chance!—"[32]

In the end, by sharing the books he loved, Jefferson made them his family's as well, their chosen companions no less than his own. When Cornelia Randolph visited the Library of Congress after her grandfather's death, she was overcome by the sight of "my old friends the books. . . . nevertheless," she reported to her sister, "I staid & stood & thought of the time when the books were ours."[33]

"The Order of Time Will Be Your Guide": Books and the Experience of Time

In one of his letters advising a young kinsman on a course of reading, Jefferson assured him that in approaching the study of history, "the order of time will be your sufficient guide." He meant that history books should be read chronologically by historical period, starting with "[t]he histories of Greece and Rome."[34] The phrase has a more resonant meaning also, however, for it epitomizes a creative project that Jefferson developed throughout his life: using his understanding of time to bring wisdom to his use of books, and using books to enrich—and, in the end, transcend—his experience of time. In particular, he believed that the choice of books to be read throughout the day should be guided by a diurnal rhythm in the powers of the mind—and the choice of books to be read across a lifetime, by natural phases in the arc of human life.

As Hannah Spahn has superbly demonstrated, Jefferson was deeply concerned throughout his life with the nature and meaning of time. "There is hardly a text by Jefferson," she notes, "from his private letters to public documents like the Declaration of Independence, that does not contain reflections on temporality, whether on the level of his personal life or on a collective historical level."[35] A "miser of his time" who unerringly structured it according to "regular and systematic" habits, a man who kept a timepiece in nearly every room of his house and made gold or silver watches his last gifts to his grandchildren, Jefferson actively sought to cultivate the wise use of time both in himself and in those around him.[36] This was particularly true in relation to young people: his (white) children, grandchildren, and other close relatives and friends; his students, protégés, and those who sought his guidance on their educations and careers. As he once told his seventeen-year-old grandson, "I have wished to know what you have entered on, what progress you have made, and how your hours are distributed. [F]or it is only by a methodical distribution of our hours, & a rigorous, inflexible observance of it that any steady progress can be made."[37]

From young manhood through old age, Jefferson advised dozens of friends on what books they should read, or what books they should ensure that their children read, particularly as formal courses of study, and most especially for education in the law.[38] And in these educational counsels, a particular form of time discipline—the necessity of reading certain kinds of books at certain times of day—is a fundamental theme. For as Jefferson explained to a young law student while still a relatively young man himself, "a great inequality is observable in the vigor of the mind at different periods of the day. [I]t's powers at these periods should therefore be attended to in marshalling the business of the day."[39] There is every reason to suppose that such counsels drew on a discipline applied in his own life.

The time scheme that followed those words is typical: "Till VIII. aclock in the morning employ yourself in Physical studies, Ethics, Religion, natural and sectarian, and Natural law. . . . From VIII. to XII. read Law. . . . From XII. to I. read Politics. . . . In the Afternoon. read History. . . . From Dark to Bed-time. Belles letters. Criticism. Rhetoric. Oratory."[40] Half a century later, the advice was similar: "[I]f you read Law from breakfast 4. or 5. hours," Jefferson told his law student grandson, "enough [time] will remain before dinner for exercise. the morning may be given to natural philosophy and Astronomy, the afternoon to Rhetoric & Belles lettres, and the night to history and ethics."[41] In both these instances, be it noted, there is no phase in the diurnal cycle except the hours of sleep which the student should regard as necessarily exempt from the companionship of books.

As these examples suggest, the daily time schemes for reading that Jefferson recommended were not altogether consistent—but neither were they arbitrary, being guided by his beliefs about "the vigor of the mind at different periods of the day" and the relation of those temporal rhythms to the distinctive demands of the subjects the student was reading. In some instances, Jefferson made those beliefs explicit, sometimes citing his own practices. The "hours the most precious for study," for example, were "those about the middle of the day"; "the afternoon . . . is the best time to spare from your studies" for other activities, such as exercise, and "[t]here are portions of the day too when the mind should be eased. Particularly after dinner it should be applied to lighter occupations"—by which he meant "light reading," less intellectually demanding books.[42]

A sampling of his guidance across the decades to half a dozen law students— as were a majority of the young people to whom such advice was given— suggests how Jefferson applied these principles in practice. The morning is most often assigned to books in the natural sciences; law books invariably and exclusively occupy the late morning and sometimes part of the afternoon; works of history are most often taken up in the evening, though sometimes in the afternoon, and volumes in other subjects, including what would now be considered the humanities, fill out the margins of the day.[43] The evening hours offer the widest choice of suggested subjects, but in old age, at least, Jefferson left no doubt about his own preference of books to complete the daily cycle: "I never go to bed," he wrote, "without an hour, or half hour's previous reading of something moral, whereon to ruminate in the intervals of sleep."[44]

If Jefferson believed that the pattern of the diurnal cycle could be wisely engaged for different kinds of reading, he also became convinced that the books best suited to enrich the mind and heart varied with life's seasons. Through this insight, his choice of books as companions was integral to how he came to understand himself and the shape of his life through time.[45]

He recorded his understanding of the books appropriate to childhood in his *Notes on the State of Virginia.* "There is a certain period of life," he wrote, "say from eight to fifteen or sixteen years of age, when the mind, like the body, is not yet firm enough for laborious and close operations. . . . The memory is then most susceptible and tenacious of impressions; and the learning of languages being chiefly a work of memory, it seems precisely fitted to the powers of this period, which is long enough too for acquiring the most useful languages antient and modern."[46] The early study of language, he wrote elsewhere, "exercises our memory while that and no other faculty is yet matured, and prevents our acquiring habits of idleness."[47]

Equally appropriate to this stage of life, with its impressionable memory, was the study of history as Jefferson first understood it: "[Children's] memories may . . . be stored with the most useful facts from Grecian, Roman, European and American history."[48] Later, however, as Spahn notes, this understanding of history as the work of receptive memory increasingly vied with a more complex understanding better associated with intellectual maturity. Jefferson "began to imagine historical studies as a more active process . . . that . . . involved not only the memory and the senses but also rational 'research and reflection' on the part of both readers and writers."[49]

Childhood for colonial British Americans was traditionally a time of religious instruction, but Jefferson would have none of it for those whose education he designed. Do not, he said, "put[ ] the Bible and Testament into the hands of the children, at an age when their judgments are not sufficiently matured for religious enquiries...." Not until late adolescence, Jefferson believed, was "reason ... mature enough to receive this object." In the meantime, the student should study mathematics, which "gives exercise to our reason, as soon as that has acquired a certain degree of strength, and stores the mind with truths which are useful in other branches of science." A student with a solid foundation in mathematics could then turn to books both of religion and of "Astronomy, Natural philosophy (or Physics) Natural history, Anatomy, Botany and Chemistry."[50]

Sensitive to the ways in which the seasons of life inflected the books proper for others, Jefferson was equally conscious of such rhythms in himself. In no area is this clearer than in his interest in poetry. With striking prescience, he predicted its flow and ebb across his life in his "Thoughts on English Prosody," written in France in the mid-1780s: "When [one is] young any composition pleases which unites a little sense, some imagination, and some rhythm, in doses however small. But as we advance in life these things fall off one by one, and I suspect we are left at last with only Homer and Virgil, perhaps with Homer alone."[51] Though he wrote these words when his interest was still acute enough to sustain the study in which they appear, they proved prophetic. At the age of fifty-eight, he explained that "in earlier life I was fond of [poetry], & easily pleased. [B]ut as [age] & cares advanced, the powers of fancy have declined. [E]very year seems to have plucked a feather from her wing, till she can no longer waft me to those sublime heights to which it is necessary to accompany the poet."[52] His words were something of an overstatement, for the scrapbooks he was even then compiling reflect an active engagement with contemporary verse—but a granddaughter with whom he shared those books confirmed the deeper truth. "In his youth he had loved poetry," she wrote, "but by the time I was old enough to observe, he had lost his taste for it, except for Homer and the great Athenian tragics, which he continued to the last to enjoy."[53]

Jefferson's love of Homer in his final years exemplifies the deepest and most intimate connection he discovered between books and the cycle of life: the value of the ancient classics and mathematics in his passage through old age. It was a theme he proclaimed repeatedly from his retirement to his death. "I have given up newspapers in exchange for Tacitus & Thucydides, for Newton & Euclid," he announced to John Adams in 1812, "& I find myself much the happier."[54] In these later years, Ellen Coolidge recalled, "I saw him more frequently with a volume of the classics in his hand than with any other book," and both his small vacation library at Poplar Forest and the Retirement Library he assembled after his library sale to Congress were distinguished by their emphasis on the works of antiquity.[55]

Certainly, he never ceased to be a maker of libraries, creating at least three and arguably as many as eight of them, depending on the terms of analysis— and his need to establish collection criteria at different stages of his life doubtless deepened his awareness of how his tastes changed over time.[56] For all its depth in the classics, the breadth of his Retirement Library, like the breadth of books he discussed in his correspondence with John Adams, somewhat belies his insistence that books of classics and mathematics were his singular choices in old age.[57] Yet when he offered to sell Congress his Monticello Library, he added a poignant note about what he wished he could withhold: "I should be willing indeed to retain a few of the books to amuse the time I have yet to pass, . . . [T]hey should be restored [to the library] at my death, which I would carefully provide for. . . . [T]hose I should like to retain would be chiefly classical and Mathematical, some few in other branches, & particularly one of the five encyclopedias in the catalogue. [B]ut this, if not acceptable, would not be urged."[58] Jefferson's late-life need for works of classical literature and mathematics was unfeigned, and the eloquence with which he expressed it invites us to consider exactly why those books meant so much.

One source of their meaning is clear: as the end of all time for him approached, these were books not bound by time. "[M]y course of reading, . . ." he said, "is of antient, rather than modern works, those which have come down to us with the approbation of ages, rather than the ephemeral casualties of the press, which have not yet obtained a character. I am old, have little time left for reading, and must therefore be choice of it."[59] When so much else was gone, these works were what remained. The classics had stood the test of time to receive "the approbation of [the] ages"; they had become in a real sense timeless, transcending the limits of history. And works of mathematics disclosed the changeless order of the universe, pointing beyond time to a divine eternity.

Books had always been for Jefferson resources of the imagination, essential to his creative achievements in architecture and landscape art.[60] Now, in old age, they also offered imaginative escape. "[W]ith one foot in the grave, . . ." as he told William Short, "my business is to beguile the wearisomness of declining life, . . . by the delights of classical reading and of Mathematical truths."

When time itself had become the endless cycle of a mill-horse, as he once told Abigail Adams, the companionship of books was his release.[61]

It was also, finally, his great consolation. To read "the Greek & Roman authors in all the beauties of their originals" was a "Luxury . . . and more now than when younger, and more susceptible of delights from other sources, when the decays of age have enfeebled the useful energies of the mind, the classic pages fill up the vacuum of ennui and become sweet composers to that rest of the grave into which we are all, sooner or later, to descend."[62]

In the evenings at Monticello, a granddaughter recalled, "[w]hen the candles were brought, all was quiet immediately, for he took up his book to read . . . and generally we followed his example and took a book—and I have seen him raise his eyes from his own book and look round on the little circle of readers, and smile and make some remark to mamma about it."[63] The bloom of light in night's darkness signaled the opening of books, for to open a book had always been for Jefferson an act of light. And in the end, his books were to him "a lamp to lighten my path thro' the dreary wilderness of time before me," his light in the darkness before death.[64]

Thomas Jefferson died in the suite of rooms that held his library, surrounded by the family that adored him, the enslaved people who served him, and—as Ellen Coolidge noticed—"his books, the beloved companions of his leisure."[65] On the table near his bed were four of them: two political pamphlets and volumes of Aristotle and Seneca—so close, when death came, that he might almost have reached to touch them with his hand.[66]

Notes

An earlier version of this essay was written and presented at the conference in the course of my work as Reference Specialist for Early American History in the Main Reading Room at the Library of Congress. I am grateful to the Library for providing the opportunity for me to begin my exploration of this topic and for allowing me to accept the generous invitation of the Robert H. Smith International Center for Jefferson Studies to make my initial findings available to other scholars and the general public. The essay has also benefited particularly from the generously shared knowledge of Mark Dimunation and Eric Frazier, of the Rare Book and Special Collections Division, Library of Congress; Diane Ehrenpreis, of the Thomas Jefferson Foundation; Endrina Tay, of the Jefferson Library, Monticello; and from the helpful comments of the anonymous reviewers for the Robert H. Smith International Center for Jefferson Studies, Monticello.

1. Ellen Wayles Randolph Coolidge, undated autobiographical fragment, Correspondence of Ellen Wayles Randolph Coolidge, Manuscript Collections, Albert and Shirley Small Special Collections Library, University of Virginia, quoted in Jan Lewis, *The Pursuit of Happiness: Family and Values in Jefferson's Virginia* (New York: Cambridge University Press, 1983), 208.

2. Ellen Wayles Randolph Coolidge (unnamed but since identified) to Henry S. Randall, 185[-], excerpted in Henry S. Randall, *The Life of Thomas Jefferson* (New York: Derby & Jackson, 1858), 3:346.

3. Jefferson to Samuel H. Smith, September 21, 1814, *PTJRS*, 7:681–84.

4. Jefferson to William F. Gray, November 8, 1818, *PTJRS*, 13:368.

5. Jefferson to Thomas Payne, October 2, 1788, *PTJ*: 13:650–52. I am indebted to Mark Dimunation for drawing my attention to this letter.

6. Douglas L. Wilson, *Jefferson's Books*, with a preface by Daniel J. Boorstin (Charlottesville: Thomas Jefferson Memorial Foundation, 1996), 27.

7. Mark Dimunation, "Thomas Jefferson Goes Shopping," Gallery Talk at the Library of Congress, October 14, 2015.

8. Endrina Tay, "Thomas Jefferson and Books," *Encyclopedia Virginia*, https://www.encyclopediavirginia.org/Jefferson_Thomas_and_Books; Wilson, *Jefferson's Books*, 47 (including photo), 52.

9. E. Millicent Sowerby, "Thomas Jefferson and His Library," *Papers of the Bibliographical Society of America* 50 (1956): 219.

10. Thomas Jefferson, *Notes on the State of Virginia* (London: J. Stockdale, 1787); *A Manual of Parliamentary Practice: For the Use of the Senate of the United States* (Washington City: Samuel Harrison Smith, 1801); *A New Translation of Volney's Ruins; or Meditations on the Revolution of Empires. Made under the Inspection of the Author*, 2 vols. (Paris, 1802) (Jefferson translated nearly all this work, but at his request his name appears nowhere in the published volumes, which were associated only with the other translator, Joel Barlow); *A Commentary and Review of Montesquieu's Spirit of Laws, Prepared for the Press from the Original Manuscript, in the Hands of the Publisher...* (Philadelphia: William Duane, 1811); *A Treatise on Political Economy: To Which is Prefixed a Supplement to a Preceding Work on the Understanding: or Elements of Ideology... by the Count Destutt Tracy; Translated from the Unpublished French Original* (Georgetown, DC: J. Milligan, 1817); *The Proceedings of the Government of the United States, in Maintaining the Public Right to the Beach of the Missisipi, adjacent to New-Orleans, against the Intrusion of Edward Livingston. Prepared for the Use of Counsel, by Thomas Jefferson* (New York: Ezra Sargeant, 1812).

11. Dickinson W. Adams and Ruth W. Lester, eds., *Jefferson's Extracts from the Gospels: "The Philosophy of Jesus" and "The Life and Morals of Jesus,"* with an introduction by Eugene R. Sheridan (Princeton, NJ: Princeton University Press, 1983); Douglas L. Wilson, ed., *Jefferson's Literary Commonplace Book* (Princeton, NJ: Princeton University Press, 1989); Jonathan Gross, ed., *Thomas Jefferson's Scrapbooks: Poems of Nation, Family, & Romantic Love Collected by America's Third President* (Hanover, NH: Steerforth Press, 2006); Kevin J. Hayes, *The Road to Monticello: The Life and Mind of Thomas Jefferson* (New York: Oxford University Press, 2008), 504; Mark Dimunation, "'The Whole of Recorded

Knowledge': Jefferson as Collector and Reader," in *The Libraries, Leadership, & Legacy of John Adams and Thomas Jefferson*, ed. Robert C. Baron and Conrad Edick Wright (Golden, CO: Fulcrum; and Boston: Massachusetts Historical Society, 2010), 29; Frederick Goff, "Freedom of Challenge (The 'Great' Library of Thomas Jefferson)," in *Thomas Jefferson and the World of Books: A Symposium Held at the Library of Congress, September 21, 1976* (Washington, DC: The Library, 1977), 14; Wilson, *Jefferson's Books*, 33; George Ticknor, in *Life, Letters and Journals of George Ticknor* (Boston, 1909), excerpt in Merrill D. Peterson, ed., *Visitors to Monticello* (Charlottesville: University Press of Virginia, 1989), 63.

12. See, e.g., David D. Hall, "The Chesapeake in the Seventeenth Century," in *A History of the Book in America*, ed. Hugh Amory and David D. Hall, vol. 1, *The Colonial Book in the Atlantic World* (New York: Cambridge University Press, 2000), 57, 75; and Karen A. Weyler, *Empowering Words: Outsiders and Authorship in Early America* (Athens: University of Georgia Press, 2013), 4, 10–11. Kevin Hayes notes that "[t]he tradition of circulating a written work in manuscript persisted much longer in the South than it did elsewhere in America." Hayes, *Road to Monticello*, 327.

13. Jefferson to Robert Skipwith, August 3, 1771, *PTJ*: 1:76–81.

14. Diane Ehrenpreis and Endrina Tay, "Enlightened Networks: Thomas Jefferson's System for Working from Home," *Transactions of the American Philosophical Society*, volume 109 (forthcoming). I am grateful to the authors for sharing this important article with me in advance of its publication. Notably, it also concludes that the piece of furniture in Jefferson's study long supposed to be a revolving book stand is not in fact suited to holding materials thicker than papers or pamphlets.

15. Isaac [Granger] Jefferson, "Life of Isaac Jefferson of Petersburg, Virginia, Blacksmith," transcription from ms. in the Manuscript Collections, Albert and Shirley Small Special Collections Library, University of Virginia, available online from the *Encyclopedia Virginia*, https://www.encyclopediavirginia.org/_Life_of_Isaac_Jefferson_of _Petersburg_Virginia_Blacksmith_by_Isaac_Jefferson_1847.

16. Dimunation, "'Whole of Recorded Knowledge,'" 28.

17. Lucia C. Stanton, *"Those Who Labor for My Happiness": Slavery at Thomas Jefferson's Monticello* (Charlottesville: University of Virginia Press, 2012), 164–66. For examples of individuals enslaved at Monticello and Poplar Forest who could read and write, see James Hemings, "Inventory of Kitchen Utensils at Monticello, [February 20, 1796]," *PTJ*: 28:610–11; Hannah to Jefferson, November 15, 1818, *PTJRS*, 13:393 and in John W. Blassingame, ed., *Slave Testimony: Two Centuries of Letters, Speeches, Interviews, and Autobiographies* (Baton Rouge: Louisiana State University Press, 1977), 14–15; John Hemmings to Jefferson and to Septimia Randolph (Meikleham), 1825, in Blassingame, *Slave Testimony*, 15–18, and John Hemmings to Jefferson, September 28, 1825, *Founders Online*, https:// founders.archives.gov/documents/Jefferson/98-01-02-5557; and Madison Hemings, interview in *Pike County* (Ohio) *Republican*, March 13, 1873, rpt. in Blassingame, *Slave Testimony*, 478, and online from the *Encyclopedia Virginia*, https://www.encyclopediavirginia .org/_Life_Among_the_Lowly_No_1_by_Madison_Hemings_March_13_1873. For evidence that Jefferson believed that slaves should be taught to read, see Israel [Gillette] Jefferson, interview in *Pike County* (Ohio) *Republican*, December 25, 1873, rpt. in Blassingame, *Slave Testimony*, 486, and online from the *Encyclopedia Virginia*,

https://www.encyclopediavirginia.org/_Life_Among_the_Lowly_No_3_by_Israel
_Jefferson_December_25_1873.

18. Madison Hemings, interview in *Pike County* (Ohio) *Republican*.

19. Sarah N. Randolph, *The Domestic Life of Thomas Jefferson* (New York: Harper &
Brothers, 1871), 45.

20. Lester J. Cappon, ed., *The Adams-Jefferson Letters: The Complete Correspondence
between Thomas Jefferson and Abigail and John Adams*, 2 vols. (Chapel Hill: University of
North Carolina Press for the Institute of Early American History and Culture at Williamsburg, VA, 1959).

21. The Marquis de Chastellux, *Travels in North America in the Years 1780, 1781, and
1782*, trans. and ed. Howard C. Rice Jr., 2 vols. (Chapel Hill: University of North Carolina Press for the Institute of Early American History and Culture, Williamsburg, VA,
1963), excerpt in Peterson, *Visitors to Monticello*, 13.

22. Jefferson to Sheldon Clark, December 5, 1825, *Founders Online*, http://founders
.archives.gov/documents/Jefferson/98-01-02-5716.

23. Gordon S. Wood, *Friends Divided: John Adams and Thomas Jefferson* (New York:
Penguin Press, 2017), 256–61; Jefferson's note is in *PTJ*, 20:290.

24. Dimunation, "'The Whole of Recorded Knowledge,'" 29; Sowerby, "Thomas Jefferson and His Library," 217; Wilson, *Jefferson's Books*, 27; Jefferson to Mercy Otis Warren,
November 25, 1790, *PTJ*, 18:77–78. For Frances Wright, see Jefferson's first letter to her,
May 22, 1820, *Founders Online*, http://founders.archives.gov/documents/Jefferson/98-01
-02-1289; her visit to Monticello with Lafayette in 1824 sealed the friendship begun with
the gift of her book.

25. Jefferson to Anne-Louise-Germaine Necker, Baronne de Staël-Holstein, July 16,
1807, *Founders Online*, http://founders.archives.gov/documents/Jefferson/99-01-02-5977;
Jefferson to David Montague Erskine, December 1, 1807, *Founders Online*, http://founders
.archives.gov/documents/Jefferson/99-01-02-6875; Anna Maria Brodeau Thornton to
Jefferson, January 15, 1808, *Founders Online*, http://founders.archives.gov/documents
/Jefferson/99-01-02-7213; David Montagu Erskine to Jefferson, January 16, 1808, *Founders
Online*, http://founders.archives.gov/documents/Jefferson/99-01-02-7215.

26. On Jefferson's library as his "sanctum sanctorum," see Margaret Bayard Smith,
*The First Forty Years of Washington Society, Portrayed by the Family Letters of Mrs. Samuel
Harrison Smith...*, ed. Gaillard Hunt (New York: C. Scribner's Sons, 1906), 70. Exam-
ples of Jefferson showing his library to visitors include ibid., 71–72; Chastellux, 12–13;
Ticknor, 63; Anna Thornton, ms. diary, excerpt in Peterson, *Visitors to Monticello*, 35;
Augustus John Foster, in Richard Beale Davis, ed., *Jeffersonian America: Notes on the
United States of America Collected in the Years 1805–6–7 and 11–12 by Sir Augustus John
Foster, Bart.* (San Marino, CA, 1954), excerpt in Peterson, *Visitors to Monticello*, 43; and
Francis Calley Gray, in Henry S. Rowe and T. Jefferson Coolidge, eds., *Thomas Jeffer-
son in 1814, Being an Account of a Visit to Monticello, Virginia* (Boston, 1924), excerpt in
Peterson, *Visitors to Monticello*, 58–60; in addition to the sources mentioned in note
25, examples of Jefferson lending his books include Johann Ludwig de Unger to Jef-
ferson, November 13, 1780, *PTJ*, 4:117–18; Jefferson to Peter Carr, March 28, 1790,
PTJ, 16:276–77; and Jefferson to James Ogilvie, January 31, 1806, *Founders Online*,

http://founders.archives.gov/documents/Jefferson/99-01-02-3156; see also Dumas Malone, *Jefferson and His Time*, vol. 6, *The Sage of Monticello* (Boston: Little, Brown, 1981), 171.

27. "Aug. 4. 1773. My Library," in James A. Bear Jr. and Lucia C. Stanton, eds., *Jefferson's Memorandum Books: Accounts, With Legal Records and Miscellany, 1767–1826* (Princeton, NJ: Princeton University Press, 1997), 1:332.

28. Jefferson to John Garland Jefferson, June 11, 1790, *PTJ*, 16:480–82; Malone, *Sage of Monticello*, 180.

29. Wilson, *Jefferson's Books*, 25; Dimunation, "Thomas Jefferson Goes Shopping."

30. James Madison to Jefferson, March 18, 1786, *PTJ*, 9:332–36. On the significance of these books to Madison's thought, see, e.g., Jack N. Rakove, *A Politician Thinking: The Creative Mind of James Madison* (Norman: University of Oklahoma Press, 2017), 39.

31. Jefferson to Martha Jefferson (Randolph), November 28, 1783, *PTJ*, 6:359–61; Ellen Wayles Randolph Coolidge to Henry S. Randall, 1856, excerpted in Randall, *Life of Thomas Jefferson*, 3:343, and on the Monticello website in *Jefferson Quotes & Family Letters* at http://tjrs.monticello.org/letter/1897; Virginia Jefferson Randolph Trist (unnamed but since identified) to Nicholas Philip Trist (unnamed but since identified), May 26, 1839, excerpted in Randall, *Life of Thomas Jefferson*, 3:350, and on the Monticello website in *Jefferson Quotes & Family Letters*, http://tjrs.monticello.org/letter/1894; Jefferson to Ellen Wayles Randolph (Coolidge), November 27, 1801, *PTJ*, 35:734–35.

32. Joseph P. Coolidge to Nicholas Philip Trist, February 11, 1829, on the Monticello website in *Jefferson Quotes & Family Letters*, http://tjrs.monticello.org/letter/1160.

33. Cornelia Jefferson Randolph to Virginia Jefferson Randolph Trist, September 13, 1827, on the Monticello website in *Jefferson Quotes & Family Letters*, http://tjrs.monticello.org/letter/1103.

34. Jefferson to Thomas Mann Randolph Jr., August 27, 1786, *PTJ*, 10:305–09.

35. Hannah Spahn, *Thomas Jefferson, Time, and History* (Charlottesville: University of Virginia Press, 2011), 17.

36. Thomas Jefferson Randolph, reminiscences of Thomas Jefferson, in Randolph, *Domestic Life*, 338; "Thomas Jefferson: Will and Codicil, 16–17 Mar. 1826, 16 March 1826," *Founders Online*, http://founders.archives.gov/documents/Jefferson/98-01-02-5963; the information about timepieces at Monticello is in Spahn, *Thomas Jefferson, Time*, 32. Spahn's first chapter, "Rational Time" (29–45), explores this concern with the use of time and its deeper implications for Jefferson's temporal worldview.

37. Jefferson to Thomas Jefferson Randolph, December 30, 1809, *PTJRS*, 2:110–11.

38. Some examples include Jefferson to Robert Skipwith, August 3, 1771, *PTJ*, 1:76–81; Jefferson to Bernard Moore, ca. 1773, in letter to John Minor, August 30, 1814, *PTJR*, 7:625–31; Jefferson to Peter Carr, August 19, 1785, *PTJ*, 8:405–08; Jefferson to Thomas Mann Randolph Jr., August 27, 1786, *PTJ*, 10:305–09; Jefferson, "Course of Reading for William G. Munford," December 5, 1798, *PTJ*, 30:594–97; and Jefferson to Nathaniel Burwell, "Enclosure: List of Recommended Books for Female Education," March 14, 1818, *PTJRS*, 12:534–35. The estimate that such lists number in the dozens is Douglas Wilson's, in *Jefferson's Books*, 50.

39. Jefferson to Bernard Moore, ca. 1773, in letter to John Minor, August 30, 1814, *PTJR*, 7:625–31.

40. Ibid.

41. Jefferson to Francis Wayles Eppes, April 9, 1822, *Founders Online*, http://founders .archives.gov/documents/Jefferson/98-01-02-2757.

42. Jefferson to Thomas Mann Randolph Jr., August 27, 1786, *PTJ*, 10:305–09; Jefferson to Peter Carr, August 19, 1785, *PTJ*, 8:405–08; Jefferson to Thomas Jefferson Randolph, December 30, 1809, *PTJRS*, 2:110–11.

43. This analysis is based on the following materials: Jefferson to Bernard Moore, ca. 1773, in letter to John Minor, August 30, 1814, *PTJR*, 7:625–31; Jefferson to Thomas Mann Randolph Jr., August 27, 1786, *PTJ*, 10:305–09; Jefferson to John Garland Jefferson, June 11, 1790, *PTJ*, 16:480–82; "Course of Reading for William G. Munford," December 5, 1798, *PTJ*, 30:594–97, and the information given about the undated, unaddressed document in the note accompanying this document; and Jefferson to Francis Wayles Eppes, April 9, 1822, *Founders Online*, http://founders.archives.gov/documents/Jefferson/98-01-02-2757.

44. Jefferson to Vine Utley, March 21, 1819, *Founders Online*, http://founders.archives .gov/documents/Jefferson/98-01-02-0245.

45. Hannah Spahn sees Jefferson's concept of the relationship between learning and the stages of life as more intricate, systematic, and comprehensive than the present essay is prepared to claim. See, for example, the structure of understanding she attributes to him in Spahn, *Thomas Jefferson, Time*, 97.

46. *Notes*, Query XIV, 147–48.

47. Jefferson to Thomas Mann Randolph Jr., August 27, 1786, *PTJ*, 10:305–09.

48. *Notes*, Query XIV, 147.

49. Spahn, *Thomas Jefferson, Time*, 105.

50. *Notes*, Query XIV, 147; Jefferson to Peter Carr, August 10, 1787, *PTJ*, 12:14–19; Jefferson to Thomas Mann Randolph Jr., August 27, 1786, *PTJ*, 10:305–09.

51. Thomas Jefferson, "Thoughts on English Prosody," in Andrew A. Lipscomb and Albert E. Bergh, eds., *The Writings of Thomas Jefferson* (Washington, DC: Issued under the Auspices of the Thomas Jefferson Memorial Association of the United States, 1903–1904), 18:448. The editors of the authoritative *Papers of Thomas Jefferson* and *Founders Online*, https://founders.archives.gov/, have concluded that Jefferson probably composed this manuscript in the summer of 1786: see the note accompanying Jefferson to Chastellux, [October 1786], *PTJ*, 10:498–99.

52. Jefferson to John Daly Burk, June 21, 1801, *PTJ*, 34:400–01.

53. See Gross, *Thomas Jefferson's Scrapbooks*; Ellen Wayles Randolph Coolidge (unnamed but since identified) to Henry S. Randall, 185[-], excerpted in Randall, *Life of Thomas Jefferson*, 3:346.

54. Jefferson to John Adams, January 21, 1812, *PTJRS*, 4:428–30; see also, for example, Jefferson to John Brazer, August 24, 1819, *Founders Online*, http://founders.archives .gov/documents/Jefferson/98-01-02-0707; and Jefferson to William Short, October 31, 1819, *Founders Online*, http://founders.archives.gov/documents/Jefferson/98-01-02-0850.

55. Ellen Wayles Randolph Coolidge (unnamed but since identified) to Henry S. Randall, 185[-], excerpted in Randall, *Life of Thomas Jefferson*, 3:346; Hayes, *Road to Monticello*, 608; Malone, *Sage of Monticello*, 190.

56. Sowerby, "Thomas Jefferson and His Library," 213; James Gilreath, "Sowerby Revirescent and Revisited," *Papers of the Bibliographical Society of America* 78 (1984): 230–31; Kevin J. Hayes, "The Libraries of Thomas Jefferson," in *A Companion to Thomas Jefferson*, ed. Francis D. Cogliano (Malden, MA: Wiley-Blackwell, 2012), 333; Dimunation, "'Whole of Recorded Knowledge,'" 24.

57. On the Retirement Library, see Hayes, *Road to Monticello*, ch. 38 (564–80).

58. Jefferson to Samuel H. Smith, September 21, 1814, *PTJRS*, 7:681–84.

59. Jefferson to Thomas Willis White, December 8, 1824, *Founders Online*, http://founders.archives.gov/documents/Jefferson/98-01-02-4757.

60. Richard Guy Wilson, "Thomas Jefferson's Classical Architecture: An American Agenda," in *Thomas Jefferson, the Classical World, and Early America*, ed. Peter S. Onuf and Nicholas P. Cole (Charlottesville: University of Virginia Press, 2011), 103; Wilson, *Jefferson's Books*, 31–32; Frederick Doveton Nichols and Ralph E. Griswold, *Thomas Jefferson, Landscape Architect* (Charlottesville: University Press of Virginia, 1978), 82, 85.

61. Jefferson to William Short, October 31, 1819, *Founders Online*, http://founders.archives.gov/documents/Jefferson/98-01-02-0850; Jefferson to Abigail Adams, January 11, 1817, *PTJRS*, 10:655–57; see also Jefferson to John Adams, May 17, 1818, *PTJRS*, 13:48.

62. Jefferson to John Brazer, August 24, 1819, *Founders Online*, http://founders.archives.gov/documents/Jefferson/98-01-02-0707.

63. Virginia Jefferson Randolph Trist (unnamed but since identified) to Nicholas Philip Trist (unnamed but since identified), May 26, 1839, excerpted in Randall, *Life of Thomas Jefferson*, 3:350, and on the Monticello website in *Jefferson Quotes & Family Letters*, http://tjrs.monticello.org/letter/1894.

64. Jefferson to John Adams, May 17, 1818, *PTJRS*, 13:48.

65. Ellen Wayles Randolph Coolidge to Henry S. Randall, May 16, 1857, extract on the Monticello website in *Jefferson Quotes & Family Letters*, http://tjrs.monticello.org/letter/466.

66. Merrill D. Peterson, *Thomas Jefferson and the New Nation: A Biography* (New York: Oxford University Press, 1970), 1008.

Forming the Body of a Library Based on the "Illimitable Freedom of the Human Mind"

ENDRINA TAY

THE LIBRARY that Thomas Jefferson formed for the University of Virginia was central to his vision for the institution. By locating it in the Rotunda, the tallest structure and central edifice in his Academical Village, Jefferson placed knowledge and reason at the center and heart of the institution he founded on the "illimitable freedom of the human mind."[1] What characterized this library? How was it put together? What did it represent, and what does it tell us about Jefferson and his vision and hopes for the University, and more broadly, the future of the American nation?

Jefferson drew from his own formative experiences and lifetime of reading to fill the shelves of the University's first library. Its inaugural collection was also an aggregation of suggested works by faculty and other individuals. Designed with the education of future republican patriots in mind, it was intended to be universal in scope. Books were chosen to support the subject areas and curricula to be taught by the professors of the eight schools,[2] and therefore included standard works while excluding more ephemeral ones. Not only were the books carefully curated, Jefferson drew up strict rules for the library to ensure that they remained in good order so as to fulfill their intended purpose. Documentary sources from the years 1824 to 1826 also reveal the chronology of how the library's collections were constituted during this early period.

Arguably one of Jefferson's "last act[s] of usefulness,"[3] the University was the culmination of a lifelong pursuit of knowledge and dedication to the practical sciences for the improvement of human society. It was to be a new model for American higher education that would embody the Enlightenment ideals of secularism, republicanism, and useful knowledge.[4] Jefferson envisaged the University as one in which "all the branches of science deemed useful at this day, shall be taught in their highest degree,"[5] and where future leaders would explore and expose "every subject susceptible of it's contemplation."[6] This forward-looking stance was to be based on a knowledge and understanding of the past. Jefferson regarded history (particularly political history and more specifically, Whig history) as both a "guide to the perfectible future through the errors of the blemished past" and as "a model of that future."[7] Thus, access and exposure for students to recorded knowledge and histories in the form of books and printed materials were key, and the University library was central to his plan.

Housed in a structure inspired by the Roman Pantheon, admired by Jefferson for its perfect proportions and as an ideal example of cubic or spherical architecture,[8] the library functioned as a storehouse and repository of human knowledge and progress for students and faculty to draw upon. It was a carefully curated collection of works that reflected Jefferson's lifetime of reading and his curiosity in all aspects of the natural and material world. The fundamental value of reading was at the heart of Jefferson's enlightened vision of an educated populace. His formative experiences under the tutelage of James Maury, William Small, and George Wythe shaped his interests and his lifelong "canine appetite for reading."[9] It was first under Maury that Jefferson learned to appreciate Latin and Greek authors in their original, a "sublime luxury" he wished to afford to other men.[10] He credited his early experiences with Maury for developing his love for the classics.[11] When asked, Jefferson would readily draw up reading lists for aspiring lawyers and other young men seeking to improve themselves. Providing students with access to the best books and the latest knowledge was therefore integral to his vision for the University of Virginia. In his *Notes on the State of Virginia*, he wrote, "[T]ime is not lost which is employed in providing tools for future operation: more especially as in this case the books put into the hands of the youth for this purpose may be such as will at the same time impress their minds with useful facts and good principles."[12] As Jefferson began to formulate his ideas of establishing a university "on a reformed plan," the vision of its library was never far from his mind.[13] In 1805 he expressed his intention to bequeath his personal library at Monticello if such an institution was to materialize.[14] Later, in 1814, when the library and scientific apparatus of the late Joseph Priestley went on sale, he even entertained the notion (albeit with little confidence at the time) that perhaps the Virginia legislature might consider acquiring his library, while also bidding for Priestley's collection, in order to build such a university. He wrote, "I have long had under contemplation, & been collecting materials for the plan of an university in Virginia which should comprehend all the sciences useful to us. . . ."[15] Nine months later, this all changed with the War of 1812. In the aftermath of the burning of the United States Capitol, Jefferson sold his 6,500-volume library in 1815 to replace the congressional library that was destroyed by the British so that Congress would have ready access to the books and legislative records it needed to govern effectively after the war. Still, he never lost sight of the university and the books he envisioned for it. As he reconstituted his library at Monticello, he formed his final collection there not only for his own pleasure reading but also for its final designee. Jefferson had the university in mind as he searched for the best editions of his favorite works of history, poetry, and philology from booksellers such as the De Bure Brothers in Paris, Lackington, Hughes & Co. in London, and John Laval in Philadelphia, among others. When he drew up his will in March 1826, three months before his death, he named the University of Virginia as the final beneficiary of his library.[16]

Amassing the library collection for the University was of vital importance to Jefferson. It was to be universal in scope and comprehensive in coverage to support an institution built on, as Roger Geiger put it, "an Enlightenment vision that valued breadth of knowledge."[17] It was to be a collection that encouraged scientific and humanistic inquiry, and so include the standard works and editions available at that time in history, mathematics, natural history, medicine, ethics, law, poetry, languages, and the arts. Some were ones he regularly included in his recommended reading lists and mentioned in numerous discussions on university curricula over many years with individuals such as Joseph Priestley, Pierre Samuel du Pont de Nemours, Thomas Cooper, Joseph Carrington Cabell, George Ticknor, and others. These included essential texts like Francis Bacon's *Novum Organum Scientiarum*, John Locke's *An Essay Concerning Human Understanding*, Lord Bolingbroke's *Letters on the Study and Use of History*, Isaac Newton's *Philosophiæ Naturalis Principia Mathematica*, and Pierre Charron's *De la Sagesse*.

The library's classification system was Baconian in its origin, but distinctly Jeffersonian in application. It reflected Francis Bacon's organization of knowledge developed in his *Advancement of Learning* and later expanded by Jean le Rond d'Alembert in Denis Diderot's *Encyclopédie*.[18] This scheme was one that Jefferson had adopted and adapted for his own sizable library at Monticello for more than fifty years. Books were organized according to Bacon's three faculties of the mind—Memory, Reason, and Imagination, which corresponded to History, Philosophy, and Fine Arts, respectively.[19] For the University, Jefferson further divided these three groups into forty-two subjects or "chapters."

Within each chapter, books were arranged in the catalog by subject and then chronologically, an arrangement Jefferson described as "sometimes analytical, sometimes chronological, & sometimes a combination of both."[20] The eight professorships to be instituted at the University were grouped around these subject areas. As one author put it, "Jefferson's educational scheme institutionalized ideas embodied in his library catalogue."[21] In his letter to Augustus B. Woodward, he wrote, "Where sciences are to be arranged in accomodation to the schools of an University, they will be grouped to coincide with the kindred qualifications of Professors. . . . for a library . . . , which was my object, their divisions and subdivisions will be made such as to throw convenient masses of books under each separate head."[22] Jefferson's scheme for the University's library was recorded on page 1 of an extant manuscript catalog of the library's holdings in 1825 by John Vaughan Kean, a student appointed in March 1825 as the fledgling institution's first librarian.[23] After Jefferson's death in 1826, this classification system was simplified and altered by University faculty such that by 1828, the eight thousand books in the library were classified into twenty-nine chapters, instead of Jefferson's original forty-two. The library catalog printed that year also departed from Jefferson's practice by alphabetizing the authors within each chapter, and translating titles in foreign languages into English.[24] By then, the books were shelved in cases according to this pared-down classification, a practice that continued until the Rotunda fire in 1895.[25]

The collection supported a University curriculum for both general and professional education that included subject electives. It was to have established and reputable works, like the *Encyclopédie Méthodique*, often too voluminous or expensive for a private library to own, so individuals would have free access to them in a public library. It was important for students at the University to gain an understanding of how ideas and conclusions had been formed, so individuals could critically examine any assumptions made. The library would thus have not only the best books in their respective branches of science but also those that were "deemed good in their day, and which consequently furnish a history of the advance of the science."[26] Several editions of classical authors would be available so students could engage in comparative study on their own. Ultimately, each chosen work should add to the library's core purpose. The collection was to be broad in scope, but far from exhaustive. With limited funds available from the legislature to build it, Jefferson had to be selective. For example, travel guides by Louis Dutens and Joseph Addison that he highly recommended in the past were omitted.[27] For the most part, the library would hold books that encouraged diverse or antithetical

1.

Books are addressed to the three faculties of

Memory   Reason   Imagination

To these belong respectively

History		Philosophy		Fine Arts
Civil	Physical pure & mixt	Mathematical	Moral	29 Architecture
1. antient	6 Physics	17 Arithmetic	19 Ethics	Gardening
2. modern foreign	7 agriculture	18 Geometry	30 Religion	30 Painting Sculpture
3. British	8 chemistry		21 L. Nature & nat.	music
4 American	anatomy 9 surgery		22 L. Equity	
5 Ecclesiastic	10 Medecine		23 L. Common	31 Poetry Epic
	11 Zoology		24 L. Merchant	32 Romance
	12 Botany		25 L. Maritime	33 Pastoral
	13 Mineralogy		26 L. Ecclesiastic	34 Didactic
	14 Technics		27 L. Foreign	35 Tragedy
	15 astronomy		28 Civil Polity	36 Comedy
	16 Geography			37 Dial. Epistles
				38 Rhetoric
				39 Criticism Theory
				40 Bibliography
				41 Philology

42.   Pol-y   gra   phi - cal

A Catalogue of the Library of the University of Virginia, ca. May 16 to December 1825, showing Jefferson's classification scheme for the University library, recorded in the hand of student John V. Kean, the first University librarian appointed in 1825 by Jefferson. (John V. Kean. Catalogue of the Library of the University of Virginia, 1825, Accession #RG-12/12/1.161, Albert and Shirley Small Special Collections Library, University of Virginia) viewpoints. For example, Jefferson declared that David Hume's *History of England* would never be read in classes. He instead prescribed for use in the classroom a republicanized abridgment of Hume in the form of John Baxter's *A New and Impartial History of England*.[28] He nevertheless permitted the thirteen-volume set of Hume's work (an edition that included Tobias Smollett's continuation), given to the University in 1825 by Bernard M. Carter, to be accessioned and retained in the library's collections for access by students.[29] Religious works were not excluded at the University as a secular institution. Rather, Jefferson regarded religion as a subset of ethics, which would be taught by the professor of moral philosophy, as opposed to a professor of divinity.

Jefferson adopted an incremental approach in building the library's collection, as public funds became available and faculty came on board. In April 1824, Francis Walker Gilmer was tasked by the Board of Visitors of the University to recruit faculty, and acquire scientific apparatus and books from Great Britain. He had a sum of $6,000 to acquire apparatus and textbooks needed in order for classes to begin in early 1825. Among the items on his checklist were instructions from Jefferson to attempt to procure from Lackington, Hughes and Co. in London the books needed for the Anglo-Saxon course to be taught in the School of Modern Languages. Jefferson supplied Gilmer with a booklist based on familiar Anglo-Saxon titles he had previously owned and later reacquired for himself after he sold his books to Congress.[30] Jefferson relied on three different sources to draw up this list. One was his manuscript catalog documenting his post-1815 library at Monticello.[31] The second was a reconstructed manuscript catalog in the hand of Nicholas Philip Trist detailing the books Jefferson had sold in 1815.[32] The last source was probably a dated Lackington bookseller's catalog that Jefferson had obtained from a previous book order in 1821, which explains the reference prices he was able to supply in the margin of his booklist for Gilmer.

Lackington turned out to be a disappointment as Gilmer found that the firm had changed hands several times since Jefferson dealt with them in 1821, and their prices were the least favorable. In mid-September 1824, armed with a budget of £800, Gilmer drew up a list of classical works to be acquired for the University by the London bookseller John Bohn from suppliers in Germany, France, and London. With the help of Samuel Parr (whom George Ticknor called "England's best and perhaps, vainest classical scholar"[33]), the educated and knowledgeable Gilmer proved to be well qualified to decide which books to buy. Having graduated from the College of William and Mary, he was a trained lawyer and well read. In his youth, he spent time at Monticello learning

Thomas Jefferson's List of Books for the Anglo-Saxon Course, ca. April 1824, that Francis Walker Gilmer was instructed to acquire for the University in Great Britain. (List of Books for Courses at the University of Virginia, 1824, Accession #7601-b, Albert and Shirley Small Special Collections Library, University of Virginia)

French from Jefferson's daughter, Martha Jefferson Randolph, and knew Jefferson's book collection and reading tastes well. Back in Virginia, Jefferson had been busy for more than two months, since June 1824, compiling his own desiderata list for the University.[34] This booklist consisted of familiar works that he had previously held in his Monticello library and sold in 1815, works that he had since acquired for his post-1815 library at Monticello, works drawn from various booksellers' catalogs in Jefferson's possession, as well as book recommendations he had received from Thomas Cooper, George Ticknor, and others.

When Jefferson arrived at the chapter on religion, he felt at a loss. Not knowing which divinity titles were worth including in his list, he turned to his close friend, retired president James Madison, who had been exposed to theology at the College of New Jersey (Princeton). He wrote, "I wish you could suggest to me any works really worthy of place in the catalogue . . . writers of celebrity in religious metaphysics . . . pray think of it and help me."[35] Jefferson incorporated a number of Madison's additions into his list, one example being William Cave's *The Lives of the Fathers in the Primitive Church.*[36]

At the end of September, Jefferson completed his desiderata booklist of 6,860 volumes estimated to cost $24,076 and shared it with Madison. With this initial nucleus, he was hopeful that by investing the University's remaining building fund in stock, they might have $1,000 a year for the foreseeable future to build up the library to become what it should be.[37] He continued to refine and add to his desiderata list such that George Ticknor, while visiting Monticello in December, observed that Jefferson "has prepared an entire catalogue of seven or eight thousand volumes for the Library of the university, neatly written in his own hand, arranged according to subjects, with an index, and priced. It must have cost him much painful and wearisome examination."[38] In November 1824, Gilmer reported to Jefferson that he had successfully procured all of Jefferson's desired Anglo-Saxon volumes from Bohn. Along with classics and works of modern literature, he also managed to acquire, inexpensively, an additional collection of mathematical works that he deemed superior to any he had seen in Great Britain. These books began to arrive at the University in their boxes, albeit somewhat damp, around January 20, 1825.[39] After unpacking the first eight boxes with Gilmer's book catalog in hand, Jefferson was pleased and expressed his approval at Gilmer's "well selected & well bought" books.[40] The rest of the Bohn shipments arrived at the University in June and July of that year. These volumes were recorded by librarian John Vaughan Kean in the manuscript catalog he maintained.[41]

Faced with the "scantiness of our building funds," gifts to the University library played a vital role in building its initial collection.[42] Shortly after the University's first classes began on March 7, 1825, Joseph Coolidge of Boston (who later became Jefferson's grandson-in-law) presented the University with a "handsome donation" of eighty-five volumes of classics and works on mathematics and philology from his personal library.[43] A native Virginian living in London, Bernard Moore Carter, offered his library of 334 volumes to the University as a "testimonial of the devotion which I cherish, for my native Country, and her Interests," which Jefferson as rector gratefully accepted.[44] Capitalizing on these substantial gifts, the Board of Visitors placed advertisements in April 1825 soliciting similar donations for the University library in the *Richmond Enquirer* and the Charlottesville *Central Gazette* newspapers. Throughout this period, Jefferson kept in close contact with and received regular updates from Kean as books were added to the shelves.[45]

In early March 1825, after funds became available, the Board of Visitors appointed the Boston firm of Cummings, Hilliard and Co. as its agent to purchase additional books that the library did not yet have. The firm had supplied classical books for Harvard College and other universities, and published mathematical texts and books in various fields. Earlier in January, Jefferson had engaged William Hilliard to supply cheaper editions for students to use as textbooks. Hilliard would have a maximum sum of $18,000 to acquire books from London, Germany, France, and America at a commission of 5 percent on the purchase price and expenses. In compiling the acquisitions list for Hilliard at this stage, Jefferson consulted his desiderata list that he had continued to update as books from Bohn arrived and gifts were received from donors, and he sought the input of faculty members. As was the case for divinity, he relied on their recommendations for subject areas where his knowledge was limited. While busily recording and classifying orders arriving from Europe and from gifts, he incorporated recommended titles submitted to him by the faculty, including those from professors Thomas Hewitt Key, Charles G. Bonnycastle, John Patton Emmet, Robley Dunglison, and George Long.[46] In late May, Jefferson reported to Hilliard that a finalized acquisitions list was forthcoming. Nicholas Trist, who had become Jefferson's grandson-in-law and personal secretary, was making a copy of the booklist for Hilliard under Jefferson's direction.[47] The order list was finally completed on June 2. Jefferson dated the catalog "June 3, 1825," and dispatched it to Hilliard, who set about immediately to fill the University's commission.[48] The first books from Hilliard arrived at the University at the end of that same month in June. From among these first volumes from Hilliard, early library circulation records reveal that Jefferson was one of the first individuals to check out volumes 2 and 3 of John Lingard's *History of England* a month later on July 28, 1825.[49] As with the books ordered by Gilmer and supplied by Bohn, these received from Hilliard were likewise

recorded by Kean in the library catalog he maintained, except that these books
from Hilliard were recorded under their respective subject classification in a
separate "supplementary" section. In April 1826, subscriptions to periodicals
for the faculty were added to Hilliard's commission.[50] Following Hilliard's
first delivery in June 1825, book deliveries continued at a steady pace for the
next year, until after Jefferson's death in July 1826 when the original budget of
$18,000 was exhausted. In a letter addressed to the Board of Visitors dated
July 11, 1826, Hilliard informed them that "the amount furnished for the purchase of Books, was altogether inadequate to the accomplishment of the Catalogue made out," and that he had no choice but to end his commission.[51]

Beyond the content of the collection, order was of paramount importance
to Jefferson, and it was critical to him that books be available when called for.
The library was temporarily located in Pavilion VII on the West Lawn while
the Rotunda was nearing completion. Jefferson appointed the first librarian,
John Vaughan Kean, in March 1825 to oversee the library collection and to ensure its order and maintenance. Kean was paid a sum of $150 a year to "keep
the books in a state of sound preservation undefiled and free from injury by
moisture or other accident, and in their stated arrangement on the shelves according to the method and order of their Catalogue."[52] Since the University
library was set up primarily as a reference collection, Jefferson insisted on a
strict system of circulation. Initially, the library was only open for one hour,
one day in the week. Students were allowed to enter the library to borrow a
book only if they had been authorized to do so by a faculty member. The numbers admitted were limited so as to secure order. No student was permitted to
take any book from the shelf himself. Nor were they permitted to read or con-
sult any book without the librarian being present. When Kean faced complaints from his fellow students on the strict regulations governing the use of
the library, he appealed to Jefferson to relax the circulation rules.[53] In response, Jefferson reminded Kean that "a book misplaced is in fact lost, as nothing but accident or a revision of the whole library book by book can ever find it
again . . . [A] library in confusion loses much of it's utility."[54] The duty of the
librarian was to prevent the books from being misplaced through carelessness.
Any change in the rule would only be permitted if Kean, as the librarian in
charge, was able to lay his hand at any time on any book so as not to disappoint
the person calling for it. William Wertenbaker, former law student and the
second librarian, appointed in early 1826 after Kean, reportedly recounted to
his son many years later, "[t]he last visit Mr. Jefferson made to the university

was to meet me for the purpose of opening the boxes of books which consti-tuted the nucleus of the present library. He manifested the warmest interest in getting everything rightly placed at an early date. With his own feeble hands he helped to unpack the books and to place them on the shelves, in the order and way he had chalked out in his mind."[55] That Jefferson was fastidious with regard to the library books was similarly demonstrated by the often cited ac-count of Jefferson, after thoroughly inspecting a shipment of books that Wertenbaker had placed on the shelf, called the librarian to him, and pointing to *Gibbon's Decline and Fall* said, "[y]ou ought not to have received that book. It should have been returned." "Why," said Wertenbaker, "it is a very handsome edition." "That may be so," said Jefferson, "but look at the back." The lettering on the spine of the book—still preserved in the University's library—read, "Gibborn's Roman Empire."[56]

Jefferson himself presented three books to the University before his death, and the only book that has survived is a volume of the *Transactions of the American Philosophical Society* from 1825. He gave it to the University in early December 1825, and it has a note by him on the front flyleaf that reads, "this vol. is given chiefly on account of the plan for an observatory pa[ge] 365-421. pl. X. by Mr. Hassler which will be worthy of attention when we have occasion to build one."[57] He was referring to Ferdinand Rudolph Hassler's plans for an observatory in Washington, DC, which were part of papers connected with the Survey of the Coast of the United States dated March 3, 1820, a survey that Jefferson had commissioned while U.S. president in 1807. He wanted the Uni-versity to have on hand such a plan for when the University was sufficiently advanced to build an observatory of its own.

Jefferson died on July 4, 1826, before construction of the Rotunda was complete. He never saw the completion of all his labors. Nor did he witness the library in its first long-term home. Yet his meticulous efforts at curating, organizing, and preserving a library collection for the University of Virginia reflected his deep commitment to its establishment. This was the institution he built with the express purpose of inculcating republican ideals in future generations who would inherit the task of safeguarding their freedoms and en-suring the survival of the American nation. Writing to Augustus Woodward as he contemplated the end of his life and his legacy a year before his death, Jefferson wrote: "I am closing the last scenes of life by fostering and fashioning an establishment for the instruction of those who are to come after us. I hope it's influence on their virtue, freedom, fame and happiness will be salutary and permanent."[58]

Notes

1. Jefferson to Antoine Louis Claude Destutt de Tracy, December 26, 1820, *Founders Online*, http://founders.archives.gov/documents/Jefferson/98-01-02-1704.

2. These were the schools of ancient languages, modern languages, mathematics, natural philosophy, natural history, anatomy and medicine, moral philosophy, and law.

3. Jefferson to Spencer Roane, March 9, 1821, *Founders Online*, http://founders.archives.gov/documents/Jefferson/98-01-02-1900.

4. Roger L. Geiger, *The History of American Higher Education: Learning and Culture from the Founding to World War II* (Princeton, NJ: Princeton University Press, 2015), 179.

5. Jefferson to George Ticknor, November 25, 1817, *PTJRS*, 12:203–5.

6. Jefferson to Antoine Louis Claude Destutt de Tracy, December 26, 1820, *Founders Online*, http://founders.archives.gov/documents/Jefferson/98-01-02-1704.

7. H. Trevor Colbourn, "Thomas Jefferson's Use of the Past," *WMQ* 15, no. 1 (January 1958): 57.

8. Richard Guy Wilson, "Thomas Jefferson's Classical Architecture: An American Agenda," in *Thomas Jefferson, the Classical World, and Early America*, ed. Peter S. Onuf and Nicholas P. Cole (Charlottesville: University of Virginia Press, 2011), 122.

9. Jefferson to John Adams, May 17, 1818, *PTJRS*, 13:48–49.

10. Jefferson to Joseph Priestley, January 27, 1800, *PTJ*, 31:339–41.

11. Dumas Malone, *Jefferson and His Time* (Boston: Little, Brown and Co., 1948), 1:44.

12. *Notes*, Query XIV, 148.

13. Jefferson to Pierre Samuel du Pont de Nemours, April 12, 1800, *PTJ*, 31:495–96.

14. Jefferson to Littleton W. Tazewell, January 5, 1805, *Founders Online*, http://founders.archives.gov/documents/Jefferson/99-01-02-0958.

15. Jefferson to Thomas Cooper, January 16, 1814, *PTJRS*, 7:124–31.

16. Jefferson bequeathed his library at Monticello to the University of Virginia at his death, but this gift was never realized. His grandson and executor, Thomas Jefferson Randolph, withheld the legacy in order to clear Jefferson's debts. It was temporarily deposited at the University for safekeeping from late 1826 until early 1829, when the books were withdrawn from the University and sold at auction in Washington, DC, from February 27 to March 11, 1829.

17. Geiger, *History of American Higher Education*, 180.

18. Jefferson adapted his library classification system from Francis Bacon's "Emanation of the Sciences," in his *Of the Advancement and Proficiencie of Learning, or The Partitions of Sciences* (1670), and Jean le Rond d'Alembert's "Système Figuré des Connoissances Humaines," published in his *Discours Préliminaire de L'Encyclopédie* in Denis Diderot's *Encyclopédie* (1781).

19. Jefferson's scheme was described in detail by Augustus B. Woodward in his 1816 publication, *A System of Universal Science* (Philadelphia: Published by Edward Earle, Harrison Hall and Moses Thomas, 1816), 208–22. Woodward discussed the topic of classifying knowledge with Jefferson and copied his scheme when visiting him, once in Washington in November 1801 and then at Monticello in May 1814.

20. Jefferson to George Watterston, March 2, 1816, *PTJRS*, 9:531–32.

21. Kevin Hayes, *The Road to Monticello: The Life and Mind of Thomas Jefferson* (New York: Oxford University Press, 2008), 619.

22. Jefferson to Augustus B. Woodward, March 24, 1824, *Founders Online*, http://founders.archives.gov/documents/Jefferson/98-01-02-4139.

23. John V. Kean, Catalogue of the Library of the University of Virginia, 1825, Accession #RG-12/12/1.161, Special Collections, University of Virginia Library. The classification scheme recorded in the front of the catalog came from Jefferson himself. This scheme was the basis for Jefferson's desiderata book list of 6,860 volumes totaling $24,076 that Jefferson compiled for the University library between June and September 1824, in the form of a manuscript volume entitled "A Catalogue of Books Forming a Body of a Library For the University of Virginia, To Be Afterwards Enlarged By Annual Additions—An Explanation of the Views on Which this Catalogue Has Been Prepared." This Jefferson document, quoted on pages 79–80 in Frederick Winslow Page, "Our Library," *Alumni Bulletin of the University of Virginia* 2, no. 3 (November 1895), was part of the University's collections and extant when Page wrote his account that was dated September 10, 1895, over a month before the Rotunda fire on October 27. This manuscript desiderata list has not been found and was presumably lost in the 1895 conflagration.

24. *Catalogue of the Library of the University of Virginia, Arranged Alphabetically Under Different Heads . . .* (Charlottesville: Gilmer, Davis & Co., 1828).

25. Page, "Our Library," 83.

26. Jefferson, "A Catalogue of Books," in Page, "Our Library," 79.

27. These were Louis Dutens's *Itinéraire des Routes les Plus Fréquentées, ou Journal de Plusieurs Voyages aux Villes Principales de l'Europe, depuis 1768 jusqu'en 1783* (Paris, 1783), and Joseph Addison's *Remarks on Several Parts of Italy, & in the Years 1701, 1702, 1703* (London, 1745), recommendations he included in his "Hints to Americans Travelling in Europe" enclosed in his letters addressed to John Rutledge Jr. and Thomas Lee Shippen, both dated June 19, 1788, *PTJ*, 13:264–76.

28. Jefferson to Cummings, Hilliard & Co., February 18, 1825, *Founders Online*, http://founders.archives.gov/documents/Jefferson/98-01-02-4976.

29. This thirteen-volume set consisted of David Hume's *The History of England: From the Invasion of Julius Caesar to the Revolution in 1688* (London: A. Strahan . . . for T. Cadell . . . and W. Davies, 1802) and Tobias Smollett's *The History of England, From the Revolution to the Death of George the Second* (London: T. Cadell . . . and R. Baldwin, 1800).

30. List of Books for Courses at the University of Virginia, 1824, Accession #7601-b, Special Collections, University of Virginia Library.

31. Jefferson's Second Library. Vol. 7, Thomas Jefferson Papers, Library of Congress, https://www.loc.gov/item/mtjbib026579/. This catalog in Jefferson's hand lists the books he acquired for, and owned in, his post-1815 Monticello library after the sale of his books to Congress.

32. Jefferson, and Nicholas Philip Trist, *Catalogue*, [1823], Library of Congress, https://www.loc.gov/item/87204942/. In 1815, Jefferson sent the original manuscript catalog (that he had created in 1812) of his library to Washington, DC, together with the books he had sold to Congress. This catalog, retained by the Librarian of Congress, George Watterston, was never returned to Jefferson and is no longer extant. To Jefferson's dismay,

Watterston produced a printed catalog from Jefferson's version that alphabetized all the book titles within each subject, thereby destroying Jefferson's carefully constructed analytical and chronological arrangement that he had painstakingly maintained in his 1812 manuscript catalog. Later, as Jefferson began to plan the University library, he had his future grandson-in-law, Nicholas Philip Trist, re-create this lost catalog (referred to today as the Trist Catalogue) that restored Jefferson's original order for the Monticello library he sold in 1815. He did this so that he would have on hand a reference list of the books in his previous library ordered by subject as he began to plan the library collection for the University of Virginia and to decide which books to include in his desiderata list. It is unclear when exactly Jefferson asked Trist to undertake this task but it could have been as early as June 1821 when Trist was at Monticello. What is clear is that Trist sent the completed manuscript catalog to Jefferson in a letter from Louisiana dated October 18, 1823, which Jefferson later endorsed as received on December 8, 1823. Apparently, Jefferson provided Trist with a copy of the 1815 printed catalog prepared by Watterston, which Jefferson had annotated to indicate his intended order for the books. Trist then made a copy of the entries in their corrected order and sent the manuscript catalog back to Jefferson, along with Jefferson's annotated copy. This 114-page Trist Catalogue differs from Jefferson's later desiderata list for the University created between June and September 1824. The Trist Catalogue was organized into forty-four chapters, while Jefferson's desiderata list was reduced to forty-two chapters. See note 34, infra.

33. George Ticknor to Jefferson, March 15, 1816, *PTJRS*, 9:559–62.

34. The desiderata list is the same manuscript volume in Jefferson's hand entitled, "A Catalogue of Books Forming a Body of a Library For the University of Virginia . . ." described in note 23. This list was created by Jefferson between June and September 1824, and it consisted not only of familiar works that he previously owned in his Monticello library and were listed in the Trist Catalogue (see note 32), but also works drawn from booksellers' catalogs and recommendations from various individuals. Jefferson subsequently revised his desiderata list several times as additional books ordered by Francis Walker Gilmer from John Bohn in London began to arrive from Europe in early 1825 and gifts of books were presented to the University. Also, as University faculty came on board, Jefferson solicited and incorporated their book recommendations into his desiderata list. None of the subsequent versions of Jefferson's desiderata list with his 1825 revisions appear to have survived. These, if any, were likely passed on to University administration following Jefferson's death in 1826, retained in the University of Virginia's archive collections, and subsequently lost in the 1895 Rotunda fire along with the original version of Jefferson's desiderata list.

35. Jefferson to James Madison, August 8, 1824, in *The Papers of James Madison: Retirement Series (PJM:RS)*, ed. David B. Mattern et al. (Charlottesville: University of Virginia Press, 2016), 3:355–56.

36. James Madison to Jefferson, September 10, 1824, *PJM:RS*, 3:373–83.

37. Jefferson to James Madison, September 24, 1824, *PJM:RS*, 3:395–96.

38. George Ticknor to Jared Sparks, December 17, 1824, in Herbert B. Adams, *The Life and Writings of Jared Sparks* (Cambridge, MA: Riverside Press, 1893), 1:344. See note 34, supra.

39. Jefferson to Francis W. Gilmer, January 20, 1825, *Founders Online*, http://founders
.archives.gov/documents/Jefferson/98-01-02-4890.

40. Jefferson to Francis W. Gilmer, March 6, 1825, *Founders Online*, http://founders
.archives.gov/documents/Jefferson/98-01-02-5023.

41. Kean, Catalogue of the Library of the University of Virginia.

42. Jefferson to James Madison, August 8, 1824, *PJM:RS*, 3:355–56.

43. Jefferson to Joseph Coolidge, April 12, 1825, *Founders Online*, http://founders
.archives.gov/documents/Jefferson/98-01-02-5128.

44. Bernard Moore Carter to Jefferson, October 10, 1824, *Founders Online*, http://
founders.archives.gov/documents/Jefferson/98-01-02-4611.

45. There is at least one extant circa 1825 manuscript inventory in Jefferson's hand,
apparently comparing the books on the library shelves against his own desiderata list, in
the Coolidge Collection of Thomas Jefferson Manuscripts at the Massachusetts Historical Society.

46. University of Virginia: Book Purchases for UVa Recommended by Key, Bonny-
castle, Emmet, and Dunglison, *Founders Online*, http://founders.archives.gov/documents
/Jefferson/98-01-02-5793.

47. In a letter from James Madison to Nicholas Trist dated October 4, 1826, Madison
recorded in a footnote, "$50 has been voted in consideration of yr. service in relation to
the Catalogue for the Library." In his reply the next day, Trist wrote, "In relation to the
catalogue, as my motive in undertaking it was to gratify Mr. Jefferson, I beg it may be
considered as work done by me for him, and as part of that gratuitously done by him for
the Uny." James Madison to Nicholas P. Trist, October 4, 1826, *Founders Online*, http://
founders.archives.gov/documents/Madison/99-02-02-0757; Nicholas P. Trist to James
Madison, October 5, 1826, *Founders Online*, http://founders.archives.gov/documents
/Madison/99-02-02-0762.

48. Thomas Jefferson, Catalog of Books for the University of Virginia Library, 1825,
Accession #38-747, Special Collections, University of Virginia Library.

49. University of Virginia Library List of Books Borrowed, 1825–1827, Accession #RG-
12/12/1.113, Special Collections, University of Virginia Library, 14. The work Jefferson
borrowed was volumes 2 and 3 of John Lingard's *A History of England, From the First Invasion by the Romans* (London, 1823), which is still extant in Special Collections, University
of Virginia Library. See DA30 .L7 1823.

50. Thomas Jefferson Docket and Note, 1826, Accession #12047, Special Collections,
University of Virginia Library.

51. William Hilliard to the Board of Visitors of the University of Virginia, July 11,
1826, Accession #11910, Special Collections, University of Virginia Library.

52. Jefferson to John V. Kean, March 30, 1825, *Founders Online*, http://founders
.archives.gov/documents/Jefferson/98-01-02-5092.

53. John V. Kean to Jefferson, May 13, 1825, *Founders Online*, http://founders.archives
.gov/documents/Jefferson/98-01-02-5221.

54. Jefferson to John V. Kean, May 16, 1825, *Founders Online*, http://founders.archives
.gov/documents/Jefferson/98-01-02-5229.

55. Daniel, Frederick, "Virginian Reminiscences of Jefferson," *Harper's Weekly* 48: 2500 (November 19, 1904).

56. Page, "Our Library," 80. This copy is extant in Special Collections, University of Virginia Library. See DG311 .G423 1821.

57. This copy is extant in Special Collections, University of Virginia Library. See Q11 .P6 Copy 2.

58. Jefferson to Augustus B. Woodward, April 3, 1825, *Founders Online*, http:// founders.archives.gov/documents/Jefferson/98-01-02-5105.

Reading Law in the Early Republic
Legal Education in the Age of Jefferson

JAMES P. AMBUSKE AND RANDALL FLAHERTY

T HE DEATH of Associate Justice William Cushing in September 1810 and President James Madison's search for a worthy replacement reminded Thomas Jefferson of the precarious state of legal education in the young United States. The Massachusetts-born Cushing was one of President George Washington's original appointments to the United States Supreme Court. Jefferson wrote to Madison—his presidential successor, and to Albert Gallatin—secretary of the treasury, of his belief that with Cushing's death "we have a chance of getting a republican majority in the supreme judiciary."[1] Finding a nominee proved difficult, however, since custom dictated that the new judge should come from New England, and Jefferson disdained the jurisprudence taught to New England lawyers as a hybrid form of Old Testament law with "a little dash of Common law, & a great mass of original notions of their own."[2] Seeking a safe choice among the prevalence of northern "tories" with presumed monarchical pretensions, Jefferson championed Levi Lincoln to take Cushing's seat.[3] Lincoln had served under Jefferson as attorney general and like Cushing hailed from Massachusetts. He was not a "correct common [law] lawyer," Jefferson wrote, but he was as good and loyal a nominee as they were likely to find from New England.

Jefferson's concern for the purity of Lincoln's jurisprudence and the Supreme Court vacancy reflected his general anxiety over the state of American law and legal education in the early republic. So many American lawyers, Jefferson lamented, had been dangerously diverted in their legal educations, forced to acquire legal knowledge under the tutelage of Tory-leaning mentors or without sufficient exposure to a full body of legal texts. Lincoln was one of many lawyers who could not overcome the teachings of their youth, Jefferson wrote to Madison: "[O]ne educated in that system can never so far eradicate early impressions as to imbibe thoroughly the principles of another system."[4] The solution, Jefferson believed, rested with schooling the future cadre of American politicians and statesmen in their youth, when they were still impressionable. With the founding of the University of Virginia in 1819, Jefferson sought to create a law curriculum at the new University that would enable the pursuit of legal knowledge from the perspective of a republican, or Revolutionary, ideology. Jefferson hoped that a hand-selected library, a required Reading list, and strict scrutiny of the republican credentials of the law professor would ensure a purity of the academic pursuit, in which law students would necessarily arrive at the right determination about American jurisprudence. Students would eschew the consolidationist and conservative thinking that was taking hold over the nation, along with the popular texts that supported this wayward thinking, and become dedicated advocates for a constrained federal government and for republican orthodoxy. In this tension between truth and philosophical exploration, the new law curriculum at the University of Virginia took shape.

Since the days of the War for Independence, Jefferson feared the persistent influence of eighteenth-century British common law in American legal life and the deference American judges continued to show for the jurisprudence of Tory, or conservative, British jurists like William Murray, Lord Mansfield, or Sir William Blackstone. He believed respect for both jurists contained the seeds of a Federalist counterrevolution that would undo both the American and Jeffersonian republican revolutions. While he acknowledged that Mansfield and Blackstone's works did have some utility, Jefferson nevertheless believed that their consistent defense of government authority and the royal prerogative in court decisions and legal treatises, especially during George III's reign, threatened to corrupt American law and the men who practiced it.

Jefferson believed that American lawyers and citizens should reject the Tory thought embodied in Mansfield and Blackstone's writings in favor of the teachings of Sir Edward Coke, the seventeenth-century jurist whose judicial opinions constrained monarchical power. Jefferson revered Coke, the author of the most important text on English common law published before the 1760s, and other Whig writers who championed the legislature's rights over the royal prerogative.[5] In his mind, the American Revolution resulted in part from the decision of mid-eighteenth-century British politicians and jurists to abandon seventeenth-century English legal precedents. Instead of an empire of liberty in which George III ruled over independent sovereign legislatures of his respective realms, the British Parliament claimed the right to legislate for the American colonies "in all cases whatsoever."[6] Mansfield and Blackstone, Jefferson believed, reinforced the British government's unjust claim to power that had made the Revolution necessary. After independence, their continued influence among American lawyers, judges, and politicians endangered the new republic, particularly due to their easily digestible prose and their broad availability. In his attempt to purge the last vestiges of Tory ideology from American law, Jefferson sought to restore it to its Whig foundations.

In the 1820s, the aging revolutionary founded the University of Virginia, an institution dedicated to the "illimitable freedom of the human mind." Jefferson expected the young men who enrolled in his University to "follow truth wherever it may lead" and to combat error with reason.[7] In the case of law, free, reasoned thought would ultimately arrive at the correct "political principles" that Jefferson believed necessary to protect liberty in Virginia and the American republic.[8] The law was central to Jefferson's conception of a republican society in which a government's authority and legitimacy rested on the consent of an independent white male citizenry who jealously guarded their rights against potential tyranny.[9]

As he neared the end of his life, Jefferson despaired over the fate of Virginia and the American union. Jefferson worried that the American experiment, riven with political division over international affairs, government power, and the expansion of slavery, would end in disunion. Only Americans who held true republican values—Jefferson's republican values—could be entrusted with Virginia's and the nation's safety. Jefferson expected the University's law students to become the nation's next generation of political leaders, and the legal curriculum at the University would ensure a proper course of republican jurisprudence.[10] The stakes were high for the new law curriculum at the University of Virginia, and in Jefferson's idealized vision for the University, law students would be free to follow the truth so long as they arrived at his preferred destination.

This essay, then, necessarily begins deep in the Anglo-American legal past before moving on to examine how the legal and political battles Jefferson waged during his life shaped his perspective on the law, the men who made it, and his vision for legal education in the early republic.

Jefferson intended the University, and the law program in particular, as the place in which "that Vestal flame" of republicanism was "to be kept alive."[11] He sought to upend an older form of legal education in the interest of molding proper, well-educated citizens capable of steering Virginia and the United States around the perilous shoals of Toryism and Federalism. That required not only a curriculum but also an extensive library filled with republican texts that would enable students to see where Blackstone, Mansfield, and other conservative jurists had forsaken Coke's jurisprudence. By pursuing the creation of a new institution, one with a comprehensive library, Jefferson sought to train lawyers to internalize the values of his American Revolution.

Jefferson and the members of the Revolutionary generation viewed the law as a historical framework for understanding human relationships and experiences. Jefferson envisioned and helped design the law curriculum at the University of Virginia with this in mind. More than a simple compilation of statutes or court decisions, the law constituted a body of historical knowledge essential for interpreting the past and shaping the present.[12] English common law, or the law common to the king's courts, was crucial in this regard. As Jefferson later explained to Philip Mazzei, the common law originated in Anglo-Saxon England in the centuries before Magna Carta. "The Common law is a *written law* the text of which is preserved from the beginning of the 13th. century downwards," he wrote, "but what preceded that is lost." Enough had been "committed to writing from time to time in the decisions of judges and treatises" to direct successive governments and law.[13] In Jefferson's rendering of English legal history, the Magna Carta marked "the point of division between the Common and Statute law."[14] Although the common law endured, Parliament made new laws by way of statute. Courts contributed to the further development of the common law by interpreting these new acts or applying past precedents to civil and criminal proceedings where statutory law was not dispositive.

While the common law's historical roots date to the Anglo-Saxon period, it gained greater permanence after the Norman Conquest. Over time it became infused with a variety of legal traditions, including civil, continental, canon, and natural law. In the seventeenth and eighteenth centuries, the Enlightenment injected reason and rational thought into the common law. Successive waves of English settlers carried this hybrid law with them to North America and the Caribbean, where they melded it with other European legal cultures.[15] For Anglo-Americans, the common law was a fundamental form of law that served as a cornerstone of the British Constitution. Subjects on both sides of the Atlantic celebrated the unwritten charter, an amalgamation of parliamentary statutes, court decisions, and legal customs, as that which made them distinct from and freer than other Europeans. While absolutist monarchs reigned in France, Spain, and other nations, the British Constitution protected the people's liberties, and constrained the king's power by making him subject to the law, including the common law. American revolutionaries would invoke the constitution and the English legal past to justify their resistance to British authority.[16]

Colonial Americans and officials in London constantly debated how much English common or statutory law actually applied to the colonies. While English and later British officials sought to extend a uniform body of law over British America, imperial officials and colonial lawyers recognized the importance of variation to accommodate local circumstances, as the historian Mary Sarah Bilder has argued. The crown granted charters authorizing colonial officials to make laws conformable to the laws of England, or at least not directly counter to them, while it acknowledged that conditions on the ground would shape their particular form.[17] In Virginia and other colonies, English laws came into force either by extension or accretion. The crown might extend the laws of the English realm by ordering colonial governments to enforce particular statutes in America, or Parliament might do so by directly naming colonies in a specific act. The Virginia House of Burgesses likewise adopted English statutes wholesale or in modified form as needed. Yet, vexing questions remained. Were English laws made after the date of settlement legally enforceable in the colonies, or did English law as it stood at the moment of the colony's founding bind them?[18]

Court cases, leading jurists, and American rebels structured the imperial debate in legal terms even as they failed to reach a consensus. In *Calvin's Case*, a 1608 proceeding before the Court of King's Bench, Sir Edward Coke ruled that the manner in which the crown acquired a new realm—either by conquest or inheritance—and the religious principles of the existing population determined how English laws could be applied. In the 1650s, Sir Matthew Hale contended that Englishmen carried English liberties and legal customs with them to the colonies, although not English law. Chief Justice Holt ruled in the 1693 case *Blankard v. Galdy* that Englishmen brought English law with them when they settled uninhabited spaces. Early seventeenth-century Virginia courts used English laws passed since the founding of Jamestown to decide cases when it proved convenient, but by the end of the century began to doubt the practice.[19] In 1681 they received encouragement from England's attorney general, Sir William Jones, who issued an opinion that English laws had no force in the colony if not so named or encompassed by its intent.[20]

In the mid-1760s, Sir William Blackstone claimed that the common law did not apply to Americans since the colonies had been acquired through conquest. He later revised his position to state that colonists had appropriated the common law for their own use. In the 1760s and 1770s, colonists who resisted

British rule argued that Parliament had no direct legislative authority over them. Whether or not English case law could or should be employed to decide legal controversies remained an open question long after independence.[21] The Revolution settled the controversy over who should rule the thirteen American colonies, but not how Americans should rule them.

With no published collections of colonial case law, Americans before the Revolution had to rely on a mix of English law reports, published compilations of parliamentary and local statutes, legal treatises, and memory of prior proceedings to adjudicate provincial disputes and define their legal relationship to the mother country.[22] Public and private libraries were central to this enterprise. The Virginia colonial government maintained an extensive law collection as part of its library in the Capitol in Williamsburg. (Sadly, most of these volumes disappeared during the Revolution.) In 1666, the General Assembly ordered county courts to procure volumes of English statutes to help local officials negotiate the boundaries between English and colonial law. Practicing attorneys like Jefferson maintained private libraries as well, although the size of a personal collection depended on one's wealth and social connections. Jefferson built or acquired a number of libraries over the course of his life, which included inherited volumes from George Wythe.[23] Patrick Henry constructed a smaller library to support his law practice, while John Adams augmented his professional library with texts from the estate of Jeremiah Gridley, a legal mentor.[24] Practicing or aspiring lawyers of lesser means often borrowed volumes from colleagues.

No author held more preeminence in the American legal mind before the Revolution than Sir Edward Coke. The famed jurist served as Elizabeth I's attorney general, and then chief justice of the Common Pleas and later King's Bench in the early years of James I's reign. Although Americans read a number of works in common that informed their understanding of power, authority, and constitutionalism in the revolutionary era—including Emerich de Vattel's *The Law of Nations* (1758), James Harrington's *The Commonwealth of Oceana* (1656), Algernon Sidney's *Discourses Concerning Government* (1698), a 1740 translation of Samuel Pufendorf's *Let Droit De La Nature Et Des Gens*, and John Locke's *Two Treatises of Government* (1689)—the revolutionary generation venerated Coke above all others as the great giver of English common law.[25] John Adams deemed him the "oracle of the Law," for "whoever is Master of his Writings is Master of the Laws of England."[26] South Carolina's wartime governor John Rutledge, who later served as the second chief justice of the U.S. Supreme Court, described Coke's *Institutes of the Lawes of England* as "almost the foundation of our law."[27] "In the study of Law the Common Law be [sic] sure deserves your first and last Attention," Jeremiah Gridley advised a young John Adams. He that "has conquered all the Difficulties of this Law" had conquered Coke's *Institutes*.[28]

Americans held Coke in such esteem for two reasons. First, they viewed Coke as a defender of English rights and liberties against monarchical and legislative corruption. As chief justice of Common Pleas and then King's Bench, Coke decided the *Case of Proclamations* (1610) that restricted the royal prerogative and declared the king subject to the law, and he hinted at the possibility of judicial review in *Dr. Bonham's Case* (1610). His opinion in *Calvin's Case* (1608) offered colonists a framework for defining the relationship between the colonists, the king, and Parliament.[29] Finally, as a member of Parliament, Coke helped to draft the Petition of Right (1628). In this major constitutional document, Parliament challenged Charles I's attempts to raise funds and quarter troops without its consent and to imprison offenders without a writ of habeas corpus.[30]

Reinforced by the Glorious Revolution of 1688, the English Bill of Rights, and political theorists of natural law and republicanism, Coke's actions gave Americans the legal language to contest Parliament's claims to sovereignty over the colonies. For example, in the 1760s colonists cited *Dr. Bonham's Case* to challenge the constitutionality of writs of assistance as well as the Stamp Act.[31] Alexander Hamilton drew on *Calvin's Case* to argue that Americans owed allegiance to the king only; Parliament had no power over them because they lived beyond Britain's borders.[32] Hamilton's argument reflected a growing American consensus that the colonies related to Great Britain only through the person of the king.

Second, Coke supplied Anglo-Americans with the most important analysis of English common law published before Blackstone's *Commentaries on the Laws of England*. Coke's four-volume *Institutes of the Lawes of England* (1628–1644) long served as *the* foundational text for law students on both sides of the Atlantic. In the early seventeenth century, Coke sought to demystify the common law as part of his broader campaign to reform and bring order to English law. The common law, as Jefferson suggested in the 1780s, had a kind of mythological quality to it. While other authors had published treatises on the common law, the legal historian David Chan Smith has argued that Coke "was conscious of the difficulty of interpreting the law. This awareness led him to take up the central problem of recovering the law's reason through method and logic."[33] By producing a systematic arrangement of the common law useful in the practice of interpreting and making law, Coke hoped to demonstrate its superiority to other forms of law by stressing its foundations in reason.

From Coke's perspective, the common law remedied legal abuses and miscarriages of justice by pointing out the unreasonableness of an action. His opinion in *Dr. Bonham's Case* seemed to suggest as much. It posited a form of judicial review by noting that "in many cases, the common law will controul acts of Parliament, and sometimes adjudge them to be utterly void: for when an act of Parliament is against common right and reason, or repugnant, or impossible to be performed, the common law will controul it, and adjudge such act to be void."[34] Coke intended his *Institutes*, along with his law reports, to help legal professionals make these distinctions. Americans like Jefferson, who fashioned themselves in the mold of seventeenth-century English Whigs who championed parliamentary rights over a stronger royal prerogative, celebrated Coke for providing some of the critical legal protections that informed their understanding of the British constitution.[35]

Americans turned to Coke's *Institutes* as the key legal text before and, to a lesser extent, after the Revolution. They studied the first volume specifically, which was an exhaustive commentary on Thomas Littleton's 1481 treatise on land tenures commonly known as *Coke on Littleton* or *Coke upon Littleton*. First published in 1628, this dense volume contains footnotes that often exceed in length the paragraphs and pages on which they comment. Copies of *Coke upon Littleton* resided in at least twenty-seven private Virginia libraries in 1776.[36] It was essential to legal education, yet maddening to read. In 1762, a young Jefferson wished "the Devil had old Cooke" as he struggled to get through the "old dull scoundrel" over the Christmas season.[37] William Bradford advised James Madison that the promise of a successful legal career made students "pore over the dry Pages of Littleton and Coke with more pleasure than those of Homer or Cicero."[38] John Quincy Adams "blunder[ed] along a few pages" one winter morning in 1788 while his cousin, William Cranch, studied the "dry pages of Coke upon Littleton" nine years later.[39] But all understood its importance to legal education. "Coke's Institutes are," as Jefferson advised a law student in 1773, "a perfect Digest of the law as it stood in his day."[40]

Despite the law's complexities, the majority of American law students had little opportunity to study this legal morass in any detail. In the eighteenth and early nineteenth centuries, the vast majority of American lawyers learned the law through private clerkships with practicing attorneys. Clerks copied legal documents, organized their mentor's papers, or filed documents with the courts, all features of daily life in a law practice. Very few colonists attended the Inns of Court in London for a comprehensive education. Aspiring attorneys spent more time learning the practical—and mundane—aspects of the legal profession than they did the law's theoretical and philosophical underpinnings.[41]

But students did gain access to their sponsor's small library. In the remaining hours of each day, men like John Adams, who clerked with James Putnam in Worcester, Massachusetts, in the late 1750s, or Jefferson, who studied under George Wythe in the early 1760s, read legal treatises, case reports, and political tracts that informed their understanding of the law and their place in the world.[42] If they read anything in this period, they read Coke and the local provincial laws. "When a young gentleman has resolved to study the law," one Virginian observed, "he applies himself to some attorney for his advice, assists him in copying a few declarations, reads the first book of Coke upon Littleton, and the Virginia laws, and then applies for a license, and begins to practice a profession . . . which he is perhaps utterly unacquainted with."[43] The self-taught Patrick Henry probably only studied for a few months at most before applying for his license.[44] By contrast, Jefferson studied over the course of at least two years.[45]

Jefferson later condemned the perils of this pedagogical imbalance. "The services [a lawyer] expected in return" for mentoring a budding attorney, he wrote to his cousin John Garland Jefferson in 1790, "have been more than the instructions have been worth." To truly study the law, he argued, "all that is necessary for a student is access to a library, and directions in what order the books are to be read."[46] Jefferson wished he had such guidance. In the early 1760s, he had purchased a copy of David Hume's *History of England*. Mesmerized by Hume's prose in his youth, his later reading taught him to see Hume as an apologist for the Stuart monarchs whose elegant book portrayed the seventeenth-century upheavals in England as a consequence of Parliament's encroachment on the royal prerogative, rather than royal infringement on the people's liberties.[47] As Jefferson planned the founding of the University of Virginia decades later, the library and its books became an integral component of the University and its mission to school lawyers in republicanism and the meaning of the American Revolution.

In 1776 Jefferson's colleagues in Virginia's Fifth Revolutionary Convention began building an eighteenth-century republican state by invoking seventeenth-century English law. As the legislative body that assumed power following the collapse of royal authority in Virginia, the Convention enacted "An ordinance to enable the present magistrates and officers to continue the administration of justice, and for settling the mode of proceedings in criminal and other cases till the same can be more amply provided for." Although work had begun on a state constitution, Virginia's legislators recognized that the demands of the war and the immediate need to preserve peace and security would "require some considerable time to compile a body of laws suited to the circumstances of the country." It was more sensible to adopt the common law and general statutes made in support of it as they stood "prior to the fourth year of the reign of king James the first," that is, 1607, the year English settlers succeeded in making a permanent settlement on Virginia soil.[48] As Jefferson outlined in his 1774 pamphlet *A Summary View of the Rights of British America*, these first Anglo-Americans, like the Saxons before them, "were the free inhabitants of the British dominions in Europe, and possessed a right, which nature has given all men" to emigrate to new lands and to make laws befitting their new society.[49] As Jefferson consequently argued, American settlers had been free to govern themselves from the moment they set foot on the continent in 1607. In 1776, the Virginia Convention declared that laws passed since 1607 by the colonial legislature, as opposed to Parliament, would be "in full force" as well until a superseding government saw fit to amend them.[50] Legislators in all but two colonies adopted similar reception statutes.[51]

By resetting the legal clock to 1607, revolutionary Virginians restored the law's foundations to what it had been in Coke's time. Wiping out nearly two centuries of legal history and debate was a conceptual move that brought the past in line with the present. It glossed over the contested nature of the transatlantic constitution in its claim that Parliament never had sovereign authority over Virginians and that the king alone united one dominion with another. Virginians pursued in practice what Jefferson had argued in *Summary View* and, later, implicitly in the Declaration of Independence. By retaining "the several acts of the general assembly of this colony now in force," the Convention preserved the English statutes that their predecessors had incorporated into Virginia law but not other parliamentary enactments.[52] Returning to first principles allowed Virginians to continue the practice of selectively appropriating English statutes as they framed a new republican government.

But the role that English common law ought to play in the new political order remained up for debate. Even as they wrote new constitutions to structure the future, Americans continued to wrestle with the past. Virginia and other states may have fixed 1607 as the year after which new English law no longer applied, but Americans could not easily ignore it. Anglo-Americans shared a legal history. Dismantling certain components of English common law and legal custom became central to Jefferson's republican project, an enterprise that culminated in his desire for Coke-centered legal education at the University of Virginia.

Beyond his contribution to Virginia's legal reform in the mid-1770s and 1780s (in which he helped the Virginia General Assembly abolish entail, primogeniture, and the established church), Jefferson launched a broader campaign against the jurisprudence of two eighteenth-century British jurists, William Murray, Lord Mansfield, and Sir William Blackstone.[53] Born in Perthshire, Scotland, Lord Mansfield joined the Court of King's Bench as chief justice in 1758 following his service as England's solicitor general and attorney general. Mansfield presided over the court during the first twenty-eight years of George III's reign.[54] Blackstone, the Vinerian Professor of English Law at Oxford University and later a judge on King's Bench and the Court of Common Pleas, authored the volumes that eventually displaced Coke's *Institutes* as the elementary text on English common law. First published between 1765 and 1769, Blackstone's *Commentaries on the Laws of England* are far less dense or complicated than Coke's *Institutes*. The volumes offered eighteenth-century readers a sophisticated, and readable, digest of the common law.[55]

From the Revolution to his death, Jefferson feared Mansfield's and Blackstone's corruption of American republicanism. If in Jefferson's mind Coke represented reason-based resistance to centralized authority, Mansfield and Blackstone embodied a Tory perspective that privileged monarchical government over the people's liberties. Similarly, and equally troubling, both men perpetuated in Jefferson's view the false notion that religion formed an integral component of the common law. "The essential principles of revealed religion are part of the common law," Mansfield argued in 1767, "so that any person reviling, subverting, or ridiculing them, may be prosecuted at common law."[56] Blackstone agreed, "for christianity is part of the laws of England."[57] Established churches reinforced state power by controlling a subject's religious beliefs; they punished nonconformists, using taxation or outright prosecution. Jefferson, who authored the Virginia Statute for Religious Freedom, expended considerable energy over the course of his life convincing himself and arguing to others that religion had never been part of the common law.[58] Disestablishment was a crucial way in which Jefferson endeavored to secure Virginia's independence from English law. Completing the Revolution meant gutting eighteenth-century Tory influence from what English law remained in place.

In 1777, Jefferson was serving in the Virginia House of Delegates, where he was engaged in the reformation of Virginia's laws, when a constitutional dispute arose between the House and the Senate.[59] The new Virginia Constitution of June 1776 forbade the Senate from amending money bills passed by the House.[60] The upper chamber could only approve or reject them. The Virginia Constitution carried the practice forward from the colonial era, which itself had been modeled after the division of powers between the two houses of Parliament. Overwhelmed with petitions for financial support from citizens affected by the Revolutionary War, the House had been lax in guarding its constitutional rights and had allowed the Senate to alter bills granting support to sufferers. In November 1777, however, the House took a stand when the Senate attempted to revise a bill granting Thomas Johnson, a captain in the Louisa County militia, a roughly £15 reimbursement for military expenditures.[61]

Jefferson's central role in defending the House's authority revealed both a strict constructionist interpretation of the constitution based on established precedent and his first serious condemnation of Blackstone's jurisprudence. If the term "money bill" in the constitution did not "immediately convey the precise idea which the framers of that act intended to express," he argued in a House committee report, the Senate ought to examine the "law and customs" of Parliament and colonial Virginia. Virginians "both under our regal and republican governments" had always recognized that "the law of parliament was their law" regarding appropriations. Irrespective of the custom's origins in the unwritten British Constitution, the Virginia Constitution expressly enumerated the House and Senate's respective powers. Only the people via their representatives in the House of Delegates could define the scope of an appropriations bill. The Senate "are at liberty to approve or reject the whole," but it could not amend the bill.[62]

The Senate protested that upholding Parliament, and "not our own Assembly, as the expositor of our Constitution" ignored the Virginia legislature's republican character. In Parliament, the Senate argued, the House of Commons represented the people; the House of Lords represented the aristocratic elements of British society more inclined to side with the crown. The framers of Virginia's constitution had chosen a different course by dividing the people's representation between the House and Senate. It had never been their intent, the Senate claimed, to deny the Senate the power to amend money bills. Besides, as the Senate argued in a counter to Jefferson's legal history, the colonial-era House of Burgesses had permitted the King's Provincial Council to alter appropriations. And yet despite its eagerness to prevent Parliament from expounding on the Virginia Constitution, the Senate could not escape the fact that Virginia's legal customs had been shaped by English law. In defense of its proposition, the Senate relied on Blackstone's *Commentaries* for its definition of "money bills." Although Blackstone's work offered greater support to Jefferson's constitutional reading of Parliamentary history, he did note one case in which the House of Lords had shorted the duration of a tax levied by the Commons.[63] To this the Virginia Senate, in almost an aside, yoked its claim.[64]

The Virginia Senate's use of Blackstone's *Commentaries* over Coke's *Institutes* is unsurprising. Americans had acquired an estimated 2,500 copies of Blackstone's book since the first volume appeared in 1765. This included roughly 1,500 copies of the first American edition, published in 1772 by the Philadelphia printer Robert Bell. Should the British have expected anything less from Americans than a robust legal defense of their rights and liberties, the whiggish Edmund Burke asked his fellow members of Parliament in a 1775 speech calling for reconciliation with the colonies? "In no country perhaps in the world," he argued, "is the law so general a study." He claimed that printers "have sold nearly as many of Blackstone's Commentaries in America as in England." Burke may have been exaggerating for effect, but only just barely. By the mid-1770s, Americans had less use for Coke now that they had Blackstone's simpler and more concise text.[65]

Jefferson spent the winter of 1777 reading through several volumes of *The History and Proceedings of The House of Commons from the Restoration to the Present Time*, Blackstone's *Commentaries*, case reports, and legal treatises as he prepared the House's rejoinder to the Senate.[66] In the finished reply, Jefferson listed numerous examples in which the Commons had defended its authority on money bills against the Lords. Moreover, it did not matter what "hidden" intent the framers of Virginia's constitution might have had when they wrote it; they incorporated the "law of parliament" into the document and "fixed" the Senate's powers regarding money bills. "Constructions" beyond the constitution's plain wording "are dangerous and not to be justified by ordinary emergencies." Whatever practices the House of Burgesses (or, indeed, the House of Delegates) might have allowed in the past no longer mattered.[67] In Jefferson's mind, the Virginia Constitution's meaning was clear.

What Jefferson objected to in particular was the Senate's "dangerous" use of Blackstone to bolster its pretensions to unenumerated authority. Blackstone, he intimated, lent greater support "to the prerogatives of the crown" than he did "the rights of the people" to give and dispose "of their own money." The authorities that Blackstone cited did, in fact, suggest that the House of Lords or even the king might alter a bill in certain circumstances, although they expressed doubts about its propriety. That Blackstone had merely de-

clared "such an experiment will hardly be repeated by the lords" in the modern era instead of "condemning [the idea] in decisive and unequivocal terms"
implied that the king or the Lords could infringe on the Commons' rights.[68]
Blackstone's reading of past precedents, Jefferson seemed to say, portended
abuse and corruption. His *Commentaries* reflected an eighteenth-century version of English law and British constitutionalism against which American republicans had rebelled. Moreover, Jefferson argued, "the judges of the common
law can take no cognizance of the law of parliament. . . . Their sayings or opinions on the subject must be ever extrajudicial."[69]

Surveying the state of American jurisprudence in 1785, Jefferson feared
that an "unexpected revolution" in English law led by Blackstone and Lord
Mansfield would infect the new republic. In addition to common law courts,
some American states had chancery courts (or courts of equity), modeled
after the British Court of Chancery, to handle legal controversies that did not
involve claims for damages. These courts had greater flexibility to resolve disputes than their common law counterparts, which rendered judgments based
on statute and case law. Mansfield, "a man of the clearest head and most seduc-
ing eloquence," had persuaded "the courts of Common law" to construe "their
text equitably. . . ." These "innovations, or civilisations of the Common Law,"
as Jefferson would later describe them, made the law less certain "under pre-
tense of rendering it more reasonable."[70] Mansfield did indeed favor incorporating principles of equity into the common law.[71] Blackstone, who found
courts of equity chaotic and almost incomprehensible, seemed to agree.[72] Jefferson believed that states with both chancery and common law courts should
forbid "all recurrence to English decisions" since Mansfield's ascension to the
bench, which might stave off the common law's perversion.[73]

Over time Jefferson grew increasingly troubled by Americans' continued reliance on these English legal authorities. Mansfield's position on seditious libel,
for example, could silence the government's critics and stifle a free press. It was
based on precedents established by Chief Justice Holt in the early eighteenth
century. Under English common law, libel was a criminal act regardless of
whether or not the statement was true. It was a crime to question the government's intent in the belief that such criticism led to disorder.[74] "Mansfield the
royalist," one legal scholar has argued, "believed at bottom that political authority emanated from the King." Challenges to that authority "were to Mansfield,
patently seditious."[75] He held that juries had no power to decide if the content of
a statement constituted seditious libel.[76] Juries could only determine the fact of
publication; the libel itself was a matter of law, which Mansfield believed only

judges could interpret. In reality, this meant that publication alone was sufficient to find a party guilty. It also meant that judges could find individuals in contempt of court for criticizing judicial officers in their official capacity.[77]

In 1788, the Pennsylvania Supreme Court employed Mansfield's rulings on seditious libel in a case involving Eleazer Oswald, the editor of the *Independent Gazetteer*. The English-born Oswald had served as a lieutenant colonel in the Continental Army and founded the *Independent Gazetteer*, a paper favoring the state's Republican faction, shortly before the war's end.[78] Oswald had a long-running feud with Thomas McKean, chief justice of the state supreme court. In 1782, Oswald published an article accusing McKean of disrespectful conduct toward military officers. McKean ordered Oswald's arrest for seditious libel and required him to post bond for his good behavior, but a grand jury twice refused to indict him. Six years later, one Andrew Browne brought suit against Oswald for libel. Following his release on bail, Oswald excoriated Browne and the state supreme court in his paper.[79] Although the Pennsylvania Constitution guaranteed freedom of the press, McKean ruled that Oswald's recent article was an attempt "to defeat and discredit the administration of justice."[80] He issued a contempt-of-court charge against Oswald, and the court found him guilty. McKean acknowledged that while some doubted the legality of the procedure, "not only my brethren and myself, but, likewise, all the judges of *England*, think, that without this power no court could possibly exist."[81] In other words, based at least in part on English law, the court possessed the power to defend its authority and reputation of its officials at the expense of a free press.[82]

Jefferson, then in Paris serving as the American ambassador to France, decried the Pennsylvania Supreme Court's use of Mansfield's jurisprudence. John Brown Cutting, an American war veteran studying law in London, supplied him with the basic outlines of Oswald's case, including McKean's use of the doctrine of attachment to hold Oswald in contempt of court.[83] McKean never cited Mansfield by name in his decision, nor did Cutting mention him in his letter, but Jefferson knew well on whose wisdom McKean had relied. "So evident a heresy in the common law," he argued, "ought not to be tolerated on the authority of two or three civilians who happen unfortunately to make authority in the courts of England." Modifying his earlier condemnation of Mansfield's case law, Jefferson now held "it essential in America to forbid that any English decision should ever be cited in a court, which has happened since the accession of Ld. Mansfeild [*sic*] to the bench." Jefferson recognized that Mansfield had authored some good opinions, particularly in the area of commercial law, "yet there is so much sly poison instilled into a great part of them, that it is better to proscribe the whole."[84] Lawyers, lacking a proper republican education, might fall prey to Mansfieldian temptation.

The ratification of the new national Constitution in 1788 heightened for Jefferson the danger of Mansfield's "sly poison" and Blackstone's seductive *Commentaries*. Americans cited both men during the ratification debates to advance arguments for or against the new federal regime. Coke merited fewer mentions, which also suggests Blackstone's wider accessibility.[85] The creation of a new national government divided Americans between supporters, who favored a more powerful federal state to better manage the nation's domestic and international affairs, and detractors, who feared it would weaken the respective states and trample on the people's individual liberties. Jefferson cautiously supported the new framework, but repeatedly urged James Madison to include a Bill of Rights "to guard the people against the federal government."[86]

By the early 1790s, Jefferson had become convinced that the emerging Federalist political party led by Alexander Hamilton and John Adams had taken up the mantle of George III's government. To Jefferson, Federalist politicians were Tories who possessed an expansive, unenumerated view of federal power that threatened the states and people. By contrast, he argued, his own Democratic-Republican opposition party (or simply "Republicans") stood as heirs to the English Whig tradition.[87] This became clearer to Jefferson when Federalists during John Adams's presidency began targeting Republican newspaper editors who criticized the government during the Quasi-War with France (1798–1800). Federal prosecutors brought criminal libel indictments first under what they claimed was federal common law and then under the Sedition Act of 1798.[88] Ironically, that act drew inspiration from a recent, liberalizing 1792 Act of Parliament, which gave juries the power to decide the truth or malice of an alleged libel.[89] Its Federalist supporters argued that the First Amendment's freedom of press clause did not protect the government's critics. They relied on formulations in Blackstone's *Commentaries* to argue that a government could silence its detractors in the interest of maintaining order and defending the state.[90]

Jefferson, Adams's vice president, rejected the idea of a federal common law of crimes and condemned the Sedition Act. When Virginia reconstituted as a republican state, he wrote to Edmund Randolph, "the nation" of Virginia "was not dissolved, was not annihilated." It simply remade itself and chose to adopt English common law as its law. The United States under the Constitution, alternatively, was a new entity. The Articles of Confederation had been a peace treaty between independent republics "for special purposes only," namely, to fight the British during the War of Independence and conduct international affairs on behalf of the several states. In Jefferson's view, the Constitution created a compact nation composed of the several states that had not existed previously.[91] The document itself was the supreme law of the land for this new nation, meaning that citizens of the constituent states had rejected, or certainly had not adopted, English common law on the federal level. No provision of the Constitution expressly gave the government the power to prosecute citizens for criminal libel.

Jefferson, along with James Madison, further emphasized this point in their secretly authored Virginia and Kentucky Resolutions of 1798 and 1799.[92] These measures, introduced in the general assemblies of those two states, argued that the Constitution was a compact between states in which its constituent members had delegated certain powers to the national government. In no instance did they grant the federal government the power to prosecute citizens for criminal seditious libel. The resolutions left unsaid that the states retained the power to bring indictments for such crimes under common law, which Republicans (occasionally with Jefferson's encouragement) did after the Jeffersonian "revolution" drove Federalists from power.[93] While the Sedition Act expired in the final days of the Adams administration, the question of a federal common law of crimes remained unresolved. In 1812, just over a decade after the Jeffersonian ascendency, the Supreme Court ruled the federal common law of crimes did not exist.[94]

Jefferson's retirement from the rigors of public life afforded him greater time to consider the dangers of English common law to American republicanism. On the eve of the War of 1812, he celebrated a legal victory over fellow Republican Edward Livingston, which raised the issue.[95] In 1807 the Napoleonic Wars, then raging in Europe, threatened to involve the United States. Acting on a request from the governor of the Louisiana Territory, Jefferson had prevented Livingston, who claimed title to a piece of land, from building improvements that could obstruct the free flow of river traffic at a perilous moment in international affairs. After Jefferson retired from the presidency, Livingston filed suit against him for illegal trespass and property confiscation in the U.S. Circuit Court for the District of Virginia. Livingston asked the court for $100,000 in damages. Jefferson prepared an exhaustive legal brief that traced legal title of the riverbed back to the kings of France and Spain, and thus to the United States via the Louisiana Purchase, but Jefferson's lawyers persuaded him that challenging the jurisdiction of the federal Circuit Court was a cheaper and more efficient legal strategy.[96] They proved right. In December 1811, Judge John Tyler (the father of the future president), joined by Chief Justice John Marshall, then riding the district circuit, drew inspiration from English common law to rule "an action of *Trespass* should be deemed a *local* Action."[97] A plaintiff could not bring suit against a party outside of the jurisdiction in which the alleged offense occurred. Federal courts in Virginia had no remedy for Livingston.

Judge Tyler sought out Jefferson's counsel several months after he had ruled in the former president's favor. What did Jefferson think, he asked, of Marshall's opinion that "decisions of British courts made since the revolution are not authority in this country ... [yet] they are entitled to that respect which is due to the opinions of wise men who have maturely studied the subject they decide."[98] In other words, Marshall based his decision on English common law even as he acknowledged that it had no formal power in the United States, and he had used both Blackstone and Mansfield to rule for Jefferson.

Jefferson offered Tyler his most comprehensive argument to date against the use of English legal authorities in American courts, even though Marshall's ruling in the Livingston case had gone in Jefferson's favor. Our ancestors, Jefferson reminded him, had adopted English common law out of convenience. As "the state of the English law at the date of our emigration, constituted the system adopted here," he argued, "we may doubt therefore the propriety" of quoting English jurists writing after the settlers' arrival in 1607. Certainly, Americans should reject "the admission of authorities" since "the accession of that king, whose reign, ab initio, was the very tissues of wrongs which rendered the Declaration [of Independence] at length necessary." This would rid American law of Mansfield and "uncanonise Blackstone." A student can find "a smattering of every thing" in Blackstone's book, "and his indolence easily persuades him that if he understands that book, he is master of the whole body of the law." Even "unlettered common people" could make a distinction between men "who have drawn their stores from the deep and rich mines of Coke Littleton" and those who only read Blackstone. Blackstone lawyers were "Ephemeral insects of the law."[99]

The War of 1812 only reinforced Jefferson's animosity toward Blackstone. The war was extremely unpopular in New England, where many citizens shared close economic ties with Great Britain. Already hurt by an embargo during Jefferson's presidency, James Madison instituted new restrictions in 1813 that further damaged the New England economy. The region's governors generally refused the federal government's request for militia; some

New England states even contemplated seceding from the Union. In Virginia, opportunistic merchants took advantage of the British invasion of the Chesapeake Bay area to sell goods to the enemy.[100] In 1814 Jefferson commiserated with New York author Horatio G. Spafford in decrying "our merchants, priests, and lawyers for their adherence to England & monarchy in preference to their own country and it's constitutions." He blamed the corruption of lawyers in part on "the substitution of Blackstone for my Lord Coke." The *Commentaries*, along with David Hume's *History of England*, "have made tories of all England, and are making tories" of young Americans. The two books had done more "toward the suppression of the liberties of man" than all of Napoleon's armies combined. English books, practices, and manners represented a greater threat to American liberty than force of arms.[101]

Jefferson devoted the last years of his life to constructing a university that would sustain his republican vision. In 1818 he described the fundamental purpose of the University of Virginia as an instrument "to form the statesmen, legislators & judges, on whom public prosperity, & individual happiness are so much to depend" and "to expound the principles & structures of government, the laws which regulate the intercourse of nations, those formed municipally for our own government, and a sound spirit of legislation, which banishing all arbitrary & unnecessary restraint on individual action shall leave us free to do whatever does not violate the equal rights of another."[102] The passage contained the hallmarks of Jefferson's republicanism and democratic idealism: limited government controlled by an informed citizenry who stood equal in rights to each other.[103] The white men who studied the law at his republican "seminary" would go forth to extinguish English common law's corrupting light forever. "Within a dozen or 20. years," a hopeful Jefferson told Madison, "a majority of our own legislature, will be from our school, & many disciples will have carried it's doctrines home with them to their several states."[104] In their hands he placed the Union's future.

Because Americans viewed the law as a means to understand the past and the present, Jefferson stressed the need for a broad legal education far more comprehensive than the majority of law students had received in the eighteenth and early nineteenth centuries. Clerking taught young men the practical aspects of the profession, but not the critical reasoning behind republican law, why it *mattered*. Over the years Jefferson recommended to students an intensive course of study with a rigorous reading schedule. "As other branches of science, especially history, are necessary to form a lawyer," he advised John

Garland Jefferson, "these must be carried on together" in the course of one's studies.[105] To another aspiring law student, written shortly before the War for Independence and reconveyed to another youth during the War of 1812, Jefferson suggested, "before you enter on the study of law a sufficient groundwork must be laid." He recommended building a foundational knowledge of Latin, French, mathematics, and natural philosophy before opening a law book. Once their legal studies began, students should "take with it such of it's kindred sciences as will contribute to eminence in it's attainment." This list of kindred subjects included "Physics, Ethics, Religion, Natural law, Belles lettres, Criticism, Rhetoric and Oratory," as a start.[106]

Jefferson believed his prescribed legal curriculum would make for a "superiority of knowledge" and a "thorough lawyer." Although it would take two or three years to complete, it ought to be done before entering a law practice. "Whenever that begins," Jefferson concluded, "there is an end of reading."[107] Clerkships afforded students very few contemplative opportunities. By moving legal training from the private office into an academy, Jefferson sought to give students the time and access to the resources they would need to become apostles of republicanism. Law would be one department among eight at the University of Virginia. Students could choose their additional courses from medicine, mathematics, chemistry, ancient languages, modern languages, natural philosophy, and moral philosophy. Students should master the law and think deeply on its place in the natural and physical worlds before they wielded it.

Selecting the right law professor to instruct young republicans was crucial. Jefferson and Madison took a more active role in the search for the law chair than they did for any other department. Their dogged search for a proper law professor went through eleven candidates and delayed the start of law classes until July 1826, a year and a half after the University opened. In the wake of the Missouri Compromise's restrictions on the expansion of slavery, and amid continued debates about the federal government's powers over internal improvements and the economy, both men feared installing a professor who favored stronger centralized national authority. Content to allow foreign-born men to hold the other professorships or delegate their recruitment to others, Jefferson argued that he and Madison were "the best judges" of prospective law professors. The law's centrality to the "character [of] our state, and the US" made it their duty "to lay down the principles which are to be taught."[108] They wanted "a native" Virginian who could bring a Virginian interest to bear against northern politicians, and a strong advocate for robust state-level authority under the Constitution.[109]

The two men scrutinized a candidate's credentials, "political orthodoxy," and powers he ascribed to Congress.[110] Richmond lawyers were suspect in their republican loyalties. They "are rank Federalists, as formerly denominated, & now Consolidationists," men who championed the federally managed consolidation of the republic through deliberate economic development and controlled territorial expansion.[111] They looked for men with "sound republican principles," disqualifying one candidate whom they observed had become a "convert to the constitutionality" of federal canal building.[112] Importantly, they required a professor who understood law beyond its everyday practical application. The new law chair ought to think "beyond the limits of technical Law." Jefferson abhorred the idea of settling for a "common-place" or a "Gothic" lawyer who could not think beyond a single text or teach anything more than municipal law.[113] He had to be "lucid" in speech and prose.[114] When called on in class or in conversation with colleagues, the law chair had to be able to enunciate his liberal and republican ideals and "speak on scientific subjects worthily of a Professor of an University."[115] If the law chair could not engage young minds or articulate reason-based jurisprudence, the law curriculum would come to naught.

When Jefferson and Madison identified John Tayloe Lomax as a candidate, they immediately inquired about his legal knowledge.[116] Did Lomax know the law "beyond the ordinary municipal law, to the law of nations, and to a more philosophical view of the general subject of the Law[?]" Lomax was not prolific for his political principles or pedagogy, but he would suffice in this late hour to find a law professor. Further, Madison heard from a trusted friend, that Lomax exhibited "advantageous elocution" and "has been a uniform sound patriot." In 1826, Lomax accepted the position, becoming the University's first law chair after six other candidates declined or died before assuming office. He served until 1830, when he resigned to become a Virginia state judge.[117]

But obtaining an appropriate republican professor was not enough. Constructing a curriculum and building a proper library centered on Sir Edward Coke, and like-minded jurists and political thinkers, were equally critical. Jefferson knew that he could never truly escape Mansfield or, especially, Blackstone. The latter's *Commentaries* were too prevalent in American society. Jefferson had even once praised their "most lucid" arrangement, but it was nothing more than "an elementary book" that "did not present all the subjects of the law in all their details." Before the Revolution, and before Blackstone's work became widely available in North America, "Coke Littleton was the universal elementary book of Law Students; and a sounder whig never wrote." For Jefferson, Coke's *Institutes* remained the foundational text on the "orthodox doctrines of the British Constitution" or what "were called English liberties." Jefferson's preferred seventeenth-century Whig view of the law had gone out of fashion when "the honied Mansfieldism of Blackstone" became the student's exclusive textbook.[118]

Jefferson would not banish Blackstone from the University, but rather dilute his influence through exposure to other texts and teachings. In Jefferson's view, men claiming to be good Whigs now sat in Congress charting the nation's future, unaware that as young men their consumption of Blackstone had turned them into Tories. Jefferson doubted they even knew "what whiggism, or republicanism" means.[119] In the event that a closet "Richm[d] lawyer, or one of that school of quondam federalism, now Consolidation," gained the law chair in the future, Jefferson believed that he had "to guard against the dissemination of such principles among our youth, and the diffusion of that poison, by a previous prescription of the texts to be followed in their discourses."[120] Madison agreed. Together, they assembled a reading list that would inculcate students with "the true doctrines of liberty" and in particular mentor students in the act of "guarding our Republican Charters against constructive violations."[121]

On March 4, 1825, Jefferson presented to the University's Board of Visitors a list of required texts "on the principles of government" for the law curriculum. The Board approved the inclusion of the political theory of Algernon Sidney's *Discourses on Government* and John Locke's "Essay concerning the true original, extent, & end, of civil govmt," which the Board pronounced as the leading sources on "the general principles of liberty and the rights of man, in nature, and in society." The Federalist Papers and the Virginia Resolution of 1799 against the Alien and Sedition Acts would give students a firm handle "on the distinctive principles of the govmt of our own state, and of that of the US. as understood and assented to when brought into the Union." Finally, students would read the Declaration of Independence as a means to interpret the federal Constitution's true meaning.[122]

The legal portion of the University's library would augment what students read in the classroom. *Coke upon Littleton* would serve as the foundational legal text in the classroom, with a library containing an extensive collection of law reports, treatises, and statutes.[123] Jefferson endeavored to democratize knowledge by building a library stocked with rare or expensive books accessible to the public. Acquiring "[g]reat standard works of established reputation" required hiring an agent with international connections.[124] In 1825 Jefferson as University rector hired Cummings, Hilliard & Company, booksellers in Boston, to purchase 3,113 titles for the University Library.[125] Jefferson included 448 law texts in his 1825 catalog sent to Cummings and Hilliard. These he categorized under chapters for Law of Nature & Nations; Chancery; Common Law; Law-Merchant; Law-Maritime; Law-Ecclesiastical; and Law-Foreign. As the highest priority, Jefferson instructed the agents to purchase *A Systematic Arrangement of Lord Coke's First Institutes of the Laws of England*, which he described as "the elementary book of the school."[126] Alongside Coke's book, Jefferson directed the Bostonians to purchase law dictionaries, equity case reports from the British High Court of Chancery, Sir Francis Bacon's *A New Abridgment of the Law*, Blackstone's *Commentaries*, Richard Wooddeson's *Lectures on the Laws of England*, and all of Baron Geoffrey Gilbert's tracts.[127]

Coke's works featured prominently in the University's first library. The shelves held one volume of Coke's *Entries* (a compilation of pleadings), seven volumes of his law reports, and three different editions of his *Institutes*. Jefferson also included works of Whig authors such as Henry Cary's *English Liberties: or, The free-born subject's Inheritance* (1719), and the 1766 revised and updated edition entitled *British Liberties*, as well as Roger Acherley's *The Britannic Constitution: or, The fundamental form of government in Britain* (1727). The library in general held works influential to American republicanism such as Henry St. John, Viscount Bolingbroke's *Letters on the State of History* (1788 edition). Jefferson had instructed his book buyers to purchase a republicanized version of Hume's *History of England*, but they bought an 1804 abridged London edition of the original work instead.[128]

In Jefferson's ideal world, the University's law students would read Coke and Whig writers first before they touched Blackstone. They would learn how Coke limited royal power, and in turn they would strive to weaken the federal government and defend the people's rights. Jefferson begrudgingly recognized Blackstone's *Commentaries* as a useful reference work, but one to be read only after they had learned to recognize its danger. And while Jefferson questioned Mansfield's jurisprudence on many fronts, and the validity of English case law since George III's ascension to the throne, they still had something to teach Virginia republicans. He ordered, and the first library contained, law reports compiled by Blackstone, Mansfield, and other jurists spanning the king's reign. Reading these reports would allow law students to trace the law's development, and to understand the wisdom of republicanism versus the tyranny of monarchy.

Unsurprisingly, Jefferson's idealized Coke-based legal education met with mixed results. While a fuller study of legal education at the University and use of its early library awaits, borrowing records and course syllabi from the late 1820s and 1830s provide a sense of what students read and what faculty taught.

According to one analysis of the books-borrowed records, between 1825 and 1828 students checked out Blackstone's *Commentaries* more frequently than Coke's *Institutes*. For example, in 1825 students borrowed Blackstone twenty-one times against Coke's seventeen. In the following year, students took home Blackstone thirteen times while Lord Coke merited only eight borrowings. In the two sessions that followed, students only borrowed Coke once, while no one borrowed Blackstone. This analysis does not account for what students may have read in the library without removing the volumes for further inspection, nor does it take into consideration evidence derived from student commonplace books, but it does point to the challenge of convincing students to read the dense Coke volumes first before imbibing the Blackstone honeypot.[129]

The disappearance of both Coke and Blackstone from the library's borrowing records may also be explained by the fact that the University's law professors assigned them as course texts. The professors used them in ways that might have caused Jefferson to question their republican commitments. Syllabi from the early 1830s show that Professor John Anthony Gardner Davis assigned Blackstone's *Commentaries* to the junior class. Seniors then read *Coke upon Littleton*. In some ways Davis's choice made sense. Blackstone served as a light introduction to English common law's core principles before they grappled with Coke's complexities. Yet Davis's curriculum ran counter ideologically to Jefferson's vision. Jefferson believed that the republic's survival hinged on making good nineteenth-century republicans by beginning their education in the seventeenth century. But Jefferson died only a few short months after he praised Coke in his letter to Madison. Davis could structure his courses as he wished. The earth, after all, belonged to the living.

Thomas Jefferson died fifty years after the Declaration of Independence severed Americans' political connection with Great Britain. And yet, as his advice to prospective law students, his vision for the University of Virginia, and his creation of its first library demonstrated, restoring American law to first principles and securing a republican revolution was a task far more difficult than he had imagined. Jefferson idealized a legal education that began with Sir Edward Coke and his *Institutes*, a book that could teach Virginia students the science of law as it had been when their ancestors arrived in North America, and help them identify the heresies of Blackstone and Mansfield.

The University, its books, and its graduates were meant to secure the promise of the American Revolution and Virginia's place in the Union. Making the common law more American and republican was a means toward that end. Amusingly, a portrait of Lord Mansfield now hangs in the University of Virginia Law Library.[130] Mansfield presides over rows of English law books, including various editions of Blackstone's *Commentaries*. His gaze is resolute, with the self-assurance of the man who ruled in the 1772 case *Somerset v. Stewart* that slavery had no foundation in English common law.[131] His portrait resides not far from class notebooks written by University law students in the early nineteenth century. They contain notes on the republican laws that justified the enslavement of the African Americans who built the physical University. Jefferson and his contemporaries could not ignore the past as they shaped the future. Neither can we.

Notes

1. Jefferson to Albert Gallatin, September 27, 1810, *PTJRS*, 3:124.

2. Jefferson to James Madison, October 15, 1810, *PTJRS*, 3:165.

3. Jefferson railed against several other potential justices, including Madison's eventual nominee, Joseph Story, whom he deemed "unquestionably a tory." Ibid., 166.

4. Jefferson added that Lord Mansfield, the chief justice of the Court of King's Bench in England during the second half of the eighteenth century, could similarly not overcome his legal schooling after his readings in Scottish Civil Law and European Continental Law shaped his interpretations of English common law. Ibid.

5. For Jefferson's conception of the past generally, see H. Trevor Colbourn, "Thomas Jefferson's Use of the Past," *WMQ* 15, no. 1 (1958): 56–70; Hannah Spahn, *Thomas Jefferson, Time, and History* (Charlottesville: University of Virginia Press, 2011).

6. The American Colonies Act, 6 Geo. 3 c 12 (1766), more commonly known as "The Declaratory Act."

7. Jefferson to William Roscoe, December 27, 1820, *Founders Online*, https://founders.archives.gov/documents/Jefferson/98-01-02-1712.

8. Jefferson to James Madison, February 17, 1826, *Founders Online*, https://founders.archives.gov/documents/Madison/04-03-02-0712.

9. On Jefferson and republicanism, see Ari Helo, "Jefferson's Conception of Republic Government," in *The Cambridge Companion to Thomas Jefferson*, ed. Frank Shuffelton (Cambridge: Cambridge University Press, 2009), 35–46.

10. Jefferson, *Principles of Government for UVa*, February 1825, *Founders Online*, https://founders.archives.gov/documents/Jefferson/98-01-02-5007; *Meeting Minutes of University of Virginia Board of Visitors*, March 4–5, 1825, March 4, 1825, *Founders Online*, https://founders.archives.gov/documents/Jefferson/98-01-02-5019.

11. Jefferson to James Madison, February 17, 1826, *Founders Online*, https://founders.archives.gov/documents/Jefferson/98-01-02-5912.

12. Bernard Bailyn, *The Ideological Origins of the American Revolution* (Cambridge, MA: Harvard University Press, 1967), 30–32.

13. Jefferson to Philip Mazzei, November [28,] 1785, *PTJ*, 9:67.

14. Jefferson to Thomas Cooper, January 16, 1814, *PTJRS*, 7:126.

15. John H. Langbein, Renée Lettow Lerner, and Bruce P. Smith, *History of the Common Law: The Development of Anglo-American Legal Institutions* (New York: Aspen, 2009); Kate Elizabeth Brown, *Alexander Hamilton and the Development of American Law* (Lawrence: University of Kansas Press, 2017), 4–5. For Jefferson's comments on the Anglo-Saxon origins of the common law, see Jefferson to George Wythe, November 1, 1778, *PTJ*, 2:229–31; Rockfish Gap Report of the University of Virginia Commissioners, August 4, 1818, *PTJRS*, 13:196–97.

16. Gordon S. Wood, *The Creation of the American Republic, 1776–1787* (Chapel Hill: University of North Carolina Press, 1998), 10, 262–63. For a cultural perspective on the American understanding of the imperial constitution, see Brendan McConville, *The King's Three Faces: The Rise and Fall of Royal America, 1688–1776* (Chapel Hill: Published for the Omohundro Institute of Early American History and Culture by the University of North Carolina Press, 2007).

17. Mary Sarah Bilder, *The Transatlantic Constitution: Colonial Legal Culture and the Empire* (Cambridge, MA: Harvard University Press, 2008), 31–39.

18. For the reception of English law in Virginia, see John Ruston Pagan, "English Statutes in Virginia, 1660–1714," in *"Esteemed Bookes of Lawe" and the Legal Culture of Early Virginia*, ed. Warren M. Billings and Brent Tarter (Charlottesville: University of Virginia Press, 2017), 57–94.

19. Bilder, *Transatlantic Constitution*, 31–39.

20. Pagan, "English Statutes in Virginia," 74.

21. Bilder, *Transatlantic Constitution*, 31–39.

22. Wood, *Creation of the American Republic*, 296–97.

23. The most comprehensive treatment of Jefferson's reading habits and libraries is Kevin J. Hayes, *The Road to Monticello: The Life and Mind of Thomas Jefferson* (New York: Oxford University Press, 2008). For extensive catalogs of Jefferson's respective libraries, see "Legacy Library: Thomas Jefferson," *LibraryThing*, https://www.librarything.com/profile/ThomasJefferson; University of Virginia Law Library, *The 1828 Catalogue Project: The First Law Library of the University of Virginia*, http://archives.law.virginia.edu/catalogue/.

24. For Henry's Library, see Kevin J. Hayes, "The Law Library of a Working Attorney: The Example of Patrick Henry," in Billings and Tarter, eds., *"Esteemed Bookes of Lawe,"* 137–56. For a useful new digital collection of Henry's writings and books, see Patrick Henry Memorial Foundation, *Patrick Henry Library*, http://www.patrickhenrylibrary.org/. For Adams and Gridley, see *The Earliest Diary of John Adams: June 1753–April 1754; September 1758–1759*, ed. L. H. Butterfield, Wendell D. Garrett, and Marc Friedlaender (Cambridge, MA: Belknap Press of Harvard University Press, 1966), 58n2.

25. Charles F. Mullett, "Coke and the American Revolution," *Economica* 38 (November 1932): 457–71.

26. John Adams to Jonathan Mason Jr., August 21, 1776, *APDE*.

27. John Rutledge to Edward Rutledge, July 30, 1769, reprinted in John Belton O'Neall, *Biographical Sketches of the Bench and Bar of South Carolina* (Charleston: S. G. Courtenay & Co., 1859), 124.

28. October 25, 1758, *Diary of John Adams*, vol. 1, *APDE*.

29. *Case of Proclamations* (1610), in *The Reports of Sir Edward Coke*, ed. George Wilson (London, Printed for J. Rivington and Sons, St. Paul's Church-Yard; W. Owen, Fleet-Street; T. Longman and G. Robinson, Pater-Noster Row; G. Kearsly, Fleet-Street; W. Flexney and W. Cater, Holborn; E. Brooke, Bell-Yard, Temple-Bar; and T. Whieldon and Co. Fleet-Street, 1777), 7:74–76; *Dr. Bonham's Case* (1610), ibid., 4:107–21; *Calvin's Case* (1608), ibid., 4:1–29.

30. For the Petition of Right, habeas corpus, and Coke's evolving views, see Paul Halliday, *Habeas Corpus: From England to Empire* (Cambridge, MA: Harvard University Press, 2012), 222–24.

31. See James Otis's arguments against in the constitutionality of the writs of assistance using Coke, in M. H. Smith, *The Writs of Assistance Case* (Los Angeles: University of California Press, 1978), 358–62.

32. Alexander Hamilton, *The Farmer Refuted: or A more impartial and comprehensive View of the Dispute between Great-Britain and the Colonies, Intended as a Further Vindication of the Congress: In Answer to a Letter From A. W. Fanner, Intitled A View of the Controversy Between Great-Britain and her Colonies: Including a Mode of determining the present Disputes Finally and Effectually, &c . . .* (New York: James Rivington, 1775). *The Papers of Alexander Hamilton Digital Edition*, ed. Harold C. Syrett (Charlottesville: University of Virginia Press, Rotunda, 2011), http://rotunda.upress.virginia.edu/founders/default .xqy?keys=ARHN.

33. David Chan Smith, *Sir Edward Coke and the Reformation of the Laws: Religion, Politics and Jurisprudence, 1578–1616* (Cambridge: Cambridge University Press, 2014), 139.

34. *Dr. Bonham's Case* (1610), in Wilson, *Reports of Sir Edward Coke*, 4:118.

35. For Jefferson's reading of Whig history, see Trevor H. Colbourn, "Thomas Jefferson's Use of the Past," *WMQ* 15, no. 1 (1958): 56–70. Ironically, Americans' perception of Coke represented a selective reading of English legal history. True, Coke did hand down decisions that curtailed the scope of the king's authority and hinted at legal mechanisms to nullify Acts of Parliament. See Smith, *Sir Edward Coke*, 1–19. More recent analysis, however, has shown that Coke's commitment to the common law earlier in his career was as much a means to protect royal authority as it was to prevent its abuses. As the fountain of justice, the king occupied a central place within the English legal system and had an implicit moral obligation to correct its misuse. Coke, these scholars argue, believed that common law remedies rooted in reason strengthened the king's authority by ensuring confidence in the judicial process and in turn shielded the king from misapplying the law. Coke's increasing skepticism of royal power only evolved over time as he struggled to reform the law and dealt with the political controversies of his day. See Smith, *Sir Edward Coke*, and Halliday, *Habeas Corpus*. For a general biography of Coke, see Catherine Drinker Bowen, *The Lion and the Throne: The Life and Times of Sir Edward Coke: 1552–1634* (Boston: Little, Brown, 1956). For his early career, see Allen D. Boyer, *Sir Edward Coke and the Elizabethan Age* (Stanford, CA: Stanford University Press, 2011).

For a useful collection of essays on Coke's writings, see *Law, Liberty, and Parliament: Selected Essays on the Writings of Sir Edward Coke*, ed. Allan D. Boyer (Indianapolis: Liberty Fund, 2004).

36. W. Hamilton Bryson, "Law Books in the Libraries of Colonial Virginians," in Billings and Tarter, eds., *"Esteemed Bookes of Lawe,"* 33. Bryson also found that Coke's law reports were the most popular case reports among colonial Virginians. Twenty full or partial copies existed in Virginia libraries (31). For Bryson's comprehensive census, see his *Census of Law Books in Colonial Virginia* (Charlottesville: University of Virginia Press, 1978).

37. Jefferson to John Page, December 25, 1762, *PTJ*, 1:3–6.

38. William Bradford to James Madison, March 4, 1774, in *The Papers of James Madison Digital Edition*, ed. J. C. A. Stagg (Charlottesville: University of Virginia Press, Rotunda, 2010), http://rotunda.upress.virginia.edu/founders/default.xqy?keys=JSMN.

39. January 16, 1788, *Diary of John Quincy Adams, APDE*; William Cranch to Abigail Adams, November 21, 1797, *APDE*.

40. Jefferson to Bernard Moore, ca. 1773, enclosed in Jefferson to John Minor, August 30, 1814, *PTJRS*, 7:627.

41. Herbert A. Johnson, "Thomas Jefferson and Legal Education in Revolutionary America," in *Thomas Jefferson and the Education of a Citizen*, ed. James Gilreath (Washington, DC: Library of Congress, 1993), 105.

42. For Jefferson's and Adams's training, see Frank Dewey, *Thomas Jefferson, Lawyer* (Charlottesville: University of Virginia Press, 1986), 9–17; Richard Alan Ryerson, *John Adams's Republic: The One, the Few, and the Many* (Baltimore: Johns Hopkins University, 2016), ch. 1.

43. *Virginia Gazette* (Rind), December 30, 1773, quoted in Jon Kukla, *Patrick Henry: Champion of Liberty* (New York: Simon & Schuster, 2017), 32.

44. Ibid.

45. Dewey, *Thomas Jefferson, Lawyer*, 10–11.

46. Jefferson to John Garland Jefferson, June 11, 1790, *PTJ*, 16:480.

47. Jefferson to William Duane, August 12, 1810, *PTJRS*, 5:5. Also Douglas L. Wilson, "Jefferson vs. Hume," *WMQ* 46, no. 1 (January 1989): 49.

48. "An ordinance to enable the present magistrates and officers to continue the administration of justice, and for settling the general mode of proceedings in criminal and other cases till the same can be more amply provided for." William Walker Hening, *The Statutes at Large; Being a Collection of all the Laws of Virginia from the First Session of the Legislature, in the year 1619* (Richmond: J.& G. Cochran, Printers, 1821), 9:127.

49. Jefferson, "A Summary View of the Rights of British America," *PTJ*, 1:121.

50. "An ordinance to enable the present magistrates and officers to continue the administration of justice, and for settling the general mode of proceedings in criminal and other cases till the same can be more amply provided for." Hening, *Statutes at Large*, 9:127.

51. Phillip I. Blumberg, *Repressive Jurisprudence in the Early American Republic: The First Amendment and the Legacy of English Law* (Cambridge: Cambridge University Press, 2010), 57–58.

52. Hening, *Statutes at Large*, 9:127.

53. For Jefferson's legal reforms, see R. B. Bernstein, *Thomas Jefferson* (New York: Oxford University Press, 2003), ch. 3. For Virginians and the law in the early Republic, see Jessica K. Lowe, *Murder in the Shenandoah: Making Law Sovereign in Revolutionary Virginia* (Cambridge: Cambridge University Press, 2019).

54. For a general biography of Lord Mansfield, see Norman S. Poser, *Lord Mansfield: Justice in the Age of Reason* (Montreal: McGill-Queen's University Press, 2013). For Mansfield's jurisprudence, see James Oldham, *English Common Law in the Age of Mansfield* (Chapel Hill: University of North Carolina Press, 2004).

55. For Blackstone, see Wilfrid Prest, *William Blackstone: Law and Letters in the Eighteenth Century* (New York: Oxford University Press, 2008). For a perspective on Blackstone's reception in America, see Mary Sarah Bilder, Maeve Marcus, and R. Kent Newmyer, eds., *Blackstone in America: Selected Essays of Kathryn Preyer* (Cambridge: Cambridge University Press, 2009).

56. Mansfield's Speech in the House of Lords on the case of *Chamberlain of London vs. Allan Evans, Esq.* is reprinted in John Holliday, *The Life of William Late Earl Mansfield* (London, 1797), 255.

57. Sir William Blackstone, *Commentaries on the Laws of England* (Philadelphia: Robert Bell, 1772), 4:59.

58. See sections 873 to 879 in Thomas Jefferson, *Legal Commonplace Book, 1762–1767*, Manuscript Division, Library of Congress, Washington, DC. See Jefferson to Thomas Cooper, January 16, 1814 and Jefferson to Thomas Cooper, February 10, 1814, *PTJRS*, 7:124–31, 190. Jefferson relied on the same material in a letter to John Adams, January 24, 1814, *PTJRS*, 7:146–51. Adams called Jefferson's research "curious and very important," but sidestepped the issue by calling religion but one of "So many Seed Plots of Division, Faction, Sedition, and Rebellion" in American society. John Adams to Jefferson, March 3, 1814, *PTJRS*, 7:217.

59. In September 1776, Jefferson resigned his seat in the Continental Congress in order to serve in the Virginia House of Delegates.

60. Virginia Constitution of June 29, 1776.

61. Petition of Thomas Johnson, [before November 11, 1777], *PTJ*, 2:45. See also the "Editorial Note" that precedes Johnson's petition for a fuller explanation of this controversy.

62. Report of the Committee of House of Delegates on Right of Senate to Alter Money Bills, [December 4, 1777], *PTJ*, 2:46–47.

63. Blackstone, *Commentaries*, 1:170.

64. Reply of Senate to House of Delegates concerning Money Bills, [December 9, 1771], *PTJ*, 2:48–49.

65. Julius S. Waterman, "Thomas Jefferson and Blackstone's Commentaries," in *Essays in the History of Early American Law*, ed. David H. Flaherty (Chapel Hill: University of North Carolina Press, 1969), 452. Louis DuPont Syle, ed., *Burke's Speech on Conciliation with the Colonies March 22, 1775* (Boston: Leach, Shewell & Sanborn, 1895), 26. The fourth volume of the first American edition of Blackstone's Commentaries contains a list of American subscribers. See "Subscribers in Virginia to Blackstone's Commentaries on the Laws of England, Philadelphia, 1771–1772," *WMQ* 1, no. 3 (1921): 183–85.

66. *The History and Proceedings of the House of Commons from the Restoration to the Present Time*, 14 vols. (London: 1742–1744). Notes on Money Bills, [before January 9, 1778], *PTJ*, 2:50–54. Jefferson may also have consulted his parliamentary commonplace book. See *Jefferson's Parliamentary Writings: Parliamentary Pocket-Book and a Manual of Parliamentary Practice*, ed. Wilbur Samuel Howell (Princeton, NJ: Princeton University Press, 2014), 61–62.

67. Communication from the House of Delegates to Senate concerning Money Bills, [January 9, 1778], *PTJ*, 2:54–55.

68. Blackstone, *Commentaries*, 1:170 ("such an experiment"); Communication from the House of Delegates to Senate concerning Money Bills, [January 9, 1778], *PTJ*, 2:58 ("condemning them in decisive").

69. Communication from the House of Delegates to Senate concerning Money Bills, [January 9, 1778], *PTJ*, 2:58. In its reply, the Senate cited several instances in which the House of Lords had amended parts of bills unrelated to appropriations. Both the Senate and Jefferson suggested a compromise whereby the Senate could amend bills in a similar fashion. In the end, the General Assembly put off a decision until the next session. The constitutional dispute was not fully resolved until the adoption of the Virginia Constitution of 1830. Reply of Senate to House of Delegates concerning Money Bills, [January 15, 1778], *PTJ*, 2:59–62; Draft of a Resolution concerning Money Bills, [before January 13, 1778], *PTJ*, 2:62. See also the "Editorial Note" preceding these documents.

70. Jefferson to Philip Mazzei, November [28,] 1785, *PTJ*, 9:71; Jefferson to Judge John Tyler, June 17, 1812, *PTJRS*, 5:135 ("innovations, or civilisations").

71. Oldham, *English Common Law*, 6.

72. W. S. Holdsworth, "Blackstone's Treatment of Equity," *Harvard Law Review* 43, no. 1 (1929): 1–32.

73. Jefferson to Philip Mazzei, November [28,] 1785, *PTJ*, 9:71.

74. Blackstone, *Commentaries*, 4:151–52.

75. Oldham, *English Common Law*, 235.

76. *Rex v. Woodfall* (1770), in *Reports of Cases Argued and Adjudged In the Court of King's Bench, During the Time of Lords Mansfield's presiding in that Court, From Michaelmas Term 30 Geo. II. 1756, to Easter Term 12 Geo. III 1772*, ed. Sir James Burrow (London: A. Strahan and W. Woodfall, 1790), 5:2661–70.

77. Oldham, *English Common Law*, 210.

78. "Major Newspapers, Printers and Policies," in *The Documentary History of the Ratification of the Constitution, Digital Edition*, ed. John P. Kaminski et al. (Charlottesville: University of Virginia Press, 2009), http://rotunda.upress.virginia.edu/founders /RNCN.html (hereinafter *DHRC*).

79. *Independent Gazetteer*, July 1, 1788.

80. *Respublica v. Oswald* (1788), in *Reports of Cases Ruled and Adjudged in the Courts of Pennsylvania, Before and Since the Revolution*, ed. A. J. Dallas (Philadelphia: T. Bradford, 1790), 324.

81. *Respublica v. Oswald*, 329.

82. For a fuller treatment of *Respublica v. Oswald*, see Saul Cornell, *The Other Founders: Anti-Federalism and the Dissenting Tradition in America* (Chapel Hill: Published for the

Omohundro Institute of Early American History and Culture by the University of North Carolina Press, 1999), 128–36. For similar cases, see Blumberg, *Repressive Jurisprudence*, 52–71.

83. John Brown Cutting to Jefferson, September 23, 1788, *PTJ*, 13:629–30.

84. Jefferson to John Brown Cutting, October 2, 1788, *PTJ*, 13:649. For a similar case involving William Duane, publisher of the pro-Jeffersonian Philadelphia newspaper *Aurora*, see Jefferson to Robert R. Livingston, May 31, 1801, *PTJ*, 34:213; Robert R. Livingston to Jefferson, May 31, 1801, *PTJ*, 34:214–16; James Madison to Jefferson, [on or before July 17, 1801], *PTJ*, 34:583–85. On Mansfield and commerce, see Oldham, *English Common Law*, 79–208. Jefferson offered his approval of one of Mansfield's decisions regarding prizes cases in Jefferson to Levi Lincoln, June 12, 1801, *PTJ*, 34:320–21.

85. Examples from the ratification debates include James Madison's reference to Blackstone's *Commentaries* as "a book which is in every man's hand," *DHRC*, 10:1382; William Findley in Pennsylvania stated that if his son "was not acquainted with the passage in Blackstone" on jury trials, "I should be justified in whipping him." *DHRC*, 2: 532. Donald Lutz found that Blackstone was the second-most-cited writer in the United States in the 1780s and the most-cited writer in the 1790s, ahead of Coke. He noted that in the colonial period of the 1760s, Coke had more citations than Blackstone. Donald Lutz, "The Relative Influence of European Writers on Late Eighteenth-Century American Political Thought," *American Political Science Review* 78, no. 1 (March 1984), 193.

86. James Madison to Jefferson, December 9, 1787, *PTJ*, 12:408–12; Jefferson to Madison, December 20, 1787, *PTJ*, 12:439–42; Jefferson to Madison, February 6, 1788, *PTJ*, 12:569–70; Madison to Jefferson, February 19, 1788, *PTJ*, 12:607–10; Madison to Jefferson, April 22, 1788, *PTJ*, 13:98–99; Madison to Jefferson, July 24–26, 1788, *PTJ*, 13:412–14; Jefferson to Madison, July 31, 1788, *PTJ*, 13:443 ("guard the people").

87. Wood, *Empire of Liberty*, 256.

88. "Chapter 40, 8 Congress, Session 1, An Act: In addition to the act entitled 'An act for the punishment of certain crimes against the United States,'" in *The Public Statutes at Large of the United States*, ed. Richard Peters (Boston: Charles C. Little and James Brown, 1848), 1:596–97.

89. 32 Geo. III c. 60 (1792).

90. Blackstone, *Commentaries*, 4:151–52; Blumberg, *Repressive Jurisprudence*, 87.

91. Jefferson to Edmund Randolph, August 18, 1799, *PTJ*, 31:170.

92. "Virginia Resolution (1798)," in *The Debates in the Several State Conventions, on the Adoption of the Federal Constitution, as Recommended by the General Convention at Philadelphia in 1787*, ed. Jonathan Elliot (Washington, DC: Taylor & Maury, 1854), 528–29; "Kentucky (1799) Resolutions," in ibid., 540–45.

93. Blumberg, *Repressive Jurisprudence*, 148–214.

94. *United States v. Hudson* (1812), in *Reports of Cases Argued and Adjudged in the Supreme Court of the United States in February Term 1812, and February Term, 1813*, ed. William Cranch (Washington, DC: Daniel Rapine, 1816), 32–34.

95. U.S. Circuit Ct. Dist. Of Va., 15 F. Cas. 660 (No. 8411) (1811). For a discussion of this case, see James F. Simon, *What Kind of Nation: Thomas Jefferson, John Marshall, and the Epic Struggle to Create the United States* (New York: Simon & Schuster, 2002), 260–65.

96. Jefferson eventually published the brief as Thomas Jefferson, *The Proceedings of the Government of the United States in Maintaining the Public Right to the Beach of the Missisip[p]i, Adjacent to New-Orleans, Against the Intrusion of Edward Livingston* (New York: [s.n.], 1812).

97. The Dismissal of *Livingston v. Jefferson*: I. John Tyler's Opinion in *Livingston v. Jefferson*, [December 4, 1811], *PTJRS*, 4:293.

98. The Dismissal of *Livingston v. Jefferson*: II. John Marshall's Opinion in *Livingston v. Jefferson*, [December 4, 1811], *PTJRS*, 4:300.

99. Jefferson to Judge John Tyler, June 17, 1812, *PTJRS*, 5:134–37.

100. For a general overview of the War of 1812, see J. C. A. Stagg, *The War of 1812: Conflict for a Continent* (Cambridge: Cambridge University Press, 2012). For enterprising Virginia merchants during the war, see Alan S. Taylor, *The Internal Enemy: Slavery and War in Virginia, 1772–1832* (New York: W. W. Norton, 2014).

101. Jefferson to Horatio G. Spafford, March 17, 1814, *PTJRS*, 7:249. For Spafford's initial letter, see Spafford to Jefferson, December 17, 1813, *PTJRS*, 7:57–58.

102. Rockfish Gap Report of the University of Virginia Commissioners, [August 4] 1818, *PTJRS*, 13:209–24.

103. Helo, "Jefferson's Conception of Republican Government," 42.

104. Jefferson to Madison, February 17, 1826, in David B. Mattern et al., eds., *The Papers of James Madison—Retirement Series* (Charlottesville: University of Virginia Press, 3 vols. to date, 2009–) (hereinafter *PJM-RS*), 3:688.

105. Jefferson to John Garland Jefferson, June 11, 1790, *PTJ*, 16:482.

106. Jefferson to Bernard Moore, c. 1773, enclosed in Jefferson to John Minor, August 30, 1814, *PTJRS*, 7:625–26.

107. Jefferson to John Garland Jefferson, June 11, 1790, *PTJ*, 16:482.

108. Jefferson to Madison, February 1, 1825, *PJM-RS*, 3:470.

109. Jefferson to Madison, November 6, 1823, *PJM-RS*, 3:155.

110. Jefferson to Madison, January 20, 1826, *PJM-RS*, 3:669.

111. Jefferson to Madison, February 1, 1825, *PJM-RS*, 3:470. Cameron Addis, *Jefferson's Vision for Education 1760–1845* (New York: Peter Lang, 2003), 107.

112. Jefferson to Madison, May 13, 1825, *PJM-RS*, 3:527–29; Madison to Jefferson, February 17, 1825, *PJM-RS*, 3:474.

113. Madison to Jefferson, January 28, 1825, *Founders Online*, https://founders.archives.gov/documents/Madison/04-03-02-0467; Jefferson to James Breckenridge, December 22, 1824, *Founders Online*, https://founders.archives.gov/documents/Jefferson/98-01-02-4802; Jefferson to Madison, January 23, 1825, *PJM-RS*, 3:465. See generally Madison to Jefferson, August 4, 1825, *PJM-RS*, 3:569. The teaching of law in terms of both practice and philosophy proved difficult to implement at the University of Virginia. In 1829, the University faculty journal published a notice that practical law would be taught to first-year students and would suffice for those interested in entering private practice, while students who remained for a second year of classes would engage in deeper studies of legal philosophy. "University Intelligence," August 5, 1829, *Virginia Literary Museum and Journal of Belles Lettres, Arts, Sciences, Etc.* 1, no. 8 (1829): 121.

114. Jefferson to Madison, May 13, 1825, *PJM-RS*, 3:528.

115. Jefferson to James Breckenridge, December 22, 1824, *Founders Online*, https://founders.archives.gov/documents/Jefferson/98-01-02-4802.

116. Francis Walker Gilmer had been named chair in 1823 and helped the University recruit faculty in Europe, but he became seriously ill after his return from Europe, which prompted Jefferson and Madison to seek other candidates for the position. Gilmer died in early 1826.

117. Jefferson to Madison, August 4, 1825, *Founders Online*, https://founders.archives.gov/documents/Jefferson/98-01-02-5432; Jefferson to John Tayloe Lomax, April 12, 1826, *Founders Online*, https://founders.archives.gov/documents/Jefferson/98-01-02-6040.

118. Jefferson to Thomas Cooper, January 16, 1814, *PTJRS*, 7:126.

119. Jefferson to Madison, February 17, 1826, *PJM-RS*, 3:688.

120. Jefferson to Joseph Carrington Cabell, February 3, 1825, *Founders Online*, https://founders.archives.gov/documents/Jefferson/98-01-02-4932.

121. Madison to Jefferson, February 8, 1825, *PJM-RS*, 3:471.

122. Principles of Government for UVa, February 1825, *Founders Online*, https://founders.archives.gov/documents/Jefferson/98-01-02-5007; Meeting Minutes of the University Board of Governors, March 4–5, 1825, *Founders Online*, https://founders.archives.gov/documents/Jefferson/98-01-02-5019.

123. Jefferson outlined his thoughts on the foundational texts for Americans studying law to Dabney Carr Terrell, and his reading recommendations mirrored those he later made to Cummings and Hilliard for the University library. He wrote to Terrell of his reading choices, specifically Lord Coke's *First Institutes*: "[T]hese give a compleat body of the law as it stood at the reign of the 1st James, an epoch the more interesting to us, as we separated at that point from English legislation, and acknolege no subsequent statuary alterations." Jefferson to Dabney Carr Terrell, February 26, 1821, *Founders Online*, https://founders.archives.gov/documents/Jefferson/98-01-02-1868.

124. Printed in Frederick W. Page, "Our Library," *Alumni Bulletin*, 2 (November 1895): 79. The original manuscript copy of Jefferson's 1825 Catalog of Books for the University of Virginia likely burned in the Rotunda fire of 1895. A copy of the 1825 Catalog, done by Nicholas P. Trist, does exist at UVA Special Collections, but this version does not include the explanatory text. Thomas Jefferson Catalog of Books for the University of Virginia Library, June 3, 1825, Acc. 38-747, Albert & Shirley Small Special Collections Library, University of Virginia (hereinafter "UVASC").

125. Jefferson to William Hilliard, June 3, 1825, *Founders Online*, https://founders.archives.gov/documents/Jefferson/98-01-02-5278. Ultimately, most of the books that Cummings and Hilliard acquired were printed in Europe, and the majority of those (1,070) were printed in England. Of the 369 law titles in the library's 1828 Catalogue, only 24 were published in the United States. Statistics on book publication location from U.Va. First Library Project, SHANTI, University of Virginia. Accessed July 14, 2015, http://www.viseyes.org/show/?base=library.

126. Jefferson to Jacob Abbot Cummings, January 17, 1825, *Founders Online*, https://founders.archives.gov/documents/Jefferson/98-01-02-4879; John Henry Thomas, *A systematic arrangement of Lord Coke's First Institute of the laws of England: on the plan of Sir*

Matthew Hale's analysis; with the annotations of Mr. Hargrave, Lord Chief Justice Hale, and Lord Chancellor Nottingham; and a new series of notes and references to the present time: including tables of parallel reference, analytical tables of contents, and a copious digested index (London: S. Brooke, 1818).

127. Jefferson to William Hilliard, August 7, 1825, *Founders Online,* https://founders .archives.gov/documents/Jefferson/98-01-02-5447; John Clarke, *Clarke's Bibliotheca Legum; Or, Complete Catalogue of the Common and Statute Law-books of the United Kingdom, with an Account of Their Dates and Prices, Arranged in a New Manner.* (London: W. Clarke and Sons, 1819).

128. Wilson, "Jefferson vs. Hume," 60.

129. Cannon Lane, "Catalogue of Borrowed Books Analysis—Final." Unpublished research, July 6, 2017. Lane served as one of the University of Virginia Law Library's public history interns in summer 2017. Lane analyzed University of Virginia Library List of Books Borrowed, 1825–1827, Accession #RG-12/12/1.113, UVASC.

130. Paolol Troubetzkoy, *Sir William Murray, Lord Mansfield,* 1932, oil on canvas, Arthur J. Morris Law Library, University of Virginia School of Law. Troubetzkov erroneously added "Sir" to Mansfield's title. His work is a copy of a 1785 portrait by Sir Joshua Reynolds that now hangs in Scone Palace, Perth, Scotland.

131. *Somerset v. Stewart* (1772), 98 E.R. 499. While Mansfield ruled that slavery had no foundation in common law, meaning that legal slavery would require an Act of Parliament, the chief justice sought to issue a narrow ruling that balanced commercial property rights against the absence of slavery in the legal code. In short, he intended his ruling to prevent the forced removal of Africans out of England, but technically their owners retained them as property, and the ruling had no legal effect in the colonies that had positive slave codes. Thus, if they left England's borders, the slaves lost the protection of Mansfield's ruling. Of course, his opinion took on a meaning greater for both slaveholders and abolitionists. See Oldham, *English Common Law,* 305–22; Derek A. Webb, "The 'Somerset' Effect: Parsing Lord Mansfield's Words on Slavery in Nineteenth Century America," *Law and History Review* 32, no. 3 (2014): 455–90; George Van Cleve, "'Somerset's Case' and Its Antecedents in Imperial Perspective," *Law and History Review* 24, no. 3 (2006): 601–45.

God and Man at the University of Virginia

CAMERON ADDIS

EFFERSON BOASTED near the end of his second presidential term that Americans had "solved, by fair experiment, the great & interesting question Whether freedom of religion is compatible with order in government and obedience to the laws," but was he right when it came to the role of religion in education?[1] Jefferson's contemporaries agreed in principle that education should reinforce democracy by teaching citizens and leaders about the world and their rights and responsibilities, but his notion that public education should emphasize scientific over scriptural revelation was controversial.

While the First Amendment provided Americans with religious freedom (especially after the Fourteenth Amendment), they have argued since the founding over religion in public schools. At the grade-school level, Catholic and Jewish parents noted that the supposed nonsectarianism emerging in nineteenth-century public schools really left pro-Protestant biases embedded in courses like history, geography, and morals.[2] Moreover, there was then a near consensus that theologians should run even public colleges. Jefferson countered that trend at the University of Virginia, where his pro-science agenda and religious heterodoxy clashed with the desires of the Protestant majority. Over the course of his half-century campaign to institute schools, he developed a curriculum that turned conventional wisdom on its head, instilling ethics based on Enlightenment universalism rather than orthodox Christianity. Confronted with the inescapability of promoting some religious stance— either explicitly or indirectly by omission—Jefferson endorsed a visionary faith at the University of Virginia based on principles of "peace, reason and morality," fending off criticism while reconciling his separationist principles with what he hoped would be a thriving but open religious culture. The result after his death was a compromise, with no strict denominational control and an inter-Protestant ecumenicalism. The University of Virginia's early religious history is both an inspirational and cautionary tale: inspirational because, within limits, its founders created an even playing field on which denominations could co-exist and exercise their freedom, but cautionary insofar as tolerance did not extend far outside mainstream Protestant faiths. The story reminds us of the tensions latent in the First Amendment right to religious freedom. The Bill of Rights, in general, protects various minorities, but sometimes only by overriding the democratic will of the majority. In founding his University, Jefferson had to subvert democracy to protect what was, by contemporary Western standards, an extreme form of republican liberty.

Jefferson's religious libertarianism began when he was studying law at the College of William and Mary in 1762, near the beginning of the revolt against Britain. The conflict immersed the precocious teenager in serious matters of politics, philosophy, and religion. The Anglicans who ran the school, despite their affiliation with the established Church of England, held liberal latitudinarian beliefs—broad by orthodox Christian standards—and Jefferson's teachers discouraged strict Calvinism and evangelical emotion. They assigned writers who described a violent Christian tradition, accentuating such lowlights of fanaticism and bigotry as the Crusades, Catholic Inquisition, Thirty Years' War, and French wars of religion. Their work gave Jefferson no appreciation of how organized faith bolstered the spirituality and sanity of everyday believers, nor did it suggest that religions might defuse, rather than necessarily promote, violence. He developed a fairly harsh and one-sided view of organized faiths that lacked appreciation for the cohesive function of churches in society. However, Jefferson never argued that organized religions should not exist (and even supported them from time to time), only that they should not dominate the public realm.

Most of the writers Jefferson read at William and Mary did not repudiate religion generally so much as they endorsed a more universal approach to Christianity. While his contemporaries studied at colleges that grew out of denominational seminaries, Jefferson read writers who saw nature as the genuine path to scientific and religious enlightenment. His religious views were similar to his contemporary William Paley's natural religion, or even intelligent design in our own time.[3]

Jefferson was a pantheist, seeing nature as animated with, rather than just created by, divinity. It followed that his take on the American Revolution's

cosmic implications strayed from the usual God and country religious nationalism one might expect from a budding statesman. In the Declaration of Independence, Jefferson kept things universal, predicating the break with Britain
on "the God of Nature" rather than the Lord or God almighty. Jefferson had
both religious and political faith. His interpretation of the Revolution was
rooted in the Jewish and Puritan traditions of a chosen people acting on behalf
of a progressive and benevolent deity, but the chosen people of the Declaration
were the universal Enlightenment diaspora rather than just the American
Protestants of nineteenth-century Manifest Destiny. This God buttressed his
otherwise unsubstantiated claim of natural rights such as civic freedom, land
ownership, and religious liberty. Republicanism and religious freedom were
compatible for Jefferson because men of the cloth, especially those associated
with monarchies, were another artificially imposed aristocracy designed to
think for the people. The potential miseducation of the people by clergy,
wrote Peter Onuf, was, for Jefferson, "the most formidable obstacle to the success of the new nation's republican experiment."[4]

Jefferson's full-blown religious separation bill (drafted in 1777) failed legislative approval in 1779 but eventually passed as the landmark 1786 Virginia
Statute for Religious Freedom. The Statute forbade even a nondenominational
inter-Protestant establishment of the sort then endorsed by Patrick Henry, and
Jefferson wrote in his autobiography that it outlawed religious discrimination
against anybody, including "the Jew and the Gentile, the Christian and Maho-
metan, the Hindoo and infidel of every denomination."[5] It was one of three accomplishments he wanted inscribed on his tombstone, along with authoring
the Declaration of Independence and creating the University of Virginia.

Simultaneously, Jefferson introduced his first education bill, which called for
public schooling to "diffuse knowledge" among an informed citizenry, but it
failed partly because it proposed a non-Christian curriculum. Virginia had a rural and dispersed population that generally opposed taxation—not a good for-
mula for public education—and religion complicated matters. Judge Edmund
Pendleton warned Jefferson that "the Rockbridge [County] Deputies want to be
Satisfied that your Bill encourages a *Presbeterian*, not a *liberal* Education."[6]

The Presbyterian rector of Hampden-Sydney Academy, Samuel Stanhope
Smith (later president of the College of New Jersey (Princeton University)),
reviewed the bill and wrote its presumed author, Jefferson, that its "chief obstacle" would arise not from funding but from the "variety of religious sentiments
[denominations] . . . each solicitous for their own preservation and jealous of
their antagonists."[7] Jefferson was not utilizing the clergy as teachers, even

though they traditionally had worked as instructors because of their literacy and familiarity with low pay. Likewise, French revolutionaries failed to establish schools because of proposed restrictions on hiring clergy as teachers.[8]

Like the philosophes he read at William and Mary, Jefferson wanted to omit biblical instruction from early education and to track selectively organized religion's checkered past in history classes.[9] He conveniently avoided confronting how these heterodox views might interfere with his endorsement of local, participatory democracy—so local as to be divided up into small wards within counties of five or six square miles and, ultimately, households and farms. He simply preferred plans that would "keep elementary education out of the hands of fanaticising preachers, who in county elections would be universally chosen. . . ."[10] Jefferson's proposed wards, inspired mainly by English "hundreds" and New England townships, evolved as he was drafting his education plan. He hoped that wards and schools would jump-start each other, writing that public education and the subdivision of counties into wards were the two subjects he would push "as long as I breathe." Jefferson considered "the continuance of republican government as absolutely hanging on these two hooks."[11] These wards, which never came about, would have comprised around a hundred families each, and each student would have been within walking distance of a school. Jefferson's focus on wards perhaps enabled him to avoid confronting the possibility that New England's educational success owed as much to its clergy as to its tight-knit townships.

Samuel Stanhope Smith warned Jefferson that the decentralization of his ward scheme conflicted with his version of religious freedom, writing that "[i]n many places the public master will be deserted by half his hundred [ward]. . . . [It is] dangerous to attempt to compel them to abide by the choice which the state may make for them in their schools, more than in their churches."[12] Rhys Isaac likewise wrote that, given his simultaneous disestablishment of the Anglican Church, many Virginians feared that Jefferson was "simply replacing parishes and pulpits with wards and teachers' desks."[13]

Smith understood that the secondary schools and university in Jefferson's pyramidal scheme for public education would influence the elementary schools, and that the competition was as much between denominations as between Christianity and infidelity: "Whatever party enjoys the preeminence in these will insensibly gain upon the others, and soon acquire the government of the state. This contest will chiefly lie betwixt the Presbyterians and the Episcopalians. The Baptists and Methodists content themselves with other kinds of illuminations than are afforded by human science." Presbyterians opposed William and Mary's capping the educational system because the bill had not gone far enough in dismantling Episcopalian influence. Smith warned Jefferson that with William and Mary serving as the capstone university in Jefferson's pyramidal plan, "the proposal will alarm the whole body of Presbyterians." As an insider, the cosmopolitan Smith lamented such sectarianism, writing that "[t]he partialities of sects indeed ought to have no place in a system of liberal education. They are the disgrace of science and would to Heaven it were possible utterly to banish them from the society of men. But such is our misfortune; they exist; and they exist in considerable force."[14]

In the colonial era, the head of Virginia's Anglican Church, the bishop of London's representative, had overseen William and Mary. However, as governor during the Revolution, Jefferson served as an ex officio visitor of his alma mater, where he eliminated the divinity department and fired the education professor because he, too, feared Anglican/Episcopalian influence on both the College and local elementary teachers, if for reasons different from those of Presbyterians. Presaging later work at the University of Virginia, he replaced these slots with posts in law, medicine, chemistry, anatomy, and modern languages. Yet Jefferson also called for a post in ecclesiastical history because, while cautioning against indoctrination, he valued knowledge *about* religions.[15]

In public, Jefferson embraced the social benefits of Jesus's teaching and stayed loosely connected to church establishments, attending Anglican or Episcopalian churches in Washington and Virginia and a Unitarian church in Philadelphia and making financial contributions to various churches.[16] He corresponded with Presbyterians like Smith and privately edited the Bible by excising supernatural passages from the New Testament. President Jefferson retained popularity among Baptists and Methodists because of his assertion of religious freedom in his "wall of separation" phrase and their minority status within certain regions such as New England.[17] On the education front, his main efforts as president were steered toward establishing a strong science curriculum and Republican stronghold at the new West Point military academy.

In retirement, Jefferson was freer to express himself and recharged his efforts at establishing public education in his home state. The earlier emphases established at William and Mary and espoused in *Notes on the State of Virginia*—generally undermining sectarian authority while endorsing religious studies and science—found expression in the curriculum, faculty, architecture, and religion of the University of Virginia (UVA).

Jefferson's pioneering Rockfish Gap Report of 1818 outlined UVA's proposed curriculum, depriving religious denominations status as the organizing principle behind Western higher education that they had enjoyed for at least a millennium. At Jefferson's University, the God of Jehovah would be dethroned and supplanted by the universal god of the philosophes. The Rockfish Report stated that "in conformity with the principles of Virginia's Constitution, which places all sects of religion on an equal footing, with the jealousies of the different sects in guarding that equality from encroachment and surprise, and with the sentiments of the legislature in favor of freedom of religion manifested on former occasions, we have proposed no professor of divinity." The professor of ethics, tasked with an unreasonably burdensome workload, would handle "proofs of the being of God, the creator, preserver, and supreme ruler of the universe, the author of all the relations of morality, and of the laws and obligations these infer." The strategy was to seek common ground on "which all sects agree" taught by scholars versed in Hebrew, Greek, and Latin.[18] Jefferson might have also mentioned the provinces of science and history, for the school's novel attempt to inculcate morals by untraditional means spread across the curriculum. Jefferson's first draft for the Rockfish Gap Report underscored his belief that church-state separation reinforced republicanism: "[T]read[ing] with awful reverence in the footsteps of our fathers . . . is the genuine fruit of alliance between church and state, the tenants [tenets] of which, finding themselves but too well in their present position, oppose all advances which might unmask their usurpations, and monopolies of honors, wealth and power, and fear every change, as endangering the comforts they now hold."[19]

It is difficult now to appreciate the radicalism of this new arrangement. By the 1820s, the trend was in the opposite direction: all American colleges, public or private, required chapel attendance, and most schools had originated around seminaries or divinity departments. Without strong colleges, it was impossible for Christians to retain their legitimacy in the elite circles they strove to be part of and affect, so they embraced education. And their students, in turn, often embraced religion. Between 1802 and 1815, there were evangelical awakenings at Yale, Williams, Middlebury, Princeton, and Dartmouth. The North American Review noted the revolutionary character of the Rockfish Gap Report in 1820 and commented on it favorably, if pessimistically. Edward Everett wrote that the journal's readers would be gratified to view portions of the report since this was the "first instance, in the world, of a university without any such [orthodox religious] provision."[20] Others had implemented nondenominational curricula before but, like the founding generation's experiment in representative democracy, Jefferson had few successful precedents to build on in founding an Enlightenment college, unless one includes his own academy at West Point. Early nondenominational experiments at Transylvania, North Carolina, and the precursors to Penn and Columbia gave way to either Presbyterian or Anglican control.[21]

Jefferson was out of step with the times, and the Rockfish Gap curriculum threatened to unravel nearly twenty years of hard work on the part of administrators to stamp out all but the most watered-down Enlightenment philosophy on America's campuses. These reformers now focused their attention on the infidel they considered the heir apparent to Thomas Paine, who had died in 1809. Jefferson's religion was similar, after all, to the deism with which Paine corrupted young minds in *The Age of Reason* (1794). After colleges managed to snuff out Paine's popularity during the Second Great Awakening revivals of the early nineteenth century, Jefferson and his cohorts emerged as the foremost public symbols of the old discredited radicalism of the French Revolution.[22] Jefferson was also trying to hire radicals such as Thomas Cooper on the faculty, in Cooper's case to teach law and science. Jailed during the Alien and Sedition unrest in 1799, Cooper was an agnostic but known as a deist because of his association with Joseph Priestley. Yale president Timothy Dwight was the most outspoken critic, fearing that the religion of Paine and Jefferson would unravel the delicate balance between liberty and order in the young republic, separating "the meat from the drink." Jefferson grouped Dwight and like-minded Virginians such as Presbyterian John Holt Rice among the men of the cloth whom he claimed were "pant[ing] to reestablish ... [the] holy inquisition" by challenging his plans for the University of Virginia.[23]

His enemies spoke in similar hyperbole, but Jefferson was only an infidel, as they charged, by the strictest definition of the term. He did not believe in scriptural revelation or the supernatural elements of biblical faiths. He rejected Jesus's divinity as a product of mythic "lore," but he admired Jesus's philosophy, as shown by his unusual cutting-and-pasting of the Bible, removing the supernatural components of the New Testament. He denied direct communication from the heavens and said of Judaism—the bedrock of the desert religions—that "the fumes of [Jews'] most disordered imaginations were recorded in their religious code, as special communications of the deity. ..."[24] For Jefferson, formal Christianity constituted an unbroken string of "dupes and imposters" led by Paul and followed by the "half reformation" of Martin Luther and John Calvin, which helped restore Jesus's doctrines, but with Calvinism having "introduced ... more new absurdities than it's leader had purged of old ones."[25] In retirement, Jefferson continued to deny Jesus's divinity, or even that Jesus himself claimed to be divine.[26]

Jefferson implemented the Scottish Common Sense School of philosophy at the University of Virginia, which was typical of early nineteenth-century colleges, including those of the Presbyterians. Common Sense bridged Enlightenment philosophy to the Christianity of Jeffersonian America. It reacted against skepticism about the limits of human knowledge by embracing God and the moderate vision of a rational and perceptible order. Common Sense conveniently doubled as common ground with Jefferson's critics and dovetailed reasonably well, but not perfectly, with his reliance on inborn morality and morals derived from studying nature and history rather than gleaned from outside supernatural forces.

Jefferson optimistically argued that the moral foundation lay *within* and relied on instinct rather than coercion. He did not see the controversy over the University's curriculum as a debate between religious morality and secular amorality or apathy. Christianity, for him, cheapened the process of personal growth because ethics enmeshed in superstitions lost their true meaning. Historians, scientists, and classical writers had broader perspectives and were better suited to awaken and develop ethics, as religions destroyed the sense of independence and responsibility requisite in a republican society.[27]

If Jefferson oversimplified when he wrote that the "dogmas in which all religions differ . . . are totally unconnected to morality," he did so in the hope that the University of Virginia would provide a universal constellation of values on which sects could agree, avoiding discrepancies in superfluous detail.[28] However, unlike the more inclusive language of the 1786 Virginia Statute, Jefferson by 1817 likely meant, by agreed-upon values, just baseline Christian tenets, described to John Adams as the "deism taught us by Jesus of Nazareth . . . ."[29] As his abridged New Testament swept clean the supernatural, his university would trim dogmatic doctrine while still exposing students to the best theological ideas through its course on moral philosophy, or ethics.

Jefferson enlisted James Madison, a former divinity student and the University of Virginia's second rector, to compile a large and comprehensive list of religious works, both pagan and Christian, dating from the first centuries after Jesus. Madison tempered Jefferson's own dogmatism in the same way he tried to moderate the University's law curriculum, for which he advocated avoiding "the two extremes, by referring to selected Standards . . . ." While no Tories made their way into UVA's law school, Madison compiled a broad cross-section of Western theology, with topics ranging from original sin, deism, natural theology, Moravians, and Quakers to the Catholic Council of Trent. His authors included Aquinas, Leibniz, Luther, Calvin, Newton, and Penn.[30]

Madison agreed that broadening students' exposure to religion was important and that an ethics course was the proper venue. As a state institution, the
University could not have an outright divinity department, which Madison
considered a direct violation of their 1786 Statute for Religious Freedom. Madison preferred overcoming short-term charges of irreligion to allowing any sect
to monopolize religion, an alternative that would have ensured "an arena of
Theological Gladiators."[31] Complementing their ethics course, their university
would also emphasize rationalism as expressed by French Physiocrats, who
shared Jefferson's dream of an agrarian utopia and hoped to use mathematics
and reason to structure society and solve its problems. For Jefferson, the most
compelling part of Physiocratic theory was sensationalist philosophy, which
argued that the human brain was comprehensible entirely (and exclusively)
through the study of chemistry. Jefferson especially liked sensationalist P. J. G.
Cabanis, who introduced Jefferson to positivism: the theory that natural
phenomena and their properties form the bases of all true knowledge.[32]

Rather than using materialism to deny the existence of God and souls,
Jefferson used it to support his pantheism—arguing that they consisted of
matter and calling the Christian heresy of immaterialism a "masked atheism."[33]
Though he did not seriously consider it, Jefferson once speculated about dividing the University of Virginia's Department of Zoology into the physical
and moral, with the latter including ideology, ethics, and religion. Underscoring his materialism, Jefferson argued that "the faculty of thought belongs to
animal history, is an important portion of it, and should there find it's place."[34]

While he never subsumed the humanities or social sciences under zoology,
Jefferson hired sensationalist professor John Patton Emmet. Emmet, the son
of Irish political rebel Thomas Addis Emmet, was unable to find work for
three years because he argued that the proximate cause of all organic formation is chemical affinity. By not accounting for an ultimate cause, or theistic
"vital principle," Emmet outraged the profession, whose members accused
him of heresy. The *American Medical Recorder* condemned Emmet as a materi-
alist and infidel. It was the last time anyone challenged the vital principle in
print until 1844, but, tellingly, he found employment at Jefferson's University
in 1825 as a professor of chemistry and medicine.[35]

The University of Virginia's architecture matched its Enlightenment curriculum. Jefferson spent his retirement absorbed in designing and oversee-
ing construction of the campus along with its curriculum. At the head of the
campus's rectangular lawn, or Academical Village, the Rotunda displaced
the traditional college chapel with a library and a proposed planetarium,

the Enlightenment temple's sanctuary. Controversy surrounded not just the building's high cost, but also the predominance of the expansive, domed library at a chapel's expense. The larger-scale Roman Pantheon on which he modeled it was a pagan temple dedicated to the planetary gods and, unlike the upward-reaching spires of Gothic cathedrals, the Rotunda's spherical dome suggested Earth and nature. A small and humble room in the basement (directly under the library) set aside for worship, drawing, and music sufficed for a chapel. Banished to the third floor at William and Mary, the library was front and center at Jefferson's University, underscoring that reason prevailed over revelation.[36]

Jefferson integrated organized religions into the plan as well. He defused opposition to the campus by inviting area denominations to build seminaries, on an equal basis, around the periphery of the University's campus. Students could attend any of the surrounding seminaries, while seminarians, in turn, were welcome to attend classes at the University. Virginia jurist St. George Tucker had suggested the idea years earlier, as had Samuel Knox, a Maryland clergyman whom Jefferson had tried unsuccessfully to hire as a faculty member.[37] Jefferson promoted the idea earlier in the Rockfish Gap Report when he wrote that having "[p]roceed[ed] this far without offence to the constitution, we have thought it proper at this point, to leave every sect to provide as they think fittest, the means of further instruction in their own peculiar tenets."[38] In 1822 he called for bridging the "chasm now existing" between science and religion by giving theological students "ready and convenient access and attendance on the scientific lectures of the University; and to maintain, by that means, those destined for the religious professions on as high a standing of science, and of personal weight and respectability, as may be obtained by others from the benefits of the University."[39] Privately, Jefferson wrote to former revolutionary Thomas Cooper—whose aforementioned aborted hiring had caused the firestorm he was now responding to—that access to a sound education for ministers in training would "soften their asperities, liberalise and neutralise their prejudices, and make the general religion a religion of peace, reason and morality."[40] As Jefferson cynically predicted, jealousies among the sects and their collective refusal to validate his experiment in ecumenicalism precluded them from initially accepting his offer. No religious organizations affiliated themselves with the University until the YMCA (Young Men's Christian Association) in 1858, because each desired a monopoly. Nonetheless, the plan helped secure state funding for the University. Jefferson's sponsor in the state legislature, Joseph Cabell, informed him that his "suggestion respecting the Religious sects has had a great influence. It is the Franklin [rod] that has drawn the Lightning from the Cloud of opposition."[41]

The seminaries-on-the-confines idea had future legal implications, as Jefferson conceded to a state board that denominations could use public University buildings for instruction so long as it was understood that they were independent of the University. Legal historian John Ragosta wrote that "Jefferson, albeit somewhat reluctantly, endorsed nondiscriminatory, 'impartial' access of religious bodies (and others) to public facilities when private facilities were lacking and public facilities were not otherwise in use." Given Jefferson and Madison's role both in founding the University of Virginia and in crafting the First Amendment, future judges like Stanley Reed—dissenting in *McCollum v. Board of Education* (1948)—used these early University of Virginia proposals to argue that the First Amendment only restricted financial aid to religion, not other church-state interactions or use of property.[42]

As Jefferson and Madison discovered when the school opened in 1825, more clouds lay on the horizon. For a variety of reasons, stemming from a disagreement between the students and European professors over how disrespectfully to treat the campus slaves, and generally including belligerent and insubordinate attitudes among the haughty and thin-skinned sons of Virginia's planters, the University suffered a disciplinary meltdown in its first years. Jefferson had rightly feared that the planters' sons, reared more in domination than submission, would be difficult to control, just as they were at William and Mary and other southern schools. He wrote Cooper that he anticipated disciplinary problems "with dismay . . . as a breaker ahead which I am far from being confident we shall be able to weather. [T]he advance of age . . . may probably spare me. . . ."[43]

Students in the University's early years received only mild reprimands or, at worst, dismissal for abusing slaves. Jefferson's final year turned out to be the school's first (1825–1826), and he suffered the indignity of realizing that his naive experiment in student self-policing and nurturing inborn morality had failed. Worse, his own distant relative, Wilson Miles Cary, presented himself as a rioting ringleader and stood first to be dismissed.[44] Jefferson had carefully dispersed the professors' dwellings amid the student dorms on the Lawn but found that most youth were not interested in philosophizing in their professors' parlors after hours the way that he had in Williamsburg, preferring instead to toss urine bottles through their professors' windows. In 1840, one rioting student shot and killed law professor and dean John Davis. Vandalism and professor-floggings were typical at contemporary religious colleges as well, making it difficult to link the University's disciplinary problems to its ethics course or lack of a proper chapel.[45]

Not so disease, which, especially in an era of rudimentary medicine, could be traced to supernatural causes. The University of Virginia suffered from the inherent disadvantage of any party subject to fundamentalist criticism, which is that any and all misfortune could easily be attributed to divine retribution. The spread-out design Jefferson had implemented, partly to avoid epidemics, failed in the late 1820s when a typhoid epidemic killed several students and slaves. A year later, after a cholera outbreak, a cadaver stolen from the medical school, wasted away to the skeleton, was found in a pond from which the dormitories drew their ice and water.[46]

This presented an opportunity for area Episcopalians and Presbyterians who were angling for greater influence on campus. The Episcopalians at William and Mary had revised their message during the Second Great Awakening, making it more evangelical than their Anglican brethren in England or revolutionary American precursors, and were now led by Reverend William Meade.[47] As the assistant bishop-elect of the Diocese of Virginia, Meade seized on the stricken students' eulogy as an opportunity to lash out at the school, with particular aim taken at its founder. Just as Presbyterians capitalized on a Richmond theater fire in 1811 to accentuate the evils of the acting profession, and no doubt aware that Jefferson conceived of the University as a counterexample to William and Mary, Meade suggested that Jefferson's infidelity had killed the students. At one point, he admitted that making such a direct link would be "idiotic" since true Christians die tragically, too, but he went on arguing exactly that. Meade noted that God "takes part in all the trivial affairs of men, and actually appoints all the accidental and seemingly irregular occurrences of life." He asked the students and faculty assembled in the Rotunda if it amounted to "superstition or weakness to wonder if these visitations have not been sent to show the rulers thereof, their entire dependence on God? The design of God, therefore, in these dispensations, and the use to be made of them by us, are as plain as they are important. When God visits us with the rod of affliction, it is that we may search our hearts, and try our ways, and turn to him."

Meade considered Jefferson and the "dignified and philosophic" French revolutionaries the "most diligent, indefatigable and daring enemies of all religion which the world ever witnessed." He compared them unfavorably to Enlightenment Christians such as Locke, Bacon, and Newton. Meade equated Jefferson's natural religion with atheism because God is "at best . . . the soul of

the world, not the creator of it." In France "the poison took effect; the conta-
gion spread far and wide and among all classes general infections prevailed."
Meade hoped that the University of Virginia could avoid that fate and turn to
Christianity, not allowing the "goddess of reason" to "set up in the form of a
lewd prostitute in the great hall of atheistic legislation." He later soft-pedaled
the message of this eulogy in his memoirs, but Meade's speech had an impact
at the time.[48] Despite protests on the part of both students and faculty to the
tenor of the bishop's sermon, his criticisms, along with the fear of more typhoid, hurt recruiting efforts enough to make the Board of Visitors consider
hiring a full-time chaplain.

The Board decided to rotate a chaplaincy among the four main Protestant
denominations: Methodist, Baptist, Episcopalian, and Presbyterian.[49] Methodists and Baptists such as James B. Taylor (who served in 1839) coveted the
post, although some evangelicals claimed that the campus was an improper
training ground. Beginning in 1835, voluntary contributions from the students
and faculty supported chaplains who performed Sunday services, weekly lectures, and a monthly concert for prayer. That same year a Sunday school and
Bible society began. Ministerial candidates won small scholarships beginning
in 1837 and could stay on campus. When Presbyterian William Maxwell addressed the University's Bible group in 1836, he said that if the school was going
to be the "nursery of republican patriots" that Jefferson and Madison had envisioned, then the Bible should be required, for it is the "best statesmen's manual
I know." The Bible would also help prevent the spirits of corruption and abolition from infecting the campus, "and twenty other spirits I will not name—all
mingling their drugs together, with infernal incantations, in the caldron of confusion, on purpose to brew up the blackest storm that has ever threatened to
destroy the vessel of state in which we are all embarked." The Board initially
rejected the idea of constructing a chapel because other denominations voiced
their intention to bar Unitarians, and that violated their view of Jefferson's legacy and his University's core principle of religious freedom and toleration.[50]

Jefferson's model of religious liberty survived at least in this compromised
form, though it fell short of the freedom prescribed by Virginia's 1786 statute.
His successors in effect diluted his purer ecumenicalism down to the statewide General Assessment model Patrick Henry had proposed in the 1784: religious worship was voluntary and pluralistic, but only within mainstream
Protestantism, defined broadly enough to include tolerating Unitarians in the
chapel. Henry had proposed that voters be taxed for maintaining Christian
churches of their choice or Christian-run seminaries.[51]

The University of Virginia's faculty prohibited Sabbath breaking in 1828 and Protestant theologians played an increasingly large role on campus as the nineteenth century wore on.[52] In addition to Jefferson's original sparse worship room, which proved too small, they converted one of the gyms under the Rotunda terraces into a nondenominational chapel in 1837 and built a new chapel in 1885. Strict impartiality was observed among the Protestant sects and many students were enthusiastic about the ministers.[53] Chaplain Taylor, in turn, attended free lectures in classics, philosophy, and chemistry. In 1832, he helped to establish the Virginia Baptist Seminary, which became Richmond College and later the University of Richmond. It is likely, given the unsustainable disciplinary problems that plagued UVA's early years and otherwise irredeemable insubordination of its gentry students, that the school's Protestant culture, and not its dispersed Academical Village or self-policing, was essential to its survival.

Dissatisfied even with this qualified ecumenicalism, clergymen kept Jefferson's University in their crosshairs. Some lambasted the decline in religion at the institution after 1835, even though a revival was arguably mounting. Journals criticized the hiring of Catholic and Jewish professors. Revolutionary France still cast its shadow a half century after the Reign of Terror. North Carolina Episcopalian Francis Lister Hawks, who considered himself a mortal enemy of Jefferson's, viewed the University as an "alliance between the civil authority and infidelity," a subject on which "revolutionary France has once read to the world an impressive lesson." Echoing Bishop Meade, Hawks accused Jefferson of "poisoning the stream at the fountain." In 1837 Professor George Tucker published a favorable Jefferson biography to counter Hawks.

But students mostly sided with Hawks, refusing to erect a statue of Jefferson at his University for twenty-five years after his death.[54] In 1910 the University erected Moses Ezekiel's sculpture of Jefferson—north of the Rotunda, facing the chapel—with an allegorical angel underneath holding a tablet that mentions the 1786 Virginia Statute for Religious Freedom followed by various names for a deity, including God-Jehovah, Brahma, Atma, Ra, Allah, and Zeus. Thanks to UVA professor Scott Harrop, the easy-to-overlook details of the angel's tablet came to light in 2014. Harrop's research unearthed Ezekiel's testimony that "under our government, they mean, and are all God—and have no other meaning and have each an equal right and protection of our just laws as Americans."[55]

The school and its founder remained easy targets, but clergy who actually visited the campus in the nineteenth century got a different impression. The

Reverend Septimus Tuston claimed to experience "nothing but kindness and courtesy" during his stay there.[56] S. H. Tyng (1800–1885), an Episcopal minister and newspaper editor from Philadelphia, confirmed the school's religious enthusiasm in an 1840 account. Tyng was a tough audience. Henry Ward Beecher once characterized him as "the one man I am afraid of," and his hatred for Jefferson kept him from touring Monticello's interior. In his first letter home from Charlottesville, before he had visited the campus, Tyng wrote: "I have never heard his name spoken with so little respect, and so much aversion, as in this very neighborhood [Charlottesville] in which he lived and died. I had never conceived his character so bad as I have found it here. His plans are all defeated. The religion of Jesus triumphs over all opposition. The whole spirit of the community has awakened against the spirit and tendency of Mr. Jefferson's example. All his greatness has perished and is forgotten because he was an infidel." Tyng changed his mind about the University of Virginia, if not Jefferson, after preaching there. Although he thought the University was set up in "direct and designed hostility to Christianity," he found that most of the faculty and students were practicing Christians, including Jefferson's biographer, George Tucker. In the Rotunda, Tyng preached to what he called the "most attentive and interested auditory of [his] entire priesthood. Not a single college in New England would've furnished me with such an attentive and respectful audience."[57]

Travel writer and sociologist Harriet Martineau (a favorite of Queen Victoria's) commented on the controversy that the humanist University caused in the North, but pointed out after visiting that the students heard a wider variety of sermons than at denominational schools. Agreeing with one of Jefferson and Madison's longtime contentions about society as a whole, she concurred that the voluntary nature of church services actually increased their attendance.[58]

Countrywide, likewise, the duo's commitment to liberty aided rather than curbed religions. While Jefferson's private fusillades against organized faith could be irrational and vindictive, the free religious market that he and Madison created thrived over the succeeding two centuries, if not in the forms he imagined.[59] Then, as now, such libertarianism was often confused with crusades against religion itself, conflicting with the wishes of the electorate. In this zero-sum view, religious neutrality equals religious hostility. Presbyterian John Holt Rice reminded newspaper readers in the 1820s that "THE UNIVERSITY OF VIRGINIA BELONGS TO THE PEOPLE OF VIRGINIA. It is their money which has founded, and will endow their institution; it is their children who are to be educated there; it is they and their posterity, who are to partake of the good or suffer the evil, which it will produce." Rice argued that the people who run a public college have no right to make independent hiring and curricular decisions. The University was "the property of the people, and they will see to it that infidelity, whether open or disguised under a Christian name, shall not taint its reputation and poison its influence."[60] Whereas for Jefferson religious freedom was fundamental to republicanism, Rice's version included the freedom of the Protestant majority to pursue its interests by influencing the democratic system—that was the "free exercise thereof" portion of the First Amendment. In short, Jefferson's crusade against denominational control brought him into direct conflict with his endorsement of participatory democracy. Yet his model at the University of Virginia is arguably good for everyone involved.

Take Yale University, for example. In *God and Man at Yale: The Superstitions of Academic Freedom* (1951), William F. Buckley Jr. echoed UVA's earlier critics, bemoaning that, in the twentieth century, Christianity there had been pushed to the margins of voluntary worship and religious studies. While Buckley did not advocate turning Yale back into a seminary, he hoped for a revival of the sort Jefferson's old nemesis Timothy Dwight led there after the Revolution. However, Yale was a Congregational school and, if Protestant leaders like Dwight had stayed in charge, it is unlikely they ever would have built the St. Thomas More Catholic Chapel and Center in 1922 where Buckley worshipped as an undergraduate. Only Jefferson's ecumenical model, and not even the watered-down version of his nineteenth-century successors, would have allowed for Buckley's Catholicism at Yale.

The multitude of American religions, far more pronounced in our time than in Jefferson's, make any agreement on religious curriculum in public schools difficult, only underscoring the need to embrace his broader vision. Jefferson's crusade for a religious education that transcended sectarianism and the merely doctrinaire remains a worthy cause with which, according to some polls, a growing number of American theologians and their followers agree.[61]

Notes

This essay is based on an earlier essay appearing in *Light & Liberty: Thomas Jefferson & the Power of Knowledge*, ed. Robert McDonald (Charlottesville: University of Virginia Press, 2012).

1. Jefferson to Virginia Baptist Associations of Chesterfield, November 21, 1808, *Founders Online*, https://founders.archives.gov/documents/Jefferson/99-01-02-9124.

2. Johann Neem, *Democracy's Schools: The Rise of Public Education in America* (Baltimore: Johns Hopkins University Press, 2017), 145.

3. Jefferson would have disagreed with Creationists' use of Intelligent Design as a cover for infiltrating Christianity into science curriculums. He was, after all, trying to disprove extinction with fossils, not Scripture.

4. Peter S. Onuf, *The Mind of Thomas Jefferson* (Charlottesville: University of Virginia Press, 2007), 139.

5. Jefferson, Autobiography Draft Fragment, July 27, 1821, *Founders Online*, https://founders.archives.gov/documents/Jefferson/98-01-02-1756.

6. Edmund Pendleton to Jefferson, May 11, 1779, *PTJ*, 2:266–67.

7. Samuel Stanhope Smith to Jefferson, March? 1779, *PTJ*, 2:246–49.

8. For context of the religious freedom law, see Jefferson to George Wythe, August 13, 1786, *PTJ*, 10:243–45. William Doyle, *The Oxford History of the French Revolution* (Oxford: Oxford University Press, 1989), 399.

9. *Notes*, Query XIV, 146–47, Query XVII, 159–60.

10. Jefferson to Joseph Cabell, November 28, 1820, *Founders Online*, https://founders.archives.gov/documents/Jefferson/98-01-02-1660.

11. Jefferson to Joseph Cabell, January 31, 1814, *PTJRS*, 7:176–77.

12. Samuel Stanhope Smith to Jefferson, March? 1779, *PTJ*, 2:246–49.

13. Rhys Isaac, *The Transformation of Virginia, 1740–1790* (Chapel Hill: University of North Carolina Press), 294.

14. Samuel Stanhope Smith to Jefferson, March? 1779, *PTJ*, 2:246–49.

15. Jefferson to Joseph Cabell, November 28, 1820, *Founders Online*, https://founders.archives.gov/documents/Jefferson/98-01-02-1660; "A Bill For Amending the Constitution of the College of William & Mary, and Substituting More Certain Revenues for Its Support," *PTJ*, 2:535–45.

16. Jefferson to Benjamin Waterhouse, July 19, 1822, and January 8, 1825, *Founders Online*, https://founders.archives.gov/documents/Jefferson/98-01-02-2965 and https://founders.archives.gov/documents/Jefferson/98-01-02-4850.

17. On New Year's Day 1802, in recognition of his support of religious freedom, President Jefferson received a 1,230-pound "mammoth cheese" ($4' \times 15''$) from the Baptist congregation of Cheshire, Massachusetts, led by Elder John Leland.

18. For the full context of the Rockfish Gap Report of the University of Virginia Commissioners, see *PTJRS*, 13:179–225.

19. Jefferson, Draft of the Rockfish Gap Report of the University of Virginia Commissioners, June 28, 1818, *PTJRS*, 13:194.

20. Edward Everett, "University of Virginia," *North American Review* 36 (January 1820): 130.

21. On the University of Pennsylvania (Jefferson called it the University of Philadelphia), see Jefferson to Caspar Wistar, August 25, 1814, *PTJRS*, 7:607–08.

22. John Holt Rice, "On the Unitarian Controversy," *Virginia Literary and Evangelical Magazine* 5 (January 1822): 31; Henry F. May, *The Enlightenment in America* (New York: Oxford University Press, 1976), 276–77.

23. Jefferson to William Short, April 13, 1820, *Founders Online*, https://founders .archives.gov/documents/Jefferson/98-01-02-1218.

24. Jefferson to William Short, August 4, 1820, *Founders Online*, https://founders .archives.gov/documents/Jefferson/98-01-02-1438.

25. Jefferson to William Short, April 13, 1820, *Founders Online*, https://founders .archives.gov/documents/Jefferson/98-01-02-1218; Jefferson to Salma Hale, July 26, 1818, *PTJRS*, 13:160 (footnote omitted).

26. For a conversation Jefferson had toward the end of his life with atheist Samuel Whitcomb on the fine line between denouncing Christian revelation while maintaining faith in God, see William Peden, "A Book Peddler Invades Monticello," *WMQ* 3, no. 6 (1949): 633–34, quoted in Kevin Hayes, *Road to Monticello: The Life and Mind of Thomas Jefferson* (Oxford: Oxford University Press, 2008), 593.

27. Jefferson to James Fishback, September 27, 1809, *PTJRS*, 1:563–66; Jefferson to Thomas Law, June 13, 1814, *PTJRS*, 7:412–15; Jefferson to John Adams, May 5, 1817, *PTJRS*, 11:311–13; see "Jefferson's Opinion On Baron d'Holbach Works," *Free Enquirer* 2, no. 13 (January 23, 1830): 102–03; Hayes, *Road to Monticello*, 582–83.

28. Jefferson to James Fishback, September 27, 1809, *PTJRS*, 1:563–66.

29. Jefferson to John Adams, May 5, 1817, *PTJRS*, 11:311–13.

30. Jefferson to William Short, October 31, 1819, *Founders Online*, https://founders .archives.gov/documents/Jefferson/98-01-02-0850. Jefferson to James Madison, August 8, 1824, and James Madison to Jefferson, September 10, 1824, *Founders Online*, https://founders .archives.gov/documents/Jefferson/98-01-02-4445 and https://founders.archives.gov /documents/Jefferson/98-01-02-4536.

31. James Madison to Edward Everett, March 19, 1823, *The Papers of James Madison: Retirement Series*, ed. David B. Mattern et al. (Charlottesville: University of Virginia Press, 2016), 3:16.

32. E. Brooks Holifield, *The Gentleman Theologians: American Theology in Southern Culture, 1795–1860* (Durham, NC: Duke University Press, 1978), 58–59; Gilbert Chinard, *Jefferson et les idéologues d'après sa correspondance inédite avec Destutt de Tracy, Cabanis, J.-B. Say, et Auguste Comte* (Baltimore: Johns Hopkins University Press, 1925), 25, 231.

33. Jefferson to John Adams, August 15, 1820, *Founders Online*, https://founders .archives.gov/documents/Jefferson/98-01-02-1458. Adrienne Koch described Jefferson as fluctuating between materialism and "vitalistic pantheism," in *The Philosophy of Thomas Jefferson* (New York: Columbia University Press, 1943), 98; Edwin S. Gaustad, *Sworn on the Altar of God: A Religious Biography of Thomas Jefferson* (Grand Rapids, MI: W. B. Eerdmans, 1996), 35.

34. Jefferson to Augustus Woodward, March 24, 1824, *Founders Online*, https://founders .archives.gov/documents/Jefferson/98-01-02-4139. At other times, Jefferson combined science and history or law and botany under history. See Daniel P. Jordan, "President's Letter," *Monticello* 11 (Spring 2000): 2.

35. George Tucker, *Memoir of the Life and Character of John P. Emmet, M.D., Professor of Chemistry and Materia Medica in the University of Virginia* (Philadelphia, 1845). Jefferson distrusted physicians generally, but he respected the more empirically minded and,

toward the end of his life, grew close to another University of Virginia medical professor, Dr. Robley Dunglison. See Dunglison, *Autobiographical Ana* [manuscript diary],
Special Collections, University of Virginia Library.

36. Mark Wenger, "Thomas Jefferson, the College of William & Mary, and the University of Virginia," *Virginia Magazine of History and Biography* 103 (July 1995): 374; Pa-
tricia C. Sherwood and Joseph Michael Lasala, "Education and Architecture: The
Evolution of the University of Virginia's Academic Village," in *Thomas Jefferson's Academical Village: The Creation of an Architectural Masterpiece,* ed. Richard Guy Wilson
(Charlottesville: Bayly Art Museum and University of Virginia Press, 1993), 71.

37. Knox was runner-up to Samuel Stanhope Smith in the American Philosophical
Society's 1796 contest to design the best educational system; "Report and Documents
Respecting the University of Virginia," *Journal of the Virginia House of Delegates, 1822–
1823:* 3–4; "Jefferson to President and Director of Literary Fund," October 7, 1822, Jeffer-
son Papers, Special Collections, University of Virginia Library; St. George Tucker,
"Sketch of a Plan for the Endowment and Establishment of a State-University in Virginia,"
January 4, 1805, Tucker-Coleman Papers, Swem Library, College of William and Mary;
"Report and Documents respecting the University of Virginia," *Norfolk & Portsmouth
Herald* 31 (January 1823).

38. Rockfish Gap Report of the University of Virginia Commissioners, *PTJRS,*
13:217–18.

39. Minutes of the Board of Visitors for the University of Virginia, October 7, 1822,
Founders Online, https://founders.archives.gov/documents/Madison/04-02-02-0504.

40. Jefferson to Thomas Cooper, November 2, 1822, *Founders Online,* https://
founders.archives.gov/documents/Jefferson/98-01-02-3137.

41. Joseph Cabell to Jefferson, February 3, 1823, *Founders Online,* https://founders
.archives.gov/documents/Jefferson/98-01-02-3303.

42. John Ragosta, *Religious Freedom: Jefferson's Legacy, America's Creed* (Charlottesville: University of Virginia Press, 2013), 193–98.

43. Jefferson to Thomas Cooper, November 2, 1822, *Founders Online,* https://
founders.archives.gov/documents/Jefferson/98-01-02-3137.

44. Cary was Jefferson's nephew on the paternal side, the son of Thomas Mann Randolph's sister.

45. On Jefferson's plans for using the professors to help police the students and to
host them in small groups in their quarters for dinner, see Jefferson to the Trustees of
the Lottery for East Tennessee College, May 6, 1810, *PTJRS,* 2:365–66; Stephen J. No-
vack, *The Rights of Youth: American Colleges and Student Revolt, 1798–1815* (Cambridge,
MA: Harvard University Press, 1977).

46. Robley Dunglison to James Madison, March 19–25, 1829, University of Virginia
Chronological File, University Archives, Special Collections, University of Virginia Library; Minutes of the University of Virginia Faculty, January 22, February 6 and 25, 1829,
418–41.

47. William Meade to John Hartwell Cocke, March 29, 1827, Cocke Family Papers,
Special Collections, University of Virginia Library.

48. William Meade, Sermon Delivered in the Rotunda of the University of Virginia on Sunday May 24, 1829 On the Occasion of the Deaths of Nine Young Men, Who Fell Victims to the Diseases Which Visited That Place During the Summer of 1828, and the Following Winter (Charlottesville, VA, 1829), Rare Pamphlets #315, Special Collections, University of Virginia Library; Meade, *Old Churches, Ministers and Families*, 2nd ed. (Philadelphia, 1910), 53–54.

49. "Student Petition" in Proctor's Records, 1830 and Rector and Visitors' Minutes, July 17, 1833, 299, University Archives, Special Collections, University of Virginia Library.

50. Joseph Martin, *A New and Comprehensive Gazetteer of Virginia and the District of Columbia* (Charlottesville, VA, 1836), 123; William Maxwell, An Address Delivered before the Bible Society of the University of Virginia, May 13th, 1836 (Charlottesville, VA, 1836), 9, 11; John B. Minor, "University of Virginia," Part 3, *The Old Dominion: A Monthly Magazine of Literature, Science and Art* 4–5 (May 15, 1870): 260; Meade, *Old Churches, Ministers and Families*, 56; George Tucker to Cabell, March 18, 1835, Cabell Deposit, and William Cabell Rives to John Hartwell Cocke, August 2, 1839, Cocke Family Papers, Special Collections, University of Virginia Library.

51. Ragosta, *Religious Freedom*, 79.

52. Minutes of the University of Virginia Faculty, July 8, 1828, 335, University Archives, Special Collections, University of Virginia Library.

53. Gessner Harrison to Dr. Peachy Harrison, April 1, 1833, Tucker-Harrison-Smith Family Papers, Special Collections, University of Virginia Library.

54. Francis Lister Hawks, ed., *A Narrative of Events Connected with the Rise and Progress of the Protestant Episcopal Church in Virginia* (New York, 1836), 179; Hawks, "The Character of Jefferson," *New York Review and Quarterly Church Journal* 1 (March 1837): 5, 7, 14–15. Some students disagreed with Hawks, arguing in the student newspaper that a statue should be built. *The Chameleon* 1 (May 9 and 16, 1831); Merrill Peterson, *The Jefferson Image in the American Mind* (New York: Oxford University Press, 1962), 127–28.

55. Lauren Jones, "Let Freedom Ring: U.VA. Professor Rediscovers Sacred Story Behind Jefferson Statue," *UVA Today*, July 2, 2014, https://news.virginia.edu/content/let-freedom-ring-uva-professor-rediscovers-sacred-story-behind-jefferson-statue.

56. Septimus Tuston, "University of Virginia," *New York Observer* [1837?], University of Virginia Chronological File, University Archives, Special Collections, University of Virginia Library.

57. Tyng was influential in the Sunday school movement, and St. Paul's Church in Philadelphia was known as "Tyng's Theater" from 1829 to 1834; S. H. Tyng, "Correspondence from Charlottesville," *Episcopal Recorder* (Philadelphia), May 27, 1840, 46, Archives of the Episcopal Church, Austin, Texas; Tyng, "For the Episcopal Recorder," *Episcopal Recorder* (Philadelphia), June 20, 1840, 50.

58. Harriet Martineau, *Retrospect of Western Travel*, 2 vols. (New York, 1838), 203–07.

59. Jefferson to Benjamin Waterhouse, June 26, 1822, *Founders Online*, https://founders.archives.gov/documents/Jefferson/98-01-02-2905; Johann Neem, "Beyond the Wall: Jefferson's Danbury Address," *Journal of the Early Republic* 17 (2007): 139–54;

Richard A. Samuelson, "What Adams Saw over Jefferson's Wall," *Commentary* 104, no. 2 (August 1997): 52–54.

60. John Holt Rice, "Literature and Science," *Virginia Evangelical and Literary Magazine* 2 (January 1819): 46–47.

61. See the Pew Forum's 2015 American Religious Landscape Study, http://www .pewforum.org/2015/05/12/americas-changing-religious-landscape.

AN EDUCATED NATION

Over the course of several decades, Thomas Jefferson meticulously planned his university. For years, he exchanged ideas on higher education with noted correspondents, especially in Europe: Alexander von Humboldt, Joseph Priestley, Thomas Cooper, Pierre Samuel du Pont de Nemours, Samuel Parr, George Ticknor, and others. As Virginians debated his proposal for a state university, the sage of Monticello fought against a rival proposal by trustees of the Washington Academy in Lexington to site the institution there. Enlisting the continued support of a sometimes-exasperated Joseph C. Cabell, he struggled doggedly—and often covertly—for funding from the state legislature.

Construction began well before Central College officially became the University of Virginia as the University's impatient founder relied on enslaved workers to lay out the grounds and construct the buildings in an Academical Village that did not provide accommodation for the slaves whose labor made the place work. Jefferson focused on what he saw as "higher" things. The pavilions he designed, featuring classical columns and Palladian proportions, would, he hoped, serve as edifying models for future southern planters, elevating their taste and sensibility. He was also concerned with who would impart the lessons to be learned within his well-designed classrooms, carefully monitoring the selection of faculty, particularly in the areas of law and politics. A lifelong maker of booklists, he obsessed about the contents and even the organization of the University library. Anxious to protect students from the pernicious influence of dogmatic theologians, he sought to maintain a rigorous wall of separation between church and state University.

Yet this was all incidental to the real story that would finally begin—after many frustrating delays—when the University opened its doors in 1825 and students and faculty finally arrived. Jefferson's mission was not to build facilities, stock the library, or hire faculty. The University would only come to life and his vision would only be fulfilled when teaching and learning began and enlightenment ensued.

The University looked to the future. Jefferson saw its primary mission as creating leaders for his beloved Commonwealth and for the nation as a whole. These would be southern leaders, certainly, but they would also be devoted to the fundamental principles that animated Jeffersonian republicans everywhere and sustained the federal union. Jefferson had always been clear that broad public education of the citizenry was the "only sure reliance for the preservation of our liberty," and he bemoaned Virginia's failure to fund basic public education for all (at least for all "free" children). But he also understood that educated, enlightened leaders were needed if the republic was to survive. Over time, other experiments in free government had always failed. And the bonds of union among the American states were still fragile, as the recent controversy over the admission of the new slave state of Missouri made so chillingly clear. An educated cadre of leaders could provide a cement of union. Years before the University was founded, he reminded a correspondent that "the boys of the rising generation are to be the men of the next, and the *sole guardians of the principles* we deliver over to them."[1]

Sadly, the long-awaited consummation of Jefferson's dream must have seemed for a time more like a nightmare. Newly arrived students, scions of the wealthy planter class, brought their thin-skinned sense of mastery, honor, and privilege with them, balking at order, discipline, and tedious lectures. Riots began within a year of the University's opening its doors. This was the predictable result of young men, especially southerners, being released from parental supervision, as Alan Taylor shows (in this volume). But Jefferson's acute, tearful, speechless distress at their youthful shenanigans spoke eloquently to his inordinately high expectations for the rising generation. For the aging founder, the University's first students embodied his hopes for the future. It was a responsibility and a burden that even the best behaved, most precociously enlightened young men anywhere in the riot-prone union would have found daunting.

Over much of the nineteenth century, the riots and disorder continued, but so too, somehow, a less exalted form of elite education also took hold. The University of Virginia proved extraordinarily successful at training leaders, producing an outsized cohort of congressmen, governors, and ambassadors;

during the Civil War, former students constituted a disproportionate number of leaders in the short-lived Confederate States of America. Perhaps Jefferson would have been pleased with this remarkable record, though the ultimate collapse of the Union would have been devastating to him and he could only have seen the Confederacy's belligerent advocacy of slavery as a "positive good" as a repudiation of his teaching. Yet in a republic, he also taught, leaders must follow the lead of a progressively enlightened people. Just as the University adapted to its students, those students—many chastened and "improved" by the growing, un-Jeffersonian influence of evangelical religion on campus— became respected leaders in their communities.

To create leaders, or at least the kind of leaders that Jefferson wanted, not just any type of education was needed. An enlightened education would be necessary. Jefferson thus was committed to ensuring that the University's students be prepared to expand the frontiers of knowledge, to obtain an education for the future. As with Jefferson's other accomplishments—ending the establishment of religion in Virginia, drafting the Declaration of Independence, erasing entail and primogeniture from the statute books—his goal for the University was to loosen the grip of the "dead hand of the past." Progressive enlightenment was his abiding ideal.

Robert S. Gibson shows (in this volume), for example, how revolutionary the University would be in the specific area of medical education. The University was also the first college or university in the United States to teach economics. Comparable investigations would likely reveal similar innovations in other disciplines as well. The school's elective curriculum became prototypical.

Johann N. Neem suggests, though, that something more fundamental was occurring at the University. Jefferson helped initiate a reorientation of higher education, moving from the traditional focus on ancient texts, which classically defined the liberal arts, to a search for greater knowledge about the world as it was, through philosophy (broadly defined) and emerging scientific and humanistic disciplines. For education, this constituted a turn outward, rather than inward, toward the future, rather than the past. This was the legacy of Jefferson's engagement in the Enlightenment and the great expansion of learning and belief in progress it inspired. While the founding of the University predates the concept of a modern research university, Jefferson's fixation on recruiting the best faculty, prohibiting them from working outside of their academic positions, and his insistence on the search for new knowledge certainly presaged it.

For years Jefferson had railed against those who placed artificial limits on the human mind and what it could achieve. In 1799 he congratulated a fellow Virginian, "I join you therefore in branding as cowardly the idea that the human mind is incapable of further advances."[2] The University of Virginia, he hoped, would put an end to such cramped thinking with a curriculum built around science and philosophy rather than rhetoric and oratory. "To Jefferson," Neem explains, "science was the site of liberation, and thus freedom, precisely because it unmoored its practitioners from the bindings of the ancients and axioms. . . . Education, then, did not refine from within a tradition, but enabled students to transcend existing boundaries to see the world anew."

Students, though, often more reactionary than their teachers, still placed a very high value on the earlier convention of learning rhetoric, oratory, and logic. As Carolyn Eastman explains, these were still the marks of a gentleman in the period. It is doubly ironic that as Jefferson set a curriculum focused on the new philosophy and science and rejected the old school emphasis on rhetoric and oratory, Virginia students formed a debating society almost immediately upon arriving on campus and then, adding insult to injury, called it the Patrick Henry Society. (This must have irritated Jefferson, who had distrusted and despised Henry for many decades. In July of 1825 a group of students broke off from the Patrick Henry Society to form the Jefferson Literary and Debating Society, today the oldest continually active collegiate debating society in America. Could it be that Jefferson had a hand in the schism?)

In fairness, Jefferson never abandoned the need for the study of rhetoric and logic, or what today might be called critical thinking. Rather, as Neem shows, he simply thought that these were precursors for further advancement and should be part of preparation for study at the University. Rhetoric was still necessary; after all, as Eastman explains, "knowledge was inert on its own, and required rhetorical persuasion to propel it into effective use in the realm of human affairs." Jefferson, one of the finest wordsmiths in history, certainly understood that. In the nineteenth-century culture, whatever Jefferson's intent, "training themselves to be orators was thus one way that University of Virginia students might attain powerful places in a wide range of American institutions." For Jefferson, though, this was only the threshold of higher education.

Of course, today the debate over education's curriculum, goals, and methods continues. Were he with us (in more than spirit), Jefferson would applaud the increased interest in STEM (science-technology-engineering-math) courses. He was an amateur scientist and dabbler and took immense satisfaction in the accelerating discoveries of his time. He would be agog at how that

The Jefferson Literary and Debating Society, the oldest continuously operating college literary society in the United States, reflected the need for gentlemen to master eloquence. (Photograph of members of Jefferson Society[?] of the University of Virginia, circa 1910?, accession no. 9061-a, Albert and Shirley Small Special Collections Library, University of Virginia)

pace of discovery has continued to increase. He would, undoubtedly, be unable to grasp fully the interest in encouraging women into STEM fields, but the desire to continue to propel humans forward, to learn new things, to drive progress is exactly what he hoped for in designing the University.

Of course, that new knowledge sought by his students was not to be limited to what we call the sciences; advances in psychology, sociology, political science, and all of the humanities would also engage his interest. He hoped that his University would lead the way in all fields, pursuing knowledge and truth. "This institution will be based on the illimitable freedom of the human mind," he explained, "for here we are not afraid to follow truth wherever it may lead, nor to tolerate any error so long as reason is left free to combat it."[3]

What is most striking, though, is to realize that as his design came to fruition in the nineteenth century, the future of his University and of university education generally were inextricably linked.

As long as the republic continues, the University will have a role in training leaders. As the University was being built, Jefferson returned to a theme
that he had raised more than a decade earlier and reminded one of the University's chief legislative patrons "that the boys of this age are to be the men of the
next; that they should be prepared to [receive] the holy charge which we are
cherishing to deliver over to them; that in establishing an institution of wisdom for them we secure it to all our future generations; . . ." Today's University students are embarked in yet another step, however halting, in the endless
progress of those future generations.[4]

Notes

1. Jefferson to Uriah Forrest, December 31, 1787, *PTJ*, 12:478. Jefferson to Samuel
Knox, February 12, 1810, *PTJRS*, 2:215 (emphasis added).

2. Jefferson to William G. Munford, June 18, 1799, *PTJ*, 31:128.

3. Jefferson to William Roscoe, December 27, 1820, *Founders Online*, https://
founders.archives.gov/documents/Jefferson/98-01-02-1712.

4. Jefferson to James Breckinridge, February 15, 1821, *Founders Online*, https://
founders.archives.gov/documents/Jefferson/98-01-02-1839.

"The Powers of Debate Should Be Sedulously Cultivated"

The Importance of Eloquence in Early American Education and the University of Virginia

CAROLYN EASTMAN

O NE OF THE THINGS we have largely forgotten about education in the nineteenth century—and more specifically about the founding of the University of Virginia—is the extent to which rhetorical talent and oral performance functioned at the center of educational practices. Schools at all levels demanded that students perform within classrooms on a daily basis and more formally on a quarterly basis, often before large public audiences. Only by exploring this world of the spoken word can we understand the means and ends of education and the origins of the University of Virginia (UVA), as well as their place within the larger political and civic culture of the nineteenth century. The defining characteristic of being a student in that era was standing in front of others and delivering carefully memorized words and information, all the while displaying one's poise and self-assurance. Why? Because nineteenth-century Americans viewed oratory as a major form of communication in a wide range of settings, from politics to religious movements to business, and because they believed that teaching skills in public speech also taught girls and boys how to listen as critical citizens.

This essay scrutinizes the place of oral performance and debate during the early years of the University of Virginia and in education more generally during the early nineteenth century in order to unpack the wider cultural prevalence of oratory and public speech. Doing so helps explain how the University was initially imagined by Thomas Jefferson and other key figures, and explains why its students sought to remake it to suit their own perceived needs. When students founded a series of student debating societies, starting almost as soon as they arrived at the new University of Virginia grounds, they sought to experience the formative culture that many of them had heard about at other

American colleges; they also knew that gaining skills in debate and public speech would help them succeed in their chosen paths in life. As the students at UVA's Jefferson Literary and Debating Society put it in their by-laws, "the faculties of the mind are excited by collision." "Especially in a country where all are free to profess and by argument maintain their opinions," they continued, "the powers of debate should be sedulously cultivated."[1] Most of all, this essay seeks to show that although Jefferson may have played up a neat contrast between orators and philosophers in some of his writings about the new school, as Johann N. Neem demonstrates elsewhere in this volume, it was impossible to mark a clear divide between the two in practice—for Jefferson himself as well as the many others who sought to realize the ideas about the University of Virginia into real-life buildings, faculty, and curricula.[2]

Oral Performance in American Schools and Young People's Mutual Education

Those of us who study education in the early republic can attest to the radical diversity of practices throughout the new United States: educational practices differed by region; between locally funded schools and expensive private academies; and by the age, sex, class, and race of the students. But all American schools shared one important thing in common: the centrality of oral performance. From elementary-level dame schools and reading schools to Latin grammar schools, academies, and colleges, students learned to display their knowledge in a series of both informal and formal public performances at which they spoke aloud, answered questions, recited oratory, and performed theatrical skits, all of which were intended to display students' grasp of both manners and the expression of feeling.

This emphasis on orality in schools began to appear by the mid-eighteenth century, largely due to the elocution movement that Americans inherited from influential British writers and educators. This movement held that knowledge was inert on its own and required rhetorical persuasion to propel it into effective use in the realm of human affairs. Leaders of this movement drew on classical instructional writings about oratory by the Roman writers recently rediscovered in their entirety: Cicero's *De Oratore* and a complete text of Quintilian's *Institutio Oratoria*. More recent assessments, like John Ward's enormously influential *A System of Oratory* (1759), which relied on Cicero and Quintilian, became instrumental within American schools and colleges.[3] Reading the Roman writers in the original Latin may have been reserved primarily for boys with lofty aims in life, but the ideas therein appeared in translated and popularized versions so frequently—even in short prefaces to the most basic American schoolbooks—that they became ubiquitous by the end of the eighteenth century.

These texts taught all students to speak well, not just those designated for the bench, the bar, and the pulpit. To be well spoken allowed a person's true character and value to shine through in every conversation. "Speaking well" meant far more than good grammar and pronunciation. It indicated an ability to convey one's ideas with proper feeling and emotion, to stand and gesture with grace, and more generally to persuade one's listeners not only with one's words, but with the way one's entire manner conveyed upright character. Whether in pursuit of an advantageous marriage, a reputation in business, or respect in one's community and church, children learned that good elocution would ease their paths forward and upward in life.[4]

Elocution worked so well in classrooms because it allowed teachers and parents to determine whether students had fully comprehended the larger meanings of the books they had read and the information they were supposed to absorb. In an era before grades, teachers and communities used public exhibitions to assess student progress. Later generations would belittle the educational practices of this era, which demanded that students memorize and recite information daily in class and more formally on exhibition days before their parents and neighbors. But at least in theory, these forms of memorization were not supposed to be rote. Elocution taught students to seek out the true meanings and feelings behind the material and to deliver it in ways that conveyed the authors' ideas and emotions to listeners. "Elocution every man must have to do. It is an essential part of every body's business," one schoolbook author insisted. "To some it may no doubt be of more consequence than to others; but to all it must be, one day or another, an object of some consequence."[5] Students in schools as far afield as the elite Philadelphia Young Ladies Academy, New York's African Free School, and the Cherokee mission school in Creekpath, Alabama, learned that the very definition of the verb *to read* meant learning to read aloud by using "suitable modulations of the voice" to convey a text's meaning clearly, as one schoolbook writer explained.[6] Educational reforms like the Lancastrian system or Horace Mann's innovations found ways to extend education to far more students, but they did not change that fundamental orientation toward oral performance.[7]

Understanding what these exhibitions looked like reveals how important they were. In Atkinson, New Hampshire, in 1787, the school's exhibition took all day: one boy delivered an oration in Latin, followed by the rest of the girls and boys delivering memorized speeches, dialogues, and tales. After a dinner break, the audience returned for more oratory and theatrical scenes. Some ambitious teachers might invite all the most prominent members of their communities with the hope of attracting attention and patronage from those figures. In Richmond, Virginia, in 1805, an all-boys academy borrowed the state Capitol building—that elegant, Jefferson-designed neoclassical building—for six straight days while its students delivered speeches and displayed their knowledge in a wide range of subjects; the schoolmaster invited all the members of the state's General Assembly. In Schenectady, New York, reviews of the school's exhibitions appeared in the local weekly magazine—and these reviews did not hold back with their criticism. One 1808 review complained that one of the child orators needed to "correct a graceless habit of bending his knee at every emphatic word," comparing him unfavorably with another student whose speech "was witty and appropriate, and performed with much taste and judgement." This ubiquitous practice of assessing students' progress by their oral performances signals the connection between education and a wider culture of oratory in the early republic—a connection that has something to teach us about both the nature of education and the centrality of oratory as a crucial mode of communication.[8]

Nor should we view this emphasis on orality merely as a curious factoid in early American history. It reveals a deep dedication to classicism; the classics taught more broadly that oratory was a marker of republicanism. As one schoolbook explained, its lessons were "intended to make republicans, to make men."[9] Today we often overlook the extent to which early Americans thought "of, through, and with the classics," as one historian has put it.[10] The classics taught Americans that republics needed to be led by great orator-leaders—figures who sought to persuade rather than coerce, and who were willing to display their debates and their rationales openly rather than conceal them. American education further popularized those concepts. In asking schoolchildren to memorize and recite the speeches of Cicero, Demosthenes, and Seneca, educators held up a vision of good leadership exemplified by eloquence: the virtuous oratory that undergirded the classical republics.

To be sure, elocution received healthy criticism during the early republic and antebellum eras, primarily from detractors who felt that in practice, poor teachers and uninspired students often produced classroom recitations and exhibition performances that revealed little real educational attainment. These critics often questioned whether the ability to memorize and recite vast amounts of text truly advanced a student's understanding of the material. One school-book entitled *The Understanding Reader* marked the difference between children who learned by rote and those who learned to understand the material, comparing them to the contrast "between a Learned Pig, which tells you the exact hour and minuite of the day, and Pope Gregory, XIII, who ascertained the exact number of hours and minutes in a Solar year. The Pig knows nothing of time, nor of those measures (hours and minutes) by which we reckon its progress." Likewise, "many of our school-boys, who pass for good readers" fail to understand their lessons.[11] This author, of course, promised to prevent his readers from becoming mere learned pigs—but his solution simply insisted on teaching elocution more effectively. Like so many of the other critics, this one had no alternative to the practices of oral performance in the classroom except that children receive the inspiration (or the prods) to understand their lessons more deeply. It was clear to no one that other modes of assessment, like written exams, would produce more substantial learning.

Learning more advanced forms of public speaking skills at the college level, especially in rhetoric classes, prepared boys to enter professions as gentlemen with firm commands of language, refined bearing, and the art of persuasion. By the end of the eighteenth century, only a fraction of American college students intended to become clergymen—a remarkable change from college attendance in the seventeenth century.[12] The ideal education for a gentleman, as John Witherspoon of Princeton influentially framed it, involved training him to be an *orator*, by which Witherspoon meant a *man of letters*: not only "the parliamentary speaker, the legal speaker, and the preacher, but also the scientific writer, the historian, the controversialist, the writer of epistles and essays and dialogues, and the poet in his minor capacities, and in his epic and dramatic might," as the historian Wilbur Samuel Howell writes.[13] By this time, parents wanted their children to acquire a power of speech because they saw it as crucial to all manner of professions that would cement their sons' status as gentlemen: most notably the law, politics, banking, and trade. Thus, even if men in such professions did not necessarily intend to perform a lot of oratory per se, skills in public speaking taught them to carry themselves like men accustomed to respect from others, possessing the bearing of one who commanded the room.

Boys and young men (and even some young women) who did not attend college may not have received the formal training as in college settings, but nevertheless knew the value of oratorical talent such that by the end of the Revolution they began to form debating and literary societies intended to

enhance their skills in public speech. Some urban settings offered a wide range
of societies to choose from: societies designed for journeymen artisans or
privileged young men of leisure, for those with strong Federalist or Republican sentiments, for those studying to become lawyers, and for those with high
literary aims. In 1791, the thirty-one-year-old Philadelphia printer Mathew
Carey "spoke once or twice" at the meeting of his literary society on the question of "[w]hether the colour of the negroes be the effect of climate & other
external causes." Reporting on the evening in his diary, Carey dismissed several of his fellow debaters variously as "a poor speaker," "a mere squib," and "a
fool," but acknowledged that one of them was a true orator.[14] In 1794, one
young man living in Brooklyn belonged to eight societies, most of which required weekly attendance at debates or the memorization and recitation of
short speeches or poetry.[15] In 1835, a twenty-two-year-old clerk in Boston's
North End dutifully recorded the specific points made by each participant in
the debates of the Northern Debating Society on questions like "Is the tax
upon minors consistent with the principles of our government?" and "whether
the measures pursued & the plans avowed by the Anti Slavery Societies of
New England are likely to produce beneficial results?"[16] The prevalence of the
extant records of such early republican and antebellum societies preserved in
archives up and down the East Coast attests to the importance their members granted these organizations: members often treated their societies' records
and minute books far more reverently than they did their own families' letters
and diaries.[17]

The sheer prevalence of these practices of training in public speaking
within and beyond formal educational settings indicates the extent to which
contemporaries saw those skills as useful to all manner of Americans, and
for a wide range of reasons. The fact that schools taught the same skills to
those in society least likely to become orators—girls, children of color, poor
children—indicates the other major purpose of elocution: to instruct everyone not only in how to speak, but how to listen and observe with heightened
critical alertness. These lessons insisted on the necessity of training children
to be skeptical listeners. As one schoolbook instructed, "Observe and mark as
well as you may, what is the temper and disposition of those persons, whose
speeches you hear, whether they be grave, serious, sober, wise, discreet persons. If they be such, their speeches commonly are like themselves, and well
deserve your attention and observation."[18] In other words, girls and boys
needed to learn skills not only in speaking well in public, but in listening critically to oratory by others. This was as fundamental to republican virtue as the

imperative for an educated and informed populace. These messages about the heightened necessity for speakers and auditors to display sharp attentiveness to one another help to illuminate a longer historical pattern in the rising importance of audiences.

Americans placed enormous value in the acquisition of good speaking skills during the early republic and antebellum eras, seeing public speech as a significant mode of communication in a republic. That emphasis mirrored an increasing prevalence of forms of public speech in a wide range of American institutions, including religion, politics, entertainment, reform, and even the self-help movement that emerged after the Civil War. Considering both the ubiquity of oral performance in schools and the existing criticisms of its weaknesses as a mode of education, it may be unsurprising that Thomas Jefferson might seek to craft a different plan for education at the college level in Virginia. But, as we shall see, one should not overestimate the extent to which such a radical change might be possible, or even preferable.

Eloquence and Oral Performance at the University of Virginia

When Thomas Jefferson plotted out the contours of Central College, he emphasized that unlike other forms of education, his university would privilege substance over style and downplay the central role of rhetorical training, as Johann Neem shows in his essay in this volume. Certainly, to speak of philosophers rather than orators constituted a shot across the bow. This grand statement reflected Jefferson's own antipathy to some of the prevailing practices at American colleges, not least his own alma mater, William and Mary, on the other side of the state, at the same time that it allowed him to declare how distinctive this new university might be. As dramatic rhetorical statements go, this was one of Jefferson's best.

As tidy as this contrast appears, and as much as Jefferson truly sought to mark his university as one exceptionally dedicated to deep scientific knowledge, we should also not underestimate two important ways that such a divide between orators and philosophers was impossible to maintain—both at the level of planning by Jefferson and others, and in the execution of the new University of Virginia. In the end, the considerable gray area between orators and philosophers illustrates better the realities of creating and opening a college in the early American republic and less the University's ideals as laid out on paper.

Jefferson harbored a lifelong distaste for public speaking and what he saw as the empty words of some talented orators—but he also demonstrated a strong appreciation for talented speakers whom he believed blended deep learning and understanding with the capacity to make those ideas meaningful in the world. For two decades, for example, he supported the career of orator and elocutionist James Ogilvie. Ogilvie taught school in Virginia for fifteen years, specializing in both elocutionary training and intensely rigorous academic education for his students. By 1807, Jefferson had entrusted to Ogilvie the education of his grandson and namesake, Thomas Jefferson Randolph. Ogilvie continued to mentor the boy even after he gave up teaching in 1808 in favor of a career as traveling speaker—a career for which Jefferson provided support, particularly in the form of letters of introduction to influential elites throughout the nation. Known in particular for his elaborate oratorical "action"—the dramatic postures, gestures, and facial expressions that accompanied his lectures—Ogilvie's lectures advocated for a greater public investment in oratory as a primary medium of communication in the United States. During an acclaimed tour that would last more than a decade and transform him into one of the nation's first celebrities, Ogilvie received criticism from some that his flair for oratorical gesture undercut the substance of his material; one newspaper writer accused him of being "all smoke and no fire."[19] Jefferson strongly disagreed with this assessment. "[H]aving myself been occasionally one of his hearers, I am safe in assuring you that no one, however learned, will hear him without instruction. none, however moral, will leave him without better impressions," he wrote to a Baltimore minister in one of the letters of introduction. This was no theater actor, Jefferson insisted. "[T]he correctness of his morals, the purity of his views and his high degree of understanding & cultivation, will not fail to impress you." "[I]n short, those who attend him once, will not fail to attend afterwards. . . ."[20] For Jefferson, Ogilvie achieved the Ciceronian ideal of undergirding his oratory with knowledge.[21]

By the time Jefferson began to seek out faculty for his new university, he likewise turned to figures with deep investments in oral performance. By deputizing Francis Walker Gilmer as a faculty member and as a recruiter of potential faculty in Europe, he demonstrated again his willingness to see considerable overlap between orators and philosophers.[22] Gilmer's education throughout his boyhood years emphasized oratorical training and deep investment in the ideals of the classical greats. By the time he studied with James Ogilvie in preparation to attend the College of William and Mary, Ogilvie believed him to be a most remarkably gifted and knowledgeable student, "probably without a rival amongst the young men of Virginia, in extent of useful information, in the range of liberal reading, in the variety, solidity and bril-

liancy of your intellectual accomplishments."[23] Gilmer's education in elocution and public speaking probably underwrote his subsequent publication, in
1816, of *Sketches of American Orators*. This volume celebrated six contemporary
political figures as oratorical heroes in the style of Demosthenes and Cicero,
and did so by focusing on the intense combination of each man's substance as
well as his style, facets that Gilmer discusses as inextricable.[24] As Gilmer explained in a letter to a friend about his *Sketches*, "The learning that I would aim
at is that of Cicero—a learning that can be instrumental in promoting the purposes of active life, in elevating the man of business into ye sage, & the mere
statement of wholesome truths, into sublime & touching eloquence."[25] By the
time Jefferson and the new Board of Visitors for the University of Virginia
began to seek out faculty members in 1824, Jefferson's health had grown delicate enough that they asked Gilmer to undertake a trip to Europe to recruit
suitable candidates.[26] This job revealed to Gilmer the extent to which some of
the most influential professors, particularly those at Scottish universities, made
use of lectures—not only as delivery mechanisms for information to students,
but for displays of erudition that could reach broader public audiences.[27]

Between Jefferson's patronage of the orator-elocutionist James Ogilvie
and his delegation to the oratory-obsessed Francis Walker Gilmer the job of
seeking out potential faculty, it becomes difficult to sustain a clear sense of
where he and his Board of Visitors might have drawn a line between orators
and philosophers. Even his ambitious proposals for an academic curriculum
included lessons in belles lettres and rhetoric.[28] And looking beyond the
vagueness of this divide in the minds of the University's founders, the persist-
ing importance of oratory and spoken-word performance becomes all the
more vivid when we examine how the new college's students found ways to
install those elocutionary practices once they arrived in 1825 and established a
series of debating and literary societies intended to permit them to organize
on their own and cultivate their gifts for debate and public speech.

Long before the University of Virginia opened its doors to students, debating societies had become so popular in American colleges that many "en-
grossed more of the interests and activities of the students than any other
aspect of college life," as James MacLachlan explains in a groundbreaking
essay on the subject. Debating societies "enrolled most of the students,
constructed—and taught—their own curricula, granted their own diplomas,
selected and bought their own books, operated their own libraries, developed
and enforced elaborate codes of conduct among their members, and set the
personal goals and ideological tone for a majority of the student body."[29]

These groups had been popular since the 1750s, and by the early republic they had evolved to provide college students with some of the amenities they felt necessary—from books and libraries to mutual assistance in developing speaking skills. As J. Jefferson Looney has explained about debating societies at what is now Princeton University, these groups "functioned as colleges *within* the College of New Jersey."[30] Jefferson himself had belonged to William and Mary's F. H. C. Society, which resembled Yale's Linonian Society and Harvard's Philomusarian Club. In some cases these clubs were officially sanctioned by colleges, but most of them sprang out of students' eagerness to create societies on their own, without college oversight. In fact, by 1800 at least eight colleges offered students a choice between rival societies, like Princeton's American Whig and Cliosophic societies, which organized debates between their members to heighten the drama of competition.[31] As one college graduate remembered, belonging to a debating society "was worth more as a part of education than the college itself, not only in a literary point of view but in manners and morals. It did most to remove boyish habits and make men of us, and men of sound and correct principles for society in after life."[32]

As a result, it should be no surprise that students at the new University of Virginia would found debating societies to provide what many commonly believed was crucial to college life. When students established the Patrick Henry Society almost immediately after arriving in Charlottesville, one of them would deliver a speech to his fellow members declaring, "Was it not societies of this sort that the youthful minds of a Robertson a Franklin and a Madison were disciplined? And has not their importance been so generally acknowledged that they have been incorporated with the very existence of almost all other American colleges, and their exercises become among the chief of the institutions?"[33] Clearly, the reputation of those college societies spread far and wide. (It is also worth noting that this member went on to become Speaker of the U.S. House of Representatives.) Several months later, by the summer of 1825, a group of sixteen students within the Patrick Henry Society would break off to form the Jefferson Literary and Debating Society—a group reportedly less prone to chaotic meetings and political radicalism, and one that within a year would enroll approximately one-third of the University's students as members.[34] Although the Patrick Henry Society proved to be short-lived, in 1831 students would add a new debating society to their choices: the Washington Society, which served as a rival to the Jefferson Society for nearly a century. Meanwhile, the law students formed the Law Society in 1833 to familiarize them with courtroom litigation and forensic debate.[35]

Like the debating societies discussed above formed by young people out-side of college settings, the Jefferson Society incorporated a range of oral per-formances each week. Meetings usually began with an oration or the reading of an essay by one of the members who had received the assignment two weeks earlier. One essayist might hold forth on the origins of language; another might elucidate a topic pertaining to metaphysics or the powers of the federal government.[36] Following this performance, the weekly debate commenced. The Society's membership was divided into four "classes" that took turns en-acting each week's debate, thus requiring each member to participate about once a month. Society rules set limits on how often each member could en-gage, thus demanding full participation from each "class" and preventing the most vociferous or aggressive from dominating the conversation. The bylaws also required that at the end of each week's debate, the full membership would vote to determine which side had proved most persuasive. The Society also sponsored a competition each year among its members for the role of Final Orator who had the honor of representing the Society by speaking at the Uni-versity Final Celebration each June.[37]

The topics they chose spanned a range of areas, thus benefiting those members who took the time to familiarize themselves with substantial infor-mation having to do with the subject. Topics like "Was the English Govern-ment justified in banishing Napoleon to St. Helena?" might reward those who scrutinized recent history and could muster evidence from British justifica-tions for that 1815 decision. "Ought capital punishment to be abolished?" might benefit those of a metaphysical or philosophical cast of mind, bringing to bear biblical and political wisdom on the question. By 1853, the Jefferson Society would engage in a furious debate over slavery.[38] Letters home from college students reveal the intense preparation and research they mustered for these debates. One such letter describes a student's pride in "addressing a public au-dience" and coming away a part of the winning side in that night's debate. As anxious as he had been before the night's proceedings began—anxieties that led him to scrutinize Lord Kames's *Elements of Criticism* in preparation—"I found great consolation in reflecting, that I should speak in company with one half of my class-mates, many of whom would succeed no better than myself."[39]

Societies like these demanded striking levels of discipline and order from their members—self-discipline that contrasted sharply with the high levels of disorder that prevailed among college students generally and particularly at the University of Virginia, as demonstrated by the essay from Ervin L. Jordan Jr. in this volume.[40] At the same time that college boys fired weapons, struck enslaved

women and men, attacked faculty, and rioted, they held themselves to the strictest of rules of conduct for the duration of their debating society meetings—
and if they broke those rules, they were fined.[41] A member appointed to open
the night's debate who failed to do so received a fine of fifty cents (about
$13.25 in today's money[42]); other delinquent members of a debate were fined
twenty-five cents. Each member of a committee who failed to "report at the
proper time" likewise received fines of fifty cents. In this fashion, the Jefferson
Society declared: "Any member shall be deemed guilty of disorder, who shall
by hissing, clapping, laughing aloud, or any other unnecessary noise whatever,
interrupt the President, or any member while speaking; or, refuse to take his
seat when ordered by the President; or, withdraw from the Hall, without the
permission of the President; or, pass between the President and any member
addressing the chair; or, address the President without rising from his seat; or,
persist in motions, resolutions or remarks which have been pronounced to be
out of order."[43]

Such an elaborate list of rules appears especially striking considering the
especially distressing behavior by Virginia students outside of Jefferson Society meetings. By 1825, the University's faculty members had threatened to resign en masse due to student disorder, riots prevailed, and Thomas Jefferson
found himself reduced to tears as he stood before the assembled body in an effort to establish better control. Not long thereafter, students "shamefully mutilated" some cows belonging to University employees; in 1840, a rioting student
shot and killed one of the University's most groundbreaking law professors.[44]
To be sure, not everyone liked the Society's restrictions; in 1834, one student
wrote in his diary of his disappointment in the Society's strict decorum:
"Too much etiquette," he wrote.[45] On the whole, however, students who
would not behave themselves for their professors or the college president were
willing to do so when they were the ones in charge. As James MacLachlan
notes, students "saw themselves in terms of the civil ideal" as citizens capable of self-government; in contrast, they saw college presidents as monarchs,
tyrants.[46]

Understanding the students' willingness to adhere to strict rules in this
one aspect of their college lives requires absorbing two important lessons
about what debating societies offered them. First, clubs provided a heady combination of comradery and competition idealized by contemporaries. As the
Jefferson Society's constitution explained, "Friendships are cemented, errors
corrected and sound principles established by society and intercourse."[47] A
contemporaneous college debating society summarized its value in similar

terms: its membership sought "mutual improvement by mutual remarks."[48] For a generation, advice literature had celebrated the *mutuality* of these friendships as providing young people with valuable opportunities to improve themselves according to the models of their peers, from their manners to their demeanor to their ability to reveal their stores of knowledge. To do so within the bonds of friendship, classmates believed, made polishing one's own rough edges far more appealing than having professors or elders do so. As one member of the Jefferson Society explained in a heartfelt tribute, "Some of my happiest and most instructive hours have been spent within these walls." William Roane Aylett continued: "I have learned here what one cannot acquire from the lips of professors, nor gather from the pages of books."[49] The sheer fact that Aylett contrasted the pleasure of learning from his peers with that obtained from his professors or from books conveys the cultural importance of mutual education and improvement during the first half of the nineteenth century.[50] Such mutuality ideally cemented friendships that would shape them long beyond their club years, helping to buttress one another's future lives and careers, and provide the alliances or support men needed as they proceeded beyond college to adulthood.

Second, the Jefferson Society and its parallel organizations at the University of Virginia and elsewhere touted the long-term value of their "mutual training" and friendship within a very specific context unique to the long nineteenth century: a broader culture of eloquence. Considering the many ways that public speech was becoming all the more significant in many areas of American public life, it is not hard to see why college students would find this training so vital. Whether it took the form of star orator-statesmen like Henry Clay and Daniel Webster in Congress, star orator-ministers like Charles Grandison Finney, star orator-educators like John Quincy Adams (named as the Boylston Professor of Rhetorick and Oratory at Harvard College in 1805), or star lyceum lecturers like Ralph Waldo Emerson, many contemporaries commented on the ways that the United States was entering a "golden age of American eloquence" that seemed to mark it as the worthy successor to the classical republics of the ancient world.[51] Nor were these elite white men the only ones to utilize oratory as a medium of communication in this era. Ecstatic evangelists held camp meetings and revivals that converted thousands with their powerful, antiauthoritarian calls to experience religion directly. Political stump speakers with radically new speaking styles such as Davy Crockett displayed the audacity to electioneer for themselves for the first time beginning in the 1820s and 1830s, ultimately changing the face of democratic politics in the United States and elsewhere in the English-speaking world. Social reformers like Frederick Douglass, Angelina Grimké, and Elizabeth Cady Stanton likewise innovated new rhetorical styles designed to alert audiences to the urgency of their causes. In all these ways, public speech was becoming more significant to American life and a wide range of social actors over the course of the nineteenth century—and college students at the University of Virginia well understood it.[52]

Training themselves to be orators was thus one way that University of Virginia students might attain powerful places in a wide range of American institutions. "By learning how to captivate, convince, and perhaps even silence their peers, young men enacted a society in which power emanated from men and for men," explains historian Timothy Williams.[53] Those who sought to enter the popular professions of the law or statesmanship viewed training in debate and oratory as vital to their success. By providing a space where young men might teach one another to "think, write, and speak," societies like these furnished "a forum for developing talents and personalities unequalled by any other facet of college life or instruction," as Thomas Harding notes.[54] If the University would not provide classes for training them in oratory or persuasive debate, they would learn it from one another.

Students were correct in believing that those talents would benefit their later careers. A history of the Jefferson Society published in 2017 contained extensive appendixes listing the dozens of alumni of the organization who went on to have notable careers in politics, the law, university administration, and literature—including U.S. president Woodrow Wilson, state governors, members of the U.S. cabinet, and sixteen officials of the Confederate States of America during the Civil War.[55] In the context of a history of the Society, of course, such lists of notable alumni imply that the education in public speech played an important role in those students' later success and the University's outsized importance in shaping American history. In this essay, however, I have sought to focus less on the University of Virginia's specific historical triumphs or its unique educational practices and more on why its *similarity* to other schools in the realm of encouraging oral performance benefited its students. I have suggested that Thomas Jefferson's proposed plan to educate philosophers rather than orators was itself more a rhetorical flourish than representative of his real belief that those categories might be neatly divided. In addition, this essay has demonstrated how much University of Virginia students eagerly sought the potent combination of training in public speaking skills, competition, friendship, and society membership that the Patrick Henry, Jefferson, and

Washington Societies provided. Even if Jefferson dreamed that students at his University might emphasize substance rather than style, students themselves knew that in order to convey the substance of their knowledge they needed the panache of practiced wordsmithing and the experience of the combat of debate. It was not merely that they saw the models of oratorical heroism in the speeches of Cicero and Demosthenes that they studied in class; they witnessed the rise of real-life orator-leaders all around them.

If some of the most famous nineteenth-century speeches remain familiar to us—Abraham Lincoln's Gettysburg Address, Frederick Douglass's What to the Slave is the Fourth of July, Sojourner Truth's impromptu Ain't I a Woman remarks, Charles Sumner's Crime Against Kansas that prompted a fellow senator to club him over the head with a cane—somehow we have lost a broader view of the wider culture of oratory of which these were a part. As one historian has explained, nineteenth-century oratorical culture "was so ubiquitous that its omnipresence has helped to render it strangely invisible. We look through it in search of material on all aspects of the period, but we fail to look at it, to interrogate it as a cultural form in its own right."[56] Recapturing the role of elocutionary training and debate at the University of Virginia and in the wider educational culture of the era permits us to see not only how contemporaries imagined schools and colleges benefiting students. It allows us to appreciate how schools' emphasis on oral performance trained children and youth to find a place in a broader culture of eloquence that defined nineteenth-century American life.

Notes

1. The Constitution of the Jefferson Society, 1837 (the original 1825 constitution has not survived; this is likely a revision of the original), in Thomas L. Howard III and Owen W. Gallogly, *Society Ties: A History of the Jefferson Society and Student Life at the University of Virginia* (Charlottesville: University of Virginia Press for the William B. Kenan Jr. Endowment Fund for the Academical Village, 2017), 259, paraphrasing Jefferson's Statute for Religious Freedom ("all men shall be free to profess, and by argument to maintain, their opinions").

2. Bruce A. Kimball, *Orators and Philosophers: A History of the Idea of Liberal Education* (New York: Columbia University Teachers College Press, 1986).

3. John Ward, *A System of Oratory, Delivered in a Course of Lectures, Publicly Read at Gresham College, London* (London: John Ward, 1759).

4. These paragraphs draw on Jay Fliegelman, *Declaring Independence: Jefferson, Natural Language, and the Culture of Performance* (Stanford, CA: Stanford University Press, 1993); Sandra M. Gustafson, *Eloquence Is Power: Oratory and Public Performance in Early America* (Chapel Hill: University of North Carolina Press for the Omohundro Institute of Early American History and Culture, 2000); G. P. Mohrmann, "Introduction," in Thomas Sheridan, *A Discourse Being Introductory to His Course of Lectures on Elocution and the English Language* (Los Angeles: William Andrews Clark Memorial Library of UCLA, 1969); John J. Mahoney, "The Classical Tradition in Eighteenth Century English Rhetorical Education," *History of Education Journal* 9, no. 4 (Summer 1958): 93–97; Carolyn Eastman, *A Nation of Speechifiers: Making an American Public after the Revolution* (Chicago: University of Chicago Press, 2009), ch. 1; and Eastman, "Oratory and Platform Culture in Britain and North America, 1740–1900," *Oxford Handbooks Online* (Oxford: Oxford University Press, 2016), http://www.oxfordhandbooks.com/view /10.1093/oxfordhb/9780199935338.001.0001/oxfordhb-9780199935338-e-33?rskey =UU2jw2&result=5.

5. Jonathan Barber, *An Introduction to the Grammar of Elocution Designed for the Use of Schools*, 2nd ed., rev. and improved (Boston: Marsh, Capen & Lyon, 1836), 17–18.

6. Daniel Adams, *The Understanding Reader, or Knowledge Before Oratory. Being a New Selection of Lessons, Suited to the Understanding and the Capacities of Youth*, 3rd ed. (1803; reprint, Leominster, MA: Salmon Wilder, 1805), iii. For information on the Young Ladies Academy and the Cherokee school, see Eastman, *Nation of Speechifiers*, 66–67, 89; on the African Free School, see Anna Mae Duane, "'Like a Motherless Child': Racial Education at the New York African Free School and in My Bondage and My Freedom," *American Literature* 82, no. 3 (September 2010): 461–88.

7. Johann Neem, *Democracy's Schools: The Rise of Public Education in America* (Baltimore: Johns Hopkins University Press, 2017).

8. See Eastman, *Nation of Speechifiers*, 29–30 (Atkinson Academy); "Course of Juvenile Education," *Enquirer* (Richmond), April 9, 1805, 2; "Local Grammar School Examination," *Pastime: A Literary Paper* (Schenectady), January 16, 1808, 241–42, spelling in the original.

9. Thomas E. Birch, *The Virginian Orator* (Richmond: Samuel Pleasants Jr., 1808), iii.

10. Eran Shalev, *Rome Reborn on Western Shores: Historical Imagination and the Creation of the American Republic* (Charlottesville: University of Virginia Press, 2009), 2. See also Caroline Winterer, *The Culture of Classicism: Ancient Greece and Rome in American Intellectual Life, 1780–1810* (Baltimore: Johns Hopkins University Press, 2002).

11. Adams, *Understanding Reader*, iii (spelling as in original).

12. Ronald Story, "Harvard and the Boston Brahmins: A Study in Institutional and Class Development, 1800–1865," *Journal of Social History* 8, no. 3 (1975): 94–121.

13. Wilbur Samuel Howell, *Eighteenth-Century British Logic and Rhetoric* (Princeton, NJ: Princeton University Press, 1971), 676.

14. Mathew Carey, diary (227A), 1787–1821, entry for March 14, 1791, Edward Carey Gardiner Collection, box 84b, Historical Society of Pennsylvania Manuscript Collections, Philadelphia.

15. John Barent Johnson diary discussed in Eastman, *Nation of Speechifiers*, 117.

16. Bradley N. Cumings, diary, 1832–1847, entries for January 23, 1835, and March 27, 1835, Massachusetts Historical Society Manuscript Collections, Boston.

17. On this subject more widely, see Albrecht Koschnik, "Let a Common Interest Bind Us Together": Associations, Partisanship, and Culture in Philadelphia, 1774–1840 (Charlottesville: University of Virginia Press, 2007); Eleanor Bryce Scott, "Early Literary Clubs in New York City," American Literature 5, no. 1 (March 1933): 3–16; David S. Shields, Civil Tongues and Polite Letters in British America (Chapel Hill: University of North Carolina Press for the Institute of American History and Culture, 1997); and Bryan Waterman, Republic of Intellect: The Friendly Club of New York City and the Making of American Literature (Baltimore: Johns Hopkins University Press, 2007).

18. Caleb Bingham, The American Preceptor Improved: Being a New Selection of Lessons for Reading and Speaking, 11th New York ed. (New York: Evert Duyckinck, 1820), 203–4.

19. "Mr. Ogilvie," Newburyport Herald, September 26, 1809, 3, reprinted from the Portsmouth Oracle.

20. Jefferson to John Glendy, June 21, 1808, Founders Online, https://founders.archives.gov/documents/Jefferson/99-01-02-8186.

21. This material is drawn from my book in progress, The Strange Genius of Mr. O: Celebrity and the Invention of the United States (Chapel Hill: University of North Carolina Press for the Omohundro Institute of Early American History and Culture, forthcoming).

22. Philip Alexander Bruce, History of the University of Virginia, 1819–1919: The Lengthened Shadow of One Man, centennial ed. (New York: Macmillan, 1920), I:344–45, 356–76.

23. Richard Beale Davis, Francis Walker Gilmer: Life and Learning in Jefferson's Virginia (Richmond: Dietz Press, 1939), 20–21, 52–55; James Ogilvie to Francis Walker Gilmer, June 20, [1812], Correspondence of Francis Walker Gilmer (Mss. 38-588), box 1, folder 34, Small Special Collections Library, University of Virginia. Ogilvie was not the only contemporary who felt this way. See John Gilmer Speed, The Gilmers in America (New York: n.p., 1897), 52–71 (similar compliments from Thomas Jefferson and others). Gilmer's education as an orator had particularly been sparked by his brother-in-law, the Richmond lawyer William Wirt, who himself had a lifelong preoccupation with the reputed brilliant oratory of Patrick Henry. Dedicating his spare hours to researching Henry's gifts for public speech, by 1817 he published a biography that included a reconstructed version of Henry's 1775 "give me liberty, or give me death" speech. In frequent letters between Wirt and Gilmer, they discuss the importance of oratory and the path to becoming a powerful speaker.

24. [Francis Walker Gilmer], Sketches of American Orators (Baltimore: Fielding Lucas Jr., 1816). After Gilmer's premature death in 1826 at the age of thirty-five, his friends published a revised and expanded edition of this pamphlet.

25. Gilmer to Hugh Legaré, October 1, 1816, Francis Walker Gilmer Correspondence, 1784–1826 (Acc. #38-588), box 2, folder 3, Small Special Collections Library, University of Virginia.

26. Bruce, History of the University of Virginia, 1:342.

27. Davis, *Francis Walker Gilmer*, 193–236; Tom F. Wright, *Lecturing the Atlantic: Speech, Print, and an Anglo-American Commons, 1830–1870* (New York: Oxford University Press, 2017), 11–16. In this regard, Scottish colleges diverged from the tutorial method of educating students that was more prevalent at Oxford and Cambridge.

28. Bruce, *History of the University of Virginia*, I:322.

29. James McLachlan, "The *Choice of Hercules*: American Student Societies in the Early 19th Century," in *The University in Society*, ed. Lawrence Stone (Princeton, NJ: Princeton University Press, 1974), II:472. See also Thomas Spencer Harding, *College Literary Societies: Their Contribution to Higher Education in the United States, 1815–1876* (New York: Pageant Press International, 1971).

30. J. Jefferson Looney, *Nurseries of Letters and Republicanism: A Brief History of the American Whig-Cliosophic Society and Its Predecessors, 1765–1941* (Princeton, NJ: Trustees of the American Whig-Cliosophic Society, 1996), 16 (emphasis added).

31. J. Jefferson Looney, "Useful without Attracting Attention: The Cliosophic and American Whig Societies of the College of New Jersey, 1765–1896," *Princeton University Library Chronicle* 64, no. 3 (Spring 2003): 389–423.

32. The unpublished memoirs of George Strawbridge (an 1802 graduate of what became Princeton University), quoted in Looney, "Useful without Attracting Attention," 391.

33. "Speech to the Patrick Henry Society," Robert Mercer Taliaferro Hunter Papers, 1826–1860 (Acc. #6662), Small Special Collections Library, University of Virginia, quoted in Howard and Gallogly, *Society Ties*, xxii.

34. Howard and Gallogly, *Society Ties*, xxi, 5–6, 18.

35. John Ritchie, *The First Hundred Years: A Short History of the School of Law of the University of Virginia for the Period 1826–1926* (Charlottesville: University Press of Virginia for the University of Virginia School of Law, 1978), 20.

36. Howard and Gallogly, *Society Ties*, 35–36.

37. Ibid., 38.

38. Ibid., 36–37.

39. James Garnett (a student at what would later be known as Princeton University), letter to Mary E. Garnett, January 1, 1814, quoted in MacLachlan, "*Choice of Hercules*," 483.

40. See also Howard and Gallogly, *Society Ties*, 26–28.

41. Rex Bowman and Carlos Santos, *Rot, Riot, and Rebellion: Mr. Jefferson's Struggle to Save the University that Changed America* (Charlottesville: University of Virginia Press, 2013).

42. Values determined by use of www.measuringworth.com.

43. Constitution of the Jefferson Literary and Debating Society, 1837, in Howard and Gallogly, *Society Ties*, 263.

44. Bowman and Santos, *Rot, Riot, and Rebellion*, 34–35, 37; Ritchie, *First Hundred Years*, 24.

45. Charles Ellis Jr. diary, Small Special Collections Library, University of Virginia, quoted in Bowman and Santos, *Rot, Riot, and Rebellion*, 96.

46. MacLachlan, "*Choice of Hercules*," 465.

47. Constitution of the Jefferson Society, 1837, in Howard and Gallogly, *Society Ties*, 259.

48. The records of the American Whig Society of the College of New Jersey [Princeton], January 13, 1817, quoted in MacLachlan, "*Choice of Hercules*," 474.

49. William Roane Aylett quoted in Howard and Gallogly, *Society Ties*, [ix].

50. On this subject more broadly, see Eastman, *Nation of Speechifiers*, 118–19; Peter Clark, *British Clubs and Societies, 1580–1800: An Associational World* (Oxford: Clarendon Press, 2000); and Daniel A. Cohen, "Arthur Mervyn and His Elders: The Ambivalence of Youth in the Early Republic," *WMQ* 43, no. 3 (July 1986): 362–80.

51. Edward G. Parker, *The Golden Age of American Oratory* (Boston: Whittemore, Niles, and Hall, 1857).

52. This paragraph draws on a range of sources including Nathan O. Hatch, *The Democratization of American Christianity* (New Haven, CT: Yale University Press, 1989); Marianne Perciaccante, *Calling Down Fire: Charles Grandison Finney and Revivalism in Jefferson County, New York, 1800–1840* (Albany: State University of New York Press, 2003); Leigh Eric Schmidt, *Holy Fire: Scotland and the Making of American Revivalism*, 2nd ed. (Grand Rapids, MI: William B. Eerdmans, 2001); Sean Scalmer, *On the Stump: Campaign Oratory and Democracy in the United States, Britain, and Australia* (Philadelphia: Temple University Press, 2017); and Angela G. Ray, *The Lyceum and Public Culture in the Nineteenth-Century United States* (East Lansing: Michigan State University Press, 2005).

53. Timothy Williams, *Intellectual Manhood: University, Self, and Society in the Antebellum South* (Chapel Hill: University of North Carolina Press, 2015), 75.

54. Harding, *College Literary Societies*, 1.

55. Howard and Gallogly, *Society Ties*, 241–45.

56. Martin Hewitt, "Aspects of Platform Culture in Nineteenth-Century Britain," *Nineteenth-Century Prose* 29, no. 1 (Spring 2002): 1. See also James Perrin Warren, *Culture of Eloquence: Oratory and Reform in Antebellum America* (State College: Pennsylvania State University Press, 1999).

From "Ancients and Axioms"
to "Every Branch of Science"

Thomas Jefferson's Philosophy
of Liberal Education

JOHANN N. NEEM

T HOMAS JEFFERSON famously argued that, in a republic, an ignorant citizenry would be easy prey for would-be tyrants. His bill to expand access to primary and secondary education and his founding of the University of Virginia are thus staples of almost all histories of American education. Jefferson, perhaps more than any other American of his generation, argued for the civic purpose of education at all levels. Yet the specific implications of his curricular proposals have remained obscure. Previous scholars have recognized the impact of the Enlightenment on Jefferson's educational ideals and have noted his commitment to secular education. To this extent, scholars are right to conclude that Jefferson's curricular proposals favored modern and new knowledge over ancient truths.[1] Jefferson's curricular ideas appear different, however, when placed within the context of a much older debate, one dating back to the ancient world. Building on Bruce Kimball's work, this essay contextualizes Jefferson's ideas within a centuries-old conversation over what is the best kind of education for citizens and civic leaders, one that prepares them to be orators or philosophers?[2] Jefferson sided with philosophy, and his commitment is reflected in his recommendations for primary and secondary education as well as his efforts to reform William and Mary College and, ultimately, to establish the new University of Virginia.

In the larger context of this much older conversation, Jefferson's curricular proposals appear less novel and, instead, grounded in a deep and contested tradition. Indeed, Jefferson's embrace of philosophy over oratory was at odds with republican thinkers in ancient Rome, Renaissance humanists, and, as Carolyn Eastman shows in her contribution to this volume, what many Americans continued to advocate into the era of the early American republic. Since ancient times, there had been a recognized tension between oratory and philosophy. Should citizens and leaders be educated primarily in rhetorical skills, as ancient sophists had argued, or should they be seekers of philosophical truth, as Plato had countered? Jefferson sided with the philosophers. American students needed not just the trivial skills of grammar, rhetoric, and logic, but also access to the new knowledge being generated by philosophical investigations of the human and natural worlds—what would become, in time, the disciplines represented by the humanities, the social sciences, and the natural sciences. The curriculum should thus be organized by subjects or domains of knowledge rather than by skills.[3]

In contrast to Jefferson's commitment to philosophy, during the colonial period and into the postrevolutionary era, most educators had emphasized the oratorical tradition, with its focus on the *studia humanitatis*, logic, and a smattering of the three branches of philosophy—natural, moral, and metaphysical. Jefferson's own education reflected the dominance of the oratorical ideal of education. In his proposals for revising education in Virginia, however, he embraced the ideal of the philosopher, a seeker of specific knowledge about the world, culminating in the Rockfish Gap Report, which laid out his ideal curriculum for education from the primary levels up through the new University of Virginia. Jefferson purposefully sought to displace ignorance by providing young people with knowledge about the world—knowledge that would allow them to be critical and thoughtful citizens and civic leaders.

Orators and Philosophers

One of the oldest debates in philosophy concerns whether one can be educated without truth. In the era of Athenian democracy, when citizens needed to speak well and effectively in order to be participants in the public spaces of the polis, a new school of teachers named sophists emerged to help people develop communication skills. These sophists, who taught people how to use language effectively, were criticized by Plato, the founder of the academic philosophical tradition. To Plato, who had witnessed his mentor Socrates condemned to death by the polis, words that were not grounded in the foundations of knowledge were dangerous. In his critique of sophistry, the *Gorgias*, named after a famous sophistic teacher, Plato's Socrates argues that knowledge is vital to speech. Doctors can speak about medicine because they have knowledge of it. This is also true, Socrates argued, for "the other arts and sciences." In response, Plato's Gorgias argues that "you don't have to learn the other arts and sciences." With rhetoric, one is "on par with the experts."[4]

The debate raged for centuries, but despite our reverence for Plato, the sophists won the argument. To be educated meant to learn how to read texts and use words. Yet Plato's critique never disappeared. The two sides were brought to a truce under Roman statesman Cicero, who argued in *The Ideal Orator,* an important text for Renaissance humanists, that oratory is best defined as "something greater, and is a combination of more arts and pursuits, than is generally supposed." One cannot be a good orator "unless [one] has gained a knowledge of all the important subjects and arts." Without knowledge, Cicero argues, "the orator's speech will remain an utterly empty, yes, almost childish verbal exercise." Cicero was kinder to philosophy than Gorgias. Society needed philosophers, but the goal of a liberal education was not to turn every one into a philosopher. Instead, the ideal orator, in Cicero's vision, would make use of philosophy in order to have an impact on the world. The ideal orator, Cicero averred, "unites wisdom and eloquence," knowledge with skills and virtue.[5]

This effort to unite wisdom to eloquence, philosophy to rhetoric, knowledge to speech, proved a winning combination. Yet, during the Renaissance, it did not achieve the balance that Cicero had sought. Instead, if anything, rhetoric regained the upper hand relative to philosophy. In his sardonic dismissal of the historiographical debate about whether the Renaissance should be interpreted as a revival of philosophical thought, Bruce Kimball has responded, "the leaders of the movement were decidedly unphilosophical."[6] This is not, of course, because they did not read. Indeed, they rediscovered many classical texts. They devoured them and modeled themselves on their ancient forebears. But that is precisely the point. For many of the most renowned Renaissance thinkers, as well as for many on-the-ground humanist educators, literature (or literary skills, arts, *techné*), was essential for forging the self. One read literature, and especially classical literature, to refine ones sensibilities and words, to achieve eloquence in public oral and written speaking. Ancient texts, not knowledge, exemplified this refined sensibility. It was a *mode* of being that humanists sought to teach through the liberal arts. The humanists, as the famed Renaissance scholar Paul Kristeller wrote, believed studying the ancients mattered less for the wisdom they imparted than because ancient texts taught students "to write and speak well."[7]

The most important Protestant synthesizer of this humanist ideal, who influenced the development of education in England and in England's North

American colonies, was Erasmus. To Erasmus, education was vital to one's development as a human being. People were made, not found. An educated human being, however, was less someone schooled in philosophy—or even the dialectics of scholasticism—but refined through words, through the study of ancient grammar and rhetoric. But, in the midst of the Reformation, Erasmus added an important addition: the truly educated person must also understand Christian ethics. Erasmus's ideal, then, was the "Christian prince," who combined Christian faith and ethics with the skills of the orator.[8]

Ancients and Axioms

Colonial education at both the primary and secondary levels was grounded in ancient learning—as reinterpreted by the revival of humanism and by Erasmus—and Protestant morality, what Robert Middlekauf has called "ancients and axioms."[9] The axioms of Christianity were to ensure moral leaders of church and state. The ancients were taught not for their insight but for language. Liberal education was grounded in the arts (techné), not philosophy. Studying Latin language and literature and, to a lesser extent, Greek, enabled people to become refined producers of language useful for pulpit and politics. Thus the trivium emphasized specific skills—grammar (the parsing of texts), rhetoric (the speaking of texts), and logic or dialectic (the analysis of texts and arguments). There is almost no specific content. Students did not need to know subject matter, for the most part. They needed to know how to analyze texts. This was not necessarily just a dry task, although, as Middlekauf and others have noted, for most students it was. Ideally, a good education produced a person able to participate in public life effectively.[10]

In New England, primary schools taught the two "r's" of reading and writing and, to a lesser extent, arithmetic. Math was not seen as a necessary skill; admission to colonial New England colleges was premised on mastery of Latin and Greek, and few students had more than basic arithmetic. Students preparing for college would attend grammar schools where they learned to parse ancient texts not for knowledge but to develop the skills of grammar, rhetoric, and logic. College itself was also bound by the principle of ancients and axioms or what scholars have called the ideal of the "Christian gentleman." At Harvard, for example, the course of study in the mid-eighteenth century emphasized ancient grammar, rhetoric, and logic, with a dose of metaphysics and ethics. In an oral culture, the capacity to speak well was of the utmost practical value for colonial elites.[11]

Virginia had a similar program, if not as robust as in New England, where New England's Calvinist ideals spurred a widespread commitment to literacy so that every person could read the Bible for her- or himself. For students who did receive a formal education, however, the ancients and axioms predominated. Colonial Virginians emphasized primary education for, in the words of one scholar, "reading, writing, and the Anglican faith."[12] In Virginia as in New England, then, students received an education shaped by Protestant humanism. They learned to be moral Christians, and philosophy—the search for substantive knowledge about the world—took a back seat to oratory.

This principled commitment to the orator over the philosopher continued after the Revolution, as Carolyn Eastman has argued.[13] The most prominent schoolbooks in the immediate postrevolutionary decades focused on the public presentation of self. The schoolbooks were called speakers, and the goal was to prepare young people for public life in a democracy. Like the celebrated Demosthenes, young people were encouraged to master the art of speaking (eloquence, in Cicero's framing), which meant developing the trivial skill of rhetoric. The end of a good education was not knowledge but the capacity to speak effectively in public. The liberal arts were not domains of philosophical knowledge—academic disciplines, as they are today—but skills or *techné*. They were *arts* that one learned through the study of ancient texts and exemplars. The purpose was to *refine*, whereas the purpose of a philosophical education was to enlighten.

This is the world in which the young Jefferson grew up. Jefferson learned Greek and Latin under the tutelage of the Reverend James Maury. While Maury himself did not believe that a classical education was suitable for everyone in Virginia, he did believe it necessary for gentlemen destined to be professionals and political leaders. It was also the necessary prerequisite for admission to Virginia's only college, William and Mary. When Jefferson matriculated, William and Mary was divided into four schools: a preparatory grammar school; the Philosophy school, which offered the bachelor's degree; the Divinity school; and a school for Native Americans.[14]

As is well known, for Jefferson, the College did not offer the kind of education that inspired him. Despite being called the Philosophy school, William and Mary's undergraduate curriculum, like that of other colleges of the era, emphasized classical language and literature—largely learned as grammar—with some courses in moral and natural philosophy. The emphasis remained on the classical liberal arts, not the modern academic disciplines and the philosophical pursuit of truth. While, according to the College's 1758 statutes, students completing grammar school would enter the "philosophy" school, the two professors to be appointed were to teach the ancients and axioms. The first "shall teach Rhetorick, Logick, and Ethicks. The other Physicks, Metaphysicks, and Mathematicks."[15] These studies were themselves preparatory for higher study in divinity. Thus, William and Mary was committed to the Renaissance organization of knowledge.

The College's focus on ancients and axioms seemed, to Jefferson, tired and dusty. He did not revere Erasmus, but instead looked to seekers of knowledge such as Bacon, Newton, and Locke. What excited Jefferson was gaining access to the new knowledge of the Enlightenment. He was inspired in part by his professor of natural philosophy, William Small. After the dismissal of a different professor, Small also taught courses in moral philosophy. Small was a modernizer, and in addition to logic and rhetoric, he taught his students the wonder of modern intellectual progress. Jefferson discovered that knowledge was always contingent, and that knowledge of the human and natural worlds— including of ethics—was something for which to strive.

Whether about the human or natural worlds, Jefferson credited his true education to have taken place in extracurricular conversations in Williamsburg. Leaving the College without a degree, Jefferson instead decided to read law under the tutelage of George Wythe, whom he met through Small. In conversations with Small and Wythe, sometimes at the table of Lieutenant Governor Francis Fauquier, Jefferson was introduced to the Enlightenment. The Enlightenment, as Caroline Winterer has recently argued, was not just about knowledge but about an attitude toward knowledge. Rather than accept knowledge as handed-down authority, the Enlightenment spirit was one of philosophical curiosity. It was about experimentation and conversation and a basic effort to make sense of the world. It required humility, because knowledge was always partial, and it favored investigation (in both natural and human affairs) over divine inheritance. Jefferson discovered the joys of philosophy from his mentors—including knowledge to be learned, new ideas to be tested, and new theories to be developed.[16]

For Jefferson, then, it was philosophy, not oratory, that inspired. As he entered political life, he would conclude that philosophy—knowledge of the human and natural worlds, and the disposition to seek new knowledge— ought to be at the heart of education. To achieve this goal he would challenge the humanist emphasis on oratory. He did not reject the trivial, classical liberal arts, but he favored the new liberal arts and sciences. For centuries, knowledge was seen as instrumental to the higher goals of oratory. Jefferson reversed the schema. To Jefferson, students should move from learning trivial skills to developing philosophical understanding by the time they entered college. To Jefferson, knowing how mattered as preparation for knowing what.

Jefferson and the Arts and Sciences

The liberal arts, as the word "art" suggests, are skills or *techné*. They are technologies of the self to produce, in Cicero's framing, a person who combined eloquence with wisdom. Jefferson, on the other hand, was less concerned with the refinement of the self than with citizens and civic leaders who were knowledgeable about the human and natural worlds. This meant that a good education should shift the balance from oratory to philosophy. And this is what Jefferson sought to do in his efforts to reform primary and higher education in Virginia. At the elementary level, the traditional liberal arts predominated, but by the time a student reached university, philosophy did. Every white Virginian must become an orator, but the end of education, at its peak, would be to graduate philosopher-leaders, Jefferson believed.

Jefferson was one of America's first and foremost advocates for public education for free children, which did not include the children of enslaved people. He believed that all white Virginians should be offered an elementary education at taxpayer expense. He proposed a pyramid structure in which the most capable students would be, as he put it, "raked from the rubbish annually," and supported at public expense at grammar school and then, ultimately, at Virginia's then-only college, William and Mary. Jefferson had two goals. First, he aspired to prepare all white Virginians for their responsibilities as citizens. Second, by providing scholarships to the most capable students, he intended to ensure that the state's leaders came from all backgrounds. He presumed that children of wealthier families would support their sons through college, so his goal was to add children from families of fewer means to the mix.[17] As he wrote John Adams, had his education bill been passed by the Virginia legislature, "worth and genius would thus have been sought out from every condition of life, and compleatly prepared by education for defeating the competition of wealth & birth for public trusts."[18]

Jefferson addressed primary and secondary education particularly at three times in his life. First, in the immediate aftermath of American independence, when he proposed his bill "to diffuse knowledge more generally through the mass of the people" and his discussion of it in Query XIV of *Notes on the State of Virginia*. Second, in the 1810s, when Virginia's leaders tried a second time to pass a bill supporting public schools. And, finally, in the Rockfish Gap Report, which provided the foundation for the University of Virginia but also discussed education at the lower levels. Although some of the details changed, the basic structure and conception remained constant. The most significant innovation was that between the 1780s and the 1810s, Jefferson replaced the grammar school with the idea of a "general school," which reflected a shift in emphasis from the traditional liberal arts to philosophy.

In his 1778 bill, Jefferson first proposed his pyramid structure, as well as a detailed curriculum. He proposed that all free young boys and girls would attend local elementary schools "gratis" where they would learn "reading, writing, and common arithmetic." The visitor of each elementary school would then select "the boy, of best genius in the school, of those whose parents are too poor to give them further education, and to send him forward to one of the grammar schools." As had long been the case, grammar schools would prepare students for college by instructing pupils in "Greek, Latin, geography, and the higher branches of arithmetic." Of this group, after six years, half would be dismissed, and the other half would be "continued three years in the study of such sciences as they shall chuse, at William and Mary college."[19]

Jefferson believed that "the first stage of this education ... wherein the great mass of the people will receive their instruction" should include, in addition to reading, writing, and arithmetic, "the most useful facts from Grecian, Roman, European and American history" and the "first elements of morality." Thus, all Virginians would have basic literacy and numeracy skills, combined with knowledge of history and ethics. For those who merited advanced study at public expense—and for those who continued thanks to the "wealth of their parents"—Jefferson argued for Greek and Latin in traditional grammar schools. He recognized that "the learning [of] Greek and Latin ... is going into disuse in Europe," but his commitment held steady because, he believed, boys between about eight and fifteen or sixteen years old were not ready for more "laborious" learning. But, he added, "I do not pretend that language is science. It is only an instrument for the attainment of science." In short, as early as the 1780s, Jefferson was reducing the curriculum of the grammar schools to instrumental purposes relative to "science," or philosophy.[20]

Jefferson remained committed to the basic outline above throughout his life, but his focus shifted to increasing access to philosophical knowledge at the level of grammar schools and in colleges. Thus, in an 1814 letter to his nephew Peter Carr, Jefferson reiterated that all Virginians in elementary schools should learn "Reading, Writing, Arithmetic, Geography." The most capable graduates of elementary schools would now enter what Jefferson called "general schools," instead of grammar schools. While grammar schools had largely emphasized ancient grammar, the curriculum at Jefferson's general schools would include the natural and human sciences (or natural and moral philosophy—the word "science" refers to organized bodies of knowledge, which at the time included what today are the natural sciences, the humanities, and the social sciences).

In the general schools, Jefferson anticipated two populations. First, there would be the children of the wealthy, who would be preparing their children to become leaders. Second, the publicly supported children who, lacking wealth, would need to learn a profession. "[B]oth of these sections will require instruction in all the higher branches of science," Jefferson argued. The result is that by 1814 Jefferson's proposed "general schools," with their emphasis on philosophy over the traditional liberal arts, look very much like the curriculum of middle and high schools as they developed over the nineteenth century. The general schools were divided into modern knowledge domains: Language, Mathematics, and Philosophy. Within each domain, were several disciplines of knowledge. Language included "1. Languages and history, antient and modern. 2. Grammar. 3. Belles Lettres. 4. Rhetoric and Oratory." Jefferson included history here "not as a kindred subject, but on the principle of economy, because both may be attained by the same course of reading." In other words, Jefferson saw history as a domain of philosophical knowledge, but concluded that it could be taught simultaneously with teaching the arts.

If language contained the liberal arts (the "ancients"), the other two were decidedly philosophical. Under mathematics, Jefferson included "1. Mathematics pure. 2. Physico-mathematics. 3. Physic. 4. Chemistry. 5. Natural history, to wit: Mineralogy. 6. botany. and 7. Zoology. 8. anatomy. 9. the Theory of Medicine." Under philosophy, Jefferson included "1. Ideology. 2. Ethics. 3. the Law of Nature & Nations. 4. Government. 5. Political economy." In short, the general schools, unlike colonial grammar schools and the grammar schools that Jefferson had supported in the 1780s, were no longer primarily about ancient language as part of the liberal arts of logic, rhetoric, and oratory. Instead, these arts were combined with philosophy into a modern "general school" of arts and sciences. The graduates of these general schools would have an education that emphasized access to knowledge as much as to the skills traditionally associated with the liberal arts.[21]

Reforming William and Mary

When it came to higher education, which Jefferson presumed would be the site for educating Virginia's future leaders, he consistently emphasized philosophy over oratory. He did so beginning with his term as governor in the midst of the Revolution when he tried to reform William and Mary's curriculum and structure. Most scholars have rightly noted his desire to limit the clergy's influence, but have been less cognizant of how Jefferson's proposals fit into the centuries-long discussion between orators and philosophers.

Jefferson's aspirations for William and Mary were first articulated as part of the broader proposals to revise Virginia laws that he and other members of the legislature were tasked with in 1778. He proposed in June 1779 "A Bill for Amending the Constitution of the College of William and Mary." At the time, the so-called Philosophy School remained largely as Jefferson had experienced it, with a professor who taught mathematics and natural philosophy, and a professor who taught grammar, logic, rhetoric, and ethics. Jefferson's bill proposed instead that a revised William and Mary have eight professors who would teach:

"moral philosophy, the laws of nature and of nations, and of the fine arts"

"law and police"

"history, civil and ecclesiastical"

"mathematics"

"anatomy and medicine"

"natural philosophy and natural history"

"ancient languages, oriental and northern"

"modern languages."

This was a fundamental reconfiguration of how knowledge would be organized at the College. The traditional liberal arts were demoted, whereas domains of knowledge were elevated.[22]

When Jefferson became Virginia's governor in 1779, he also became rector of the College. With the support of William and Mary's visitors, he initiated some of the changes that his bill had proposed. William and Mary established new professorships in law, medicine, the arts, and modern languages. Mandatory chapel attendance was also abolished. Yet until the charter was altered by the legislature, William and Mary could have only six professorships, and thus there were limits to what Jefferson could accomplish. Nonetheless, in his proposal and his actions we see his effort to switch the basis of higher education from the oratorical tradition to that of the philosopher-leader.

Reflecting on his efforts in 1814 as well as his growing interest in a new university, Jefferson proclaimed, "I have long entertained the hope that this our native state would take up the subject of education, and make an establishment, either with or without incorporation into that of William & Mary, where *every branch of science*, deemed useful at this day, should be taught in it's highest degree."[23]

The Rockfish Gap Report

The culminating statement of Jefferson's education program is the Rockfish Gap Report. For Jefferson, this was a high-stakes moment. Virginians were divided over whether to sponsor a new university or invest in primary schools, and they were also divided over whether to locate the new university in Jefferson's Charlottesville (as he wanted) or on the western side of the Appalachians. Jefferson was committed to the establishment of a new university that would achieve the goals that he had failed to achieve with William and Mary. At a time of growing religiosity and partisan rancor, moreover, Jefferson aspired to establish a public-minded university that would graduate the kinds of leaders that he believed Virginia and the United States most needed.[24]

When Virginia's leading lights met in the Rockfish Gap in the Blue Ridge Mountains, Jefferson played an outsized role in shaping the report delivered to the legislature. Scholars are correct to note that Jefferson purposefully emphasized a modern, secular curriculum that challenged inherited assumptions. "Some good men, and even of respectable information, consider the learned sciences as useless acquirements," he noted in the Rockfish Gap Report. A good education, Jefferson and the commissioners of the Report continued, "engrafts a new man on the native stock." This "new man" would be a philosopher, not simply an orator, the Report made clear. The new university would take for granted that truth is not handed down but sought through scientific or philosophical inquiry. The commissioners condemned those who believed "that the condition of man cannot be ameliorated, that has been must ever be, and that to secure Ourselves . . . , we must tread with awfull reverence in the footsteps of our fathers." Education, then, did not refine from within a tradition, but enabled students to transcend existing boundaries to see the world anew. This is truly the Enlightenment's call for courage and progress.

The curriculum for the new university leaned toward the modern disciplines of knowledge, with the older liberal arts taking a smaller role than before. For the new university, the Rockfish Gap Report proposed the following "groups" of knowledge, each to be assigned to a professor:[25]

"I   Languages Antient
- Latin
- Greek
- Hebrew

II   Languages Modern
- French
- Spanish
- Italian
- German
- Anglo-Saxon

III   Mathematics Pure
- Algebra
- Fluxions
- Geometry   elementary
-     Trancendental
- Architecture   Military
-     Naval

IV   Physico-Mathematics
- Mechanics
- Statics
- Dynamics
- Pneumatics
- Acoustics
- Optics
- Astronomy
- Geography

V
- Physics or Natural Philosophy
- Chemistry
- Mineralogy

VI
- Botany
- Zoology
- Anatomy

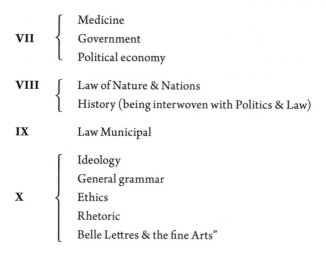

As can be seen, there was still a role for the *artes liberales*. Students would still be exposed to ancient language and literature as well as rhetoric. But the bulk of the teaching would come from mathematics, the natural sciences, and the humanities and social sciences. Domains of knowledge—of truth— would replace domains defined by the skills that they imparted. Philosophy would predominate over the arts or *techné*. A good leader must not only be able to speak and argue effectively, but must have knowledge of the human and natural worlds. A graduate of the proposed university—which in time would become the University of Virginia—would be immersed in the arts and sciences, not the ancients and axioms of old.

There is some ground for irony that Jefferson, who deeply disliked Plato, should embrace the Platonic tradition of education. The thing to remember is that Jefferson's dislike of Plato had to do with Plato's metaphysics, not his understanding of education. To Plato, truth was embodied in ideal forms. To Jefferson, grounded in the empiricism of the Enlightenment, truth emerged through evidence, whether it be of the human or natural worlds. Thus, Jefferson condemned Plato's "mysticisms incomprehensible to the human mind . . . ." Ministers of the established church benefited from Platonic idealism because it allowed them to found their own earthly authority on "a basis of impenetrable darkness whereon to rear fabrications as delirious, of their own invention."[26] But Jefferson did not reject Plato's premise that the leaders of a republic needed to be seekers of truth through knowledge, rather than sophists who could convince but did not have the knowledge to lead effectively.

It should be added that the Rockfish Gap Report was concerned primarily with civic leaders. Jefferson also believed that there would be an important role for Americans versed in applied rather than liberal knowledge. It was this impetus that animated his commitment to the military academy at West Point, where future officers would learn to apply scientific knowledge to further military goals and to improve American society.[27] Jefferson was not opposed to applied learning, but considered it distinct from liberal education. At his University of Virginia, students would be immersed in a liberal environment in which they would learn the leading edge of scientific and philosophical knowledge about the human and natural worlds.

The Federalists on Jefferson's Philosophizing

Like Aristophanes's portrayal of Socrates in the ancient Greek comedy *The Clouds*, so Jefferson was presented by political opponents as someone who sought useless knowledge through his curious but ultimately ridiculous philosophical investigations. Indeed, while to many Americans Jefferson's scientific temper and commitments earned him respect (he was president of the American Philosophical Society for eighteen years), to Federalists, including those associated with the rival American Academy of Arts and Sciences, there was something suspect and humorous in Jefferson's scientific investigations. Josiah Quincy, then-president of the Massachusetts Historical Society, a member of the American Academy of Arts and Sciences, and a future president of Harvard, mocked Jefferson's explorations into the existence of a mammoth or mastodon: "If he happen to have his scale and dividers in his pocket, and should submit to the drudgery of making a drawing and description, for the benefit of the curious, he will have ill luck indeed, if, in consequence of these rare exertions, he be not elevated, for life, to the presidency of the American philosophical society."[28]

In her brilliant discussion of the topic, Linda Kerber suggests two reasons for Federalists' dismissal of Jefferson's scientific credentials, as well as those of the Republican-dominated American Philosophical Society. First, the American Philosophical Society embraced natural history, which involved the empirical study of the natural world through specific pieces of evidence. To many Federalists, this kind of democratic science was nothing more than trying to make sense of the world through random stuff that one found. In contrast, scientists at the American Academy of Arts and Sciences tended to study astronomy and mathematics, which dealt in large abstract models. This also had, Kerber adds, the important corollary that one could sense the divine hand in the formation of an orderly universe governed by God's abstract laws, whereas natural history produced questions (for example, about shells on top of mountains, or the age of the earth) that questioned the existence of a divine plan.[29]

Kerber is no doubt correct, but as my reference to *The Clouds* suggests, there is more to think about. Should the philosopher be a free investigator "in the clouds," or be somehow connected organically to the moral and cultural demands of the polity? Does philosophical speculation evade its value by allowing its investigators free reign? Plato and Jefferson thought philosophers— people trained in the search for knowledge about the world—should rule. Aristophanes and the Federalists found that notion laughable. To skeptics of philosophy, the quest for knowledge must always be grounded in morality and social need. In short, knowledge must serve and be subordinate to the demands of the engaged public orator. To many Federalist scientists, Jefferson and his colleagues in the American Philosophical Society seemed to seek knowledge for its own sake without virtue or social value.

Of course, members of both the American Academy of Arts and Sciences and the American Philosophical Society embraced science, promoted philosophical investigation, and sought knowledge. What distinguished them, as Kerber's subtle analysis suggests, is their temper, how they placed science within the order of things. To Federalists such as Quincy, science had to be moored to rather than liberated from other goods. To Jefferson, science was the site of liberation, and thus freedom, precisely because it unmoored its practitioners from the bindings of the ancients and axioms.

This debate raged among those concerned with education in the early republic. It concerned as well the status of classical language and literature. As suggested above, Jefferson in the 1810s replaced his support for traditional grammar schools with new "general schools." Many Americans agreed; private academies and new public high schools were increasingly modeled on the modern organization of knowledge. They continued to offer an ancient track for students seeking admission to college, but for others, they offered English-language instruction in modern subjects. The general high school, organized around domains of knowledge rather than *techné*, was quickly replacing the grammar school.[30]

Conclusion

Jefferson proposed that students should be exposed to "every branch of science" rather than the "ancients and axioms" that had once defined what it meant to be educated. And that is what happened. Increasingly, American common schools emphasized English over ancient languages. Academic skills mattered, especially at the elementary level, where the new trivium of reading, writing, and arithmetic reigned. Orality continued to be central to pedagogy and public culture, but as students advanced, the formal curriculum shifted during the nineteenth century toward disciplinary knowledge in academic subjects. Grammar schools declined as advanced students focused on modern academic subjects like history and political economy and chemistry and astronomy in private chartered academies and new public high schools (Jefferson's "general schools"). Latin and Greek continued to be taught, but their relative importance faded, as they were no longer essential to what it meant to being educated.

At the higher education level, too, a shift toward philosophy is evident, especially after the establishment of the Johns Hopkins University, America's first research university, which emphasized scholarly research in the humanities, social sciences, and natural sciences. The process was never complete; learning knowledge requires skills, and American schools and universities continued to care about character and virtue. And indeed, for Jefferson, academic pursuits were not ends in themselves; they were always connected to civic life. Thus, the University of Virginia's primary mission was to prepare the republic's leaders, and the primary and secondary system existed to educate citizens.[31] But to do so, Jefferson was clear, requires not just teaching the skills associated with the traditional liberal arts, but also democratizing access to the knowledge generated by modern academic disciplines. Jefferson's ideal graduate was a republican philosopher-leader.

Notes

1. On Jefferson and the Enlightenment, see, e.g., Joseph F. Kett, "Education," in *Thomas Jefferson: A Reference Biography*, ed. Merrill Peterson (New York: Scribner, 1986), 233–52; Paul H. Mattingly, *American Academic Cultures: A History of Higher Education* (Chicago: University of Chicago Press, 2017), ch. 2; Jennings Wagoner, *Thomas*

Jefferson and the Education of a New Nation (Bloomington, IN: Phi Delta Kappa Educational Foundation, 1976). The classic work is Henry Steele Commager, *Jefferson, Nationalism, and the Enlightenment* (New York: G. Braziller, 1975). On Jefferson as modernizer, see Roger Geiger, *The History of American Higher Education: Learning and Culture from the Founding to WWII* (Princeton, NJ: Princeton University Press, 2015), ch. 3; James Axtell, *Wisdom's Workshop: The Rise of the Modern University* (Princeton, NJ: Princeton University Press, 2016), ch. 3; George Oberle, "Institutionalizing the Information Revolution: Debates over Knowledge Institutions in the Early American Republic" (PhD diss., George Mason University, 2016), 51–123. Linda Kerber, *Federalists in Dissent: Imagery and Ideology in Jeffersonian America* (Ithaca, NY: Cornell University Press, 1970), ch. 3. On Jefferson and religion, see esp. Cameron Addis, *Jefferson's Vision for Education, 1760–1845* (New York: Peter Lang, 2003).

2. Bruce Kimball, *Orators and Philosophers: A History of the Idea of Liberal Education* (New York: Teachers College Press, 1986).

3. In a prior essay I argued that Jefferson's educational proposals would encourage the development of citizens' individual and civic capabilities. This essay argues that to do so Jefferson sought to democratize not just education in general, but one premised on knowledge. See Johann N. Neem, "'To Diffuse Knowledge More Generally through the Mass of the People': Thomas Jefferson on Individual Freedom and the Distribution of Knowledge," in *Light and Liberty: Thomas Jefferson and the Power of Knowledge*, ed. Robert M. S. McDonald (Charlottesville: University of Virginia Press, 2012), 47–74. But for a skeptical appraisal of Jefferson's democratic commitments, see Darren Staloff, "The Politics of Pedagogy: Thomas Jefferson and the Education of a Democratic Citizenry," in *The Cambridge Companion to Thomas Jefferson*, ed. Frank Shuffleton (New York: Cambridge University Press, 2009), ch. 9.

4. All quotes from Plato, *Gorgias*, trans. Tom Griffith, ed. Malcolm Schofield (Cambridge: Cambridge University Press, 2010).

5. All quotes from Cicero, *On The Ideal Orator*, trans. James May and Jakob Wise (New York: Oxford University Press, 2001).

6. Kimball, *Orators and Philosophers*, 77.

7. Paul Kristeller, *Renaissance Thought: The Classic, Scholastic, and Humanist Strains* (New York: Harper and Row, 1961), 13. See also Olaf Pedersen, *The First Universities: Studium Generale and the Origins of University Education in Europe* (Cambridge: Cambridge University Press, 1997), 196–204; Kimball, *Orators and Philosophers*, 82–87; Herbert M. Kliebard, "The Decline of Humanistic Studies in the American School Curriculum," in *The Humanities in Precollegiate Education*, part 2, ed. Benjamin Ladner (Chicago: National Society for the Study of Education, 1984), 7–30, esp. 8–10; James Turner, *Philology: The Forgotten Origins of the Modern Humanities* (Princeton, NJ: Princeton University Press, 2014). See also Robert E. Proctor, *Defining the Humanities: How Rediscovering a Tradition Can Improve Our Schools*, 2nd ed. (Bloomington: Indiana University Press, 1998).

8. Kimball, *Orators and Philosophers*, 87–90; Erika Rummel, "Desiderius Erasmus," in *The Stanford Encyclopedia of Philosophy* (Winter 2017), ed. Edward N. Zalta, https://plato.stanford.edu/archives/win2017/entries/erasmus/. Erasmus's "On the

Method of Study," trans. Brian McGregor, in *Collected Works of Erasmus: Literary and Educational Writings*, ed. Craig R. Thompson (Toronto: University of Toronto Press, 1978), 24:661–91.

9. Robert Middlekauf, *Ancients and Axioms: Secondary Education in Eighteenth-Century New England* (New Haven, CT: Yale University Press, 1963). See also Kliebard, "Decline of Humanistic Studies."

10. Carolyn Eastman, *A Nation of Speechifiers: Making an American Public after the Revolution* (Chicago: University of Chicago Press, 2009).

11. Geiger, *History of American Higher Education*, chs. 1–2; Lawrence Cremin, *American Education: The Colonial Experience, 1607–1783* (New York: Harper and Row, 1970), ch. 7; Kimball, *Orators and Philosophers*, 133–41; Frederick Rudolph, *Curriculum: A History of the American Undergraduate Course of Study since 1636* (San Francisco: Jossey-Bass, 1977), ch. 1.

12. Robert J. Vejnar III, "The State of Education in Colonial Virginia," *International Social Science Review* 77, no. 1–2 (2002): 16–31.

13. Eastman, *Nation of Speechifiers*.

14. My discussion of Jefferson's childhood education relies primarily on Kevin J. Hayes, *The Road to Monticello: The Life and Mind of Thomas Jefferson* (New York: Oxford University Press, 2008), chs. 3–5.

15. Statutes of the College of William and Mary (1758), https://www.encyclopediavirginia.org/The_Statutes_of_the_College_of_William_and_Mary_in_Virginia_1758.

16. Carolyn Winterer, *American Enlightenments: Pursuing Happiness in the Age of Reason* (New Haven, CT: Yale University Press, 2016).

17. *Notes*, Query XIV, 146–49. My discussion of Jefferson's bill and citations to other scholars on whom I rely can be found in Neem, "'To Diffuse Knowledge.'"

18. Jefferson to John Adams, October 28, 1813, *PTJRS*, 6:565.

19. *Notes*, Query XIV, 146. See Jefferson, "A Bill for the More General Diffusion of Knowledge," *PTJ*, 2:526–35.

20. *Notes*, Query XIV, 147–48.

21. Jefferson to Peter Carr, September 7, 1814, *PTJRS*, 7:637–38.

22. On Jefferson's reforms at William and Mary, see Mark R. Wenger, "Thomas Jefferson, the College of William and Mary, and the University of Virginia," *Virginia Magazine of History and Biography* 103, no. 3 (July 1995): 339–74; Jefferson, "A Bill for Amending the Constitution of the College of William and Mary, and Substituting More Certain Revenues for Its Support" (June 18, 1779), *PTJ*, 2:535–43.

23. Jefferson to Peter Carr, September 7, 1814, *PTJRS*, 7:636 (emphasis added).

24. Addis, *Jefferson's Vision*.

25. Rockfish Gap Report of the University of Virginia Commissioners, August 4, 1818, *PTJRS*, 13:212–14.

26. Jefferson to William Short, October 31, 1819, *Founders Online*, https://founders.archives.gov/documents/Jefferson/98-01-02-0850. See also Jefferson to John Adams, August 22, 1813, *PTJRS*, 6:438–40.

27. Jennings Wagoner Jr., and Christine Coalwell McDonald, "Mr. Jefferson's Academy: An Educational Interpretation," in *Thomas Jefferson's Military Academy: Founding*

West Point (Charlottesville: University of Virginia Press, 2004), 118–53; Oberle, *Institutionalizing the Information Revolution*, ch. 2.

28. "Climenole, No. 8" (March 24, 1804), quoted in Kerber, *Federalists in Dissent*, 73.

29. Kerber, "The Objects of Scientific Inquiry," in Kerber, *Federalists in Dissent*, ch. 3.

30. On public high schools, see Kliebard, "Decline of Humanistic Studies"; Jürgen Herbst, *The Once and Future School: 350 Years of American Secondary Education* (New York: Routledge, 1996); Johann N. Neem, *Democracy's Schools: The Rise of Public Education in America* (Baltimore: Johns Hopkins University Press, 2017), ch. 2. On academies, see Mark Boonshoft, "Creating a 'Civilized Nation': Religion, Social Capital, and the Cultural Foundations of Early American State Formation" (PhD diss., Ohio State University, 2015); J. M. Opal, *Beyond the Farm: National Ambitions in Rural New England* (Philadelphia: University of Pennsylvania Press, 2008), 96–125; Mary Kelley, *Learning to Stand and Speak: Women, Education, and Public Life in America's Republic* (Chapel Hill: University of North Carolina Press, 2006); Nancy Beadie and Kimberley Tolley, eds., *Chartered Schools: Two Hundred Years of Independent Academies in the United States, 1727–1925* (New York: Routledge, 2002); Theodore R. Sizer, ed., *The Age of the Academies* (New York: Bureau of Publications, Teachers College, Columbia University, 1964).

31. See Alan Taylor, "The Virtue of an Educated Voter," *American Scholar* 85, no. 4 (Autumn 2016): 18–27.

The University Survives

PREPARING A VOLUME of essays on the history of a university is an odd endeavor in some respects, not unlike writing a biography of a person who still lives. We can only write an introduction, with anticipation of what is to come. The past is prologue, as Shakespeare quipped, but the "earth belongs . . . to the living," the sage of Monticello assured us.

Still, Jefferson understood as much as anyone that the careful and honest study of history provides an essential platform from which to understand the present and plan for the future, no less so for a university and for the role of education in a republic. This volume and the conference on which it was based have been pursued in that spirit.

A collection of essays on the early history of the University of Virginia is, unsurprisingly, largely defined by the University's founder, as was the school in its early years and to some extent still today. So much of what was unique and different at the University of Virginia in its design and youth came directly from Jefferson. Ralph Waldo Emerson once remarked: "An institution is the lengthened shadow of one man." Rarely has that statement been so true as in the case of the University of Virginia. Few, if any, universities owe so much to the vision of one man, and his spiritual presence in Charlottesville is inescapable.

Undoubtedly there were important innovations at the University. Historians of education have long credited Jefferson and his University for helping to launch the movement toward an elective curriculum, now a foundation for higher education in the United States and around the world. The change has had truly revolutionary consequences. No less important was his determination to free education from the grips of religion and religious orthodoxy, an innovation that Jefferson pursued on a broader political landscape as well.

Focusing more specifically, a look at medical education suggests marked improvements were made at the founding of the University of Virginia. Inquiries into other fields may yield similar discoveries.

Of course, academic papers on very particular aspects of the founding of the University of Virginia—from cataloging books, to specifying which British jurists should be read for understanding the common law, to the whimsical possibility of using the inside of the Rotunda's dome as a large easel for astronomy studies—should not hide the more fundamental point about why a university was being built and what it hoped to achieve.

Certainly, in the 1820s, Jefferson saw the University as a means to limit the spread of what he saw as pernicious northern and Federalist ideas, including immediate abolitionism, with which he believed too many Virginian and other southern students were being infected at northern universities. At the time of the University's construction, Jefferson was undoubtedly focused on protecting and promoting the interest of Virginia and its southern neighbors, a focus sharpened by the sectional crisis at the time of the Missouri Compromise—Jefferson's "fire bell in the night." He envisioned educating leaders for his state and nation, but southern leaders in particular. And time would show that many graduates of the University would play critical roles in the Confederate Army and government.

Yet, focusing solely on that result distorts Jefferson's broader vision. Jefferson had been advocating the formation of a public university since at least 1779 and saw it as an important institution to provide the leadership necessary in a republic, a leadership that should promote the "natural aristocracy" of merit and protect the sinews of a representative republic. His unlikely alliance with Joseph C. Cabell in obtaining legislative approval for the University was driven by a mutual commitment to the benefits of education for the students and the nation and, equally important, for the development of knowledge and progress of mankind. The University's legacy of slavery must be explored, understood, and confronted, but it is not the legacy that drove Jefferson's initial commitment to a university, nor the one that he intended to leave.

Even beyond the critical advantages to be found in the pursuit of knowledge, Jefferson was deeply conscious of not just the role that higher education played in teaching a student facts and theories about biology, history, and philosophy, but also the role of the intimate interactions of students and mentors, young people exploring the universe and their own developing personhood with educators deeply interested in both. While he emphasized the fundamental flaws he found in the program at William and Mary at the end of the eighteenth and beginning of the nineteenth century, he was always grateful for the broader education he received there. Jefferson first experienced the Enlightenment at Williamsburg, dedicating himself thereafter to the pursuit of truth, science, and progress—all in the name of humanity and on behalf of the community of other scholars and seekers. This was the source of his passionate commitment to constructing the University of Virginia, choosing its faculty, and implementing what he saw as important innovations, even his elaborate, detailed plans for organizing the library and controlling the circulation of books. It was these high hopes that left Jefferson so sad—literally tearful and speechless—in the wake of student riots. The University was his hope not just for Virginia, the South, and the nation, but ultimately for the ongoing progress of enlightenment everywhere.

We still believe that this is the mission of the University of Virginia. Today, students and graduates explore the frontiers of knowledge and dedicate themselves to serving their communities and the larger world. The breadth of the University's reach alone speaks to the possibilities. In 1825, the University of Virginia opened with sixty-eight students, mostly sons of wealthy white planters, and eight faculty members. Today, almost 23,000 undergraduate and graduate students of every ethnicity, creed, color, and background join with

The University survives in its students, faculty, alumni, and mission. (Image courtesy of Sanjay Suchak, University of Virginia)

over 3,000 faculty members in studies encompassing all realms of knowledge. Over 200,000 living alumni touch virtually all possible human pursuits around the diverse corners and byways of the world. The contributions of the University and its graduates are vast and expanding.

The University "survives," to adapt John Adams's dying declaration about Jefferson on July 4, 1826, the day the two old friends died. The University survives, much as the Declaration of Independence and Jefferson's Virginia Statute for Religious Freedom survive. Each is a living organism with unbounded potential for the future. Our failing, and the failings of the founders of the nation and the University, do not define the future of enlightened possibilities available through education, democracy, and freedom of the mind. The construction, staffing, and curriculum at the early University of Virginia were designed with that in mind.

As he neared his death, Jefferson famously wrote a letter celebrating the coming fiftieth anniversary of the adoption of the Declaration of Independence. The sage of Monticello wrote,

> [M]ay it be to the world . . . the Signal of arousing men to burst, the chains under which Monkish ignorance and superstition had persuaded them to bind themselves, and to assume the blessings & security of self-government . . . the general spread of the light of science has already laid open to every view the palpable truth that the mass of mankind has not been born, with saddles on their backs, nor a favored few booted and spurred, ready to ride them legitimately, by the grace of god. These are grounds of hope for others.[1]

The same could be said of the University.

Note

1. Jefferson to Roger C. Weightman, June 24, 1826, *Founders Online*, https://founders .archives.gov/documents/Jefferson/98-01-02-6179.

Contributors

CAMERON ADDIS is Professor of History at Austin Community College (ACC). He is the author of *Jefferson's Vision for Education* (listed on the Library of Congress Select Jefferson Bibliography) and articles in the *Journal of the Early Republic, Journal of Texas Music History,* and *Mercury Magazine.* A fellow at the International Center for Jefferson Studies in 1997–1998, he is currently director of ACC's annual History Symposium and has been nominated three times for ACC Teacher of the Year. He is author-webmaster of History Hub (Creative Commons, 2012–), a free digital textbook.

JAMES P. AMBUSKE is Farmer Postdoctoral Fellow in Digital Humanities at the University of Virginia Law Library. He was a contributor to the edited collection, *The Eighteenth Centuries: Global Networks of Enlightenment.* He is currently at work on a book titled "Emigration and Empire: America and Scotland in the Revolutionary Era" as well as a chapter on Scottish loyalism during the American Revolution for a volume to be published by the University of Edinburgh Press. He comanages the Scottish Court of Session Digital Archive Project and the 1828 Catalogue Project at the University of Virginia Law Library, and is pursuing projects centered on transatlantic legal history and the reign of George III.

CAROLYN EASTMAN is Associate Professor of History at Virginia Commonwealth University. Her research is particularly concerned with the cultural and intellectual history of early America and the Atlantic world; political culture; and the history of print, oral, and visual media. She has written about Americans' fascination with Indian eloquence after the Revolution, schoolgirls' vindication of female oratorical excellence, and debates over the best means of advocating world peace during the antebellum era. Her book, *A Nation of Speechifiers: Making an American Public after the Revolution,* received the James Broussard Best First Book Prize from the Society for Historians of the Early American Republic (SHEAR).

RANDALL FLAHERTY is Special Collections Librarian at the University of Virginia Law Library, where she supports research in the Library's archival, rare book, and digital collections. Her dissertation focused on the politics and global geography of trade in the early American republic. She is completing a book titled *Maritime Frontier: Early American Merchants and the Commercial Republic, 1760–1830*.

ROBERT S. GIBSON, MD, MACP, is Professor of Medicine Emeritus at the University of Virginia. In 1992, he was named the Lockhart B. McGuire Professor of Medicine. He has received numerous teaching awards from the School of Medicine, University at large, State Council of Higher Education, and from national organizations. In 2003, he was deemed a Laureate Educator, and in 2006, he received Mastership recognition from the American College of Physicians. He has authored or coauthored more than 300 publications. In 2010, he was elected president of the Clinical Staff and served two three-year terms. Presently, he devotes more time and energy to his work on the early history of the University of Virginia School of Medicine.

DOUGLAS J. HARNSBERGER is a historical architect and architectural historian at Legacy Architecture in Swarthmore, Pennsylvania. For his master's thesis in architectural history at the University of Virginia, he researched the American applications of Delorme's method, where over twenty laminated wooden domes were erected during the early American neoclassical period, from 1801 to 1825. His research brought him back to Charlottesville in 2013 as a Jefferson Scholar at the International Center for Jefferson Studies to study Thomas Jefferson's novel "Age of Enlightenment" design ideas for the 1824 Rotunda Delorme Dome at the University.

JURRETTA JORDAN HECKSCHER is Reference Specialist for Early American History in the Main Reading Room at the Library of Congress. Her work at the Library includes the development of research resources about the American founding era generally and Thomas Jefferson in particular. Her current scholarship focuses on the cultural history of Virginia's Natural Bridge, including its Jeffersonian connections. She received the Ralph Henry Gabriel Dissertation Prize of the American Studies Association for her study on the significance of the dance and movement traditions forged by enslaved Africans and African Americans in the greater Chesapeake region.

ELLEN HICKMAN is Associate Editor at *The Papers of Thomas Jefferson: Retirement Series* at the Thomas Jefferson Foundation. She is currently coediting the seventeenth volume of the series, the sixteenth volume on which she has worked. She also gathers and researches contemporary visitor accounts of Monticello and maintains a database of known visitors to Monticello during Jefferson's lifetime.

ERVIN L. JORDAN JR. is Associate Professor and research archivist at the University of Virginia's Albert and Shirley Small Special Collections Library. He specializes in Civil War and African American history and is the author of three books including *Black Confederates* and *Afro-Yankees in Civil War Virginia*, named one of 1995's best nonfiction books by *Publisher's Weekly*. He has contributed to a variety of academic and general publications including *Voices from within the Veil: African Americans and the Experience of Democracy*, essays exploring the four-hundred-year journey of African Americans in America. He contributed a chapter, "Perseverance and Resilience: African Americans at the University of Virginia," in *The Key to the Door: Experiences of Early African American Students at the University of Virginia*. He has published more than sixty articles, essays, and book chapters and is presently researching a comprehensive bicentennial history of African Americans at the University. Since 2015 he has been an affiliated faculty at the John L. Nau III Center for Civil War History at the University of Virginia.

JOSEPH MICHAEL LASALA is a 1991 graduate of the University of Virginia's School of Architecture. He coauthored the book *Thomas Jefferson's Academical Village: The Creation of an Architectural Masterpiece*, a project that helped launch his career as an author and editor catering to architects. Recently retired from publishing after twenty-five years, he has returned to his favorite pursuit—studying the architectural drawings of Thomas Jefferson. He is now working on a multimedia database that will update and greatly expand the one-hundred-year-old definitive book about Jefferson's drawings, Fiske Kimball's *Thomas Jefferson Architect*, using the latest twenty-first century analytical methods and digital enhancements.

NEVEN LEDDY is a historian of the eighteenth-century Atlantic World— defined broadly to include the Alps and the Mississippi. Originally trained as a cultural and intellectual historian, he integrates methodologies borrowed from migration and diaspora studies in his teaching and research. His research focuses on the experience of education at home and abroad, as well as of migration in the eighteenth century. He has taught at seven Canadian universities (and counting), in departments ranging from Sociology and Conflict Studies to History and the Humanities.

J. JEFFERSON LOONEY is the Daniel P. Jordan Editor of the Papers of Thomas Jefferson at the Thomas Jefferson Foundation. He is the founding editor in chief of *The Papers of Thomas Jefferson: Retirement Series*. Fifteen volumes of this definitive edition of Jefferson's writings and correspondence between 1809 and 1826 have been published, and a sixteenth is in press. He was formerly editor and project director of the *Dictionary of Virginia Biography*, and he is the author or editor of several works on the history of Princeton University.

MAURIE D. McINNIS is Professor of American Studies and the Jacob and Frances Sanger Mossiker Chair in the Humanities at the University of Texas at Austin, where she is also executive vice president and provost. She is an award-winning author, most recently of *Slaves Waiting for Sale: Abolitionist Art and the American Slave Trade*. McInnis has also worked extensively with historic sites and museums including serving as curator for "To Be Sold: Virginia and the American Slave Trade" at the Library of Virginia in Richmond in 2015. In 2012, she cofounded the digital humanities project called JUEL at the University of Virginia, which is in the process of digitizing and transcribing all of the University's early records.

JOHANN N. NEEM is Professor of History at Western Washington University. He is author of *Democracy's Schools: The Rise of Public Education in America* and *Creating a Nation of Joiners: Democracy and Civil Society in Early National Massachusetts*. He is coeditor of the forthcoming essay collection *Jeffersonians in Power: The Rhetoric of Opposition Meets the Realities of Governing*. His book *What's the Point of College?* will be published in 2019.

PETER S. ONUF is a senior research fellow at the Robert H. Smith International Center for Jefferson Studies and Thomas Jefferson Foundation Professor of History Emeritus at the University of Virginia. Onuf has written extensively on sectionalism, federalism, and political economy, with a particular emphasis on the political thought of Thomas Jefferson. With his brother, political theorist Nicholas G. Onuf, he collaborated on *Nations, Markets, and War: Modern History and the American Civil War*, a history of international law and order in the Atlantic states' system during the Age of Revolutions and early nineteenth century. He is also the author of *The Mind of Thomas Jefferson* and a coauthor, with Annette Gordon-Reed, of *"Most Blessed of the Patriarchs": Thomas Jefferson and the Empire of the Imagination*. His most recent book is *Jefferson and the Virginians: Democracy, Constitutions, and Empire*. An elected member of the American Academy of Arts and Sciences, he is also a founding cohost of the public radio program and podcast *BackStory*.

ANDREW J. O'SHAUGHNESSY is Vice President of the Thomas Jefferson Foundation and the Saunders Director of the Robert H. Smith International Center for Jefferson Studies. He oversees the archaeology and research departments, as well as the Jefferson Library, *The Papers of Thomas Jefferson: The Retirement Series*, and the Center's domestic and international fellowship program. He also arranges domestic and international conferences. He is the author of *An Empire Divided: The American Revolution and the British Caribbean*. His most recent book, *The Men Who Lost America: British Leadership, the American Revolution and the Fate of the Empire*, received eight national awards including the New York Historical Society American History Book Prize, the George Washington Book Prize, and the Society of Military History Book Prize. He is a coeditor of *Old World, New World: America and Europe in the Age of Jefferson* and a coeditor of the *Jeffersonian America* series published by the University of Virginia Press. A Fellow of the Royal Historical Society, he has been an editor of the *Journal of American History* and the *Journal of the Early Republic*.

JOHN A. RAGOSTA is a historian at the Robert H. Smith International Center for Jefferson Studies. Ragosta has taught law and history at the University of Virginia, George Washington University, and Oberlin, Hamilton, and Randolph Colleges. He has published in scientific, legal, and history journals, and authored *Religious Freedom: Jefferson's Legacy, America's Creed* and *Wellspring of Liberty: How Virginia's Religious Dissenters Helped to Win the American Revolution & Secured Religious Liberty*. His most recent book is *Patrick Henry: Proclaiming a Revolution*. Before returning to academia, he was a trade and litigation partner at Dewey Ballantine, LLP.

ENDRINA TAY is Associate Foundation Librarian for Technical Services at the Jefferson Library at the Thomas Jefferson Foundation. She joined

Monticello in 2002. Since 2004, she has also been project manager for Thomas Jefferson's Libraries, a project currently under way in collaboration with LibraryThing.com, to build a comprehensive and publicly accessible inventory of the books Jefferson owned, read, and recommended during his lifetime. Her publications include "Unquestionably the Choicest Collection of Books in the U.S: The 1815 Sale of Thomas Jefferson's Library to the Nation," in *Commonplace: The Journal of Early American Life*, and "Thomas Jefferson and Books," in the *Encyclopedia Virginia*.

ALAN TAYLOR holds the Thomas Jefferson Foundation Chair at the University of Virginia. His eight books include *William Cooper's Town: Power and Persuasion on the Frontier of the Early Republic* and *The Internal Enemy: Slavery and War in Virginia*, both of which won the Pulitzer Prize in American History. His most recent book is *American Revolutions: A Continental History, 1750–1804*. His essay in this collection derives from his forthcoming book, *Thomas Jefferson's Education*, which examines the social and political context for education in Virginia from the 1750s to the 1820s, with an emphasis on Jefferson's experiences as a student at the College of William and Mary and his role in creating the republican postwar alternative, the University of Virginia.

Index

Recent Books in the Jeffersonian America Series

Nature's Man: Thomas Jefferson's Philosophical Anthropology, Maurizio Valsania

Religious Freedom: Jefferson's Legacy, America's Creed, John Ragosta

Sons of the Father: George Washington and His Protégés, Robert M. S. McDonald, editor

Paine and Jefferson in the Age of Revolutions, Simon P. Newman and Peter S. Onuf, editors

Era of Experimentation: American Political Practices in the Early Republic, Daniel Peart

Collegiate Republic: Cultivating an Ideal Society in Early America, Margaret Sumner

Amelioration and Empire: Progress and Slavery in the Plantation Americas, Christa Dierksheide

Becoming Men of Some Consequence: Youth and Military Service in the Revolutionary War, John A. Ruddiman

Patriotism and Piety: Federalist Politics and Religious Struggle in the New American Nation, Jonathan J. Den Hartog

Between Sovereignty and Anarchy: The Politics of Violence in the American Revolutionary Era, Patrick Griffin, Robert G. Ingram, Peter S. Onuf, and Brian Schoen, editors

Citizens of a Common Intellectual Homeland: The Transatlantic Origins of American Democracy and Nationhood, Armin Mattes

The Haitian Declaration of Independence: Creation, Context, and Legacy, Julia Gaffield, editor

Confounding Father: Thomas Jefferson's Image in His Own Time, Robert M. S. McDonald

Blood from the Sky: Miracles and Politics in the Early American Republic, Adam Jortner

Pulpit and Nation: Clergymen and the Politics of Revolutionary America, Spencer W. McBride

Jefferson's Body: A Corporeal Biography, Maurizio Valsania

Jefferson on Display: Attire, Etiquette, and the Art of Presentation, G. S. Wilson

Jeffersonians in Power: The Rhetoric of Opposition Meets the Realities of Governing, Joanne B. Freeman and Johann N. Neem, editors

The Founding of Thomas Jefferson's University, John A. Ragosta, Peter S. Onuf, and Andrew J. O'Shaughnessy, editors